D1482789

Strategic Planning: Selected Readings

Revised

Edited by

J. William Pfeiffer, Ph.D., J.D.

San Diego • Toronto • Amsterdam • Sydney

Pfeiffer & Company
8517 Production Avenue
San Diego, California 92121
619 578-5900 FAX: 619 578-2042

Contents

Preface

This book of selected readings about strategic planning represents the best, most relevant, and most insightful articles on the topic spanning the last decade or so. Some are classics and others will be. Many of them changed the ways management thought about their organizations: their purposes, objectives, and methods for obtaining those objectives in both prosperous and adverse times.

The articles are organized along the line of the Applied Strategic Planning (ASP) Model developed by Pfeiffer & Company over several years and in conjunction with much field testing and evaluation of existing models in the field of strategic planning. The model was first published in *The 1985 Annual: Developing Human Resources* and has since been available in various forms for use in different stages of the planning process. The ASP Model has several distinctive elements that set it apart from others that have generally been available. These specific additions build upon the traditional strategic planning steps and enhance the model to make it a more usable and effective guide. First, it includes an organizational "values scan" as one of the initial steps to be taken in the planning process. Second, it labels the core strategic planning activity as "strategic business modeling," a dynamic process that couples an assessment of internal capabilities with external threats and opportunities in the organization's environment. Third, it specifically identifies "integrating action plans" as a first step of implementing the strategic plan within the operational control systems of the organization. The overview to the readings is based on the original article on the ASP Model and serves as the basic structure around which the readings are organized.

This book is divided into four sections that broadly correspond with the main stages of the strategic planning process as described in the overview. Each section has an introduction that specifically explains how the articles in that section relate to the overall model. Significant highlights are presented from the articles, which are also individually abstracted for the convenience of the reader. Please review the section introductions to obtain the most out of the articles.

Although the point is not emphasized throughout this text, the model and readings also directly apply to not-for-profit organizations, governmental agencies, and small businesses. The planning steps, for the most part, are identical to those in the corporations that are specifically cited; and the issues and concerns are just as real for these other types of organizations. Some articles have more relevance to an organization that is experiencing extensive change or entering new markets, for example, but all the material contains concepts that any manager will find of interest and value.

I wish to acknowledge that Dewey Johnson, Ph.D., did the basic research for "The History of Strategic Planning," included in the appendix. Dr. Johnson is a professor in the department of management and marketing, School of Business, California State University, Fresno. A special thanks also goes to our managing editor, Mary Kitzmiller, who supervised the editorial work for both the original edition and this revised version.

J. William Pfeiffer
San Diego, California
April, 1991

Overview

Applied Strategic Planning: A Revised Model for Organizational Growth and Vitality

Leonard D. Goodstein
J. William Pfeiffer
Timothy M. Nolan

Most organizations do some type of long-range or strategic planning, and the formal strategic planning process has been used for over thirty years. However, our experience as consultants to a variety of organizations has convinced us that most strategic planning processes are poorly conceptualized and poorly executed; the strategic plan rarely impacts the day-to-day decisions made in the organization. To be successful, a strategic planning process should provide

---

Based on an article in L.D. Goodstein & J.W. Pfeiffer (Eds.), *The 1985 Annual: Developing human resources*, San Diego, CA: University Associates, 1985. Since the publication of the original version of this article seven years ago, the authors collectively have used this model in applied strategic planning with over 100 different organizations—organizations of various sizes, in profit, not-for-profit, and public organizations, and in various types of industries. This revision of our model is based upon this collective experience and the reports from numerous friends and colleagues who have also used our model during this period.

the criteria for making organizational decisions at all levels and should provide a template against which all such decisions can be evaluated.

When a consultant asks the managers of an organization about its strategic plan, they frequently look pained or embarrassed and begin to search through their files to find the plan, which obviously is nonfunctional. All too often, strategic planning is seen as a top management or staff exercise that has little to do with the actual running of the organization.

A Definition of Strategic Planning

Strategic planning is the process by which an organization envisions its future and develops the necessary procedures and operations to achieve that future. This vision of the future state of the organization provides both the direction in which the organization should move and the energy to begin that move. The envisioning process is very different from long-range planning—the simple extrapolation of statistical trends or forecasts—and it is more than attempting to anticipate the future and prepare accordingly. Envisioning involves a belief that aspects of the future can be influenced and changed by what we do now. The model of strategic planning presented here helps an organization to understand that the strategic planning process does more than plan for the future; it helps the organization to *create* its future.

Strategic planning is, however, more than just an envisioning process. It requires the setting of clear goals and objectives and the attainment of those goals and objectives within specified periods of time in order to reach the planned future state. Thus, targets must be attainable. The goals and objectives developed within the strategic planning process should provide the organization with its core priorities and a set of guidelines for virtually all day-to-day managerial decisions.

This definition of strategic planning focuses on the *process* of planning, not the plan that is produced. Although documents delineating mission statements, strategic business models, critical success indicators, competitor analyses, and so on do emerge from the planning process, it is the process of self-examination, the confrontation of difficult choices, and the establishment of priorities that characterize successful strategic planning. Documents too often are merely filed away until a revision is mandated by some external force.

Strategic planning also is a reiterative process. Strategic planning and strategic management—the day-to-day implementation of the strategic plan—are the most important, never-ending tasks of management, especially top management. Once a strategic planning cycle is completed, the task of management is to ensure its implementation and then plan when to begin the next planning cycle, typically on an annual basis. The future, by definition, always faces us; thus, organizations always must be in the simultaneous processes of planning and implementing plans. Applied strategic planning produces future-driven decision-making tools and a process for sustaining that future focus.

A New Strategic Planning Model

The new model (see Figure 1) of strategic planning is based on existing models but differs in content, emphasis, and process. This model is intended to be especially useful for medium-sized and small organizations and is as useful for nonprofit organizations as it is for business and industrial organizations. The use of this model in an organization's strategic planning will provide both new direction and new energy to that organization. The model differs from others in its continual concern with application and implementation, not only after its completion but at every step along the way; hence the title "Applied Strategic Planning Model." The purpose of this article is to provide an overview of the model. A more complete description of the model is found in Pfeiffer, Goodstein, and Nolan (1989).

Planning To Plan

The prework of the strategic planning process involves answering a host of questions and making a number of decisions, all of which are critically important to the eventual success or failure of the entire planning process. The questions include: How much commitment is there to the planning process? Who should be involved? How can we involve absent stakeholders? How long will it take? What do we need to know in order to plan successfully? Who should develop the

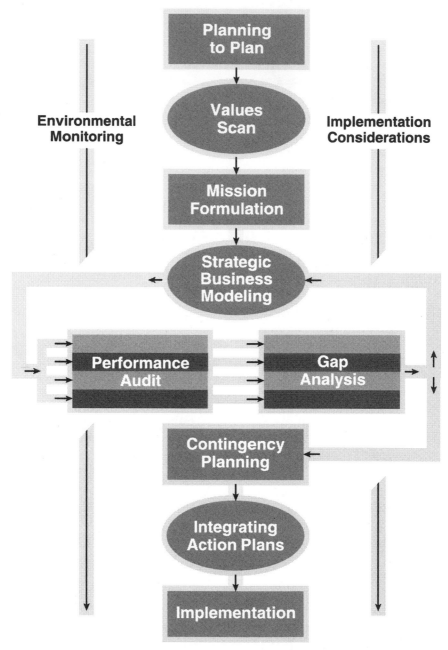

Figure 1. The Applied Strategic Planning Model

data? Planning to plan includes developing the answers to these questions and making these decisions prior to the initiation of any actual planning process. It is critically important not to rush into the process without clarifying various expectations, considering who will and who will not be involved, and so on. These issues must be resolved before the decision to plan can be made.

The first step in planning to plan is to make certain that there is organizational commitment to the process—that the key people in the organization, especially the chief executive officer (CEO), see the planning process as important and are willing to invest time and effort in the process in a way that is visible to the rest of the organization. Steiner (1979) defines the CEO as the person or persons with the authority to manage the organization. Steiner (p. 80) points out that the CEO can be the president, the president and the executive vice president, or some other combination of individuals; in the case of a division of an organization, this authority can be exercised by a divisional manager or the like. What is critical is that this authority must be actively involved in the planning process in a highly visible way to signify commitment.

Once commitment from the chief executive officer is secured, the next concern is to identify the planning team. The CEO should be involved, especially in the early stages, as should other key people in the organization. The model presented here requires top-management involvement on a continuous basis. At the same time, both input to the process and reactions to decisions that are being reached must be solicited from a broadly representative group of people in the organization. To be effective, a planning team should be able to observe and process its own group dynamics. This means that the planning team probably should not exceed ten to twelve permanent members. Who should be involved, what the selection process should be, how to deal with organizational members who feel that they should have been included, how to solicit input and feedback regularly from various segments of the organization, and so on, are matters that need to be addressed with both candor and sensitivity by those initiating the strategic planning process. Among the factors to be considered in making these decisions are the size of the organization, its structure, the various stakeholder groups that exist, and the organization's history in dealing with issues of general organizational importance. Again, these issues should be resolved prior to the initiation of any actual planning.

Although it has been suggested that the planning process be assigned to a staff group, we believe that deciding the future course of an organization is the task of top management—a task that cannot and should not be delegated. The proper role of staff in this process is to serve as a resource to the management planning group, to conduct research, generate data, and develop alternative ways of integrating and implementing the action steps that emerge from the planning process.

There are two kinds of decisions that organizations make: strategic decisions and strategically driven decisions. Senior management of the organization needs to be intimately involved with the first of these, as that is clearly an executive function, perhaps the most important executive function. The senior management needs to make certain that the second, strategically driven decisions, are properly made and implemented. This is strategic management—the execution of the strategic plan. Applied strategic planning is intended to build or increase the strategic management capacity of the organization by involving senior management directly in the planning process.

Another issue that must be dealt with is how long the process will take. As with many such processes, developing a strategic plan usually takes longer than anticipated. It often is difficult to ascertain how much consensus already exists within the management team on a variety of issues, how much team building the team has undergone, how available the necessary data will be, and what the resources of the organization are for developing data that do not exist. Without the answers to such questions, it is not possible to predict how long the process will take.

Realistically, an organization should expect to spend ten to fifteen days in the initial round of the planning process, depending on its size, complexity, and skills—especially its skills in problem identification and problem solving. With each repetition of the process, the time may be reduced by half, until a minimum of two to four days is required annually.

In an ideal model, the process can be completed in nine to twelve months. In such circumstances, the planning group would meet fairly regularly, perhaps every six weeks, for two or three days at a time. Ideally, the group would work effectively toward consensus, develop a mission statement that is rapidly and enthusiastically endorsed by the organization, and then develop strategic plans expeditiously. The resulting action plans then would be developed, tested, integrated, and implemented promptly. But it is more likely that significant stumbling blocks will arise at various points in the sequence, blocks that must be addressed and resolved before the group can move on.

One way in which these stumbling blocks and confrontations can most expeditiously and effectively be addressed is by the use of an organizational consultant, especially one skilled in both the strategic planning process *and* group dynamics. The authors of this article have spent much of their professional time over the past five years engaged in this process of facilitating strategic planning sessions. Our collective judgment is that it is the rare and exceptional organization that can manage the planning process effectively without such consultation help. Part of the planning to plan process thus involves the decision about the use of consultation help and how it might best be secured, either externally or internally.

Another issue is where the strategic planning sessions should be conducted. The site must be away from the interruptions of daily work. A retreat-type setting often is conducive to the kind of envisioning and confrontation that is involved in strategic planning. The type of facility that might be used for a team-building session probably would be appropriate for a strategic planning session.

The Values Scan

A values scan is an examination of the values of the members of the planning team, the current values of the organization, the organization's philosophy of operations, the assumptions that the organization ordinarily uses in its operations, the organization's preferred culture, and, finally, the values of the stakeholders in the organization's future. In this values scan, the planning team moves from an individual focus to a broader examination of the organization and how it works as a social system. The values scan is the first formal step of this strategic planning model, an emphasis that is different from that found in most strategic planning models.

This step also involves an examination of the personal values of the individual members of the team. Rokeach (1973) defines a value as "an enduring belief that a specific mode of conduct or end-state of existence is personally or socially preferable to an opposite or converse mode of conduct or end-state of existence" (p. 5). An individual for whom risk taking is an important personal value will envision a very different organizational future than will a person who holds security as a high personal value. Likewise, the goals and dreams of an individual who holds professional reputation as a value and is less interested in power will be different from those of a person with the opposite priorities.

These differences have clear implications for the organization's future direction, its structure, decision-making processes, and all other work of the management team. If the differences in values are not identified, clarified, and understood, there can be little agreement about how the organization's future meets the personal expectations of the individual members of the management group. Once there is clarity on the personal values of the members of the planning team and an agreement as to how whatever differences in values have emerged can be managed, the strategic planning process can move ahead. This stage of applied strategic planning is very much a values-clarification process, and the actual strategic plan for an organization represents the operational implementation of the shared values-based vision of the management team.

Once the individual values of the management planning team have been worked through, the desired values of the organization as a whole must be considered. These organizational values will be played out in the future behavior of the organization. To avoid an overly abstract discussion of these preferred future behaviors, the group may identify some recent organizational decisions that caused them pride and some that caused them concern or shame. The sharing of these feelings and exploration of the underlying reasons for them provide a useful demonstration to the planning group of the truism that all management decisions are values based.

An organization's values are organized and codified into its philosophy of operations, that is, the way the organization approaches its work. Some organizations have explicit, formal statements of philosophy, such as the Five Principles of Mars, the multinational candy corporation (see Figure 2).

---

1. **Quality**
   The consumer is our boss, quality is our work, and value for money is our goal.
2. **Responsibility**
   As individuals, we demand total responsibility from ourselves; as associates, we support the responsibilities of others.
3. **Mutuality**
   A mutual benefit is a shared benefit; a shared benefit will endure.
4. **Efficiency**
   We use resources to the fullest, waste nothing, and do only what we can do best.
5. **Freedom**
   We need freedom to shape our future; we need profit to remain free.

Figure 2. Sample Statement of Philosophy

These formal statements integrate the organization's values with the way it does business. Value-driven organizations such as Mars spend a good deal of time and energy disseminating and tracking the impact of their philosophy on all organizational behavior. All employees are expected to know the philosophy and to use it in their daily work, and there are serious sanctions against any violation of the philosophy by an organizational member.

The decision by McNeil Consumer Products Company—a wholly owned subsidiary of Johnson & Johnson—to withdraw Tylenol from the retail shelves, once it was learned it had been contaminated by some unknown external parties, was made promptly and in accordance with the Johnson & Johnson Credo—their explicit philosophy of operation.

All organizations have philosophies of operation, whether or not these are stated explicitly, and all organizations disseminate their philosophies and evaluate organization members on conformance to those philosophies. If an organization's philosophy of operations is implicit, it is necessary to make it explicit as part of the strategic planning process. The strategic plan must fit the philosophy or the philosophy must be modified—a difficult task at best.

An organization's philosophy of operations includes a series of assumptions about the way things work and the way in which decisions are made. Such assumptions in the profit-making sector include "No profit can be made doing business with the government" or "Allowing a labor union to organize our hourly production people would destroy this company." In the not-for-profit sector, typical assumptions are: "If we do not spend all of this year's budget, it will be cut next time" and "You have to go along to get along." Some general assumptions are that the organization's growth is assured by an expanding and more affluent population or that there never will be a satisfactory substitute for the organization's major product or service.

Unless such assumptions are examined in terms of their current validity and relevance—whether or not they ever were true or relevant—the organization will continue to assume that they are true and operate accordingly. Thus, an important part of the strategic planning process is to identify the assumptions that the organization makes about its environment, its markets, its operations, and how things do or should work and to examine their validity.

One function of the strategic planning consultant is to make certain that these assumptions are surfaced and addressed by the management team. This ordinarily requires some courage on the part of the consultant to confront these somewhat touchy issues and on the part of the management team as it moves through uncharted waters, questioning basic assumptions and beliefs.

Organizations develop a culture over time, in a similar fashion to the way societies in general develop cultures. Schein (1985) defines culture as a set of *shared* assumptions: (a) about the world and the way it works, (b) values about what is right and wrong based upon those assumptions, (c) beliefs about what are or should be the consequences of those values; and (d) norms about expected behavior. Of these factors—which lie at the heart of most of our actions in social systems—only the behaviors are directly observable. All the rest, much of which is unconscious, must be inferred from that behavior.

Although there is behavioral evidence about the organization's culture everywhere—in the organization's physical structures and sites, in how it greets or guards itself from outsiders, in its "war stories" told about the good (or bad) old days, in those regarded as the organization's heroes and villains, in the rites and rituals of the organization, and so on—all this must be decoded. And this decoding is rather difficult as it involves drawing inferences about the underlying meaning and significance of behavior, a frequently controversial task. It thus often becomes one of the tasks that needs to be initiated and managed by the strategic planning consultant.

An organization's culture provides the social context in and through which the organization performs its work. It guides the organization's members in decision making, how time and energy are invested, which facts are examined with care and which are summarily rejected, which options are looked favorably upon from the start, which types of people are selected to work for and in the organization, and practically everything else that is done in the organization.

Clearly the culture of an organization will either facilitate or hinder both the strategic planning process itself and the implementation of whatever plan that process produces. A formal assessment of the organization's culture and its potential impact on the implementation of the strategic plan is ordinarily performed as part of the performance audit and gap analysis phases of the applied strategic planning process. But often a discussion of the organization's culture—especially the roots of that culture in the assumptions, values, and beliefs of the management team—will begin during the values scan and is a useful and important part of that phase, providing a link to a further discussion of these issues later on.

A scan of organizational values requires a stakeholder analysis as well. Stakeholders are those individuals, groups, and organizations who will be impacted by or interested in the organization's strategic plan. They must be identified, and their concerns must be determined (that is, how their resources, status, freedom of action, relationships, and activities may appear to them to be impacted by shifts or changes in the organization's direction). Stakeholders typically include: employees (including managers), clients or customers, suppliers, governments, unions, creditors, owners, shareholders, and members of the community who believe that they have a stake in the organization, regardless of whether or not such a belief is accurate or reasonable.

Once the stakeholders are identified, the impact of various future states on different stakeholders can be considered as they are developed as part of the strategic planning process. It is important to identify who the planning team regards as significant stakeholders early in the values scan. If this is not done until later in the process, a more selective list may emerge. The stakeholders are the various constituencies that need to be considered by the strategic planning team.

The values scan is the most important and one of the most difficult phases of the applied strategic planning process. It requires an in-depth analysis of the most fundamental beliefs that underlie organizational life, especially organizational decision making. Such analysis is rare in the experience of many managers and thus can be a long and painful experience. But without such confrontation, unresolved differences in assumptions, values, beliefs, and philosophy will surface continually in the planning process, blocking forward movement and interfering with the development of a functional strategic plan. Once the differences in the management group are surfaced and clarified, and some level of agreement reached about how differences are to be resolved in the future so that they do not interfere with the planning process, it is time to move on to the next phase of the process.

Mission Formulation

Mission formulation involves developing a clear statement of what business the organization is in (or plans to be in)—a concise definition of the purpose that the organization is attempting to fulfill in society and/or the economy. In formulating its mission, an organization must answer three primary questions: (a) *What* function does the organization perform?; (b) For *whom* does the organization perform this function?; and (c) *How* does the organization go about filling this function? Often organizations add a fourth question to this list: *Why* does this organization exist?

Most organizations tend to answer the "what" question in terms of the goods or services produced. Manufacturers of detergents see themselves as in the "soap business," and gasoline producers see themselves as in the "oil business." As Levitt (1960) pointed out some three decades ago, such myopia prevents organizations both from seeing new opportunity from growth and expansion and from responding to threats and challenges.

The recommended alternative is to answer the question in terms of the customer or client needs that the organization attempts to meet. If an organization identifies itself as meeting certain public needs, it will be more sensitive to identifying and treating those needs, more likely to develop new products and services to meet those needs, and less likely to experience obsolescence and decline. If a detergent manufacturer sees itself as being in the business of providing a mechanism for helping people to clean their garments, or if gasoline producers see themselves as being in the business of providing sources of energy to consumers, many new options are open to them—ultrasonic cleaners, solar and wind power generators, and so on.

In the not-for-profit sector, answering the question of *what* function the organization serves is critical. For example, once a large metropolitan library became clear that its function was the dissemination of information, and not merely distributing books, options for new services became apparent, as did new community support.

Successful organizations try to identify value-satisfying goods and services that meet the needs of the public and include these considerations in their mission formulations. The major issue in mission formulation typically is achieving consensus on how broadly or narrowly to answer the "what" question.

Identifying the "who" is the second concern of mission formulation. No organization, no matter how large, can meet all the needs of all possible clients or customers. The mission formulation requires a clear identification of what portion of the total potential customer base an organization identifies as its primary target. The process of sorting out the potential customer or client base and identifying which portion should be sought out by the organization typically is called market segmentation.

Markets can be segmented in many ways: geographically, financially, ethnically, and so on. The needs of Sun Belt consumers are different from those of Frost Belt consumers. Federal Express serves customers who are willing to spend more than the price of ordinary postage to ensure next-day delivery of packages. Kosher foods have devout consumers, as do soul foods. General Motors has five traditional automobile lines, each designed for consumers in different economic strata.

Understanding the market place is also important for the not-for-profit sector, especially those that are publicly funded. Clarity about the two kinds of the critical clients—those who control the funding sources and those who are the recipients of the organization's service—and meeting the needs and expectations of both sets of clients are important ingredients of success in this arena.

Once the planning team has identified what the organization does and for whom, the next step is deciding *how* the organization will proceed to achieve these targets. The "how" can involve a marketing strategy, such as being the low-cost producer or the technological leader or the high-quality manufacturer; it may involve a distribution system, such as regional warehouses or evening classes in factories or no-appointment medical treatment facilities. It may involve customer service or personalized selling or any of a variety of processes through which an organization can deliver products or services to a defined consumer group.

The question of *why* an organization performs the functions that it does—the existential question—frequently is an important one for both profit-oriented and not-for-profit organizations. Many organizations feel that they need to include some simple statement of their raison d'être as part of their mission statements. It can appear as the "heart" in the diagram of the triangular relationship of the "What," "Who," and "How" questions (as in Figure 3). For example, the mission statement of the Johnsonville Sausage Company, of Johnsonville, Wisconsin, includes the following: "We, here at Johnsonville, have a moral responsibility to become the best sausage company ever established . . . ." whereas the Center for Creative Leadership in Greensboro, North Carolina, states, "Our mission is to encourage and develop creative leadership and effective management for the good of society overall." While not all organizations choose to include such a statement—nor should they be required to do so— such statements are often a natural outgrowth of the organizational-level values scan, and the planning model conveniently allows the inclusion of such a statement.

One more important factor must be considered as part of mission formulation: the identification and prioritizing of the organization's driving forces. Tregoe and Zimmerman (1980) identify nine basic categories of driving forces. These are:

1. *Products or Services Offered.* The organization is committed primarily to improving a product or service, such as retail banking, corn-sugar refining, or automotive manufac-

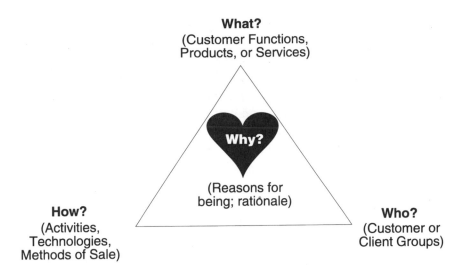

What?
(Customer Functions,
Products, or Services)

Why?

(Reasons for
being; rationale)

How?
(Activities,
Technologies,
Methods of Sale)

Who?
(Customer or
Client Groups)

Figure 3. The Basic Elements of the Organizational Model

turing, and limits its strategy for a time to increasing efficiency and improving quality in production and service.

2. *Market Needs.* Market-driven organizations continually survey potential customers to discover unfilled needs for goods
and services. Once these are identified, the organization
develops products to fill those needs.

3. *Technology.* Organizations that are technology driven continually try to develop products and services based on the
latest scientific breakthroughs.

4. *Production Capability.* Capacity-driven organizations have
a primary commitment to keeping their existing production
capability utilized (e.g., to have hospital beds filled or to
have aluminum ingots on the back loading dock ready to be
shipped).

5. *Method of Sale.* The method of sale, such as door-to-door
selling, direct mail, premiums and bonus programs, and so
on, directs the strategy of these organizations.

6. *Method of Distribution.* Some organizations are driven by their current method of distribution, which may be regional warehouses, manufacturer's representatives, pipelines, and so on.

7. *Natural Resources.* Certain types of organizations are driven by their dependency on natural resources such as coal, timber, petroleum, metals, or land.

8. *Size and Growth.* Organizations that are driven by set goals regarding size and growth constantly strive for continuing significant growth above current performance.

9. *Profit/Return on Investment.* Many organizations set high requirements about profit margins or return on investments and make decisions to achieve those goals.

Although Tregoe and Zimmerman recommend that all nine of these driving forces be considered in strategic planning, they argue that an organization must be clear about which factor is its only driving force—and organizations, according to them, can have only one such driver; when decisions are to be made that require choosing among these nine considerations, the decision makers in the organization must have mutual understanding about whether their goal is to emphasize profit, or research and development, or the development of a sales force in order to achieve growth, or some other factor that will be the single driving force behind the organization's strategy.

We, on the other hand, have found it to be more useful to have the strategic planning team prioritize the driving forces from one to nine in terms of their perceived relative importance, rather than to attempt to identify a single one. The importance of gaining consensus on these priorities should be apparent. Most major, strategic decisions that organizations make involve the allocation of resources according to a set of priorities. When there are inadequate resources or the choices are incompatible, the rank order of the nine strategic areas will determine how resources are to be allocated or which direction will be chosen. A consensual rank order, with the most important driving force in first place, enables the planning team to make otherwise difficult decisions rather easily.

Once the questions of "what," "who," and "how," and probably "why," are answered and the driving forces identified, these elements can be woven into the organization's mission statement. This should be a brief (one hundred words or less) statement that identifies the basic business the organization is in. The mission statement, which should be known to all members of the organization and understood by them, answers the questions of what the organization does, for whom, and how, and identifies the organization's major, strategic, driving force. By providing this information for both internal and external use, the organization identifies its distinctive competence(s)—those distinctive products or services offered by the organization that set it apart from its competitors. The following is a good example of a mission statement:

> The Alpha Corporation is a low-cost manufacturer and marketer of consumable food-service items for home and industrial use. We intend to maintain our position as a market leader by meeting customer needs and providing a high level of quality and service while maintaining a sufficiently high level of earnings to satisfy our investors.

Developing a mission statement can be an extremely difficult and time-consuming task, but one that the planning group must complete before moving to the next step. Developing, editing, and reaching consensus on such a statement requires skill, patience, and understanding. However, the mission statement provides an enormously valuable management tool to an organization: it clearly charts its future direction and establishes a basis for organizational decision making. The next step is for each major unit of the organization to develop its own mission statement. Unit mission statements should be more focused and more limited than that of the total organization, but they clearly must be derived from the organizational mission statement.

Strategic Business Modeling

Strategic business modeling is not an extrapolation of what the organization is now doing. It is not a long-range plan to do more of the same, only better. In this phase of the process, the planning team is asked to conceptualize a series of specific future scenarios. It is also asked to identify the steps necessary for achieving those scenarios, who will be responsible for those steps, and when those steps can be accomplished. And the strategic business models that are developed should reflect the values and the overall mission created in the earlier stage of the planning process.

Strategic business modeling thus involves establishing the quantified business objectives of the organization. The process of strategic business modeling consists of four major elements:

1. Identifying the major lines of business (LOBs) or strategic profile that the organization will develop to fulfill its mission;

2. Establishing the critical success indicators (CSIs) that will enable the organization to track its progress.

3. Identifying the strategic thrusts, that is, those tasks that will be performed to bring the LOBs and CSIs into reality, with a timetable and the designation of the persons responsible for each thrust; and

4. Determining the culture required to support the desired LOBs, CSIs, and strategic thrusts.

Each of these four elements must be determined, individually, carried through the next two phases (performance audit and gap analysis), and—if necessary—looped back and revised in the strategic business modeling phase before moving on to the next element.

The LOB analysis involves deciding the mix of products and/or services the organization will offer in the future. After each such LOB is identified, the relative size of that LOB must be agreed upon —in terms of gross revenue, marketing required, profit potential, investment required, and so on. The LOB analyses allow an organization to change its product/service mix—to drop those that no longer meet market needs, that have become unprofitable, that require too much investment to maintain, etc. For example, as a result of its strategic business modeling a law firm decided to abandon its maritime-law and patent-law practices, as the volume of such work no longer justified maintaining these as LOBs. A government agency decided on the basis of its planning process to reduce its heavy focus on MIS consulting and to begin instead to focus on general management consultation. Pie charts are often used to illustrate LOBs, because the data lend themselves to that particular format.

As the organization conceptualizes its future, it must identify the specific means of measuring its progress toward that future— setting the CSIs for the organization. CSIs are typically a mix of hard financial figures such as sales, margins, and return on investment (ROI) and soft indices of success, such as opinions of customers about service, employee morale, and the like. Other measures—such as the number of new product launches and new markets established—can be included as long as they are clear, quantifiable, and trackable. Priorities need to be set for these CSIs to make certain that the most important indices of being "on track" have been established and will be closely monitored over time. A timetable for reaching particular levels for each of these indices also must be established.

The strategic thrusts are the directions that the planning team intends for the organization to take for its LOBs in order to achieve the CSIs. Strategic thrusts are *what* the team plans to do to reach its strategic goals. During strategic business modeling, the thrusts are determined without concern for *how* they will be accomplished. To illustrate the difference between LOBs, CSIs, and strategic thrusts, we can look at a bakery, for example, whose LOBs include fresh breads, boxed cookies, and frozen pastries. Its CSIs may include 12 percent profit and 20 percent growth. But its strategic thrusts might include expanding the territory into other states or acquiring delicatessen and restaurant trade.

Relative to determining the required culture, two questions are important: (1) What common values do members of the organization need to share to achieve the desired future? and (2) What are the cultural specifications required to achieve success? For example, a major international airline set a 20 percent increase in customer satisfaction as one of its CSIs, as measured by reductions in passenger complaints, reports from focus groups and questionnaires, employee reports, and a variety of other sources. To achieve such a dramatic increase in customer satisfaction, a market-oriented culture is required—one sensitive to the critical importance of meeting passenger needs and willing and able to provide "seamless service." After the culture requirement has been set, the degree to which such a culture is present or absent in the organization is ascertained in the performance audit phase of the planning process.

That applied strategic planning is distinctively different from long-range planning becomes most clear in the strategic business modeling process. Long-range planning tends to be merely an extension of what an organization is doing already. The Alpha Corporation may plan to sell more units through its existing distribution network. A hospital may plan to open a satellite clinic. But both of these plans involve only slight variations in or expansion of the product or service offered in existing markets. Such typical long-range planning often is myopic and unduly constraining. When an organization focuses heavily on that area of the market that it currently occupies, it overlooks other possible markets. Thus, for example, Alpha might not consider developing other products, such as low-cost, nonconsumable items, or new markets, such as international, whereas the hospital might consider preventative health programs and so on. Strategic business modeling, in contrast, provides a template against which the organization can measure its future-oriented decisions.

Several considerations are critical to the success of this stage. First, the modeling must be congruent with and build on the identified values and mission of the organization. Second, the modeling must be done in a context of proactive futuring: the belief that, although no one can fully predict the future, it is possible to anticipate significant aspects of the future, to conceptualize a desired end state for the organization taking those anticipated aspects of the future into account, and to work proactively to make that desired future state occur. Within this context, the organization takes responsibility for its own future rather than assigning that responsibility to unseen external forces. Third, strategic business modeling involves a heavy emphasis on focused creativity, a free-flowing generation of ideas that involves many alternative options for the organization to consider. Success in this phase of the process is most likely to be attained when there is a maximum creative output within *realistic* boundaries. There is little or no point in the Alpha Corporation's planning team considering a new business focus unless the corporation is strongly committed to that new path and has the willingness to commit its resources to following that path. The next steps of the planning process—performance audit and gap analysis—are intended to identify whether or not Alpha, or any organization, has the necessary resources, because commitment alone is *not* sufficient to achieve success.

Performance Audit

Once the planning team has envisioned the future the organization wants to have, the team must develop a clear understanding of the organization's current performance in a process called the performance audit. It is important that the envisioning of the future precede any in-depth analysis of the organization's current performance and capacity. All too often such an analysis will limit the options that the planning team considers.

The internal performance audit examines the *recent* performance of the organization in terms of the basic performance indices — cash flow, growth, staffing patterns, quality, technology, operations, service, profit, ROI, cash flow, and so on—that have been identified as critical in the strategic profile. The purpose of the performance audit is to provide the data with which the "gap analysis"—the determination of to what degree the strategic business model is a realistic and workable one—can be conducted.

The performance audit is a focused effort that involves the simultaneous study of the internal strengths and weaknesses of the organization and the external opportunities and threats that may positively or negatively affect the organization in its efforts to achieve a desired future. The acronym SWOT represents these four factors (strengths, weaknesses, opportunities, and threats) that must be considered in an effective performance audit. The SWOT analysis is the major way of validating the strategic business model.

What is necessary here is detached objectivity and a willingness to realistically evaluate the internal strengths and weakness of the organization, as painful as such an analysis may be. An important part of this internal analysis is the evaluation of the organization's present structure: Is the present organizational structure likely to be supportive with the achievement of the new mission and LOBs?

Any data that can help the organization to better understand its present capabilities for doing its work should be included in the performance analysis. Such data might include life cycles of existing products, employee productivity, scrap rate, inventory turnover, facilities (including capacity and condition), and management capability. The important question that the performance audit must answer is whether or not the organization has the capability to successfully implement its strategic business plan and thus achieve its mission. Therefore, in planning the performance audit, special attention must be paid to securing the hard data that will indicate the organization's capacity to move in the identified strategic direction.

The performance audit must also include information about the forces outside the organization that might have an impact on achieving success in reaching its goals—the opportunities and threats of the SWOT analysis. As part of this external analysis the planning team must study competitors, suppliers, markets and customers, economic trends, labor-market conditions, and governmental regulations on all levels that can affect the organization, positively or negatively. This information should include a consideration of both current and future trends—a longitudinal perspective. In the game of chess, this is called "down-board thinking"; the chess players must not only decide on their immediate moves, but must also look "down board," consider their opponents' possible responses to their moves, and plan a number of possible moves ahead. So also must an organization say, "If I do this, my competitor (or customers, or supplier, or governmental agency, or whomever) will do that, then I will need to . . . ."

One of the most important sets of data is the competitor analysis, which profiles organizations that are in the same business or aiming for the same market segment of clients or customers. The competitor analysis should include "creative crossovers"—items that are sold or services that are delivered for similar reasons. For example, one of the chief competitors of Cross pens during the holiday seasons is not another pen manufacturer but the billfold industry, because both pen-and-pencil sets and billfolds are frequently purchased as holiday gifts for men. Because the competitor analysis usually required some research, and—as an additional benefit—to increase awareness of the marketplace, we recommend that each member of the planning team have responsibility for conducting an analysis of one to three competitors.

Much, but not all, of the data required for the performance audit will be available in organizations that have good management information systems, including financial reporting systems. Furthermore, although data bases may be available (inside or outside the organization), the organization may need to hire or reassign financial staff to research, validate, and analyze the data. This is a crunch point in many organizations: the ability—in terms of time, personnel, expertise, and so on—to handle and report on the data. However, it is a critical step that must be completed adequately.

One major emphasis of the performance-audit analysis should be a strategic business unit (SBU) analysis. A strategic business unit is a division, department, or product line that is a business unto itself within the organization; for example, the loan department in a bank, the home-furnishings division of a large department store, or the pharmacy in a large "drugstore." The SBU analysis should identify which aspects of the business are losing money, how strengths can be reinforced and weaknesses eliminated, and so on.

It should be obvious by now that the performance audit and subsequent analysis are some of the most detailed and time-consuming aspects of the strategic planning process. However, without this important, detailed information, the basis for planning is incomplete and shaky. In addition, the need for candor, openness, and nondefensiveness during the performance audit cannot be underestimated. An organization that fools itself during the performance audit is almost certain to find itself with an unworkable plan. Obviously, under such circumstances, the time and effort put into the strategic planning process will result in a travesty.

Gap Analysis

After the performance audit is complete, it is necessary to identify gaps between the current performance of the organization and the desired performance required for the successful realization of its strategic business model. This gap analysis is a comparison of the data generated during the performance audit with that requisite for executing its strategic plan, that is, a *reality test.* Furthermore, the gap analysis requires the development of specific strategies to bridge each gap identified. That is, for each such gap, the planning team must *return* to the strategic business modeling phase and rework the model until the gap is closed. For this reason, the Applied Strategic Planning Model (Figure 1) depicts an arrow running backwards from the gap analysis to the strategic business modeling phase, in addition to the arrows running forward from strategic business modeling to the performance audit and then to the gap analysis. Several repetitions of this process may be necessary before the gaps can be closed. Occasionally, the mission statement may even need to be modified in the process.

If the gap analysis reveals a substantial disparity between the performance audit and the strategic profile or the strategies identified for achieving it, the design or functioning of the organization may need to be re-examined. Obviously, either the strategic business model, or the organization, or both need to be modified in order to close the gaps between the plan and the organization's capacity.

In general, there are four basic approaches to closing gaps between the organization's current and desired state: (a) Lengthen the time frame for accomplishing the objective—the current allocation of resources is appropriate, but it will take more time to achieve these goals than initially planned; (b) reduce the size or scope of the objective—the vision was appropriate, but lesser or somewhat modified objectives are more achievable and less risky; (c) reallocate resources to achieve goals—these goals can be achieved only by focusing existing resources that have been spread too thin; and (d) obtain new resources—new talent, products, markets, or capital are necessary to achieve desired goals. Each of these approaches needs to be considered carefully each time a gap is encountered and needs to be closed.

Events never quite work out as anticipated, but strategic plans need to be developed nevertheless. The typical planning process focuses quite appropriately on the highest-probability events but this focus can result in an incomplete set of plans. Contingency planning involves the development of specific action(s) when lower-probability events occur, but only those lower-probability events that would have important consequences for the organization.

A significant part of the gap analysis is the comparison of the strategic business model with the outcome of the values scan and the mission statement, in order to ascertain that the things the organization is proposing to do are consistent with its culture. As has been noted earlier, plans that do not take into account and build on the organization's culture are not likely to succeed. This portion of the gap analysis requires the same degree of openness, candor, and confrontation that should have typified the original values scan. The gap analysis is important because it tests the organization's "wants" against reality; in effect, it is the anchor that keeps the plan from floating off in an unguided, or misguided, direction.

Contingency Planning

The next phase, contingency planning, involves: (a) identifying the most important internal and external threats to, and opportunities for, the organization, especially those involving other than the most-likely scenarios; (b) developing trigger points to initiate action steps for each contingency; and (c) agreeing on which action steps will be taken for each of these trigger points. In our model, contingency planning is placed *outside* the linear phases of the model (see Figure 1) because those phases are based on the more-likely scenarios.

Among the kinds of internal threats that are often identified by planning teams are the death or severe disability of an "irreplaceable" key staff member (e.g., the director of research and development or the orchestra's principal soloist), the destruction of a key facility (e.g., a manufacturing plant or the computer room), a prolonged strike, and so on.

Internal opportunities would include the unanticipated opportunity to commercialize a chance invention or a cash infusion by the settlement of long-standing litigation, whereas external opportunities would include the sudden opening of new markets (e.g., what occurred in Eastern Europe, the availability of new technology or equipment, and so on). Certainly not all such contingencies can be anticipated, but careful attention to the early warning signs of such critically important changes can assist an organization both to conduct and to execute effective contingency planning.

Aside from "universal" external threats such as war, economic collapse, and the like, each type of business or organization is subject to a specific set of contingencies that must be planned for. For example, producers of building materials are heavily influenced by new housing starts which, in turn, are a function of interest rates and general economic conditions. In developing its strategic business model, a producer of building materials may identify several alternative futures, each based on different volumes of housing starts. Housing starts, in turn, are influenced by a variety of governmental actions; the elimination of mortgage deductions on personal income taxes clearly would be a threat to housing starts, while a large governmental program to subsidize single-family homes would be an opportunity. The strategic business model of the building-materials producer would assume that neither of these two events would be likely to occur, but contingency plans would be developed on the basis of both possibilities.

The SWOT analysis performed earlier as part of the performance audit should provide some useful clues as to where contingencies may develop. These may have been passed over lightly as part of the earlier analysis but now become more important in contingency planning.

Contingency planning is based on the assumption that the ability to forecast accurately the significant factors that will affect the organization is somewhat limited, especially in terms of variations in those factors. However, the planning team should be able to identify the factors themselves, such as interest rates, employment, housing starts, foreign currency exchange rates, and so on, and develop alternative plans based on possible variations in these factors. Thus, contingency planning provides the organization with a variety of business modeling strategies that can be used with a variety of scenarios, each of which can be evaluated and planned for.

Contingency planning should also identify a number of key indicators that will trigger an awareness of the need to re-examine the adequacy of the strategy currently being followed. A "trigger point" could be an actual or anticipated increase in the price of a critical raw material, in the price of fuel, or in the interest rate, or it could be a sharp, unexpected positive turnaround in the economy that offers the possibility for expansion and growth. When a trigger point is identified as having been reached, two levels of response should be generated:

1. *Higher-level monitoring.* No precipitant action should be taken; in fact, no action may be required. However, the *possibility* of a need for a change in main-line assumptions should be noted, and indicators should be watched.

2. *Action.* At this level, the decision is made that conditions are different, and some contingency plan is implemented or some aspect of a strategy is modified.

The end of 1990 and the early months of 1991 saw a rapid increase in the price of oil and the threat and then the reality of war in the Gulf while the world economy was experiencing a recession— all of which had profound consequences for airlines, both domestic and international. Had the airlines had adequate contingency plans with any or all of these variables as trigger points, they could have taken earlier and more functional actions, saving several of them from having to seek the protection of bankruptcy.

Integrating Action Plans

Once the gaps revealed in the gap analysis phase of the planning process have been closed to a manageable level, the various units of the organization—functional and business—need to develop detailed operational plans based on the overall organizational plan, plans with budgets and timetables. Together, these unit action plans become the tactical plan of the organization.

In each of the separate business units—for organizations that are arrayed in business units—detailed business plans need to be developed based on the newly established strategic directions. On the functional level, financial plans, sales and marketing plans, human and capital resources plans, and so on, are needed.

For example, in a human resources plan, current and future needs for staffing on the managerial, supervisory, technical, production, and administrative levels would be developed for the time period of the plan. Such an action plan would take into account employee turnover, staffing needs, recruitment and training programs, and costs and would include contingency plans.

Each action plan developed by a functional group or business unit in the organization also must be understood and agreed to by each of the other functional groups in the organization. This process often is difficult, because once the model is developed and plans are made, each part of the organization begins to compete for limited resources in order to attain its objectives, achieve the planned growth, and so on. Several departments simultaneously may require the services of the graphics department, need a new computer program, or produce something that requires the support of the sales staff or the mailing department. All these actions have timing and budget implications as well. It is imperative that each of the functional units within the organization understands the impact of such competition and agrees to the planned allocation of resources both to itself and to the other functional units.

The planning team then will identify the gaps in and between the combined action plans, how these can be closed, and what the impact of the gaps might be on the successful execution of the strategic business model. The integration of the action plans involves putting together all the pieces in order to ascertain how the overall plan will work and where the potential trouble spots are. Most of this integration should occur in the budgetary process.

Each constituent action plan must be checked against the organizational values scan and mission statement to determine whether the proposed actions and directions are consistent with what the organization has said it wants to be. This check may reveal a need for further clarification of the values, mission, and strategic business model of the organization so that all action plans are developed with the same overall objectives and assumptions.

Environmental Monitoring

Throughout their existence, organizations need to be aware of what is happening in their environments that might affect them, and this is especially true during the planning process. Four separate but overlapping environments, in particular, should be monitored: (a) the macro environment, (b) the industry environment, (c) the competitive environment, and (d) the organization's internal environment. These should be surveyed in depth to contribute to planning to plan, the values scan, the strategic business model, and so on. The environmental monitoring process also will identify a variety of factors, both internal and external to the organization, to be considered as part of the strategic planning process. In fact, one of the extra benefits of strategic planning is that the organization gains a better understanding of how environmental monitoring should be done.

Factors to be considered as part of the macro-environmental-monitoring process include social factors such as demographics, technological factors such as the large-scale use of microcomputers, economic factors such as interest rates, and political factors such as increasing governmental deregulation. Among the factors to be considered as part of the industry environment are the structure of the industry, how the industry is financed, the degree of governmental presence, the typical products used in the industry, and

Finally, the involvement of key members of the organization, the examination of the social and psychological underpinnings of the organization, the constant environmental surveillance, and the ongoing awareness of the need for implementation throughout the planning process produce a broader and yet more detailed, more immediately applicable plan than that which results from using other models. This truly is Applied Strategic Planning, an activity that provides criteria for making important day-to-day decisions in organizations.

References

Levitt, T. (1960, July-August). Marketing myopia. *Harvard Business Review,* pp. 45-56. Reprinted in *Harvard Business Review,* September-October 1975, pp. 26-28, 33-34, 38-39, 44, 173-174, 176-181.

Pfeiffer, J.W., Goodstein, L.D., & Nolan, T.M. (1986). *Applied strategic planning: A how to do it guide.* San Diego, CA: University Associates.

Pfeiffer, J.W., Goodstein, L.D., & Nolan, T.M. (1989). *Shaping strategic planning: Frogs, dragons, bees, and turkey tails.* Glenview, IL: Scott, Foresman, and San Diego, CA: University Associates.

Rokeach, M. (1973). *The nature of human values.* New York: Free Press.

Schein, E.H. (1985). *Organizational culture and leadership: A dynamic view.* San Francisco: Jossey-Bass.

Steiner, G.A. (1979). *Strategic planning: What every manager should know.* New York; Free Press.

Tregoe, B.B., & Zimmerman, J.W. (1980). *Top management strategy: What it is and how to make it work.* New York: Simon & Schuster.

I.
Perspective on the Need to Plan

Introduction

Strategic planning, the process by which an organization envisions its future and develops the necessary procedures and operations to achieve that future, has become an institutionalized process in most companies over the last few decades. Often, however, the planning process involves a formal development of a plan which then has little impact on the day-to-day operations of the firm. When a strategic plan is nonfunctional or dysfunctional, it is usually due to a planning process that is poorly conceptualized and poorly executed. A successful planning process does not end with a formal document that is then put aside, but rather it taps the lifeblood of the organization in a way that permanently changes the way its members think and act.

This strong bias that a strategic plan is an active, vital process that has a significant impact on the organization is reflected in "The Why and How of Planning," our first article in this section. In it the author advocates that planning should imply change and initiate immediate actions to obtain optimal results in a fixed time period, usually one year. He emphasizes that a plan is a continuing process (not simply a written document) by which a business is kept on course.

Planning to Plan

Effective strategic planning starts with effective preplanning, an important step that helps to ensure that subsequent steps in the process go smoothly. The gist of preplanning involves asking and answering a series of questions and making numerous decisions in the process. If these preplanning questions are rushed or skipped, the process is later likely to become bogged down or involve extensive backtracking as preplanning concerns are addressed in a piecemeal fashion throughout the process. These questions include the following:

How much commitment is there to strategic planning? In order to be effective, strategic planning must start with a clear commitment from the chief executive officer (CEO). Support from other key staff and line managers is also essential. This commitment to the process is best confirmed by the CEO and the other key managers in a visible way (i.e., in verbal and written statements made to all members of the organization). Organizational commitment should also extend to the board of directors, whose function is not to formulate strategy, but to review it.

Who should be involved in the process? Those individuals who make up the strategic planning activity should be expected to work together as a team for a set cycle of the planning process, usually a one-year period. The team should consist of members from top management as well as representative individuals from other key power groups within the organization. The planning team should ideally be composed of from five to twelve members.

How long will the process take? Ideally, the planning process takes from eight to twenty days, generally scheduled in alternating two- and three-day fully focused sessions, each six weeks apart. Although this may seem like an excessively long period of time to tie up a group of key personnel, the issues that are discussed in-depth are the same issues the group members would normally be addressing in a much less efficient manner as an ongoing part of implementing their individual responsibilities.

Formal strategic planning provides a systematic and organized approach to addressing the most important issues that guide day-to-day operations in the organization. This systematic approach should be done under a somewhat ideal set of circumstances that involve the accessibility of key personnel, extensive internal and external data, and "quality" time that is free of interruptions, so that choices can be better evaluated and rational decisions more clearly made. When done effectively, the resulting strategic plan will serve as a road map and reference guide for managers, saving extensive amounts of time in the day-to-day operations of their jobs as the "right" decisions are made easily and more frequently. In addition, the strategic planning process allows for key decisions to be addressed a single time in a comprehensive manner rather than dozens, if not hundreds, of times by isolated managers acting independently. On an overall basis, effective strategic planning saves the organization significant amounts of expensive management time while simultaneously enhancing the quality of management decisions.

The entire process can be completed in six to nine months if the planning group meets regularly, perhaps every six weeks. Of course, when the time frame depends on a host of variables (such as the cohesiveness of the group, the extent of problems and opportunities that the organization faces, the availability of necessary data, and the ability to obtain needed data that does not exist), the time involved to effectively complete the strategic planning process is often underestimated.

What is expected to be accomplished? At the outset, all members of the planning team should have an understanding of what the process will—and will not—involve. This clarification will help to focus expectations and minimize hidden agenda by team members. The third article in this section, "Strategic Intent," advocates stretching and building new competitive advantages through strategic planning.

What information is needed for the process? An extensive amount of historical, competitive, environmental, and operational data will be needed throughout the planning process. Early identification by the planning team as to what information will be needed allows time for missing data to be gathered and available when required.

Where should the process be conducted? Usually the process is best conducted in an off-site facility that allows minimal interruptions and permits the group of individuals to develop into a team, working together to achieve mutual goals.

The Values Scan

An essential starting point to the strategic planning process is a discussion of values: of members of the planning team, the organization, and important stakeholders in the organization (employees, customers, suppliers, owners, creditors, unions, etc.). This examination seeks to identify and clarify underlying assumptions about the organization's culture, mode of operations, and philosophy of business, which will serve as a foundation for the rest of the planning process. Once there is clarity and consensus on values, the strategic planning process can move ahead. If the time and effort is not taken at this initial stage to clarify values, delays in the process will be inevitable later when statements and goals are identified as functions of unresolved conflicts in values.

A strategic planning process needs to thoroughly identify and clarify the underlying organizational values that exist in the company prior to establishing objectives and strategies that will work. The alternative approach of attempting to change the organization's values is a complex and difficult task, which is not generally recommended.

Other Early Issues

Also early in the strategic planning process several other issues must be faced. The last article in this section, "Begin Strategic Planning by Asking Three Questions" focuses on the company's directions, environment, and strategic choices. The three questions are "Where are you going? What is the environment? How do you get there?" The author introduces the mission statement and discusses ways to identify specific goals and objectives and establish strategies for achieving each. He stresses the importance of environmental monitoring to identify and understand changing trends that will affect the company. Examples are given to illustrate strategies that were used to affect market shares.

1

The Why and How
of Planning

Abstract

Planning should imply change. An organization does not need to "plan" if it intends to continue doing the same thing. The reason a lot of planning is never done is not because people dislike planning; it is because they dislike change.

Plans are made for action. Not any action; the right action. The purpose of planning is to initiate an immediate act that has the maximum probability of optimal results over some time period (long enough to give people control over the future). Objectives should be defined, and then a decision should be made on what needs to be done immediately to start attaining those objectives.

Why plan? Planning is conducted not to attempt to predict the future (an unprobable task), but because it's the best chance for survival in a world that is constantly changing.

What is planning? Planning is simply a technique for establishing and maintaining a sense of direction so that you can work consistently to make progress in that direction. It is directive rather than restrictive. It questions convention and suggests innovation.

Planning is a continuing process by which a business is kept on course. Planning is not finished when a planning document is published. The written plan is a record of the progression of the enterprise as it was preceived at a certain fixed point in time. The document shows the relationships of various activities anticipated in the future. It provides a point of reference against which subsequent developments can be measured so that corrective action can be taken. If a plan is going to work, it must be worked, that is, actively implemented.

How do you plan? You decide realistically what you want to accomplish, given an objective assessment of the resources available. Then you plot an idealized course of a reasonable way to get there, making adjustments along the way as they are needed.

The Why and How of Planning

Merritt L. Kastens

I wonder how many speeches, articles, essays, books, seminars, and inter-office memoranda have been written on this subject. You would think that by now somebody would have said it so that it stayed said. I am sure that the trouble is that if you say it right, it sounds too simple—and if you say it complicated, it isn't right.

The physicists have an article of faith that the ultimate solution is always simple—"elegant" they like to call it. My old physics prof loved to invoke the "KISS Principle" although he didn't invent it— "KEEP IT SIMPLE, STUPID." It's a good slogan for thinking about planning, too. Which doesn't make it easy. Ask any designer. It's that simple little basic black dress that is the hardest to bring off well. If it doesn't quite come out right , you have to stick a ruffle or a big cloth flower on it. If the car design doesn't quite look like you want it to, stick another strip of chrome on it. I'm afraid that's what a lot of people do with their planning systems if they don't work right— stick another gadget or set of forms or some new labels on it.

Unfortunately the gadgets, the black boxes, yes, even the smooth-talking consultants don't work. Gentlemen, *you have to think, you*

Reprinted by permission. "The Why and How of Planning," by Merritt L. Kastens in *Managerial Planning,* July-August 1979, pp. 33-35.

have to be honest with yourselves, you have to make up your mind—
and you've got to do something. Now that's very simple to say; it's
even simple to understand—but a lot of people find it very difficult
to do. They want a magic formula and it just doesn't exist—there ain't
no free lunch. It's tough work—sometimes unpleasant, it makes your
mental muscles ache. It's like golf; it's really a very simple game—
but it ain't easy.

So now that I've cleared myself with the truth-in-advertising boys,
let's talk about planning. But why? Why should we bother?

Well, I'll tell you one thing: there is no need to bother if you don't
plan to change something. You don't need to plan to keep doing the
things you have been doing. You've all been around long enough
that I presume you are pretty good at the things you have been doing.
You can do them by reflex, maybe in your sleep. You don't need a
fancy plan for that. "Planning for change" is a redundancy. There
is no other kind that means anything.

That's one of the reasons that a lot of planning doesn't get done.
It isn't that people don't like planning; it's that they don't like change.
This is a real problem and you might as well face up to it, in yourself
as well as in others.

However, paradoxically, planning for change is exactly why good
planning does get done. That's how and why formal planning got
started some...[thirty-seven] years ago. It got started in the industries
that were subject to the greatest changes—mostly technological
changes. The accelerating rate of change was shaking them to pieces.
They had to invent an orderly process to deal with change if they
were going to survive—and formal planning was born.

Now that "future shock" is endemic in almost every enterprise,
you find planning almost everywhere. However, there still is a spectrum. The more aggressive and rapidly changing an industry, the
more and better planning you will find in its companies. There also
have been some pretty convincing attempts to prove a correlation
between planning competence and growth and profitability. Change,
gentlemen, is the name of the game. The point is precisely to "grasp
this sorry scheme of things entire and shape it closer to our hearts
desire." If that makes some of you uncomfortable, I'm sorry.

Now the next thing to remember is that you plan in order to *do*
something. You plan for an *Action*. Actually it isn't very hard to get

people to do something—although as day-to-day managers, it may not always seem that way. No, most people will *do* things in the same way that your knee jerks when the shrink hits it with that little rubber hammer. The trouble is they do the wrong things, often for the wrong reasons. The late Robert Hutchins used to say, "Don't just do something; stand there." Presumably while you're standing there, you might be thinking. But ultimately you have to act. *The purpose of planning is to initiate an immediate act which has the maximum probability of optimal results over some time period.* A pretty simple statement but pregnant with significance.

Immediate action: you don't plan future actions. You decide on your future actions in the future, on the basis of plans that you will make in the future. Why commit yourself to a future action before you have to? Presumably you will learn something between now and that "future" which you might want to use to modify that future decision. However, if you don't take any action at all, the planning is a futile exercise. So you must do something and do it now, but you want to do something that has the *maximum probability* of turning out the way you want it to. You don't look for certainty. That would be presumptuous. But you want the best odds you can get in your favor. Peter Drucker in his inimitable style says planning deals with "the futurity of present decisions." In other words it helps you make present action decisions that have the best chance of favorable consequences not just in the present but in the future as well.

Optimal results is loaded. As beauty is in the eye of the beholder, so optima are in the minds of the planners. They sound nice and mathematical but they are subjective as hell. Don't let that spook you. But you *are* going to have to declare yourself. How much excitement do you want? How much security? What will you risk? How long are you willing to wait? They are all in "optimal."

Over some period of time is a cop-out. It has to be. How long is a long range plan? Lincoln said a man's legs should be long enough to reach from his body to the ground. A long range plan must be long enough to give you control over the future you are trying to create for your enterprise. The number of years will vary with the industry, the size of the company, the nature of your markets and, very importantly, with the scope of the ambitions you have for the enterprise.

So why do you plan? Not to predict the future—because you're kidding yourself if you think you can. Not to lock yourself into a lot of pre-determined actions because that is likely to be as disastrous as persisting in what you have been doing in the past. You plan in order to find out what the hell is going on and because it gives you the only chance of getting a grip on the future success of the enterprise. You plan because you're bruised and bloody from being knocked around by events that you don't undertand and from finding yourself in corners when it is too late to do anything about getting out of them. You plan because you're tired of managing from crisis to crisis, of constantly putting out fires—or more likely stumbling around in the hot ashes. You plan, not because it's fun. It's not, but it can be exciting. You plan, not because it's a new management fad. After. . . [thirty-seven] years it is well beyond that stage. You plan because it's your best chance for survival in a world that is changing as fast as ours is. Furthermore, I'll clue you; if you're going to be a manager, it's a lot more pleasant when you know what you're doing.

All right, so it's good for you. Every manager should do it. It builds strong companies eight ways. But what is it? Planning is simply a technique for establishing and maintaining a sense of direction so that you can work consistently to make progress in that direction. It is directive rather than restrictive. It questions convention and suggests innovation.

When a ship sets out to sail from point A to point B, it has to pick out a direction. In order to select that direction, the skipper needs to know a minimum of two things: where is point A and where is point B. For identical reasons, if we want to set a direction for business, we have to know at least where we are and where we want to arrive.

Don't say you want to make money. That doesn't tell you anything. A ship is to sail. A business is to make money. That's definition, not direction.

Do you want to go to Hong Kong or Hoboken? To a considerable degree it depends on whether you have a canoe or supertanker. If you set out to sail around the world in a canoe, you had better be a very good sailor—and be prepared to accept the ultimate risk. Be honest about your abilities and your resources. And then decide how much risk you want to take.

Merchantmen, a long time ago, would set out and go pretty much where the winds took them. They'd do business wherever they hit land. Some of them got rich on a single voyage. A lot of them ended up on the bottom of the Mediterranean. A lot of businesses were run that way once. Not any more.

The single, central, essential concept of planned management is to pick your objectives first and then decide what you have to do *now* to start attaining them. Picking proper objectives is a matter of judgment. Planning won't do it for you although it will help you analyze the objectives' feasibility. But if the judgment is bad, good planning will only help you to get to the wrong place expeditiously.

When the ship's captain has picked his destination, the first thing he does is call his navigator to bring up the charts. They will tell him where his is relative to where he wants to go. They will also tell him something about prevailing winds, current sets, and channels through the tight places. He and the navigator will then lay out a course using their judgment and skill to decide what short cuts they will risk and what areas they will give a wide berth.

The manager who has set his objectives calls in his planners and their charts. These will be market surveys, industry analyses, cash flow forecasts, and whatever other pertinent information is available. They plot a course from where they are to where they want to get.

Does the skipper actually expect to sail the course he has drawn on the chart? Not likely! The sea is not that accommodating. But the captain has a navigator and the navigator will spend his time finding out where the ship is. He may have a charthouse full of fancy electronic gear or he may use a sextant. The Polynesians do it with crossed sticks. But the job is to get a "fix" so that adjustments can be made to get back on course. If the weather is rough, the course corrections may be substantial.

So, the manager has his planners. They too may have a room full of electronic computers. They too have their charts and their equivalents of loran tables and the Coast Pilot and maybe even of the crossed sticks. Their job, too, is to maintain a "fix" and propose mid-course corrections. They don't set the objectives and they don't steer the ship. They don't decide what risks to take. They do have a major responsiblity for seeing that the course is maintained as efficiently as conditions permit. If they are wise they will know that conditions will never be quite what anybody expected.

Note, please, that you do not leave the navigator on the beach once the course has been set. Navigation is a continuing process by which the ship is kept progressing toward its destination.

So, too, planning is a continuing process by which a business is kept on course. Planning is not finished when a planning document is published. The physical "plan" is a record of the progression of the enterprise as it was preceived at a certain fixed point in time. The document shows the relationships of various activities anticipated in the future. It hypothesizes responses that will be made to certain expected challenges. But the physical plan is a stop-action photograph. It is obsolete by the time it comes out of the typewriter because already some conditions will have changed. It is an idealized representation, and no experienced manager should expect it to predict with fidelity what will actually happen.

What the written plan does do is provide a point of reference against which subsequent realities can be measured so that appropriate corrective action can be taken quickly and surely. But to fulfill that function, it must be "worked." The written plan won't do it sitting on a shelf in a fancy binder marked "PLAN."

Furthermore, a plan if it is going to work, needs a reliable information feedback. If you don't know where you are, you don't know whether you are on the planned course or not and so you have no way of taking any corrective action. And you can't find out where you are by counting the engine revolutions. You have to know where you are relative to the world outside.

So, how do you plan? You decide realistically what you want to accomplish given an objective assessment of the resources available. Then you plot an idealized course of a reasonable way to get there. Then you start out—but you pay attention. You take your regular fixes so that you know where you are and can get back on the course before you fetch up on the reefs.

There are lots of charts and navigational aids you can use. The electronic gadgetry is extremely valuable. But even if you do it with crossed sticks, the principles are the same.

2

Matching Corporate Culture and Business Strategy

Abstract

This article aims to show how to gauge the likely impact of an organization's culture on the chances for success of future business strategies. Culture is defined as a pattern of beliefs and expectations shared by the organization's members. (It is different from an organization's climate, which measures whether those expectations are being met. While climate is often transitory, tactical, and manageable over the relatively short term, culture is usually long-term and strategic in nature.) Culture is capable of blunting or significantly altering the intended impact of even well-thought-out changes in an organization. The methodology for dealing with culture takes four steps:

Step 1. Define the relevant culture and subcultures in the organization using meetings and interviews to identify central norms.

Step 2. Organize the information about the firm's culture in terms of manager's tasks and their key relationships.

Step 3. Assess the risk that the company's culture presents to the realization of the planned strategic effort.

Step 4. Identify and focus on those aspects of the company's culture that are highly important to strategic success and incompatible with the organizational approaches that are planned.

When culture and strategy do not match, managers' choices include (1) ignoring the culture (often impossible); (2) managing around the culture (through unique approaches to implementation); (3) trying to change the culture to fit the strategy (difficult); and (4) changing the strategy to fit the culture (sometimes unavoidable).

The third option (changing the culture) involves coordinated efforts by top leadership to change their own behavior, the signals they send to subordinates, as well as the firm's structure, systems, and people's skills.

Matching Corporate Culture and Business Strategy

Howard Schwartz
Stanley M. Davis

Which are the well-run companies? Are they the star performers so often referred to in articles about good management and organization—GE, GM, IBM, Texas Instruments? Not to mention the Mitsubishis, Sonys, ICIs, Phillipses, and Siemenses of the world? Whatever your list, a discussion of what makes these firms tops will involve notions of their strategic sense, their clear organization, their management systems, and their excellent top people. Even then, a description generally ends up with statements about some vague thing called corporate "style" or "culture." Apparently, the well-run corporations of the world have distinctive cultures that are somehow responsible for their ability to create, implement, and maintain their world leadership positions.

Coca-Cola and Pepsi, Hertz and Avis, Mars and Hershey are direct competitors within their industries. No doubt their strategies differ significantly. No less doubtfully, so do their companies' cultures. All one has to do to get a feel for how the different cultures of competing businesses manifest themselves is to spend a day visiting each. Of course there are patterns in the trivia of variations in dress, jargon, and style—but there is something else going on as well. There are characteristic ways of making decisions, relating to bosses, and choosing people to fill key jobs.

These mundane routines buried deep in companies' cultures (and subcultures) may be the most accurate reflections of why things work the way they do, and of why some firms succeed with their strategies where others fail. And if we can get at the way in which these minutiae determine an organization's ability to create and to carry out strategy—that is, if we can learn how to evaluate corporate culture—we can also learn a great deal about how to manage a large organization through a period of strategic change.

There are many examples of corporate cultures that, though once a source of strength, have become major obstacles to success. In 1978, for instance, AT&T announced that it was making a major strategic shift—from a service-oriented telephone utility to a market-oriented communications business. Chairman J. D. deButts went on intracompany TV to announce to every employee that "we will become a marketing company." To implement this new strategy, AT&T has had to undertake the largest organizational transformation in the history of U.S. industry. One out of every three of the one million jobs in AT&T will be changed. Despite the major changes in structure, in human resources, and in support systems, there is a general consensus both inside and outside AT&T that its greatest task in making its strategy succeed will be its ability to transform the AT&T culture. It will probably be a decade before direct judgments should be made as to its success. In the meantime, however, we are concerned with how to get your hands around an organization's culture.

One man who tried was Walter Spencer, the former president of Sherwin-Williams Company. For six years Spencer tried to turn around a firm that suffered from an overabundance of unprofitable products that could not, it seemed, be cut; from antiquated plant and equipment that could not be written off; and from a deeply entrenched manufacturing bias on the part of the board of directors, who were sitting in the capital-goods-oriented city of Cleveland. Speaking of his attempt to transform Sherwin-Williams from a production-oriented company to a marketing-oriented one, Spencer said, "When you take a 100-year-old company and change the culture of the organization, and try to do that in Cleveland's traditional business setting—well, it takes time. You just have to keep hammering away at everybody." After six years of such "hammering away," Spencer resigned, saying the job was no longer any fun. He had dented but not changed the culture.

Corporate cultures impose powerful influence on the behavior of managers. As the examples given above suggest, a business that is shifting its strategic direction may find its culture a source of strength or of weakness. It is possible to evaluate this elusive aspect of organization that appears to be so intimately linked with strategic success or failure. One can gauge the likely impact an organization's culture will have on the chances for success of future business strategies, and it is the aim of this article to show how to do so.

Strategy and Organization

Most people realize intuitively that corporate organizations designed to implement strategy are a lot more than the boxes and lines on an organization chart. Despite this awareness, managers often behave as though organizing a business to execute a new strategy is primarily a question of redrawing the boxes. In such a situation they frequently ask "What is the right structure for dividing and coordinating work?"

Executives are generally aware, however, that a corporation's management systems, and the skills and experience of its people, are as much a part of its organization as its structure. Organizations cannot function without some degree of regularized, formal information flows, policies, procedures, and meetings through which the essential tasks of the business are carried out. Organizations are also built upon the skills, experience, and needs of the people who compose them. It has also become clear that corporations have distinct cultures.

Anthropologist Clyde Kluckhohn has usefully defined culture as "the set of habitual and traditional ways of thinking, feeling, and reacting that are characteristic of the ways a particular society meets its problems at a particular point in time." A corporation's culture, similarly, is reflected in the attitudes and values, the management style, and the problem-solving behavior of its people.

Organizational theorists and executives agree that the best answer to the question, "How should we organize to pursue a particular strategy?" depends on a complex set of trade-offs among structure, systems, people, and culture. No organization will perform well in a competitive environment unless these four dimensions of organization are internally consistent and fit the strategy. While a great deal is known about managing the first three dimensions—structure, systems, and people—there is little more than an intuitive sense about how to manage the fourth dimension of organization—culture—and we will therefore limit ourselves in this article to matching corporate culture and business strategy.

What Corporate Culture Is (and Isn't)

Most executives with whom we have discussed corporate culture are comfortable with the idea that their companies have such a dimension. They are unsure, however, about what the word means in a business context and what use they could make of a better understanding of their own organization's culture. It was suggested earlier that an understanding of culture might reduce the risk of failure. Before describing how, it is important to clarify what we mean by culture and to illustrate how a company's culture can be usefully understood.

One way to understand culture is to understand what it is not. Many large corporations, for instance, periodically undertake climate surveys to "take the temperature" of their organizations. But climate is not culture. Climate is a measure of whether people's expectations about what it *should* be like to work in an organization are being met. Measurements of climate can be very helpful in pinpointing the causes of poor employee motivation, such as unclear organizational goals, dissatisfaction with compensation, inadequate advancement opportunities, or biased promotion practices. Action to address these sources of dissatisfaction tends to improve motivation. Improved motivation ought to result in improved performance, and by and large the evidence suggests that it does.

Culture, on the other hand, is a pattern of beliefs and expectations shared by the organization's members. These beliefs and expectations produce norms that powerfully shape the behavior of individuals and groups in the organization. So, while climate measures whether expectations are being met, culture is concerned with the nature of these expectations themselves.

For example, Douglas McGregor's early notions about management style, Theory X and Theory Y, were reflections of two distinct views of life leading to two different managerial cultures. Theory X was based on the belief that employees were inherently unwilling to work, and this led to a set of attitudes and norms that emphasized coercive controls and hierarchy. Theory Y assumed that employees were self-actualizing and produced a culture that emphasized self-control and collaboration. In either case the climate could be "good" or "bad," depending on whether the employee's own view of life fit the prevailing managerial culture.

What climate really measures, then, is the fit between the prevailing culture and the individual values of the employees. If employees have adopted the values of the prevailing culture, the climate is "good." If they have not, the climate is "poor," and motivation and presumably performance suffer. If, for example, the culture includes the belief that individuals should know where they stand, but the performance appraisal process does not allow for this, climate and motivation will very likely suffer.

While climate is often transitory, tactical, and manageable over the relatively short term, culture is usually long-term and strategic. It is very difficult to change. Culture is rooted in deeply held beliefs and values in which individuals hold a substantial investment as the result of some processing or analysis of data about organizational life. (Technically speaking, these beliefs and values are manifestations of the culture, not the culture itself.) These beliefs and values create situational norms that are evidenced in observable behavior. This behavior then becomes the basis for the formation of beliefs and values out of which norms flow. This closed circuit of culture development, which is illustrated in Figure 1, accounts for much of the tenacity that organizational cultures exhibit. In most groups, individuals who violate these cultural norms are pressured to conform and may be ostracized unless norms change to accommodate those who deviate from them.

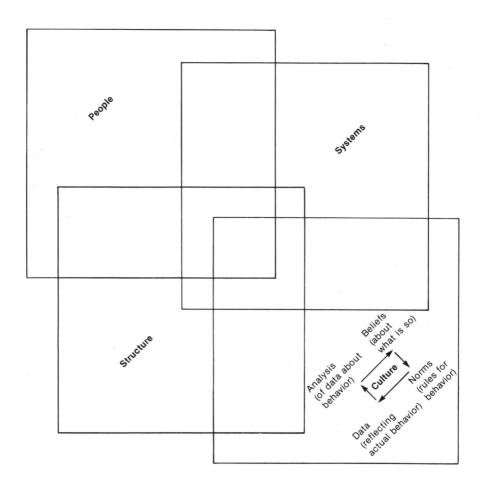

Figure 1. Culture Development in an Organization

Culture Reflects What Has Worked in the Past

Recent research by Richard F. Vancil, which was aimed at understanding the behavior of decentralized profit-center managers, suggests that the primary influence on their behavior is top-management behavior, "which, in turn, reflects their [top management's] philosophies of management and style of leadership." While top-management tasks may be similar in most decentralized firms, their approach to these tasks may be quite different. The choices senior managers make about their approach to management tasks, about how they spend their time, and about the structure of their relationships with each other and with their subordinates will "clearly produce different behavior on the part of profit center managers in . . . different firms." Such choices were found to be "the single most important determinant of a profit center manager's perception of his [or her] autonomy."

Anthropologist C.S. Ford has defined culture as "composed of responses which have been accepted because they have met with success." The choices top managers make reflect their view of reality —the values, beliefs, and norms that served them and the company well during their own rise to power. It is these choices that continually reaffirm the corporation's culture and reinforce the expected behavior across the organization.

Many executives have learned the hard way that reaching the top rungs of their organizations does not necessarily confer a license to violate the corporate culture. Studies of small-group behavior tell us that groups tend to choose as leaders those who most embody the norms of the group. One of the dilemmas of leadership in a changing business environment is the need to violate the norms on which the leader's selection was based. Deep resentment and resistance nearly always result.

The former chairman of a large oil corporation, for example, led his company through a major restructuring to prepare it for a world of reduced crude oil margins, less-favorable tax treatment, and the possibility of forced vertical divestiture. Other steps he took included a major commitment to strategic planning, an influx of outside professionals to staff the planning effort, attempts to change marketing from its traditional obsession with volume to a focus on profit contribution, turnover in many key executive posts, and emphasis on diversification outside the energy field.

To many of his former peers, this executive's behavior was an unfathomable violation of the cherished beliefs on which the corporation's culture was based. He realized, however, that the effect of the firm's culture was to place restrictive limits on the strategic options the executive group would consider and to seriously hamper the firm's ability to execute a new strategic direction. Predictably, as soon as he resigned, the company's leadership group returned to the time-tested patterns of action that had served them and the company well in the past.

As this oil executive discovered, culture is capable of blunting or significantly altering the intended impact of even well-thought-out changes in an organization. A lack of fit between culture and planned changes in other aspects of organization may result in the failure of a new measure to take hold. All too often the result is, "We tried but it didn't work the way we thought it would." Something has to give. In this case, either the culture is changed to fit the strategy or the strategy is changed to fit the culture.

Measuring Cultural Risk

Most attempts to define organizational culture leave managers who have tried it at a loss. The usual product is a list of eight or ten phrases describing the informal rules that govern the interaction of management team members. This may appear useful until an attempt is made to judge from the list whether a proposed strategy will find that the culture is amenable to its execution.

Such efforts have been disappointing because managers have had no method for thinking through the relationship between culture and the critical success factors on which strategy is contingent. The way to fathom this relationship is to recognize that the four components of an organization—structure, systems, people, and culture—determine important managerial behavior. They influence the way in which major management tasks are carried out and critical management relationships formed.

An organization's culture can also be described by its management in terms of the way their tasks are typically handled in the context of these key relationships (see Figure 2). Then, once culture and the other organizational dimensions have been defined in similar terms, their compatibility can be systematically assessed.

In Figure 2, each of the lines is to be filled in to describe how a particular task is handled in the context of a particular relationship. The table serves as a checklist and a way to spot interaction between the cultural characteristics of each level of relationship and between the various managerial tasks. The richness of the analysis is particularly useful for identifying the underlying patterns that must be understood in any attempt to change aspects of the culture or in seeking the means to manage around it.

This framework is helpful in assigning meaning to the anecdotes in which much of the data about organizational norms are stored. We have also found it useful to help interpret what we see in management meetings and to analyze records of how executives and managers spend their time. As is true when any management tool is used for the first time, internal support services and/or external consultants are often helpful.

Tasks	Relationships			
	Companywide	Boss-subordinate	Peer	Interdepartment
Innovating				
Decision making				
Communicating				
Organizing				
Monitoring				
Appraising and rewarding				

Figure 2.   Corporate Culture Matrix

Figure 3 is a simplified presentation of the results of a cultural analysis. Adding across the rows of the table in Figure 2 will provide a composite portrait of how the organization tends to handle particular kinds of tasks. Adding down the columns will portray the way in which each type of relationship is typically structured. For ease of communication, we have displayed only the results of the rows and columns, not the material in each cell.

The degree of control that managers have over culture is very limited in comparison with the degree of control they have over structure, systems, and people's skills. Indeed, most of the risk surrounding organizational shifts arises from the relative immutability of the organization's culture. Because an organization's current culture is relatively fixed, it is most useful for a manager who wants to effect a strategic change to ask: How compatible with the existing culture are the other organizational elements—structure, systems, and people—through which a shift in strategic direction is to be implemented?

It is then possible to highlight those task/relationship areas where major problems exist. If these problems involve task relationship areas that would be critical to the success of the new strategy, they represent sources of cultural risk that must command major management attention.

Does the Culture Fit the Strategy?

To illustrate how cultural risks can be identified and managed in an organization, it is useful to look at the strategy and culture of the international banking division of a major money center bank. (This example was developed as a composite of the strategies and cultures of several such banks.) The international division has developed a strategy to grow its off-shore correspondent banking business. Many months were spent in creating a sound, market-based plan.

In the arcane world of international correspondent banking, profits are earned by U.S. multinational banks through the collection and issuance of letters of credit, foreign exchange trading, loans

Relationships	Culture Summary
Companywide	Preserve your autonomy. Allow area managers to run the business as long as they meet the profit budget.
Boss-subordinate	Avoid confrontations. Smooth over disagreements. Support the boss.
Peer	Guard information; it is power. Be a gentleman or lady.
Interdepartment	Protect your department's bottom line. Form alliances around specific issues. Guard your turf.
Tasks	**Culture Summary**
Innovating	Consider it risky. Be a quick second.
Decision making	Handle each deal on its own merits. Gain consensus. Require many sign-offs. Involve the right people. Seize the opportunity.
Communicating	Withhold information to control adversaries. Avoid confrontations. Be a gentleman or lady.
Organizing	Centralize power. Be autocratic.
Monitoring	Meet short-term profit goals.
Appraising and rewarding	Reward the faithful. Choose the best bankers as managers. Seek safe jobs.

**Figure 3. Summary of Cultural Risk Assessment
(international banking division)**

and loan participations, and other banking services provided to foreign banks. Income is taken as fees, interest payments, and as spreads earned on deposit balances.

To succeed in this business, the services of numerous foreign branches must be carefully coordinated with those in New York, Chicago, London, and other global money centers. Operational support for money transfer and other services must be of high quality. Response time to customer inquiries must be short. A high level of calling officer quality and customer contact is needed to add value to what is otherwise a commodity-like service. It is also important to hold costs to a minimum.

Implementation of a new strategic plan in the international division postulated these eight major changes:

Structure

1. Dedicate an organization to the foreign correspondent banking market. (Previously this market had been managed by each geographic area.)

2. Establish a matrix structure between the new line of business organization and the geographic areas.

3. Place predominant decision-making authority with key correspondent banking personnel rather than leaving it with geographic managers.

4. Use an intergroup team (both correspondent bankers at headquarters and local offices in the field) to improve international money transfer.

Systems

5. Coordinate closely with other bank operations units.

6. Develop a management information system to measure account profitability.

People

7. Increase continuity in client relationships.

8. Attract superior personnel from within the bank to this new line of business organization.

In any industry or company that is implementing major strategic shifts, success depends on successfully combining the culture with changes in organizational structure, management systems, and people to produce desired behavior. Where changes in any of these three aspects of organization are aimed at behavior that is crucial to success, the risk that performance will suffer increases if the culture rejects or alters their impact. Can the proposed strategy be successfully implemented in the international division culture? What are the cultural risks? What is their source?

Figure 3 is a summary of the culture of the international banking division of our composite money center bank. It was actually developed through a series of individual and small group interviews in several such banks. Executives and managers were asked to describe the survival rules (that is, "the way the game is played") as if they were coaching a new member of the organization. The result was a collection of simply stated imperatives that are the norms implicitly accepted by the group. These statements were summarized into patterns that represent the principal shared expectations about behavior, and the summaries were fed back to small groups of managers to develop agreement among them on definitions of the central norms in the culture of the international division.

The categories used, which reflect the language and meanings within the division, were chosen to help the managers organize their impressions. Relationships were defined from each manager's point of view and included those between bosses, subordinates, and peers within the division; between the international banking division and other banking divisions, such as domestic corporate banking; and with the bank's top management.

The resulting summary of the international banking division culture characterized individual area managers as feudal barons. Each had been in place from five to seven years. As long as their profit contribution goals were met, they operated with almost complete autonomy. To preserve that autonomy, their concern for short-term performance was paramount. Planning and decision making were undisciplined, excessively personalized, and focused on each individual deal. Subordinates were highly adverse to taking risks. So many people were involved in signing off on a loan decision that it was difficult to hold anyone truly accountable for results.

There was, furthermore, a veneer of mannerliness and colleagueship that inhibited frank and honest confrontations to resolve conflicts in the bank's best interest. Information, jealously guarded, was used to manipulate and control adversaries. Political intrigues abounded, with advancement often going to people most loyal to immediate supervisors. As a result of these cultural aspects of our composite division, innovation was risky and received little support. Anything the area manager decided to address was quickly picked up by subordinates. Opportunism was more important than strategy. Not surprisingly, the organization very quickly fell into second place behind more innovative, effective competitors.

The international division's culture described in this analysis appears on the surface to be an obstacle to the successful implementation of the eight-point correspondent banking program. But it is equally unrealistic either to forge ahead; to launch a difficult, expensive, and time-consuming effort to change the culture; or to abandon the strategy as unworkable. What is needed is a careful analysis to determine the degree and source of cultural risk involved. Then policy makers can make decisions about which specific aspects of culture might be changed and how the strategy might be modified to increase the chances of success.

Cultural Risk Assessment

Each of the eight organizational approaches outlined in the international division's implementation plan is aimed at influencing the tasks and relationships of managers, credit officers, and bank operations personnel. Approaches that run counter to the cultural norms of the international banking division will encounter resistance. Others, more compatible with the culture, will be more readily accepted. Some of the behavior sought is particularly crucial to the success of the strategy. The degree of cultural risk, therefore, depends on the answers to these two questions: How important is each organizational approach to the success of the strategy? How compatible is each approach with the division's current culture?

Significant risks result from organizational approaches that are highly important to the success of the proposed strategy but not compatible with the existing culture. Each organizational approach under consideration was therefore reviewed. The results suggested where the implementation plan should be changed to manage around the culture, or where efforts to change the culture might be necessary. There are times when it is better to manage around the culture than to attempt to change it, and there are times when the strategy itself should be modified or abandoned.

Figure 4 shows management's judgments about the cultural risks involved in implementing the strategic plan. The proposed matrix organization and the attraction of outstanding personnel were judged to be the most troublesome aspects of the plan. Each was found to be particularly important to the success of the growth strategy objectives, yet each was highly incompatible with the current culture of the banking group.

Importance to Strategy

The importance of each organizational approach to strategy is relatively easy to assess if the strategy itself has been well thought through. An organizational approach, such as dedicating an organization to the offshore correspondent banking market, is important to strategy if the intended behavior affects a critical success factor. In this case it is difficult to see how a key competitive edge (that is, closer coordination between foreign branches and domestic headquarters) could otherwise be achieved.

The proposed matrix structure is aimed at achieving a balance between the resource claims of the correspondent banking line of business and the other corporate and personal banking businesses the bank operates in each area. It is essential to the bank's long-term performance that these trade-offs be made with the bank's total interests in mind. Top people must be recruited to gain the credibility

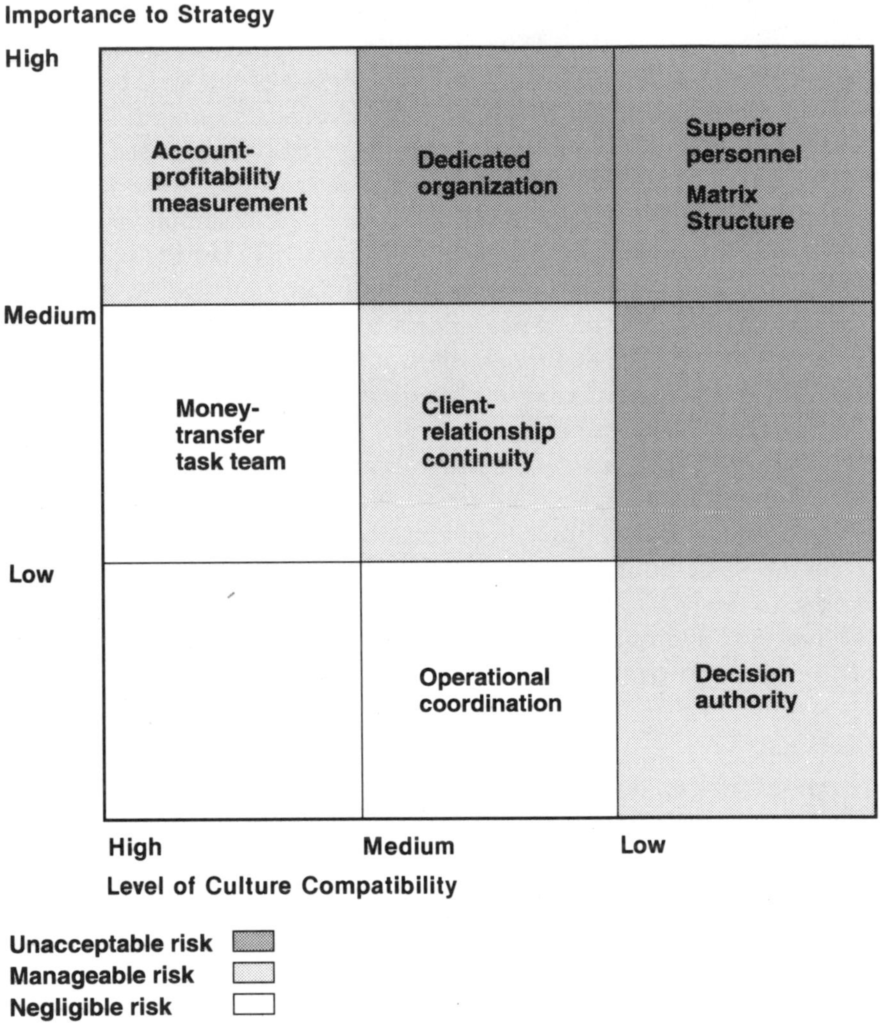

Importance to Strategy

Figure 4. Assessing Cultural Risk

necessary to win the cooperation required from other departments in the bank.

In assessing the importance of each organizational approach to strategy, we have found it useful to ask:

1. *What specific behavior is the organizational approach designed to encourage?* (How will key management tasks be affected? How will important relationships be affected?)

2. *How is this behavior linked to critical success factors?* (What specific customer needs or requirements is the behavior intended to satisfy? What competitive advantage will be gained in the marketplace? What impact will such behavior have on costs? What impact will this behavior have on such external factors as government, regulatory agencies, the financial community, public opinion, prospective employees?) The discipline of this approach forces planners and executives to think hard about the relationship between a business plan and the organization designed to carry out that plan.

Cultural Compatibility

The planned matrix structure and the attraction of top people to the correspondent banking business were both judged to have low compatibility with the international division culture. The lack of open resolution of conflict apparent in the culture, combined with the division's customary deal-oriented decision making and the subjectivity with which the reward system operated, made the success of the matrix structure unlikely without major cultural change.

Attracting top people to staff the matrix was a key success factor. In this culture, advancement by association rather than by performance had been the rule. Status and prestige were conferred on those who managed the largest corporate client relationships. Correspondent banking has never been a place to go to get ahead. Turnarounds more often failed than succeeded. In such an environment, what was the likelihood that top talent could be attracted into major jobs to turn around an international correspondent banking business?

To determine the plan's compatibility with the culture, we asked: How much change is involved in key tasks and relationships? How adaptable is the culture? How skilled is the management?

In this example, the amount of change envisioned seemed unrealistic given the current culture. Perhaps if the culture valued adaptability, as in some high-technology firms where organization is continuously forming and reforming, such change could be accommodated. In any case, strong leadership, skilled at managing a complex organization through change, would be necessary. In the bank's case, both adaptability and leadership experienced at managing change were lacking.

The case of the international banking division is not unusual. Many months of study and hundreds of thousands of dollars in consulting fees were spent in devising a tightly woven, well-documented strategy that would be responsive to customer needs, and in making good use of the bank's competitive strengths in a very attractive market. The organization plan fit the strategy, but it did not fit the culture. For that reason it was almost certain to fail, unless adjustments—either to strategy or to culture—were made.

It is not difficult to see why the problem faced by the bank is so common to other firms and industries. In many industries and in many companies, organizational cultures do not value adaptability. Most executives and managers are not particularly skilled or experienced at managing complex change. The cultural risks may be significant even where the changes contemplated do not represent an overwhelming challenge to the existing culture. A culture that values the status quo over adaptability, as most do, and that is led by executives and managers who have limited experience with strategic change, may find even modest change deceptively difficult.

Cultural Risk Can Be Managed

The case of the international banking division illustrated how a cultural risk analysis can help management pinpoint where the implementation of a proposed strategy is likely to encounter serious cultural difficulties. One or more of the organizational approaches planned may fall into the unacceptable risk zone shown in Figure 4. If so, the options available to reduce the risks to manageable proportions should be reviewed. Anything that makes the implementation plan more compatible with the culture, or reduces the strategic significance of the behavior sought, tends to reduce cultural risk. Depending on the strategy chosen, the choices open include the following: (1) Ignore the culture; (2) manage around the culture by changing the implementation plan; (3) try to change the culture to fit the strategy; and (4) change the strategy to fit the culture, perhaps by reducing performance expectations.

Can the impact of a company's culture be safely ignored?—The position taken to preserve established ways of doing business is, nearly always, to maintain the status quo. We have argued that culture can seldom be ignored when making informed management decisions.

Should ways be sought to manage around the culture?—In certain circumstances, yes. Consider, for example, a multibillion-dollar industry leader facing several major threats to its record of outstanding growth and profitability. A study is launched to consider restructuring around major markets. After formally assessing the cultural risks of such a move, the proposal is rejected as too radical and too inconsistent with the company's functional culture to warrant the risk. As a positive alternative, a major increase in planning and coordination personnel is begun.

To further illustrate the action implications of managing around a firm's culture, Figure 5 outlines four typical strategies that companies might pursue and the "right" organizational approaches to implement them. The third column summarizes a number of central aspects of the cultures of each of four companies. In each case none of the "right" organizational approaches is compatible with the company's culture. In the fourth column alternative organizational approaches that are more compatible with its culture are suggested to accomplish the same ends for each firm.

Managers familiar with the situation of each case, of course, are best equipped to determine the most appropriate options. Generally speaking, organization is aimed at achieving an appropriate degree of specialization, coordination, and motivation. A limited number of devices are available to achieve each objective, but in each case there is likely to be more flexibility than we often allow ourselves to see. Thinking of an organization as four components—structure, systems, people, and culture—helps keep the focus on the results sought rather than on the means chosen to get there. It is thus possible for corporations to evolve unique approaches to management processes. They meet competitive

	Strategy	"Right" approach	Cultural barriers	Alternative approaches
Company A	Diversify product and market.	Divisionalize.	Centralized power. One-man rule. Functional focus. Hierarchical structure.	Use business teams. Use explicit strategic planning. Change business measures.
Company B	Focus marketing on most profitable segments.	Fine tune reward system. Adjust management-information system.	Diffused power. Highly individualized operations. Relationship-oriented managers.	Dedicate full-time personnel to each key market.
Company C	Extend technology to new markets.	Set up matrix organization.	Multiple power centers. Functional focus.	Use program coordinators. Set up planning committees. Get top management more involved.
Company D	Withdraw gradually from declining market and maximize cash throw-offs.	Focus organization specifically. Fine-tune rewards. Ensure top-management visibility.	New-business driven. Innovators rewarded. State-of-the-art operation.	Sell out.

Figure 5. How to Manage Around Company Culture

challenges by finding more culturally compatible ways to implement their strategies.

Should an attempt be made to change the culture to fit the strategy?—Although extremely difficult to accomplish, culture can, and in some instances must, be changed. However, this is a lengthy process requiring considerable resources, and should not be entered into lightly. There are three prerequisites for changing a culture. First of all, the strategy and all its elements must be explicitly stated. Second, the current culture must be analyzed and made tangible. Finally, the strategy must be reviewed in the context of the culture to determine where the risks are.

An organization's culture is best altered by gradually reducing the perceived differences between current norms and the new behavior, increasing the value that the culture places on adaptability, and enhancing the ability of the managers involved to effect the desired change. There are several interrelated management techniques utilized in changing the culture. However, all steps must be prefaced by strong top leadership creating the pressure for change coupled with new top-management behavior that sets the example. It is also necessary to have a united front at the top for the sake of sending consistent messages to other managers. The pivotal word is commitment—the commitment to initiate the cultural change and the staying power to see it through.

Managers cannot be expected to change the manner in which they approach their tasks and relationships unless they are fully aware of the behavior required to get things done in the new culture, as well as to enhance their development and advancement in the firm. In short, they must know how to behave and be rewarded for behaving properly. It may be stating the obvious to say that the culture change should be coordinated with other planned internal changes in management systems and organization structure. The result will be mutual and positive reinforcement of the overall strategic change.

The company's management information and compensation systems are valuable tools in effecting change, particularly when used in conjunction with an intensive management education program. The latter both stimulates the managers to change and gives them the tools to facilitate the change in culture. It is also useful to conduct pilot programs for implementing key areas of the new strategy under controlled conditions in an effort to create an environment of success and enhance the acceptance of the new culture.

In all these activities, it is important to set priorities that focus on issues that are strategically significant, while concentrating on those elements of the culture where change is important to success. In fact, it may not be desirable to totally change the culture—only those parts of it that demonstrate high cultural risk.

Should strategy be changed to one that is more compatible with the existing culture?—A good example of this occurs when two organizations with distinctly different cultures merge. The results may fall far short of expectations. The Rockwell-North American merger in 1968 was sought by both firms for its synergistic potential. Rockwell, looking for new technologies and new products for commercial markets, saw North American as a place where "scientific longhairs" threw away ideas every day that could be useful to Rockwell. North American, in turn, was attracted to Rockwell's commercial manufacturing and marketing muscle.

Four years after the merger, some markets failed to develop as expected, and there were also problems in bridging the two cultures. As then-CEO Robert Anderson lamented, the aerospace people weren't used to commercial problems. "We kept beating them on the head to diversify, but every time they'd try it, they'd spend a lot of money on something that, when all is said and done, there was no market for, or they overdesigned for the market." The depth of the culture problem was foreshadowed by North American President John Atwood, who saw opportunity for improvement but felt that none of it would do any good unless they continued their basic line of business: aerospace engineering. Rockwell's company culture looked at the world as a rough-and-tumble place where profit margins dominate decision making. North American's environment was more noble. Some 60 well-paid Ph.D.s, for example, spent only 20 percent of their time on company business and were free to devote the rest as they chose to basic research. This was not compatible with Rockwell's obsession about controlling costs and margins.

Over a decade has passed since the merger, and Rockwell continues to have problems with its strategy of capitalizing on North

American's scientific strengths to develop important new commercial businesses. Put simply, the poor cultural fit of these two firms has restricted their ability to implement the most desirable strategy for the combined firms.

A strategy in serious cultural trouble is likely to require some combination of the three types of actions—that is, manage around the culture, change the culture, and modify the strategy—to bring cultural risk into the manageable zone. Any business decision involves a risk/reward trade-off. Cultural risk analysis is a means to clarify organizational risks that frequently go unmanaged and result in unanticipated problems.

A Top-Management Perspective

We have discussed the management of cultural risk from the viewpoint of the general manager of a single business unit. The manager of a portfolio of businesses, such as a group executive in charge of a number of businesses or the chief executive officer managing an entire corporation through a period of strategic redirection, can also use a cultural risk analysis to identify priorities for future change. These executives need to know:

- How much cultural risk is there in my portfolio of businesses, each with its own strategy and approach to implementation?
- How is this risk spread across my businesses?
- What are the specific sources of cultural risk, and do any patterns emerge across my portfolio?
- If too many important business units are at significant cultural risk, is the total corporate strategy endangered?

To answer these questions, a group executive or CEO must know how many business units in the group or corporation are faced with unacceptable cultural risk. The source of such risk anywhere within the corporation must be understood; so must the potential impact on corporate performance.

So far, corporate culture has been discussed in a post-strategy-formulation context. However, it is the perceptive manager who elects to address the issue of culture before it becomes a barrier to making strategy happen. There are several areas in which cultural analysis at the front-end can pay dividends later.

Formulating strategy.—Strategies are built on management's assumptions about many external factors. But a corporation's culture filters top management's perspective, often limiting the strategic options they are prepared to consider seriously. Defining the central values of a company's culture can remove old taboos that have unnecessarily constrained past strategic decision making.

Competitive analysis.—As culture conditions the direction of a company's strategic choices, a competitor's own culture conditions its strategic decisions and the effectiveness of their implementation. Understanding a competitor's corporate culture can provide useful clues to how that firm will behave in the competitive environment.

Managing cultural formation.—Rapidly growing companies, such as high-technology firms, often find that the ideals and values of the founding group or individual are lost as the culture becomes institutionalized through formalized organizational structures, reporting systems, and controls. Managing the process of cultural formation in relationship to the more tangible aspects of organization can help preserve the original driving force of the company.

Merger planning.—The failure to successfully integrate the disparate cultures of merging companies, as in the previously cited North American-Rockwell example, is often the cause of considerable problems in turnover and productivity. Early definition of culture in both companies and the identification of cultural compatibility and cultural risk facilitate a smoother transitional period and the realization of the desired synergy.

Installing a planning system.—Experience demonstrates that there is a long lead time (often four to five years) in achieving good results from a formal planning system. One reason is the often dramatic change in how managers are required to approach their tasks and relationships. This change is frequently very stressful and, therefore, a natural inhibiting factor. Considering culture's role in planning can shorten the installation process to two or three years.

behavior and the signals they send to their subordinates and others in the organization. Such changes must be reinforced by shifts in management processes, information and reward systems, reporting relationships, and people's skills. Major changes in management personnel, including adding outsiders as a source of new skills and new cultural patterns, are often necessary. Massive management education may be required. A cultural risk analysis helps identify the need for such costly and difficult decisions and provides a practical way to evaluate cultural change options against possible changes in the strategy to create a better match with the existing culture.

Selected Bibliography

A number of authors have recognized that organizations do in fact have cultures. Several have focused on identifying the elements that should be included in a definition of organizational culture. Andrew M. Pettigrew provides a useful compendium of these approaches in his article "On Studying Organizational Cultures" *(Administrative Science Quarterly,* December 1979). The recent work of William G. Ouchi, *Theory Z* (Addison-Wesley, 1981) describes a Japanese-oriented management philosophy as a better model for organizational cultures in U.S. businesses. Douglas McGregor's *The Human Side of Enterprise* (McGraw-Hill, 1960) describes the roots of the current U.S. model.

The difficulty of changing an organization's culture and one way of systematically approaching the task is described by Stan Silverzweig and Robert F. Allen in "Changing the Corporate Culture" *(Sloan Management Review,* Spring 1976). The decisive impact that culture can have on managerial behavior and business performance is discussed by Richard F. Vancil in *Decentralization: Ambiguity by Design* (Dow Jones-Irwin, 1978).

Issues involving culture are frequently reported in the business press, although the articles may not specifically refer to culture as the problem. Examples include those we cite in the text: For the North American-Rockwell merger, see "North American Tries to Advance Under Fire," *Business Week,* June 3, 1967, and "Forget the Magic

Mergers," *Forbes,* July 15, 1972; for the AT&T example, see Bro Uttal's "Selling Is No Longer Mickey Mouse at AT&T," *Fortune,* July 17, 1978; and for the Sherwin-Williams example, see Harold Seneker's "Why CEOs Pop Pills (And Sometimes Quit)," *Fortune,* July 12, 1978.

Finally, an excellent description of a major corporation's culture from the viewpoint of a former insider is provided in *On a Clear Day You Can See General Motors,* by J. Patrick Wright (Avon, 1980).

3

Strategic Intent

Abstract

Most of the dramatic successes in business strategy over the last decade have come from organizations that were not threats a few years ago. The major factor in these successes was the ability to innovate on a competitive basis—an ability created by a competitive obsession termed "strategic intent."

Strategic intent is an expression of ambition and leadership that is not constrained by current resources. It includes focusing and sustaining the organization's energy over time, even as circumstances change. Unlike most current planning, which results in small increments of improvement measured by short-term financial indicators, strategic intent requires the organization to stretch as it builds new competitive advantages for obtaining additional resources.

There are four suggested approaches to achieving competitive innovation:

1. **Build layers of competitive advantage.** An organization is better able to withstand the risks of competitive innovation as it broadens and deepens its base of competitive advantage.

2. **Search for loose bricks.** Enter markets in which the competitors are weakest, surprising them with varying tactics.

3. **Change the terms of engagement.** Never compete on the industry leader's terms; instead, redefine the boundaries of the industry to your advantage.

4. **Compete through collaboration.** Use joint ventures to your advantage, learning your competitors' weaknesses as you serve the industry.

Strategic intent places significant responsibility on top managers. They are expected (1) to create a sense of urgency, (2) to develop a competitor focus throughout the organization, (3) to provide employees with the skills they need, (4) to take on a new challenge only as the organization is ready for it, and (5) to establish clear targets of performance and review progress regularly.

In addition, top managers must preserve the broadest view of their competitive marketplace to maintain the strategic intent, and they must create a sense of responsibility for formulating effective strategy throughout the organization. This reciprocal responsibility on the part of managers and employees helps to keep strategic planning from becoming an elitist activity.

Strategic Intent

Gary Hamel and C. K. Prahalad

Today managers in many industries are working hard to match the competitive advantages of their new global rivals. They are moving manufacturing offshore in search of lower labor costs, rationalizing product lines to capture global scale economies, instituting quality circles and just-in-time production, and adopting Japanese human resource practices. When competitiveness still seems out of reach, they form strategic alliances—often with the very companies that upset the competitive balance in the first place.

Important as these initiatives are, few of them go beyond mere imitation. Too many companies are expending enormous energy simply to reproduce the cost and quality advantages their global competitors already enjoy. Imitation may be the sincerest form of flattery, but it will not lead to competitive revitalization. Strategies based on imitation are transparent to competitors who have already mastered them. Moreover, successful competitors rarely stand still. So it is not surprising that many executives feel trapped in a seemingly endless game of catch-up—regularly surprised by the new accomplishments of their rivals.

For these executives and their companies, regaining competitiveness will mean rethinking many of the basic concepts of strategy.[1] As "strategy" has blossomed, the competitiveness of Western
companies has withered. This may be coincidence, but we think not.
We believe that the application of concepts such as "strategic fit"
(between resources and opportunities), "generic strategies" (low
cost vs. differentiation vs. focus), and the "strategy hierarchy"
(goals, strategies, and tactics) have often abetted the process of
competitive decline. The new global competitors approach strategy
from a perspective that is fundamentally different from that which
underpins Western management thought. Against such competitors,
marginal adjustments to current orthodoxies are no more likely to
produce competitive revitalization than are marginal improvements
in operating efficiency. (The insert, "Remaking Strategy" [page 69],
describes our research and summarizes the two contrasting
approaches to strategy we see in large, multinational companies.)

Few Western companies have an enviable track record anticipating the moves of new global competitors. Why? The explanation
begins with the way most companies have approached competitor
analysis. Typically, competitor analysis focuses on the existing
resources (human, technical, and financial) of present competitors.
The only companies seen as a threat are those with the resources to
erode margins and market share in the next planning period.
Resourcefulness, the pace at which new competitive advantages are
being built, rarely enters in.

In this respect, traditional competitor analysis is like a snapshot
of a moving car. By itself, the photograph yields little information
about the car's speed or direction—whether the driver is out for a
quiet Sunday drive or warming up for the Grand Prix. Yet many

---

[1]Among the first to apply the concept of strategy to management were
H. Igor Ansoff in *Corporate Strategy: An Analytic Approach to Business
Policy for Growth and Expansion* (New York: McGraw-Hill, 1965) and Ken-
neth R. Andrews in *The Concept of Corporate Strategy* (Homewood, IL:
Dow Jones-Irwin, 1971).

managers have learned through painful experience that a business's initial resource endowment (whether bountiful or meager) is an unreliable predictor of future global success.

Think back. In 1970, few Japanese companies possessed the resource base, manufacturing volume, or technical prowess of U.S. and European industry leaders. Komatsu was less than 35% as large as Caterpillar (measured by sales), was scarcely represented outside Japan, and relied on just one product line—small bulldozers—for most of its revenue. Honda was smaller than American Motors and had not yet begun to export cars to the United States. Canon's first halting steps in the reprographics business looked pitifully small compared with the $4 billion Xerox powerhouse.

If Western managers had extended their competitor analysis to include these companies, it would merely have underlined how dramatic the resource discrepancies between them were. Yet by 1985, Komatsu was a $2.8 billion company with a product scope encompassing a broad range of earth-moving equipment, industrial robots, and semiconductors. Honda manufactured almost as many cars worldwide in 1987 as Chrysler. Canon had matched Xerox's global unit market share.

The lesson is clear: assessing the current tactical advantages of known competitors will not help you understand the resolution, stamina, and inventiveness of potential competitors. Sun-tzu, a Chinese military strategist, made the point 3,000 years ago: "All men can see the tactics whereby I conquer," he wrote, "but what none can see is the strategy out of which great victory is evolved."

Companies that have risen to global leadership over the past 20 years invariably began with ambitions that were out of all proportion to their resources and capabilities. But they created an obsession with winning at all levels of the organization and then sustained that obsession over the 10- to 20-year quest for global leadership. We term this obsession "strategic intent."

On the one hand, strategic intent envisions a desired leadership position and establishes the criterion the organization will use to chart its progress. Komatsu set out to "Encircle Caterpillar." Canon sought to "Beat Xerox." Honda strove to become a second Ford—an automotive pioneer. All are expressions of strategic intent.

At the same time, strategic intent is more than simply unfettered ambition. (Many companies possess an ambitious strategic intent yet fall short of their goals.) The concept also encompasses an active management process that includes: focusing the organization's attention on the essence of winning; motivating people by communicating the value of the target; leaving room for individual and team contributions; sustaining enthusiasm by providing new operational definitions as circumstances change; and using intent consistently to guide resource allocations.

Strategic intent captures the essence of winning. The Apollo program—landing a man on the moon ahead of the Soviets—was as competitively focused as Komatsu's drive against Caterpillar. The space program became the scorecard for America's technology race with the USSR. In the turbulent information technology industry, it was hard to pick a single competitor as a target, so NEC's strategic intent, set in the early 1970s, was to acquire the technologies that would put it in the best position to exploit the convergence of computing and telecommunications. Other industry observers foresaw this convergence, but only NEC made convergence the guiding theme for subsequent strategic decisions by adopting "computing and communications" as its intent. For Coca-Cola, strategic intent has been to put a Coke within "arm's reach" of every consumer in the world.

Strategic intent is stable over time. In battles for global leadership, one of the most critical tasks is to lengthen the organization's attention span. Strategic intent provides consistency to short-term action, while leaving room for reinterpretation as new opportunities emerge. At Komatsu, encircling Caterpillar encompassed a succession of medium-term programs aimed at exploiting specific weaknesses in Caterpillar or building particular competitive advantages. When Caterpillar threatened Komatsu in Japan, for example, Komatsu responded by first improving quality, then driving down costs, then cultivating export markets, and then underwriting new product development.

Strategic intent sets a target that deserves personal effort and commitment. Ask the chairmen of many American corporations how they measure their contributions to their companies' success and you're likely to get an answer expressed in terms of shareholder wealth. In a company that possesses a strategic intent, top management is more likely to talk in terms of global market leadership. Market share leadership typically yields shareholder wealth, to be sure. But the two goals do not have the same motivational impact. It is hard to imagine middle managers, let alone blue-collar employees, waking up each day with the sole thought of creating more shareholder wealth. But mightn't they feel different given the challenge to "Beat Benz"—the rallying cry at one Japanese auto producer? Strategic intent gives employees the only goal that is worthy of commitment: to unseat the best or remain the best, worldwide.

Many companies are more familiar with strategic planning than they are with strategic intent. The planning process typically acts as a "feasibility sieve." Strategies are accepted or rejected on the basis of whether managers can be precise about the "how" as well as the "what" of their plans. Are the milestones clear? Do we have the necessary skills and resources? How will competitors react? Has the market been thoroughly researched? In one form or another, the admonition "Be realistic!" is given to line managers at almost every turn.

But can you *plan* for global leadership? Did Komatsu, Canon, and Honda have detailed, 20-year "strategies" for attacking Western markets? Are Japanese and Korean managers better planners than their Western counterparts? No. As valuable as strategic planning is, global leadership is an objective that lies outside the range of planning. We know of few companies with highly developed planning systems that have managed to set a strategic intent. As tests of strategic fit become more stringent, goals that cannot be planned for fall by the wayside. Yet companies that are afraid to commit to goals that lie outside the range of planning are unlikely to become global leaders.

Although strategic planning is billed as a way of becoming more future oriented, most managers, when pressed, will admit that their strategic plans reveal more about today's problems than tomorrow's opportunities. With a fresh set of problems confronting managers at the beginning of every planning cycle, focus often shifts dramatically from year to year. And with the pace of change accelerating in most industries, the predictive horizon is becoming shorter and shorter. So plans do little more than project the present forward incrementally. The goal of strategic intent is to fold the future back into the present. The important question is not "How will next year be different from this year?" but "What must we do differently next year to get closer to our strategic intent?" Only with a carefully articulated and adhered to strategic intent will a succession of year-on-year plans sum up to global leadership.

Just as you cannot plan a 10- to 20-year quest for global leadership, the chance of falling into a leadership position by accident is also remote. We don't believe that global leadership comes from an undirected process of intrapreneurship. Nor is it the product of a skunkworks or other techniques for internal venturing. Behind such programs lies a nihilistic assumption: the organization is so hidebound, so orthodox ridden that the only way to innovate is to put a few bright people in a dark room, pour in some money, and hope that something wonderful will happen. In this "Silicon Valley" approach to innovation, the only role for top managers is to retrofit their corporate strategy to the entrepreneurial successes that emerge from below. Here the value added of top management is low indeed.

Sadly, this view of innovation may be consistent with the reality in many large companies.[2] On the one hand, top management lacks any particular point of view about desirable ends beyond satisfying shareholders and keeping raiders at bay. On the other, the planning format, reward criteria, definition of served market, and belief in accepted industry practice all work together to tightly constrain the range of available means. As a result, innovation is necessarily an isolated activity. Growth depends more on the inventive capacity of individuals and small teams than on the ability of top management to aggregate the efforts of multiple teams towards an ambitious strategic intent.

---

[2]Robert A. Burgelman, "A Process Model of Internal Corporate Venturing in the Diversified Major Firm," *Administrative Science Quarterly*, June 1983.

In companies that overcame resource constraints to build leadership positions, we see a different relationship between means and ends. While strategic intent is clear about ends, it is flexible as to means—it leaves room for improvisation. Achieving strategic intent requires enormous creativity with respect to means: witness Fujitsu's use of strategic alliances in Europe to attack IBM. But this creativity comes in the service of a clearly prescribed end. Creativity is unbridled, but not uncorralled, because top management establishes the criterion against which employees can pretest the logic of their initiatives. Middle managers must do more than deliver on promised financial targets; they must also deliver on the broad direction implicit in their organization's strategic intent.

Strategic intent implies a sizable stretch for an organization. Current capabilities and resources will not suffice. This forces the organization to be more inventive, to make the most of limited resources. Whereas the traditional view of strategy focuses on the degree of fit between existing resources and current opportunities, strategic intent creates an extreme misfit between resources and ambitions. Top management then challenges the organization to close the gap by systematically building new advantages. For Canon this meant first understanding Xerox's patents, then licensing technology to create a product that would yield early market experience, then gearing up internal R&D efforts, then licensing its own technology to other manufacturers to fund further R&D, then entering market segments in Japan and Europe where Xerox was weak, and so on.

In this respect, strategic intent is like a marathon run in 400-meter sprints. No one knows what the terrain will look like at mile 26, so the role of top management is to focus the organization's attention on the ground to be covered in the next 400 meters. In several companies, management did this by presenting the organization with a series of corporate challenges, each specifying the next hill in the race to achieve strategic intent. One year the challenge might be quality, the next total customer care, the next entry into new markets, the next a rejuvenated product line. As this example indicates, corporate challenges are a way to stage the acquisition of new competitive advantages, a way to identify the focal point for employees' efforts in the near to medium term. As with strategic intent, top management is specific about the ends (reducing product development times by 75%, for example) but less prescriptive about the means.

Like strategic intent, challenges stretch the organization. To preempt Xerox in the personal copier business, Canon set its engineers a target price of $1,000 for a home copier. At the time, Canon's least expensive copier sold for several thousand dollars. Trying to reduce the cost of existing models would not have given Canon the radical price-performance improvement it needed to delay or deter Xerox's entry into personal copiers. Instead, Canon engineers were challenged to reinvent the copier—a challenge they met by substituting a disposable cartridge for the complex image-transfer mechanism used in other copiers.

Corporate challenges come from analyzing competitors as well as from the foreseeable pattern of industry evolution. Together these reveal potential competitive openings and identify the new skills the organization will need to take the initiative away from better positioned players. The exhibit, "Building Competitive Advantage at Komatsu," illustrates the way challenges helped that company achieve its intent.

For a challenge to be effective, individuals and teams throughout the organization must understand it and see its implications for their own jobs. Companies that set corporate challenges to create new competitive advantages (as Ford and IBM did with quality improvement) quickly discover that engaging the entire organization requires top management to:

Create a sense of urgency, or quasi crisis, by amplifying weak signals in the environment that point up the need to improve, instead of allowing inaction to precipitate a real crisis. (Komatsu, for example, budgeted on the basis of worst case exchange rates that overvalued the yen.)

Develop a competitor focus at every level through widespread use of competitive intelligence. Every employee should be able to benchmark his or her efforts against best-in-class competitors so that the challenge becomes personal. (For example, Ford showed production-line workers videotapes of operations at Mazda's most efficient plant.)

Provide employees with the skills they need to work effectively —training in statistical tools, problem solving, value engineering, and team building, for example.

Corporate Challenge	Protect Komatsu's home market against Caterpillar	Reduce costs while maintaining quality	Make Komatsu an international enterprise and build export markets	Respond to external shocks that threaten markets	Create new products and markets
Programs	**early 1960s** Licensing deals with Cummins Engine, International Harvester, and Bucyrus-Erie to acquire technology and establish benchmarks **1961** Project A (for Ace) to advance the product quality of Komatsu's small- and medium-sized bulldozers above Caterpillar's **1962** Quality Circles company-wide to provide training for all employees	**1965** C D (Cost Down) program **1966** Total C D program	**early 1960s** Develop Eastern bloc countries **1967** Komatsu Europe marketing subsidiary established **1970** Komatsu America established **1972** Project B to improve the durability and reliability and to reduce costs of large bulldozers **1972** Project C to improve payloaders **1972** Project D to improve hydraulic excavators **1974** Establish presales and service department to assist newly industrialized countries in construction projects	**1975** V-10 program to reduce costs by 10% while maintaining quality; reduce parts by 20%; rationalize manufacturing system **1977** ¥-180 program to budget company-wide for 180 yen to the dollar when exchange rate was 240 **1979** Project E to establish teams to redouble cost and quality efforts in response to oil crisis	**late 1970s** Accelerate product development to expand line **1979** Future and Frontiers program to identify new businesses based on society's needs and company's know-how **1981** EPOCHS program to reconcile greater product variety with improved production efficiencies

Building Competitive Advantage at Komatsu

Give the organization time to digest one challenge before launching another. When competing initiatives overload the organization, middle managers often try to protect their people from the whipsaw of shifting priorities. But this "wait and see if they're serious this time" attitude ultimately destroys the credibility of corporate challenges.

Establish clear milestones and review mechanisms to track progress and ensure that internal recognition and rewards reinforce desired behavior. The goal is to make the challenge inescapable for everyone in the company.

It is important to distinguish between the process of managing corporate challenges and the advantages that the process creates.

Whatever the actual challenge may be—quality, cost, value engineering, or something else—there is the same need to engage employees intellectually and emotionally in the development of new skills. In each case, the challenge will take root only if senior executives and lower level employees feel a reciprocal responsibility for competitiveness.

We believe workers in many companies have been asked to take a disproportionate share of the blame for competitive failure. In one U.S. company, for example, management had sought a 40% wage-package concession from hourly employees to bring labor costs into line with Far Eastern competitors. The result was a long strike and, ultimately, a 10% wage concession from employees on the line. However, direct labor costs in manufacturing accounted for less than 15% of total value added. The company thus succeeded in demoralizing its entire blue-collar work force for the sake of a 1.5% reduction in total costs. Ironically, further analysis showed that their competitors' most significant cost savings came not from lower hourly wages but from better work methods invented by employees. You can imagine how eager the U.S. workers were to make similar contributions after the strike and concessions. Contrast this situation with what happened at Nissan when the yen strengthened: top management took a big pay cut and then asked middle managers and line employees to sacrifice relatively less.

Reciprocal responsibility means shared gain and shared pain. In too many companies, the pain of revitalization falls almost exclusively on the employees least responsible for the enterprise's decline. Too often, workers are asked to commit to corporate goals without any matching commitment from top management—be it employment security, gain sharing, or an ability to influence the direction of the business. This one-sided approach to regaining competitiveness keeps many companies from harnessing the intellectual horsepower of their employees.

Creating a sense of reciprocal responsibility is crucial because competitiveness ultimately depends on the pace at which a company embeds new advantages deep within its organization, not on its stock of advantages at any given time. Thus we need to expand the concept of competitive advantage beyond the scorecard many managers now use: Are my costs lower? Will my product command a price premium?

Few competitive advantages are long lasting. Uncovering a new competitive advantage is a bit like getting a hot tip on a stock: the first person to act on the insight makes more money than the last. When the experience curve was young, a company that built capacity ahead of competitors, dropped prices to fill plants, and reduced costs as volume rose went to the bank. The first mover traded on the fact that competitors undervalued market share—they didn't price to capture additional share because they didn't understand how market share leadership could be translated into lower costs and better margins. But there is no more undervalued market share when each of 20 semiconductor companies builds enough capacity to serve 10% of the world market.

Keeping score of existing advantages is not the same as building new advantages. The essence of strategy lies in creating tomorrow's competitive advantages faster than competitors mimic the ones you possess today. In the 1960s, Japanese producers relied on labor and capital cost advantages. As Western manufacturers began to move production offshore, Japanese companies accelerated their investment in process technology and created scale and quality advantages. Then as their U.S. and European competitors rationalized manufacturing, they added another string to their bow by accelerating the rate of product development. Then they built global brands. Then they deskilled competitors through alliances and outsourcing deals. The moral? An organization's capacity to improve existing skills and lean new ones is the most defensible competitive advantage of all.

∿

To achieve a strategic intent, a company must usually take on larger, better financed competitors. That means carefully managing competitive engagements so that scarce resources are conserved. Managers cannot do that simply by playing the same game better—making marginal improvements to competitors' technology and business practices. Instead, they must fundamentally change the game in ways that disadvantage incumbents—devising novel approaches to market entry, advantage building, and competitive warfare. For smart competitors, the goal is not competitive imitation but competitive innovation, the art of containing competitive risks within manageable proportions.

Four approaches to competitive innovation are evident in the global expansion of Japanese companies. These are: building layers of advantage, searching for loose bricks, changing the terms of engagement, and competing through collaboration.

The wider a company's portfolio of advantages, the less risk it faces in competitive battles. New global competitors have built such portfolios by steadily expanding their arsenals of competitive weapons. They have moved inexorably from less defensible advantages such as low wage costs to more defensible advantages like global brands. The Japanese color television industry illustrates this layering process.

By 1967, Japan had become the largest producer of black-and-white television sets. By 1970, it was closing the gap in color televisions. Japanese manufacturers used their competitive advantage—at that time, primarily, low labor costs—to build a base in the private-label business, then moved quickly to establish world-scale plants. This investment gave them additional layers of advantage—quality and reliability—as well as further cost reductions from process improvements. At the same time, they recognized that these cost-based advantages were vulnerable to changes in labor costs, process and product technology, exchange rates, and trade policy. So throughout the 1970s, they also invested heavily in building channels and brands, thus creating another layer of advantage, a global franchise. In the late 1970s, they enlarged the scope of their products and businesses to amortize these grand investments, and by 1980 all the major players—Matsushita, Sharp, Toshiba, Hitachi, Sanyo—had established related sets of businesses that could support global marketing investments. More recently, they have been investing in regional manufacturing and design centers to tailor their products more closely to national markets.

These manufacturers thought of the various sources of competitive advantage as mutually desirable layers, not mutually exclusive choices. What some call competitive suicide—pursuing both cost and differentiation—is exactly what many competitors strive for.[3]

---

[3]For example, see Michael E. Porter, *Competitive Strategy* (New York: Free Press, 1980).

Using flexible manufacturing technologies and better marketing intelligence, they are moving away from standardized "world products" to products like Mazda's mini-van, developed in California expressly for the U.S. market.

Another approach to competitive innovation—searching for loose bricks—exploits the benefits of surprise, which is just as useful in business battles as it is in war. Particularly in the early stages of a war for global markets, successful new competitors work to stay below the response threshold of their larger, more powerful rivals. Staking out underdefended territory is one way to do this.

To find loose bricks, managers must have few orthodoxies about how to break into a market or challenge a competitor. For example, in one large U.S. multinational, we asked several country managers to describe what a Japanese competitor was doing in the local market. The first executive said, "They're coming at us in the low end. Japanese companies always come in at the bottom." The second speaker found the comment interesting but disagreed: "They don't offer any low-end products in my market, but they have some exciting stuff at the top end. We really should reverse engineer that thing." Another colleague told still another story. "They haven't taken any business away from me," he said, "but they've just made me a great offer to supply components." In each country, their Japanese competitor had found a different loose brick.

The search for loose bricks begins with a careful analysis of the competitor's conventional wisdom: How does the company define its "served market"? What activities are most profitable? Which geographic markets are too troublesome to enter? The objective is not to find a corner of the industry (or niche) where larger competitors seldom tread but to build a base of attack just outside the market territory that industry leaders currently occupy. The goal is an uncontested profit sanctuary, which could be a particular product segment (the "low end" in motorcycles), a slice of the value chain (components in the computer industry), or a particular geographic market (Eastern Europe).

When Honda took on leaders in the motorcycle industry, for example, it began with products that were just outside the conventional definition of the leaders' product-market domains. As a result, it could build a base of operations in underdefended territory and then use that base to launch an expanded attack. What many competitors failed to see was Honda's strategic intent and its growing competence in engines and power trains. Yet even as Honda was selling 50cc motorcycles in the United States, it was already racing larger bikes in Europe—assembling the design skills and technology it would need for a systematic expansion across the entire spectrum of motor-related businesses.

Honda's progress in creating a core competence in engines should have warned competitors that it might enter a series of seemingly unrelated industries—automobiles, lawn mowers, marine engines, generators. But with each company fixated on its own market, the threat of Honda's horizontal diversification went unnoticed. Today companies like Matsushita and Toshiba are similarly poised to move in unexpected ways across industry boundaries. In protecting loose bricks, companies must extend their peripheral vision by tracking and anticipating the migration of global competitors across product segments, businesses, national markets, value-added stages, and distribution channels.

Changing the terms of engagement—refusing to accept the front runner's definition of industry and segment boundaries—represents still another form of competitive innovation. Canon's entry into the copier business illustrates this approach.

During the 1970s, both Kodak and IBM tried to match Xerox's business system in terms of segmentation, products, distribution, service, and pricing. As a result, Xerox had no trouble decoding the new entrants' intentions and developing countermoves. IBM eventually withdrew from the copier business, while Kodak remains a distant second in the large copier market that Xerox still dominates.

Canon, on the other hand, changed the terms of competitive engagement. While Xerox built a wide range of copiers, Canon standardized machines and components to reduce costs. Canon chose to distribute through office-product dealers rather than try to match Xerox's huge direct sales force. It also avoided the need to create a national service network by designing reliability and serviceability into its product and then delegating service responsibility to the dealers. Canon copiers were sold rather than leased, freeing Canon from the burden of financing the lease base. Finally, instead of selling to the heads of corporate duplicating departments, Canon appealed to secretaries and department managers who wanted distributed copying. At each stage, Canon neatly sidestepped a potential barrier to entry.

Canon's experience suggests that there is an important distinction between barriers to entry and barriers to imitation. Competitors that tried to match Xerox's business system had to pay the same entry costs—the barriers to imitation were high. But Canon dramatically reduced the barriers to entry by changing the rules of the game.

Changing the rules also short-circuited Xerox's ability to retaliate quickly against its new rival. Confronted with the need to rethink its business strategy and organization, Xerox was paralyzed for a time. Xerox managers realized that the faster they downsized the product line, developed new channels, and improved reliability, the faster they would erode the company's traditional profit base. What might have been seen as critical success factors—Xerox's national sales force and service network, its large installed base of leased machines, and its reliance on service revenues—instead became barriers to retaliation. In this sense, competitive innovation is like judo: the goal is to use a larger competitor's weight against it. And that happens not by matching the leader's capabilities but by developing contrasting capabilities of one's own.

Competitive innovation works on the premise that a successful competitor is likely to be wedded to a "recipe" for success. That's why the most effective weapon new competitors possess is probably a clean sheet of paper. And why an incumbent's greatest vulnerability is its belief in accepted practice.

Through licensing, outsourcing agreements, and joint ventures, it is sometimes possible to win without fighting. For example, Fujitsu's alliances in Europe with Siemens and STC (Britain's largest computer maker) and in the United States with Amdahl yield manufacturing volume and access to Western markets. In the early 1980s, Matsushita established a joint venture with Thorn (in the United Kingdom), Telefunken (in Germany), and Thomson (in France), which allowed it to quickly multiply the forces arrayed against Philips in the battle for leadership in the European VCR business. In fighting larger global rivals by proxy, Japanese companies have adopted a maxim as old as human conflict itself: my enemy's enemy is my friend.

Hijacking the development efforts of potential rivals is another goal of competitive collaboration. In the consumer electronics war, Japanese competitors attacked traditional businesses like TVs and hi-fis while volunteering to manufacture "next generation" products like VCRs, camcorders, and compact disc players for Western rivals. They hoped their rivals would ratchet down development spending, and in most cases that is precisely what happened. But companies that abandoned their own development efforts seldom reemerged as serious competitors in subsequent new product battles.

Collaboration can also be used to calibrate competitors' strengths and weaknesses. Toyota's joint venture with GM, and Mazda's with Ford, give these automakers an invaluable vantage point for assessing the progress their U.S. rivals have made in cost reduction, quality, and technology. They can also learn how GM and Ford compete—when they will fight and when they won't. Of course, the reverse is also true: Ford and GM have an equal opportunity to learn from their partner-competitors.

The route to competitive revitalization we have been mapping implies a new view of strategy. Strategic intent assures consistency in resource allocation over the long term. Clearly articulated corporate challenges focus the efforts of individuals in the medium term. Finally, competitive innovation helps reduce competitive risk in the short term. This consistency in the long term, focus in the medium term, and inventiveness and involvement in the short term provide the key to leveraging limited resources in pursuit of ambitious goals. But just as there is a process of winning, so there is a process of surrender. Revitalization requires understanding that process too.

Given their technological leadership and access to large regional markets, how did U.S. and European companies lose their apparent birthright to dominate global industries? There is no simple answer. Few companies recognize the value of documenting failure. Fewer still search their own managerial orthodoxies for the seeds for competitive surrender. But we believe there is a pathology of surrender (summarized in "The Process of Surrender" [page 70]) that gives some important clues.

It is not very comforting to think that the essence of Western strategic thought can be reduced to eight rules for excellence, seven S's, five competitive forces, four product life-cycle stages, three generic strategies, and innumerable two-by-two matrices.[4] Yet for the past 20 years, "advances" in strategy have taken the form of ever more typologies, heuristics, and laundry lists, often with dubious empirical bases. Moreover, even reasonable concepts like the product life cycle, experience curve, product portfolios, and generic strategies often have toxic side effects: They reduce the number of strategic options management is willing to consider. They create a preference for selling businesses rather than defending them. They yield predictable strategies that rivals easily decode.

Strategy "recipes" limit opportunities for competitive innovation. A company may have 40 businesses and only four strategies—invest, hold, harvest, or divest. Too often strategy is seen as a positioning exercise in which options are tested by how they fit the existing industry structure. But current industry structure reflects the strengths of the industry leader; and playing by the leader's rules is usually competitive suicide.

Armed with concepts like segmentation, the value chain, competitor benchmarking, strategic groups, and mobility barriers, many managers have become better and better at drawing industry maps. But while they have been busy map making, their competitors have been moving entire continents. The strategist's goal is not to find a niche within the existing industry space but to create new space that is uniquely suited to the company's own strengths, space that is off the map.

This is particularly true now that industry boundaries are becoming more and more unstable. In industries such as financial services and communications, rapidly changing technology, deregulation, and globalization have undermined the value of traditional

---

[4]Strategic frameworks for resource allocation in diversified companies are summarized in Charles W. Hofer and Dan E. Schendel, *Strategy Formulation: Analytical Concepts* (St. Paul, MN: West Publishing, 1978).

industry analysis. Map-making skills are worth little in the epicenter of an earthquake. But an industry in upheaval presents opportunities for ambitious companies to redraw the map in their favor, so long as they can think outside traditional industry boundaries.

Concepts like "mature" and "declining" are largely definitional. What most executives mean when they label a business mature is that sales growth has stagnated in their current geographic markets for existing products sold through existing channels. In such cases, it's not the industry that is mature, but the executives' conception of the industry. Asked if the piano business was mature, a senior executive in Yamaha replied, "Only if we can't take any market share from anybody anywhere in the world and still make money. And anyway, we're not in the 'piano' business, we're in the 'keyboard' business." Year after year, Sony has revitalized its radio and tape recorder businesses, despite the fact that other manufacturers long ago abandoned these businesses as mature.

A narrow concept of maturity can foreclose a company from a broad stream of future opportunities. In the 1970s, several U.S. companies thought that consumer electronics had become a mature industry. What could possibly top the color TV? they asked themselves. RCA and GE, distracted by opportunities in more "attractive" industries like mainframe computers, left Japanese producers with a virtual monopoly in VCRs, camcorders, and compact disc players. Ironically, the TV business, once thought mature, is on the verge of a dramatic renaissance. A $20 billion-a-year business will be created when high definition television is launched in the United States. But the pioneers of television may capture only a small part of this bonanza.

Most of the tools of strategic analysis are focused domestically. Few force managers to consider global opportunities and threats. For example, portfolio planning portrays top management's investment options as an array of businesses rather than as an array of geographic markets. The result is predictable: as businesses come under attack from foreign competitors, the company attempts to abandon them and enter others in which the forces of global competition are not yet so strong. In the short term, this may be an appropriate response to waning competitiveness, but there are fewer and fewer businesses in which a domestic-oriented company can find refuge. We seldom hear such companies asking: Can we move into emerging markets overseas ahead of our global rivals and prolong the profitability of this business? Can we counterattack in our global competitors' home markets and slow the pace of their expansion? A senior executive in one successful global company made a telling comment: "We're glad to find a competitor managing by the portfolio concept—we can almost predict how much share we'll have to take away to put the business on the CEO's 'sell list.'"

Companies can also be overcommitted to organizational recipes, such as strategic business units and the decentralization an SBU structure implies. Decentralization is seductive because it places the responsibility for success or failure squarely on the shoulders of line managers. Each business is assumed to have all the resources it needs to execute its strategies successfully, and in this no-excuses environment, it is hard for top management to fail. But desirable as clear lines of responsibility and accountability are, competitive revitalization requires positive value added from top management.

Few companies with a strong SBU orientation have built successful global distribution and brand positions. Investments in a global brand franchise typically transcend the resources and risk propensity of a single business. While some Western companies have had global brand positions for 30 or 40 years or more (Heinz, Siemens, IBM, Ford, and Kodak, for example), it is hard to identify any American or European company that has created a new global brand franchise in the last 10 to 15 years. Yet Japanese companies have created a score or more—NEC, Fujitsu, Panasonic (Matsushita), Toshiba, Sony, Seiko, Epson, Canon, Minolta, and Honda, among them.

General Electric's situation is typical. In many of its businesses, this American giant has been almost unknown in Europe and Asia. GE made no coordinated effort to build a global corporate franchise. Any GE business with international ambitions had to bear the burden of establishing its credibility and credentials in the new market alone. Not surprisingly, some once-strong GE businesses opted out of the difficult task of building a global brand position. In contrast, smaller Korean companies like Samsung, Daewoo, and Lucky Gold Star are busy building global-brand umbrellas that will ease market entry for a whole range of businesses. The underlying principle is simple: economies of scope may be as important as economies of scale in entering global markets. But capturing economies of scope demands interbusiness coordination that only top management can provide.

We believe that inflexible SBU-type organizations have also contributed to the deskilling of some companies. For a single SBU, incapable of sustaining investment in a core competence such as semiconductors, optical media, or combustion engines, the only way to remain competitive is to purchase key components from potential (often Japanese or Korean) competitors. For an SBU defined in product-market terms, competitiveness means offering an end product that is competitive in price and performance. But that gives an SBU manager little incentive to distinguish between external sourcing that achieves "product embodied" competitiveness and internal development that yields deeply embedded organizational competences that can be exploited across multiple businesses. Where upstream component manufacturing activities are seen as cost centers with cost-plus transfer pricing, additional investment in the core activity may seem a less profitable use of capital than investment in downstream activities. To make matters worse, internal accounting data may not reflect the competitive value of retaining control over core competence.

Together a shared global corporate brand franchise and shared core competence act as mortar in many Japanese companies. Lacking this mortar, a company's businesses are truly loose bricks—easily knocked out by global competitors that steadily invest in core competences. Such competitors can coopt domestically oriented companies into long-term sourcing dependence and capture the economies of scope of global brand investment through interbusiness coordination.

Last in decentralization's list of dangers is the standard of managerial performance typically used in SBU organizations. In many companies, business unit managers are rewarded solely on the basis of their performance against return on investment targets. Unfortunately, that often leads to denominator management because executives soon discover that reductions in investment and head count—the denominator—"improve" the financial ratios by which they are measured more easily than growth in the numerator—revenues. It also fosters a hair-trigger sensitivity to industry downturns that can be very costly. Managers who are quick to reduce investment and dismiss workers find it takes much longer to regain lost skills and catch up on investment when the industry turns upward again. As a result, they lose market share in every business cycle. Particularly in industries where there is fierce competition for the best people and where competitors invest relentlessly, denominator management creates a retrenchment ratchet.

The concept of the general manager as a movable peg reinforces the problem of denominator management. Business schools are guilty here because they have perpetuated the notion that a manager with net present value calculations in one hand and portfolio planning in the other can manage any business anywhere.

In many diversified companies, top management evaluates line managers on numbers alone because no other basis for dialogue exists. Managers move so many times as part of their "career development" that they often do not understand the nuances of the businesses they are managing. At GE, for example, one fast-track manager heading an important new venture had moved across five businesses in five years. His series of quick successes finally came to an end when he confronted a Japanese competitor whose managers had been plodding along in the same business for more than a decade.

Regardless of ability and effort, fast-track managers are unlikely to develop the deep business knowledge they need to discuss technology options, competitors' strategies, and global opportunities substantively. Invariably, therefore, discussions gravitate to "the numbers," while the value added of managers is limited to the financial and planning savvy they carry from job to job. Knowledge of the company's internal planning and accounting systems substitutes for substantive knowledge of the business, making competitive innovation unlikely.

When managers know that their assignments have a two- to three-year time frame, they feel great pressure to create a good track record fast. This pressure often takes one of two forms. Either the manager does not commit to goals whose time line extends beyond his or her expected tenure. Or ambitious goals are adopted and squeezed into an unrealistically short time frame. Aiming to be number one in a business is the essence of strategic intent; but imposing a three- to four-year horizon on the effort simply invites disaster. Acquisitions are made with little attention to the problems of integration. The organization becomes overloaded with initiatives. Collaborative ventures are formed without adequate attention to competitive consequences.

Almost every strategic management theory and nearly every corporate planning system is premised on a strategy hierarchy in which corporate goals guide business unit strategies and business unit strategies guide functional tactics.[5] In this hierarchy, senior management makes strategy and lower levels execute it. The dichotomy between formulation and implementation is familiar and widely accepted. But the strategy hierarchy undermines competitiveness by fostering an elitist view of management that tends to disenfranchise most of the organization. Employees fail to identify with corporate goals or involve themselves deeply in the work of becoming more competitive.

The strategy hierarchy isn't the only explanation for an elitist view of management, of course. The myths that grow up around successful top managers—"Lee Iacocca saved Chrysler," "De Benedetti rescued Olivetti," "John Sculley turned Apple around"—perpetuate it. So does the turbulent business environment. Middle managers buffeted by circumstances that seem to be beyond their control desperately want to believe that top management has all the answers. And top management, in turn, hesitates to admit it does not for fear of demoralizing lower level employees.

The result of all this is often a code of silence in which the full extent of a company's competitiveness problem is not widely shared. We interviewed business unit managers in one company, for example, who were extremely anxious because top management wasn't talking openly about the competitive challenges the company faced. They assumed the lack of communication indicated a lack of awareness on their senior managers' part. But when asked whether they

---

[5]For example, see Peter Lorange and Richard F. Vancil, *Strategic Planning Systems* (Englewood Cliffs, NJ: Prentice-Hall, 1977).

were open with their own employees, these same managers replied that while they could face up to the problems, the people below them could not. Indeed, the only time the work force heard about the company's competitiveness problems was during wage negotiations when problems were used to extract concessions.

Unfortunately, a threat that everyone perceives but no one talks about creates more anxiety than a threat that has been clearly identified and made the focal point for the problem-solving efforts of the entire company. That is one reason honesty and humility on the part of top management may be the first prerequisite of revitalization. Another reason is the need to make participation more than a buzzword.

Programs such as quality circles and total customer service often fall short of expectations because management does not recognize that successful implementation requires more than administrative structures. Difficulties in embedding new capabilities are typically put down to "communication" problems, with the unstated assumption that if only downward communication were more effective—"if only middle management would get the message straight" —the new program would quickly take root. The need for upward communication is often ignored, or assumed to mean nothing more than feedback. In contrast, Japanese companies win, not because they have smarter managers, but because they have developed ways to harness the "wisdom of the anthill." They realize that top managers are a bit like the astronauts who circle the earth in the space shuttle. It may be the astronauts who get all the glory, but everyone knows that the real intelligence behind the mission is located firmly on the ground.

Where strategy formulation is an elitist activity it is also difficult to produce truly creative strategies. For one thing, there are not enough heads and points of view in divisional or corporate planning departments to challenge conventional wisdom. For another, creative strategies seldom emerge from the annual planning ritual. The starting point for next year's strategy is almost always this year's strategy. Improvements are incremental. The company sticks to the segments and territories it knows, even though the real opportunities may be elsewhere. The impetus for Canon's pioneering entry into the personal copier business came from an overseas sales subsidiary —not from planners in Japan.

The goal of the strategy hierarchy remains valid—to ensure consistency up and down the organization. But this consistency is better derived from a clearly articulated strategic intent than from inflexibly applied top-down plans. In the 1990s, the challenge will be to enfranchise employees to invent the means to accomplish ambitious ends.

We seldom found cautious administrators among the top managements of companies that came from behind to challenge incumbents for global leadership. But in studying organizations that had surrendered, we invariably found senior managers who, for whatever reason, lacked the courage to commit their companies to heroic goals—goals that lay beyond the reach of planning and existing resources. The conservative goals they set failed to generate pressure and enthusiasm for competitive innovation or give the organization much useful guidance. Financial targets and vague mission statements just cannot provide the consistent direction that is a prerequisite for winning a global competitive war.

This kind of conservatism is usually blamed on the financial markets. But we believe that in most cases investors' so-called short-term orientation simply reflects their lack of confidence in the ability of senior managers to conceive and deliver stretch goals. The chairman of one company complained bitterly that even after improving return on capital employed to over 40% (by ruthlessly divesting lackluster businesses and downsizing others), the stock market held the company to an 8:1 price/earnings ratio. Of course the market's message was clear: "We don't trust you. You've shown no ability to achieve profitable growth. Just cut out the slack, manage the denominators, and perhaps you'll be taken over by a company that can use your resources more creatively." Very little in the track record of most large Western companies warrants the confidence of the stock market. Investors aren't hopelessly short term, they're justifiably skeptical.

We believe that top management's caution reflects a lack of confidence in its own ability to involve the entire organization in revitalization—as opposed to simply raising financial targets. Developing faith in the organization's ability to deliver on tough goals, motivating it to do so, focusing its attention long enough to internalize new capabilities—this is the real challenge for top management. Only by rising to this challenge will senior managers gain the courage they need to commit themselves and their companies to global leadership.

Remaking Strategy

Over the last ten years, our research on global competition, international alliances, and multinational management has brought us into close contact with senior managers in America, Europe, and Japan. As we tried to unravel the reasons for success and surrender in global markets, we became more and more suspicious that executives in Western and Far Eastern companies often operated with very different conceptions of competitive strategy. Understanding these differences, we thought, might help explain the conduct and outcome of competitive battles as well as supplement traditional explanations for Japan's ascendance and the West's decline.

We began by mapping the implicit strategy models of managers who had participated in our research. Then we built detailed histories of selected competitive battles. We searched for evidence of divergent views of strategy, competitive advantage, and the role of top management.

Two contrasting models of strategy emerged. One, which most Western managers will recognize, centers on the problem of maintaining strategic fit. The other centers on the problem of leveraging resources. The two are not mutually exclusive, but they represent a significant difference in emphasis—an emphasis that deeply affects how competitive battles get played out over time.

Both models recognize the problem of competing in a hostile environment with limited resources. But while the emphasis in the first is on trimming ambitions to match available resources, the emphasis in the second is on leveraging resources to reach seemingly unattainable goals.

Both models recognize that relative competitive advantage determines relative profitability. The first emphasizes the search for advantages that are inherently sustainable, the second emphasizes the need to accelerate organizational learning to outpace competitors in building new advantages.

Both models recognize the difficulty of competing against larger competitors. But while the first leads to a search for niches (or simply dissuades the company from challenging an entrenched competitor), the second produces a quest for new rules that can devalue the incumbent's advantages.

Both models recognize that balance in the scope of an organization's activities reduces risk. The first seeks to reduce financial risk by building a balanced portfolio of cash-generating and cash-consuming businesses. The second seeks to reduce competitive risk by ensuring a well-balanced and sufficiently broad portfolio of advantages.

Both models recognize the need to disaggregate the organization in a way that allows top management to differentiate among the investment needs of various planning units. In the first model, resources are allocated to product-market units in which relatedness is defined by common products, channels, and customers. Each business is assumed to own all the critical skills it needs to execute its strategy successfully. In the second, investments are made in core competences (microprocessor controls or electronic imaging, for example) as well as in product-market units. By tracking these investments across businesses, top management works to assure that the plans of individual strategic units don't undermine future developments by default.

Both models recognize the need for consistency in action across organizational levels. In the first, consistency between corporate and business levels is largely a matter of conforming to financial objectives. Consistency between business and functional levels comes by tightly restricting the means the business uses to achieve its strategy—establishing standard operating procedures, defining the served market, adhering to accepted industry practices. In the second model, business-corporate consistency comes from allegiance to a particular strategic intent. Business-functional consistency comes from allegiance to intermediate-term goals, or challenges, with lower level employees encouraged to invent how those goals will be achieved.

The Process of Surrender

In the battles for global leadership that have taken place during the last two decades, we have seen a pattern of competitive attack and retrenchment that was remarkably similar across industries. We call this the process of surrender.

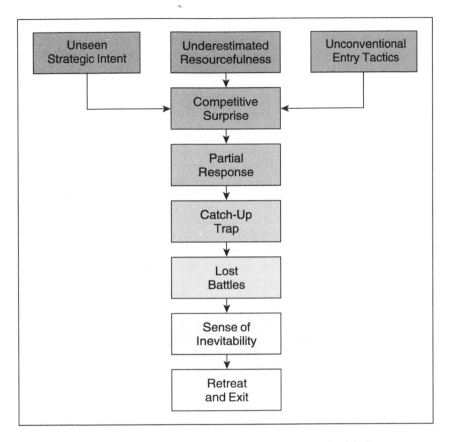

When Does Surrender Become Inevitable?

The process started with unseen intent. Not possessing long-term, competitor-focused goals themselves, Western companies did not ascribe such intentions to their rivals. They also calculated the threat posed by potential competitors in terms of their existing resources rather than their resourcefulness. This led to systematic underestimation of smaller rivals who were fast gaining technology through licensing arrangements, acquiring market understanding from downstream OEM partners, and improving product quality and manufacturing productivity through companywide employee involvement programs. Oblivious of the strategic intent and intangible advantages of their rivals, American and European businesses were caught off guard.

Adding to the competitive surprise was the fact that the new entrants typically attacked the periphery of a market (Honda in small motorcycles,

Yamaha in grand pianos, Toshiba in small black-and-white televisions) before going head-to-head with incumbents. Incumbents often misread these attacks, seeing them as part of a niche strategy and not as a search for "loose bricks." Unconventional market entry strategies (minority holdings in less developed countries, use of nontraditional channels, extensive corporate advertising) were ignored or dismissed as quirky. For example, managers we spoke with said Japanese companies' position in the European computer industry was nonexistent. In terms of brand share that's nearly true, but the Japanese control as much as one-third of the manufacturing value added in the hardware sales of European-based computer businesses. Similarly, German auto producers claimed to feel unconcerned over the proclivity of Japanese producers to move upmarket. But with its low-end models under tremendous pressure from Japanese producers, Porsche has now announced that it will no longer make "entry level" cars.

Western managers often misinterpreted their rivals' tactics. They believed that Japanese and Korean companies were competing solely on the basis of cost and quality. This typically produced a partial response to those competitors' initiatives: moving manufacturing offshore, outsourcing, or instituting a quality program. Seldom was the full extent of the competitive threat appreciated—the multiple layers of advantage, the expansion across related product segments, the development of global brand positions. Imitating the currently visible tactics of rivals put Western businesses into a perpetual catch-up trap. One by one, companies lost battles and came to see surrender as inevitable. Surrender was not inevitable, of course, but the attack was staged in a way that disguised ultimate intentions and sidestepped direct confrontation.

4

Begin Strategic Planning by Asking Three Questions

Abstract

This article deals with three questions that must be asked by top management for effective strategic planning to occur. The questions focus on the company's directions, environment, and strategic choices.

Where are you going? *To determine where a company is going, management must develop or define: (a) a corporate mission, (b) a scope of operations, and (c) specific goals or objectives. The corporate mission is a statement of what business the company is in. The scope of operations tells where the company is doing business and what the product-market is. The goals and objectives should be specific and clearly defined based on the business's mission and scope.*

What is the environment? *Before determining the strategies necessary to achieve the goals, it is necessary to analyze the internal and external environment within which the company operates. The internal analysis includes a management audit, an examination of the firm's financial condition, and an analysis of its existing products and strategies. The external analysis, or environmental scanning, seeks to identify changing social, economic, political, and technological developments that may affect the company. Each of the trends or factors that are identified need to be weighed as to whether it is a threat or an opportunity to the company. Alternatives are then evaluated for response to the threats and opportunities that are most likely to occur. Finally, a gap analysis is conducted between where the company is and where it wants to be, and goals of the company are revised as they are determined to be unrealistic.*

How do you get there? *Strategy provides a method for attaining desired objectives. Each company has to design a strategy that fits its particular needs. Effective strategies tend to meet three criteria: (1) they are attainable—i.e., realistic and can be achieved in a reasonable period of time, (2) they are compatible with other objectives of the firm, and (3) they are definable—i.e., can be measured and tracked.*

Begin Strategic Planning by Asking Three Questions

Benton E. Gup

Many business concerns and nonprofit organizations want to use strategic planning but they do not know what it is, or how to begin the process. The terms "strategy" and "strategic planning" are defined in various ways. Alfred Chandler defined strategy as "...the determination of basic long-term goals and objectives of an enterprise, and the adoption of courses of action and the allocation of resources necessary for carrying out these goals."[1] Peter Drucker defined strategic planning as "...the continuous process of making present entrepreneurial *(risk-taking) decisions* systematically and with the greatest knowledge of their futurity; organizing the *efforts* needed to carry out these decisions; and measuring the results of these decisions against the expectations through organized,

Reprinted by permission. "Begin Strategic Planning by Asking Three Questions," by Benton E. Gup in *Managerial Planning,* November/December 1979, pp. 28-31, 35.

[1]Alfred D. Chandler, Jr. *Strategy and Structure: Chapters in the History of the Industrial Enterprise* (Cambridge, Mass.: The M.I.T. Press, 1962), p. 13.

systematic feedback."[2] Both statements deal with the same topic, but from different perspectives. In order to avoid arguments over semantics, the terms strategy and strategic planning as used here refer to major action programs that are used by an organization to achieve its mission and goals.

Having defined strategic planning, it is equally important to point out what is *not* strategic planning. According to Peter Drucker, strategic planning is not:[3]

1. The application of quantitative techniques to business decisions. It is analytical thinking and a commitment of resources to action.

2. It is not forecasting. In fact, strategic planning is necessary *because* we are unable to forecast beyond a short time span with any degree of precision. Entrepreneurs upset forecasts by bringing about innovations that by definition alter the course of economic, social, and political events.

3. Strategic planning does not deal with decisions that are made in the future. It deals with decisions that are made today that will affect the future.

4. Strategic planning does not eliminate risk. It helps management weigh the risks that it must take.

One way to begin strategic planning is by asking the proper questions. This article deals with three questions that must be asked by top management. The first question focuses on the directions that the company is going. The second question concerns the environment that the company must operate in. The final question deals with the strategic choices that the company must make.

Where Are You Going?

There is a saying that "if you do not know where you are going, it does not make any difference what road you take to get there." This saying has important implications for management because they have

---

[2]Peter F. Drucker, *Management: Tasks, Responsibilities, Practices* (New York, Harper & Row, Publishers, 1974), p. 125.

[3]*Ibid.*, pp. 123-125.

to know where they want to go or else strategic planning is a waste of time! To determine where a company is going, management must develop: a) a corporate mission, b) a scope of operations, and c) specific goals or objectives.

The Corporate Mission

Defining the corporate mission is the most important decision in the planning process as the purpose of the corporate mission is to state the nature of the company's business. This mission can be defined narrowly or in broad general terms as demonstrated by Exhibit 1.

The breadth or narrowness of the corporate mission has an important effect upon operations. A good illustration of this is the Mobil Corporation. Mobil has been known as an oil company for most of its history. The mission of an oil company is to produce and sell oil and related products. However, in recent years there have been dramatic changes in the oil economies of the world that caused management to reappraise their corporate mission. Today Mobil is an *energy* company instead of an *oil* company. The word "energy" has a much broader meaning than the word "oil" since "energy" includes oil, gas, coal, the sun, nuclear power, and other sources. In addition to becoming an energy company, Mobil implemented a diversification program that included the following acquisitions: one of the world's largest retail stores (Montgomery Ward), the nation's largest manufacturer of paperboard packaging (Container Corporation), real estate developments, and chemical companies.

Narrow Lines of Business	Broad Lines of Business
Oil	Energy
Banking	Financial Services
Soap	Personal Hygiene Products
Newspaper	Communications
Guard Service	Security
Movie Theater	Entertainment

Exhibit 1. Corporate Missions

Similarly, many banks have formed holding companies in order to broaden their lines of business. Bank holding companies are permitted by the Board of Governors of the Federal Reserve System to engage in the activities listed in Exhibit 2, as well as other activities. A bank holding company located in New York City can own a finance company, or even a mortgage banking company, that has offices located throughout the United States. Thus, the bank holding company can operate in a wider geographic area than a "traditional" bank. Note that all of the activities of the holding companies are closely related to banking. In contrast, it is difficult to see the common thread between an oil company (Mobil), Montgomery Ward, and Container Corporation. Such combinations create more complex problems for planners and management than business concerns that have a common thread. The important point is that the definition of the corporate mission determines the broad limits of a company's growth.

Finance Company

Mortgage Banking Companies

Factoring Companies

Leasing Companies

Underwriting Credit Life Insurance

Data Processing

Operating an Industrial Loan Company

Investing in Community Development Projects

Source: Regulation Y; Federal Reserve Bulletin

Exhibit 2. Selected Activities of Bank Holding Companies

Scope

The corporate mission tells *what* business a company is in and the scope tells *where* they are doing business and their product-market. For example, the mission and scope of First National City Corporation is to "provide any worthwhile financial service *anyplace* in the

world permitted by law."[4] Most business concerns have a less ambitious geographic scope. One reason for the limited geographic
scope is that many companies are regulated by federal or state
governments. Regulations dictate where the airlines can fly, where
banks can establish branches, where trucks can haul commodities,
and where many other businesses of a "quasi-utility" nature can
operate. Other factors that limit the scope of a corporation's business
activity are transportation costs, location of natural resources,
availability of labor and customers, and competition. Although this
list is not exhaustive, it is sufficient to demonstrate that there are
many factors that limit the geographic area that a business serves.

The concept of "scope" also refers to particular product-markets.
Many industries contain such a wide range of products that some
companies specialize in one or two products. The fast food industry,
for example, consists largely of firms that specialize in hamburgers,
pizza, fish, Mexican food, or other specialty foods. Thus, the
product-market scope for Pizza Hut is pizza.

Goals

Once the mission and scope are established, it is necessary to determine specific goals. Such goals should be clearly defined in order
to avoid ambiguity. To say that the goal is "growth" or a "reasonable
rate of return" raises questions about what is meant by growth and
what is a reasonable rate of return. This problem can be avoided
by stating explicit objectives such as those shown in Exhibit 3.
However, not all corporate goals can be measured in terms of dollars
or ratios. For example, social goals and those dealing with consti-
tuents (customers, employees, suppliers, etc.) may have to be stated
in general terms. "To assure a challenging and satisfying work environment for our employees, compensating them accordingly for

---

[4]Statement by Walter B. Wriston, October 1970. Emphasis added by
author. Appears in Alexander A. Robichek, Alan B. Coleman, and George
H. Hempel, Management of Financial Institutions: Notes and cases, Second Edition (Hinsdale, Ill.: Dryden Press, 1976), p. 616.

their services and recognizing them for outstanding dedication to the Association"[5] is an example of such a goal.

It is important to keep in mind that corporate goals are not static like words carved in granite. They can be changed when conditions, management, or the stockholders demand change.

In summary, the corporate mission, scope, and goals make it clear where the company wants to go. The next task is to determine how to achieve the corporation's goals.

---

1. Earnings per share—growth trend	15%
2. Sales growth trend	15%
3. Return on sales	7%
4. Return on assets	13%
5. Return on total investments	21%

Exhibit 3. Corporate Goals for the Next Five Years

What Is the Environment?

Before determining the strategies necessary to achieve the goals, it is necessary to analyze the internal and external environment within which the company operates. The purpose of this analysis is to provide information about a company's strengths, weaknesses, potential threats, and opportunities.

Introspection

Introspection means self examination. The function of introspection is to determine the current *internal* condition of the firm and its existing markets. Introspection consists of a management audit, an examination of the firm's financial condition, and an analysis of their existing markets and strategies. It provides answers to the following questions. Is management capable of coping with future challenges? Are personnel recruitment, compensation, and training programs good enough to attract and retain the people that are

---

[5]*1976 Annual Report,* Sooner Federal Savings and Loan Association.

required to achieve the corporate goals? How strong is the firm's balance sheet and what is the quality of earnings? Can existing markets yield greater profits? As a result of introspection, one bank discovered that it was doing a poor job cross-selling its products. Very few of the depositors were borrowers from the bank, and very few of the borrowers had deposits at that bank. This discovery led to a strategy to improve cross-selling. Another firm discovered that reducing its debt-to-equity ratio from 40 percent debt to 30 percent debt would result in increasing the rating on its debt securities from A to A_a. Finally, a major bank found that the biggest obstacle to its growth was a shortage of competent people.

The External Environment

According to a leading authority on planning, "external forces not under corporate control are and will be dominant in determining corporate destiny."[6] In other words, management must understand changing social, economic, political, and technological developments that may affect them now and in the future. For example, the shock of the 1973 oil embargo forced many companies to evaluate their sources and uses of energy. Baker International Corporation, a major producer of tools for oil and gas exploration, analyzed the energy factors affecting them in two ways—one was over a long time period and the other was over a short time period.[7]

In the long run, Baker International Corporation foresaw four important trends. First, the world's standard of living is based on energy. Second, the world would be dependent on hydrocarbons for the remainder of the 20th century. Third, there is an imbalance between those that use energy and those that supply it. Moreover, the capital generated by energy consumption is not being entirely reinvested in energy resource development. Finally, there is only a finite amount of oil and natural gas available for world usage.

-----

[6]A statement by Michael J. Kami, President, Corporate Planning, Inc., presented at the Fifth International Planning Conference, Cleveland, Ohio, July 20, 1976.

[7]Baker International Corporation, *1976 Annual Report.*

In the short run, it was noted that the production of oil and natural gas in the United States declined despite the rising demands for energy products. Furthermore, [it was noted] that the economics and incentives of energy exploration remained in doubt while the government contemplated new regulatory policies. Finally, the cost of exploration continued to rise due to inflation and problems associated with drilling in frontier areas. Baker used this information to determine if the trends represented threats or opportunities to the future development of the company.

Threats and Opportunities

Changing economic and social conditions that threaten some firms may offer golden opportunities for other firms. For example, rising crime rates have contributed to the introduction of many new products and services such as burglar alarms, locks, T.V. monitors and various types of security services. On the other side of the coin, many companies have to pay for products and services mentioned above to avoid being robbed. The net effect is reduced earnings for those companies. Accordingly, each of the trends or factors considered in the external environment has to be weighed as to whether it is a threat or opportunity to a particular company.

Evaluating Alternatives

Once particular threats or opportunities have been identified as warranting further study, the process of evaluating their potential costs and benefits begins to determine if they are feasible or if some alternative must be found. However, each investment alternative must be evaluated on its own merits. Such an evaluation may include a feasibility study, pro forma projections, and the discounting of future expenses and revenues to their present value. Then the potential investments must be evaluated in a portfolio context in order to determine if any "synergy" exists, and how it affects the overall risk and returns of the firm.

The Gap

At this stage of the planning process, one should have a firm understanding of the "gap" that exists between the current position of the firm and the desired position. After evaluating the threats and opportunities, if the gap is insurmountable, the goals of the firm should be revised as they are unrealistic. However, if the gap can be closed by expansion or diversification of the firm, the next step is to develop appropriate strategies.

How Do You Get There?

The function of strategy is to provide a method for achieving particular goals. The following examples from Eastern Airlines illustrate strategies that were used by that airline to affect their market share.[8]

Develop Strategies

From Eastern's point of view, there were three strategic options that would affect market share. Option 1 was strategic superiority which means giving the best possible service to customers. Such service includes on-time arrivals and departures, on-time in-flight service, and on-time baggage handling. TWA initiated such a program but has had to pay the price in terms of higher fuel bills and potential revenue losses due to missed connections. Therefore, in considering this option Eastern chose not to be the best in all its areas in the United States but rather to concentrate on Atlanta where it chose strategic superiority by offering more flights from Atlanta than any other airline.

Option 2 is strategic equivalence which means matching the competition. When National Airlines offered "no frills" flights, Eastern matched this competition by also offering "no frills" flights in order to protect its share of the market.

Option 3 is strategic inferiority which means being inferior to the competition. This option is now being used by Pan American World Airlines which has reduced its employment and suspended services in a variety of markets. In addition, Pan American exhanged

---

[8]A presentation by Alfred E. Brescia, Direction of Economic Research and Forecasting, Eastern Air Lines, Inc., before the Planning Executives Institute, Corporate Planning Conference, Atlanta, Georgia, March 17-18, 1977.

routes with TWA and American Airlines in an effort to reduce its scope of operations. Eastern chose not to use this strategy.

Each company has to design a strategy that fits its particular needs. Thus, Eastern Airlines chose to develop strategies to achieve a larger share of the market. On the other hand, Dart Industries, a manufacturer and marketer of consumer products, chemicals and plastics, developed the following strategy to achieve certain financial goals.[9]

1. Correct or eliminate loss divisions;
2. Pursue new manufacturing efficiencies and cost controls;
3. Eliminate products that do not add to the profitability or to an improved return on investment;
4. Constantly improve the quality of our research programs;
5. Make new capital commitments which have the potential of a return that will contribute to the attainment of our goal— which is 15% return on stockholders' equity.

The above examples from Eastern Airlines and Dart Industries illustrated strategies to achieve market share and financial goals respectively. In each case, the strategies met certain criteria for their respective companies. First, they were attainable, or stated otherwise, the strategies were realistic and could be achieved in a reasonable period of time. Second, the strategies were compatible with other objectives of the firm. Finally, the strategies were definable as they could be measured and tracked. This is important because it allows management to observe the success or failure of their decisions.

Contingency Plans

An important part of developing strategies is to make contingency plans in order to shorten the reaction times to certain situations. In addition, contingency planning keeps surprises to a minimum since the threats and opportunities of the situations have already been examined.

---

[9]Dart Industries, Inc., Annual Report, 1975.

Operations *Plans*

The strategies that have been developed have to be followed by an operating plan that results in *management actions.* The operating plan explains who is responsible for particular functions and when they are to be accomplished. Finally, the operations plan provides for continuous or periodic reviews. If the strategies are not working they should be reviewed, analyzed, and changed if necessary.

Conclusion

This article outlines the major elements of strategic planning. The elements are grouped into three categories that are posed as questions. The questions and a summary of the elements of strategic planning are shown in Exhibit 4. The first question deals with the mission, scope and goals of the firm. This is the most important question. However, most of the time and effort in planning is spent on the next two questions. The second question explores the internal and external condition of the firm. The answers to this question provide information about the gap between the desired and current position of the firm, and about potential investment opportunities. The final question concerns several strategies that can be used to achieve particular market shares and financial goals.

Questions	To Obtain Answers
1. **Where are you going?**	a) Determine the corporate mission.
	b) Determine the scope of operations.
	c) Establish specific goals.
2. **What is environment?**	a) Examine the internal condition of the firm.
	b) Examine the external environment.
3. **How do you get there?**	a) Develop strategies.
	b) Develop contingency plans.

Exhibit 4. Elements of Strategic Planning

II.
Clarifying
the Mission

Introduction

If there is a cornerstone to the strategic planning process, it lies with defining the company's mission statement. All else in the strategic planning process should follow directly from the mission statement, which clearly charts the future direction of the company and establishes a basis for ongoing organizational decision making. Effective mission statements answer three questions: (1) *What* function does the organization perform? (2) For *whom* does the organization perform this function? and (3) *How* does the organization go about filling this function? Organizations sometimes add a fourth question: *Why* does this organization exist?

1. What function does the organization perform? This is a clear statement about what business the organization is in. Novice strategic planners make the mistake of defining their company in terms of the products that are produced and sold. Such a definition is too restrictive and tends to prevent the organization from pursuing new opportunities for growth and expansion as well as to keep the organization from effectively responding to threats and challenges as they arise. Instead, an organization should define its mission in terms of the customer or client needs that the organization is attempting to meet, that is, what value-satisfying goods or services the organization offers its customers. Ideally, this customer-oriented mission statement should be future oriented and should not just relate to current or historical activities of the firm. The major issue to be decided in the mission formulation is how broadly or narrowly to answer this "what" question.

The crucial strategic question, "What business are we in?," is well addressed in "Marketing Myopia," our first selection in this section. In it the author first advocated the insight that organizations should define their industries more broadly to take advantage of growth opportunities. He suggested that strategic planning be a dynamic process that examines the future markets that the company wants to be in, rather than simply examining the current products that are produced by the firm for existing markets. This article went on to be a classic that has shaped and prompted strategic planning efforts throughout American industry for over two decades.

2. For whom does the organization perform this function? Within the broad market potential defined in Number 1, the organization needs to more specifically segment the portion of the market the firm seeks to target. This segmentation can be done a number of different ways, including geographically, financially, qualitatively, and ethnically. An effective mission statement will clearly determine the boundaries of the competitive arena in which the organization will operate.

The second article in this section, "Corporate Mission Statements: The Bottom Line," lists eight key components of mission statements. These include, among other things, the specification of target customers and markets.

"Making Quality a Fundamental Part of Strategy," our third article in this section, emphasizes the importance of the quality dimension in a successful competitive strategy. It states that quality is more a matter of the consumers' perception than of the production of a defect-free product. The authors contend that quality is a cost-effective and profitable variable that should be a fundamental part of the top management's responsibility when developing strategic plans and that quality should be built into the value system of the organization.

3. How does the organization go about filling this function? After Questions 1 and 2 are adequately agreed on, Question 3 should be addressed by key members of the organization. It involves specific strategies that the organization will attempt in order to achieve the desired targets, usually in a way that takes advantage of the organization's primary technologies, that is, the firm's unique competitive advantage or distinctive competence. The strategies can and do vary greatly from organization to organization and often involve integral aspects of the business operations, such as marketing, distribution, and pricing strategies. An effective mission statement should provide guidance as to how resources will be allocated to the different demands within the organization.

The last article in this section, "Competitive Advantage: The Cornerstone of Strategic Thinking," addresses the "how" question of strategic planning. It emphasizes the meaning and importance of "competitive advantage," especially given the growing uncertainty in the business environment and the increased intensity of global competition. The article explains how a competitive advantage may be obtained in a specific market.

5

Marketing Myopia

Abstract

[This article is a classic that has sold over 265,000 reprints since it was initially published in 1960 by the Harvard Business Review. It presented a new and challenging insight: that organizations should define their industries more broadly to take advantage of growth opportunities. It prompted companies to ask themselves the now well-known strategic question: "What business are we in?"]

Every major industry was once a growth industry. Each industry's assumed strength lay in the apparently unchallenged superiority of its product. If an industry's growth has been threatened or has slowed or stopped, the reason is not market saturation; the reason is a failure of management. Many industries have declined because the short-sighted management failed to define the business properly. For example, if railroad companies had identified themselves as being in the transportation business rather than in the railroad business, they could have added cars, trucks, airplanes, and even telephones. They defined their business wrong because they were product-oriented instead of customer-oriented.

The history of every dead or dying growth industry shows a self-deceiving cycle of bountiful expansion and undetected decay. Four conditions will usually guarantee this cycle: (1) the belief that growth is assured by an expanding and more affluent population; (2) the belief that there is no competitive substitute for the industry's major product; (3) too much faith in mass production and in the advantages of rapidly declining unit costs as output rises; and (4) preoccupation with a product that lends itself to carefully controlled scientific experimentation, improvement, and manufacturing cost reduction.

Mass production generates pressure to move the product. What is usually emphasized, however, is selling—not marketing. Selling focuses on the needs of the seller, but marketing considers the needs of the buyer. A truly marketing-minded firm tries to create value-satisfying goods and services that consumers will want to buy. What it offers for sale is determined not by the seller but by the buyer.

Marketing Myopia

Theodore Levitt

*How can a company ensure its continued growth? In 1960
"Marketing Myopia" answered that question in a new and
challenging way by urging organizations to define their industries broadly to take advantage of growth opportunities.
Using the archetype of the railroads, Mr. Levitt showed how
they declined inevitably as technology advanced because they
defined themselves too narrowly. To continue growing, companies must ascertain and act on their customers' needs and
desires, not bank on the presumptive longevity of their products. The success of the article testifies to the validity of its
message. It has been widely quoted and anthologized, and
HBR has sold more than 265,000 reprints of it. The author of
14 subsequent articles in HBR, Mr. Levitt is one of the
magazine's most prolific contributors. In a retrospective com-
mentary, he considers the use and misuse that have been made
of "Marketing Myopia," describing its many interpretations and
hypothesizing about its success.*

*At the time of the article's publication, Theodore Levitt
was lecturer at the Harvard Business School. Now a full professor there, he is the author of six books.*

Every major industry was once a growth industry. But some that are now riding a wave of growth enthusiasm are very much in the shadow of decline. Others which are thought of as seasoned growth industries have actually stopped growing. In every case the reason growth is threatened, slowed, or stopped is *not* because the market is saturated. It is because there has been a failure of management.

Fateful purposes: The failure is at the top. The executives responsible for it, in the last analysis, are those who deal with broad aims and policies. Thus:

The railroads did not stop growing because the need for passenger and freight transportation declined. That grew. The railroads are in trouble today not because the need was filled by others (cars, trucks, airplanes, even telephones), but because it was *not* filled by the railroads themselves. They let others take customers away from them because they assumed themselves to be in the railroad business rather than in the transportation business. The reason they defined their industry wrong was because they were railroad-oriented instead of transportation-oriented; they were product-oriented instead of customer-oriented.

Hollywood barely escaped being totally ravished by television. Actually, all the established film companies went through drastic reorganizations. Some simply disappeared. All of them got into trouble not because of TV's inroads but because of their own myopia. As with the railroads, Hollywood defined its business incorrectly. It thought it was in the movie business when it was actually in the entertainment business. "Movies" implied a specific, limited product. This produced a fatuous contentment which from the beginning led producers to view TV as a threat. Hollywood scorned and rejected TV when it should have welcomed it as an opportunity—an opportunity to expand the entertainment business.

Today TV is a bigger business than the old narrowly defined movie business ever was. Had Hollywood been customer-oriented (providing entertainment), rather than product-oriented (making movies), would it have gone through the fiscal purgatory that it did? I doubt it. What ultimately saved Hollywood and accounted for its recent resurgence was the wave of new young writers, producers, and directors whose previous successes in television had decimated the old movie companies and toppled the big movie moguls.

There are other less obvious examples of industries that have been and are now endangering their futures by improperly defining their purposes. I shall discuss some in detail later and analyze the kind of policies that lead to trouble. Right now it may help to show what a thoroughly customer-oriented management *can* do to keep a growth industry growing, even after the obvious opportunities have been exhausted; and here there are two examples that have been around for a long time. They are nylon and glass—specifically, E. I. duPont de Nemours & Company and Corning Glass Works.

Both companies have great technical competence. Their product orientation is unquestioned. But this alone does not explain their success. After all, who was more pridefully product-oriented and product-conscious than the erstwhile New England textile companies that have been so thoroughly massacred? The DuPonts and the Cornings have succeeded not primarily because of their product or research orientation but because they have been thoroughly customer-oriented also. It is constant watchfulness for opportunities to apply their technical know-how to the creation of customer-satisfying uses which accounts for their prodigious output of successful new products. Without a very sophisticated eye on the customer, most of their new products might have been wrong, their sales methods useless.

Aluminum has also continued to be a growth industry, thanks to the efforts of two wartime-created companies which deliberately set about creating new customer-satisfying uses. Without Kaiser Aluminum & Chemical Corporation and Reynolds Metals Company, the total demand for aluminum today would be vastly less.

Error of analysis: Some may argue that it is foolish to set the railroads off against aluminum or the movies off against glass. Are not aluminum and glass naturally so versatile that the industries are bound to have more growth opportunities than the railroads and movies? This view commits precisely the error I have been talking about. It defines an industry, or a product, or a cluster of know-how so narrowly as to guarantee its premature senescence. When we mention "railroads," we should make sure we mean "transportation." As transporters, the railroads still have a good chance for very considerable growth. They are not limited to the railroad business as such (though in my opinion rail transportation is potentially a much stronger transportation medium than is generally believed).

What the railroads lack is not opportunity, but some of the same managerial imaginativeness and audacity that made them great. Even an amateur like Jacques Barzun can see what is lacking when he says:

"I grieve to see the most advanced physical and social organization of the last century go down in shabby disgrace for lack of the same comprehensive imagination that built it up. [What is lacking is] the will of the companies to survive and to satisfy the public by inventiveness and skill."[1]

Shadow of Obsolescence

It is impossible to mention a single major industry that did not at one time qualify for the magic appellation of "growth industry." In each case its assumed strength lay in the apparently unchallenged superiority of its product. There appeared to be no effective substitute for it. It was itself a runaway substitute for the product it so triumphantly replaced. Yet one after another of these celebrated industries has come under a shadow. Let us look briefly at a few more of them, this time taking examples that have so far received a little less attention:

Dry cleaning—This was once a growth industry with lavish prospects. In an age of wool garments, imagine being finally able to get them safely and easily clean. The boom was on.

Yet here we are 30 years after the boom started and the industry is in trouble. Where has the competition come from? From a better way of cleaning? No. It has come from synthetic fibers and chemical additives that have cut the need for dry cleaning. But this is only the beginning. Lurking in the wings and ready to make chemical dry cleaning totally obsolescent is that powerful magician, ultrasonics.

Electric utilities—This is another one of those supposedly "no-substitute" products that has been enthroned on a pedestal of invincible growth. When the incandescent lamp came along, kerosene lights were finished. Later the water wheel and the steam engine

---

[1]Jacques Barzun, "Trains and the Mind of Man," *Holiday*, February 1960, p. 21.

were cut to ribbons by the flexibility, reliability, simplicity, and just plain easy availability of electric motors. The prosperity of electric utilities continues to wax extravagant as the home is converted into a museum of electric gadgetry. How can anybody miss by investing in utilities, with no competition, nothing but growth ahead?

But a second look is not quite so comforting. A score of nonutility companies are well advanced toward developing a powerful chemical fuel cell which could sit in some hidden closet of every home silently ticking off electric power. The electric lines that vulgarize so many neighborhoods will be eliminated. So will the endless demolition of streets and service interruptions during storms. Also on the horizon is solar energy, again pioneered by nonutility companies.

Who says that the utilities have no competition? They may be natural monopolies now, but tomorrow they may be natural deaths. To avoid this prospect, they too will have to develop fuel cells, solar energy, and other power sources. To survive, they themselves will have to plot the obsolescence of what now produces their livelihood.

Grocery stores—Many people find it hard to realize that there ever was a thriving establishment known as the "corner grocery store." The supermarket has taken over with a powerful effectiveness. Yet the big food chains of the 1930s narrowly escaped being completely wiped out by the aggressive expansion of independent supermarkets. The first genuine supermarket was opened in 1930, in Jamaica, Long Island. By 1933 supermarkets were thriving in California, Ohio, Pennsylvania, and elsewhere. Yet the established chains pompously ignored them. When they chose to notice them, it was with such derisive descriptions as "cheapy," "horse-and-buggy," "cracker-barrel storekeeping," and "unethical opportunists."

The executive of one big chain announced at the time that he found it "hard to believe that people will drive for miles to shop for foods and sacrifice the personal service chains have perfected and to which Mrs. Consumer is accustomed."[2] As late as 1936, the National Wholesale Grocers convention and the New Jersey Retail

---

[2]For more details see M. M. Zimmerman, *The Super Market: A Revolution in Distribution* (New York, McGraw-Hill Book Company, Inc., 1955), p. 48.

Grocers Association said there was nothing to fear. They said that the supers' narrow appeal to the price buyer limited the size of their market. They had to draw from miles around. When imitators came, there would be wholesale liquidations as volume fell. The current high sales of the supers was said to be partly due to their novelty. Basically people wanted convenient neighborhood grocers. If the neighborhood stores "cooperate with their suppliers, pay attention to their costs, and improve their service," they would be able to weather the competition until it blew over.[3]

It never blew over. The chains discovered that survival required going into the supermarket business. This meant the wholesale destruction of their huge investments in corner store sites and in established distribution and merchandising methods. The companies with "the courage of their convictions" resolutely stuck to the corner store philosophy. They kept their pride but lost their shirts.

Self-deceiving cycle: But memories are short. For example, it is hard for people who today confidently hail the twin messiahs of electronics and chemicals to see how things could possibly go wrong with these galloping industries. They probably also cannot see how a reasonably sensible businessman could have been as myopic as the famous Boston millionaire who 50 years ago unintentionally sentenced his heirs to poverty by stipulating that his entire estate be forever invested exclusively in electric streetcar securities. His posthumous declaration, "There will always be a big demand for efficient urban transportation," is no consolation to his heirs who sustain life by pumping gasoline at automobile filling stations.

Yet, in a casual survey I recently took among a group of intelligent business executives, nearly half agreed that it would be hard to hurt their heirs by tying their estates forever to the electronics industry. When I then confronted them with the Boston streetcar example, they chorused unanimously, "That's different!" But is it? Is not the basic situation identical?

In truth, *there is no such thing* as a growth industry, I believe. There are only companies organized and operated to create and capitalize on growth opportunities. Industries that assume themselves to be riding some automatic growth escalator invariably descend

---

[3]Ibid., pp. 45-47.

into stagnation. The history of every dead and dying "growth" industry shows a self-deceiving cycle of bountiful expansion and undetected decay. There are four conditions which usually guarantee this cycle:

1. The belief that growth is assured by an expanding and more affluent population.
2. The belief that there is no competitive substitute for the industry's major product.
3. Too much faith in mass production and in the advantages of rapidly declining unit costs as output rises.
4. Preoccupation with a product that lends itself to carefully controlled scientific experimentation, improvement, and manufacturing cost reduction.

I should like now to begin examining each of these conditions in some detail. To build my case as boldly as possible, I shall illustrate the points with reference to three industries—petroleum, automobiles, and electronics—particularly petroleum, because it spans more years and more vicissitudes. Not only do these three have excellent reputations with the general public and also enjoy the confidence of sophisticated investors, but their managements have become known for progressive thinking in areas like financial control, product research, and management training. If obsolescence can cripple even these industries, it can happen anywhere.

Population Myth

The belief that profits are assured by an expanding and more affluent population is dear to the heart of every industry. It takes the edge off the apprehensions everybody understandably feels about the future. If consumers are multiplying and also buying more of your product or service, you can face the future with considerably more comfort than if the market is shrinking. An expanding market keeps the manufacturer from having to think very hard or imaginatively. If thinking is an intellectual response to a problem, then the absence of a problem leads to the absence of thinking. If your product has an automatically expanding market, then you will not give much thought to how to expand it.

One of the most interesting examples of this is provided by the petroleum industry. Probably our oldest growth industry, it has an enviable record. While there are some current apprehensions about its growth rate, the industry itself tends to be optimistic.

But I believe it can be demonstrated that it is undergoing a fundamental yet typical change. It is not only ceasing to be a growth industry, but may actually be a declining one, relative to other business. Although there is widespread unawareness of it, I believe that within 25 years the oil industry may find itself in much the same position of retrospective glory that the railroads are now in. Despite its pioneering work in developing and applying the present-value method of investment evaluation, in employee relations, and in working with backward countries, the petroleum business is a distressing example of how complacency and wrongheadedness can stubbornly convert opportunity into near disaster.

One of the characteristics of this and other industries that have believed very strongly in the beneficial consequences of an expanding population, while at the same time being industries with a generic product for which there has appeared to be no competitive substitute, is that the individual companies have sought to outdo their competitors by improving on what they are already doing. This makes sense, of course, if one assumes that sales are tied to the country's population strings, because the customer can compare products only on a feature-by-feature basis. I believe it is significant, for example, that not since John D. Rockefeller sent free kerosene lamps to China has the oil industry done anything really outstanding to create a demand for its product. Not even in product improvement has it showered itself with eminence. The greatest single improvement—namely, the development of tetraethyl lead—came from outside the industry, specifically from General Motors and DuPont. The big contributions made by the industry itself are confined to the technology of oil exploration, production, and refining.

Asking for trouble: In other words, the industry's efforts have focused on improving the *efficiency* of getting and making its product, not really on improving the generic product or its marketing. Moreover, its chief product has continuously been defined in the narrowest possible terms, namely, gasoline, not energy, fuel, or transportation. This attitude has helped assure that:

Major improvements in gasoline quality tend not to originate in the oil industry. Also, the development of superior alternative fuels comes from outside the oil industry, as will be shown later.

Major innovations in automobile fuel marketing are originated by small new oil companies that are not primarily preoccupied with production or refining. These are the companies that have been responsible for the rapidly expanding multipump gasoline stations, with their successful emphasis on large and clean layouts, rapid and efficient driveway service, and quality gasoline at low prices.

Thus, the oil industry is asking for trouble from outsiders. Sooner or later, in this land of hungry inventors and entrepreneurs, a threat is sure to come. The possibilities of this will become more apparent when we turn to the next dangerous belief of many managements. For the sake of continuity, because this second belief is tied closely to the first, I shall continue with the same example.

Idea of indispensability: The petroleum industry is pretty much persuaded that there is no competitive substitute for its major product, gasoline—or if there is, that it will continue to be a derivative of crude oil, such as diesel fuel or kerosene jet fuel.

There is a lot of automatic wishful thinking in this assumption. The trouble is that most refining companies own huge amounts of crude oil reserves. These have value only if there is a market for products into which oil can be converted—hence the tenacious belief in the continuing competitive superiority of automobile fuels made from crude oil.

This idea persists despite all historic evidence against it. The evidence not only shows that oil has never been a superior product for any purpose for very long, but it also shows that the oil industry has never really been a growth industry. It has been a succession of different businesses that have gone through the usual historic cycles of growth, maturity, and decay. Its overall survival is owed to a series of miraculous escapes from total obsolescence, of last-minute and unexpected reprieves from total disaster reminiscent of the Perils of Pauline.

Perils of petroleum: I shall sketch in only the main episodes.

First, crude oil was largely a patent medicine. But even before that fad ran out, demand was greatly expanded by the use of oil in kerosene lamps. The prospect of lighting the world's lamps gave rise to an extravagant promise of growth. The prospects were similar to those the industry now holds for gasoline in other parts of the world. It can hardly wait for the underdeveloped nations to get a car in every garage.

In the days of the kerosene lamp, the oil companies competed with each other and against gaslight by trying to improve the illuminating characteristics of kerosene. Then suddenly the impossible happened. Edison invented a light which was totally nondependent on crude oil. Had it not been for the growing use of kerosene in space heaters, the incandescent lamp would have completely finished oil as a growth industry at that time. Oil would have been good for little else than axle grease.

Then disaster and reprieve struck again. Two great innovations occurred, neither originating in the oil industry. The successful development of coal-burning domestic central-heating systems made the space heater obsolescent. While the industry reeled, along came its most magnificent boost yet—the internal combustion engine, also invented by outsiders. Then when the prodigious expansion for gasoline finally began to level off in the 1920s, along came the miraculous escape of a central oil heater. Once again, the escape was provided by an outsider's invention and development. And when that market weakened, wartime demand for aviation fuel came to the rescue. After the war the expansion of civilian aviation, the dieselization of railroads, and the explosive demand for cars and trucks kept the industry's growth in high gear.

Meanwhile, centralized oil heating—whose boom potential had only recently been proclaimed—ran into severe competition from natural gas. While the oil companies themselves owned the gas that now competed with their oil, the industry did not originate the natural gas revolution, nor has it to this day greatly profited from its gas ownership. The gas revolution was made by newly formed transmission companies that marketed the product with an aggressive ardor. They started a magnificent new industry, first against the advice and then against the resistance of the oil companies.

By all the logic of the situation, the oil companies themselves should have made the gas revolution. They not only owned the gas; they also were the only people experienced in handling, scrubbing, and using it, the only people experienced in pipeline technology and transmission, and they understood heating problems. But, partly because they knew that natural gas would compete with their own sale of heating oil, the oil companies pooh-poohed the potentials of gas.

The revolution was finally started by oil pipeline executives who, unable to persuade their own companies to go into gas, quit and organized the spectacularly successful gas transmission companies. Even after their success became painfully evident to the oil companies, the latter did not go into gas transmission. The multibillion dollar business which should have been theirs went to others. As in the past, the industry was blinded by its narrow preoccupation with a specific product and the value of its reserves. It paid little or no attention to its customers' basic needs and preferences.

The postwar years have not witnessed any change. Immediately after World War II the oil industry was greatly encouraged about its future by the rapid expansion of demand for its traditional line of products. In 1950 most companies projected annual rates of domestic expansion of around 6% through at least 1975. Though the ratio of crude oil reserves to demand in the Free World was about 20 to 1, with 10 to 1 being usually considered a reasonable working ratio in the United States, booming demand sent oil men searching for more without sufficient regard to what the future really promised. In 1952 they "hit" in the Middle East; the ratio skyrocketed to 42 to 1. If gross additions to reserves continue at the average rate of the past five years (37 billion barrels annually), then by 1970 the reserve ratio will be up to 45 to 1. This abundance of oil has weakened crude and product prices all over the world.

Uncertain future: Management cannot find much consolation today in the rapidly expanding petrochemical industry, another oil-using idea that did not originate in the leading firms. The total United States production of petrochemicals is equivalent to about 2% (by volume) of the demand for all petroleum products. Although the petrochemical industry is now expected to grow by about 10% per year, this will not offset other drains on the growth of crude oil consumption. Furthermore, while petrochemical products are many and growing, it is well to remember that there are nonpetroleum sources of the basic raw material, such as coal. Besides, a lot of plastics can be produced with relatively little oil. A 50,000-barrel-per-day oil refinery is now considered the absolute minimum size for efficiency. But a 5,000-barrel-per-day chemical plant is a giant operation.

Oil has never been a continuously strong growth industry. It has grown by fits and starts, always miraculously saved by innovations and developments not of its own making. The reason it has not grown in a smooth progression is that each time it thought it had a superior product safe from the possibility of competitive substitutes, the product turned out to be inferior and notoriously subject to obsolescence. Until now, gasoline (for motor fuel, anyhow) has escaped this fate. But, as we shall see later, it too may be on its last legs.

The point of all this is that there is no guarantee against product obsolescence. If a company's own research does not make it obsolete, another's will. Unless an industry is especially lucky, as oil has been until now, it can easily go down in a sea of red figures— just as the railroads have, as the buggy whip manufacturers have, as the corner grocery chains have, as most of the big movie companies have, and indeed as many other industries have.

The best way for a firm to be lucky is to make its own luck. That requires knowing what makes a business successful. One of the greatest enemies of this knowledge is mass production.

Production Pressures

Mass-production industries are impelled by a great drive to produce all they can. The prospect of steeply declining unit costs as output rises is more than most companies can usually resist. The profit possibilities look spectacular. All effort focuses on production. The result is that marketing gets neglected.

John Kenneth Galbraith contends that just the opposite occurs.[4] Output is so prodigious that all effort concentrates on trying to get rid of it. He says this accounts for singing commercials, desecration of the countryside with advertising signs, and other wasteful and vulgar practices. Galbraith has a finger on something real, but

---

[4]*The Affluent Society* (Boston, Houghton Mifflin Company, 1958), pp. 152-160.

he misses the strategic point. Mass production does indeed generate great pressure to "move" the product. But what usually gets emphasized is selling, not marketing. Marketing, being a more sophisticated and complex process, gets ignored.

The difference between marketing and selling is more than semantic. Selling focuses on the needs of the seller, marketing on the needs of the buyer. Selling is preoccupied with the seller's need to convert his product into cash, marketing with the idea of satisfying the needs of the customer by means of the product and the whole cluster of things associated with creating, delivering, and finally consuming it.

In some industries the enticements of full mass production have been so powerful that for many years top management in effect has told the sales departments, "You get rid of it; we'll worry about profits." By contrast, a truly marketing-minded firm tries to create value-satisfying goods and services that consumers will want to buy. What it offers for sale includes not only the generic product or service, but also how it is made available to the customer, in what form, when, under what conditions, and at what terms of trade. Most important, what it offers for sale is determined not by the seller but by the buyer. The seller takes his cues from the buyer in such a way that the product becomes a consequence of the marketing effort, not vice versa.

Lag in Detroit: This may sound like an elementary rule of business, but that does not keep it from being violated wholesale. It is certainly more violated than honored. Take the automobile industry.

Here mass production is most famous, most honored, and has the greatest impact on the entire society. The industry has hitched its fortune to the relentless requirements of the annual model change, a policy that makes customer orientation an especially urgent necessity. Consequently the auto companies annually spend millions of dollars on consumer research. But the fact that the new compact cars are selling so well in their first year indicates that Detroit's vast researches have for a long time failed to reveal what the customer really wanted. Detroit was not persuaded that he wanted anything different from what he had been getting until it lost millions of customers to other small car manufacturers.

How could this unbelievable lag behind consumer wants have been perpetuated so long? Why did not research reveal consumer preferences before consumers' buying decisions themselves revealed the facts? Is that not what consumer research is for—to find out before the fact what is going to happen? The answer is that Detroit never really researched the customer's wants. It only researched his preferences between the kinds of things which it had already decided to offer him. For Detroit is mainly product-oriented, not customer-oriented. To the extent that the customer is recognized as having needs that the manufacturer should try to satisfy, Detroit usually acts as if the job can be done entirely by product changes. Occasionally attention gets paid to financing, too, but that is done more in order to sell than to enable the customer to buy.

As for taking care of other customer needs, there is not enough being done to write about. The areas of the greatest unsatisfied needs are ignored, or at best get stepchild attention. These are at the point of sale and on the matter of automotive repair and maintenance. Detroit views these problem areas as being of secondary importance. That is underscored by the fact that the retailing and servicing ends of this industry are neither owned and operated nor controlled by the manufacturers. Once the car is produced, things are pretty much in the dealer's inadequate hands. Illustrative of Detroit's arm's-length attitude is the fact that, while servicing holds enormous sales-stimulating, profit-building opportunities, only 57 of Chevrolet's 7,000 dealers provide night maintenance service.

Motorists repeatedly express their dissatisfaction with servicing and their apprehensions about buying cars under the present selling setup. The anxieties and problems they encounter during the auto buying and maintenance processes are probably more intense and widespread today than 30 years ago. Yet the automobile companies do not *seem* to listen to or take their cues from the anguished consumer. If they do listen, it must be through the filter of their own preoccupation with production. The marketing effort is still viewed as a necessary consequence of the product, not vice versa, as it should be. That is the legacy of mass production, with its parochial view that profit resides essentially in low-cost full production.

What Ford put first: The profit lure of mass production obviously has a place in the plans and strategy of business management, but it must always *follow* hard thinking about the customer. This is one

of the most important lessons that we can learn from the contradic-
tory behavior of Henry Ford. In a sense Ford was both the most
brilliant and the most senseless marketer in American history. He
was senseless because he refused to give the customer anything but
a black car. He was brilliant because he fashioned a production
system designed to fit market needs. We habitually celebrate him
for the wrong reason, his production genius. His real genius was
marketing. We think he was able to cut his selling price and therefore
sell millions of $500 cars because his invention of the assembly line
had reduced the costs. Actually he invented the assembly line
because he had concluded that at $500 he could sell millions of cars.
Mass production was the *result* not the cause of his low prices.

Ford repeatedly emphasized this point, but a nation of production-oriented business managers refuses to hear the great lesson he
taught. Here is his operating philosophy as he expressed it
succinctly:

"Our policy is to reduce the price, extend the operations, and
improve the article. You will notice that the reduction of price comes
first. We have never considered any costs as fixed. Therefore we
first reduce the price to the point where we believe more sales will
result. Then we go ahead and try to make the prices. We do not
bother about the costs. The new price forces the costs down. The
more usual way is to take the costs and then determine the price;
and although that method may be scientific in the narrow sense,
it is not scientific in the broad sense, because what earthly use is
it to know the cost if it tells you that you cannot manufacture at a
price at which the article can be sold? But more to the point is the
fact that, although one may calculate what a cost is, and of course
all of our costs are carefully calculated, no one knows what a cost
ought to be. One of the ways of discovering . . . is to name a price
so low as to force everybody in the place to the highest point of efficiency. The low price makes everybody dig for profits. We make
more discoveries concerning manufacturing and selling under this
forced method than by any method of leisurely investigation."[5]

---

[5]Henry Ford, *My Life and Work* (New York, Doubleday, Page & Company, 1923), pp. 146-147.

Product provincialism: The tantalizing profit possibilities of low unit production costs may be the most seriously self-deceiving attitude that can afflict a company, particularly a "growth" company where an apparently assured expansion of demand already tends to undermine a proper concern for the importance of marketing and the customer.

The usual result of this narrow preoccupation with so-called concrete matters is that instead of growing, the industry declines. It usually means that the product fails to adapt to the constantly changing patterns of consumer needs and tastes, to new and modified marketing institutions and practices, or to product developments in competing or complementary industries. The industry has its eyes so firmly on its own specific product that it does not see how it is being made obsolete.

The classical example of this is the buggy whip industry. No amount of product improvement could stave off its death sentence. But had the industry defined itself as being in the transportation business rather than the buggy whip business, it might have survived. It would have done what survival always entails, that is, changing. Even if it had only defined its business as providing a stimulant or catalyst to an energy source, it might have survived by becoming a manufacturer of, say, fanbelts or air cleaners.

What may some day be a still more classical example is, again, the oil industry. Having let others steal marvelous opportunities from it (e.g., natural gas, as already mentioned, missile fuels, and jet engine lubricants), one would expect it to have taken steps never to let that happen again. But this is not the case. We are now getting extraordinary new developments in fuel systems specifically designed to power automobiles. Not only are these developments concentrated in firms outside the petroleum industry, but petroleum is almost systematically ignoring them, securely content in its wedded bliss to oil. It is the story of the kerosene lamp versus the incandescent lamp all over again. Oil is trying to improve hydrocarbon fuels rather than develop *any* fuels best suited to the needs of their users, whether or not made in different ways and with different raw materials from oil.

Here are some things which nonpetroleum companies are working on:

Over a dozen such firms now have advanced working models of energy systems which, when perfected, will replace the internal combustion engine and eliminate the demand for gasoline. The superior merit of each of these systems is their elimination of frequent, time-consuming, and irritating refueling stops. Most of these systems are fuel cells designed to create electrical energy directly from chemicals without combustion. Most of them use chemicals that are not derived from oil, generally hydrogen and oxygen.

Several other companies have advanced models of electric storage batteries designed to power automobiles. One of these is an aircraft producer that is working jointly with several electric utility companies. The latter hope to use off-peak generating capacity to supply overnight plug-in battery regeneration. Another company, also using the battery approach, is a medium-size electronics firm with extensive small-battery experience that it developed in connection with its work on hearing aids. It is collaborating with an automobile manufacturer. Recent improvements arising from the need for high-powered miniature power storage plants in rockets have put us within reach of a relatively small battery capable of withstanding great overloads or surges of power. Germanium diode applications and batteries using sintered-plate and nickel-cadmium techniques promise to make a revolution in our energy sources.

Solar energy conversion systems are also getting increasing attention. One usually cautious Detroit auto executive recently ventured that solar-powered cars might be common by 1980.

As for the oil companies, they are more or less "watching developments," as one research director put it to me. A few are doing a bit of research on fuel cells, but almost always confined to developing cells powered by hydrocarbon chemicals. None of them are enthusiastically researching fuel cells, batteries, or solar power plants. None of them are spending a fraction as much on research in these profoundly important areas as they are on the usual run-of-the-mill things like reducing combustion chamber deposit in gasoline engines. One major integrated petroleum company recently took a tentative look at the fuel cell and concluded that although "the companies actively working on it indicate a belief in ultimate success...the timing and magnitude of its impact are too remote to warrant recognition in our forecasts."

One might, of course, ask: Why should the oil companies do anything different? Would not chemical fuel cells, batteries, or solar energy kill the present product lines? The answer is that they would indeed, and that is precisely the reason for the oil firms having to develop these power units before their competitors, so they will not be companies without an industry.

Management might be more likely to do what is needed for its own preservation if it thought of itself as being in the energy business. But even that would not be enough if it persists in imprisoning itself in the narrow grip of its tight product orientation. It has to think of itself as taking care of customer needs, not finding, refining, or even selling oil. Once it genuinely thinks of its business as taking care of people's transportation needs, nothing can stop it from creating its own extravagantly profitable growth.

'Creative destruction': Since words are cheap and deeds are dear, it may be appropriate to indicate what this kind of thinking involves and leads to. Let us start at the beginning—the customer. It can be shown that motorists strongly dislike the bother, delay, and experience of buying gasoline. People actually do not buy gasoline. They cannot see it, taste it, feel it, appreciate it, or really test it. What they buy is the right to continue driving their cars. The gas station is like a tax collector to whom people are compelled to pay a periodic toll as the price of using their cars. This makes the gas station a basically unpopular institution. It can never be made popular or pleasant, only less unpopular, less unpleasant.

To reduce its unpopularity completely means eliminating it. Nobody likes a tax collector, not even a pleasantly cheerful one. Nobody likes to interrupt a trip to buy a phantom product, not even from a handsome Adonis or a seductive Venus. Hence, companies that are working on exotic fuel substitutes which will eliminate the need for frequent refueling are heading directly into the outstretched arms of the irritated motorist. They are riding a wave of inevitability, not because they are creating something which is technologically superior or more sophisticated, but because they are satisfying a powerful customer need. They are also eliminating noxious odors and air pollution.

Once the petroleum companies recognize the customer-satisfying logic of what another power system can do, they will see that they have no more choice about working on an efficient, long-lasting fuel (or some way of delivering present fuels without bothering the motorist) than the big food chains had a choice about going into the supermarket business, or the vacuum tube companies had a choice about making semiconductors. For their own good the oil firms will have to destroy their own highly profitable assets. No amount of wishful thinking can save them from the necessity of engaging in this form of "creative destruction."

I phrase the need as strongly as this because I think management must make quite an effort to break itself loose from conventional ways. It is all too easy in this day and age for a company or industry to let its sense of purpose become dominated by the economies of full production and to develop a dangerously lopsided product orientation. In short, if management lets itself drift, it invariably drifts in the direction of thinking of itself as producing goods and services, not customer satisfactions. While it probably will not descend to the depths of telling its salesmen, "You get rid of it; we'll worry about profits," it can, without knowing it, be practicing precisely that formula for withering decay. The historic fate of one growth industry after another has been its suicidal product provincialism.

Dangers of R&D

Another big danger to a firm's continued growth arises when top management is wholly transfixed by the profit possibilities of technical research and development. To illustrate I shall turn first to a new industry—electronics—and then return once more to the oil companies. By comparing a fresh example with a familiar one, I hope to emphasize the prevalence and insidiousness of a hazardous way of thinking.

Marketing shortchanged: In the case of electronics, the greatest danger which faces the glamorous new companies in this field is not that they do not pay enough attention to research and development, but that they pay *too much* attention to it. And the fact that the fastest growing electronics firms owe their eminence to their heavy emphasis on technical research is completely beside the point.

They have vaulted to affluence on a sudden crest of unusually strong general receptiveness to new technical ideas. Also, their success has been shaped in the virtually guaranteed market of military subsidies and by military orders that in many cases actually preceded the existence of facilities to make the products. Their expansion has, in other words, been almost totally devoid of marketing effort.

Thus, they are growing up under conditions that come dangerously close to creating the illusion that a superior product will sell itself. Having created a successful company by making a superior product, it is not surprising that management continues to be oriented toward the product rather than the people who consume it. It develops the philosophy that continued growth is a matter of continued product innovation and improvement.

A number of other factors tend to strengthen and sustain this belief:

1. Because electronic products are highly complex and sophisticated, managements become top-heavy with engineers and scientists. This creates a selective bias in favor of research and production at the expense of marketing. The organization tends to view itself as making things rather than satisfying customer needs. Marketing gets treated as a residual activity, "something else" that must be done once the vital job of product creation and production is completed.

2. To this bias in favor of product research, development, and production is added the bias in favor of dealing with controllable variables. Engineers and scientists are at home in the world of concrete things like machines, test tubes, production lines, and even balance sheets. The abstractions to which they feel kindly are those which are testable or manipulatable in the laboratory, or, if not testable, then functional, such as Euclid's axioms. In short, the managements of the new glamour-growth companies tend to favor those business activities which lend themselves to careful study, experimentation, and control—the hard, practical realities of the lab, the shop, the books.

What gets shortchanged are the realities of the *market*. Consumers are unpredictable, varied, fickle, stupid, shortsighted, stubborn, and generally bothersome. This is not what the engineer-managers say, but deep down in their consciousness it is what they believe. And this accounts for their concentrating on what they know and what they can control, namely, product research, engineering, and production. The emphasis on production becomes particularly attractive when the product can be made at declining unit costs. There is no more inviting way of making money than by running the plant full blast.

Today the top-heavy science-engineering-production orientation of so many electronics companies works reasonably well because they are pushing into new frontiers in which the armed services have pioneered virtually assured markets. The companies are in the felicitous position of having to fill, not find markets; of not having to discover what the customer needs and wants, but of having the customer voluntarily come forward with specific new product demands. If a team of consultants had been assigned specifically to design a business situation calculated to prevent the emergence and development of a customer-oriented marketing viewpoint, it could not have produced anything better than the conditions just described.

Stepchild treatment: The oil industry is a stunning example of how science, technology, and mass production can divert an entire group of companies from their main task. To the extent the consumer is studied at all (which is not much), the focus is forever on getting information which is designed to help the oil companies improve what they are now doing. They try to discover more convincing advertising schemes, more effective sales promotional drives, what the market shares of the various companies are, what people like or dislike about service station dealers and oil companies, and so forth. Nobody seems as interested in probing deeply into the basic human needs that the industry might be trying to satisfy as in probing into the basic properties of the raw material that the companies work with in trying to deliver customer satisfactions.

Basic questions about customers and markets seldom get asked. The latter occupy a stepchild status. They are recognized as existing, as having to be taken care of, but not worth very much real thought or dedicated attention. Nobody gets as excited about the customers in his own backyard as about the oil in the Sahara Desert. Nothing illustrates better the neglect of marketing than its treatment in the industry press.

The centennial issue of the *American Petroleum Institute Quarterly,* published in 1959 to celebrate the discovery of oil in Titusville, Pennsylvania, contained 21 feature articles proclaiming the industry's greatness. Only one of these talked about its achievements in marketing, and that was only a pictorial record of how service station architecture has changed. The issue also contained a special section on "New Horizons," which was devoted to showing the magnificent role oil would play in America's future. Every reference was ebulliently optimistic, never implying once that oil might have some hard competition. Even the reference to atomic energy was a cheerful catalogue of how oil would help make atomic energy a success. There was not a single apprehension that the oil industry's affluence might be threatened or a suggestion that one "new horizon" might include new and better ways of serving oil's present customers.

But the most revealing example of the stepchild treatment that marketing gets was still another special series of short articles on "The Revolutionary Potential of Electronics." Under that heading this list of articles appeared in the table of contents:

"In the Search for Oil"

"In Production Operations"

"In Refinery Processes"

"In Pipeline Operations"

Significantly, every one of the industry's major functional areas is listed, *except* marketing. Why? Either it is believed that electronics holds no revolutionary potential for petroleum marketing (which is palpably wrong), or the editors forgot to discuss marketing (which is more likely, and illustrates its stepchild status).

The order in which the four functional areas are listed also betrays the alienation of the oil industry from the consumer. The industry is implicitly defined as beginning with the search for oil and ending with its distribution from the refinery. But the truth is, it seems to me, that the industry begins with the needs of the customer for its products. From that primal position its definition moves steadily backstream to areas of progressively lesser importance, until it finally comes to rest at the "search for oil."

Beginning & end: The view that an industry is a customer-satisfying process, not a goods-producing process, is vital for all businessmen to understand. An industry begins with the customer and his needs, not with a patent, a raw material, or a selling skill. Given the customer's needs, the industry develops backwards, first concerning itself with the physical *delivery* of customer satisfactions. Then it moves back further to *creating* the things by which these satisfactions are in part achieved. How these materials are created is a matter of indifference to the customer, hence the particular form of manufacturing, processing, or what-have-you cannot be considered as a vital aspect of the industry. Finally, the industry moves back still further to *finding* the raw materials necessary for making its products.

The irony of some industries oriented toward technical research and development is that the scientists who occupy the high executive positions are totally unscientific when it comes to defining their companies' overall needs and purposes. They violate the first two rules of the scientific method—being aware of and defining their companies' problems, and then developing testable hypotheses about solving them. They are scientific only about the convenient things, such as laboratory and product experiments.

The reason that the customer (and the satisfaction of his deepest needs) is not considered as being "the problem" is not because there is any certain belief that no such problem exists, but because an organizational lifetime has conditioned management to look in the opposite direction. Marketing is a stepchild.

I do not mean that selling is ignored. Far from it. But selling, again, is not marketing. As already pointed out, selling concerns itself with the tricks and techniques of getting people to exchange their cash for your product. It is not concerned with the values that the exchange is all about. And it does not, as marketing invariably does, view the entire business process as consisting of a tightly integrated effort to discover, create, arouse, and satisfy customer needs. The customer is somebody "out there" who, with proper cunning, can be separated from his loose change.

Actually, not even selling gets much attention in some technologically minded firms. Because there is a virtually guaranteed market for the abundant flow of their new products, they do not actually know what a real market is. It is as if they lived in a planned economy, moving their products routinely from factory to retail outlet. Their successful concentration on products tends to convince them of the soundness of what they have been doing, and they fail to see the gathering clouds over the market.

Conclusion

Less than 75 years ago American railroads enjoyed a fierce loyalty among astute Wall Streeters. European monarchs invested in them heavily. Eternal wealth was thought to be the benediction for anybody who could scrape a few thousand dollars together to put into rail stocks. No other form of transportation could compete with the railroads in speed, flexibility, durability, economy, and growth potentials.

As Jacques Barzun put it, "By the turn of the century it was an institution, an image of man, a tradition, a code of honor, a source of poetry, a nursery of boyhood desires, a sublimest of toys, and the most solemn machine—next to the funeral hearse—that marks the epochs in man's life."[6]

Even after the advent of automobiles, trucks, and airplanes, the railroad tycoons remained imperturbably self-confident. If you had told them 60 years ago that in 30 years they would be flat on their backs, broke, and pleading for government subsidies, they would have thought you totally demented. Such a future was simply not considered possible. It was not even a discussable subject, or an askable question, or a matter which any sane person would consider worth speculating about. The very thought was insane. Yet a lot of insane notions now have matter-of-fact acceptance—for example, the idea of 100-ton tubes of metal moving smoothly through the air 20,000 feet above the earth, loaded with 100 sane and solid citizens casually drinking martinis—and they have dealt cruel blows to the railroads.

What specifically must other companies do to avoid this fate? What does customer orientation involve? These questions have in part been answered by the preceding examples and analysis. It would take another article to show in detail what is required for

---

[6]Jacques Barzun, "Trains and the Mind of Man," *Holiday*, February 1960, p. 20.

specific industries. In any case, it should be obvious that building an effective customer-oriented company involves far more than good intentions or promotional tricks; it involves profound matters of human organization and leadership. For the present, let me merely suggest what appear to be some general requirements.

Visceral feel of greatness: Obviously the company has to do what survival demands. It has to adapt to the requirements of the market, and it has to do it sooner rather than later. But mere survival is a so-so aspiration. Anybody can survive in some way or other, even the skid-row bum. The trick is to survive gallantly, to feel the surging impulse of commercial mastery; not just to experience the sweet smell of success, but to have the visceral feel of entrepreneurial greatness.

No organization can achieve greatness without a vigorous leader who is driven onward by his own pulsating *will to succeed.* He has to have a vision of grandeur, a vision that can produce eager followers in vast numbers. In business, the followers are the customers.

In order to produce these customers, the entire corporation must be viewed as a customer-creating and customer-satisfying organism. Management must think of itself not as producing products but as providing customer-creating value satisfactions. It must push this idea (and everything it means and requires) into every nook and cranny in the organization. It has to do this continuously and with the kind of flair that excites and stimulates the people in it. Otherwise, the company will be merely a series of pigeonholed parts, with no consolidating sense of purpose or direction.

In short, the organization must learn to think of itself not as producing goods or services but as *buying customers,* as doing the things that will make people *want* to do business with it. And the chief executive himself has the inescapable responsibility for creating this environment, this viewpoint, this attitude, this aspiration. He himself must set the company's style, its direction, and its goals. This means he has to know precisely where he himself wants to go, and to make sure the whole organization is enthusiastically aware of where that is. This is a first requisite of leadership, for *unless he knows where he is going, any road will take him there.*

If any road is okay, the chief executive might as well pack his attaché case and go fishing. If an organization does not know or care where it is going, it does not need to advertise that fact with a ceremonial figurehead. Everybody will notice it soon enough.

Retrospective Commentary

Amazed, finally, by his literary success, Isaac Bashevis Singer reconciled an attendant problem: "I think the moment you have published a book, it's not any more your private property. . . . If it has value, everybody can find in it what he finds, and I cannot tell the man I did not intend it to be so." Over the past 15 years, "Marketing Myopia" has become a case in point. Remarkably, the article spawned a legion of loyal partisans—not to mention a host of unlikely bedfellows.

Its most common and, I believe, most influential consequence is the way certain companies for the first time gave serious thought to the question of what businesses they are really in.

The strategic consequences of this have in many cases been dramatic. The best-known case, of course, is the shift in thinking of oneself as being in the "oil business" to being in the "energy business." In some instances the payoff has been spectacular (getting into coal, for example) and in others dreadful (in terms of the time and money spent so far on fuel cell research). Another successful example is a company with a large chain of retail shoe stores that redefined itself as a retailer of moderately priced, frequently purchased, widely assorted consumer specialty products. The result was a dramatic growth in volume, earnings, and return on assets.

Some companies, again for the first time, asked themselves whether they wished to be masters of certain technologies for which they would seek markets, or be masters of markets for which they would seek customer-satisfying products and services.

Choosing the former, one company has declared, in effect, "We are experts in glass technology. We intend to improve and expand that expertise with the object of creating products that will attract customers." This decision has forced the company into a much more systematic and customer-sensitive look at possible markets and users, even though its stated strategic object has been to capitalize on glass technology.

Deciding to concentrate on markets, another company has determined that "we want to help people (primarily women) enhance their beauty and sense of youthfulness." This company has expanded its line of cosmetic products, but has also entered the fields of proprietary drugs and vitamin supplements.

All these examples illustrate the "policy" results of "Marketing Myopia." On the operating level, there has been, I think, an extraordinary heightening of sensitivity to customers and consumers. R&D departments have cultivated a greater "external" orientation toward uses, users, and markets—balancing thereby the previously one-sided "internal" focus on materials and methods; upper management has realized that marketing and sales departments should be somewhat more willingly accommodated than before; finance departments have become more receptive to the legitimacy of budgets for market research and experimentation in marketing; and salesmen have been better trained to listen to and understand customer needs and problems, rather than merely to "push" the product.

A Mirror, Not a Window

My impression is that the article has had more impact in industrial-products companies than in consumer-products companies—perhaps because the former had lagged most in customer orientation. There are at least two reasons for this lag: (1) industrial-products companies tend to be more capital intensive, and (2) in the past, at least, they have had to rely heavily on communicating face-to-face the technical character of what they made and sold. These points are worth explaining.

Capital-intensive businesses are understandably preoccupied with magnitudes, especially where the capital, once invested, cannot be easily moved, manipulated, or modified for the production of a variety of products—e.g., chemical plants, steel mills, airlines, and railroads. Understandably, they seek big volumes and operating efficiencies to pay off the equipment and meet the carrying costs.

At least one problem results: corporate power becomes disproportionately lodged with operating or financial executives.

If you read the charter of one of the nation's largest companies, you will see that the chairman of the finance committee, not the chief executive officer, is the "chief." Executives with such backgrounds have an almost trained incapacity to see that getting "volume" may require understanding and serving many discrete and sometimes small market segments, rather than going after a perhaps mythical batch of big or homogeneous customers.

These executives also often fail to appreciate the competitive changes going on around them. They observe the changes, all right, but devalue their significance or underestimate their ability to nibble away at the company's markets.

Once dramatically alerted to the concept of segments, sectors, and customers, though, managers of capital-intensive businesses have become more responsive to the necessity of balancing their inescapable preoccupation with "paying the bills" or breaking even with the fact that the best way to accomplish this may be to pay more attention to segments, sectors, and customers.

The second reason industrial products companies have probably been more influenced by the article is that, in the case of the more technical industrial products or services, the necessity of clearly communicating product and service characteristics to prospects results in a lot of face-to-face "selling" effort. But precisely because the product is so complex, the situation produces salesmen who know the product more than they know the customer, who are more adept at explaining what they have and what it can do than learning what the customer's needs and problems are. The result has been a narrow product orientation rather than a liberating customer orientation, and "service" often suffered. To be sure, sellers said, "We have to provide service," but they tended to define service by looking into the mirror rather than out the window. They *thought* they were looking out the window at the customer, but it was actually a mirror—a reflection of their own product-oriented biases rather than a reflection of their customers' situations.

A Manifesto, Not a Prescription

Not everything has been rosy. A lot of bizarre things have happened as a result of the article:

Some companies have developed what I call "marketing mania"—they've become obsessively responsive to every fleeting whim of the customer. Mass production operations have been converted to approximations of job shops, with cost and price consequences far exceeding the willingness of customers to buy the product.

Management has expanded product lines and added new lines of business without first establishing adequate control systems to run more complex operations.

Marketing staffs have suddenly and rapidly expanded themselves and their research budgets without either getting sufficient prior organizational support or, thereafter, producing sufficient results.

Companies that are functionally organized have converted to product, brand, or market-based organizations with the expectation of instant and miraculous results. The outcome has been ambiguity, frustration, confusion, corporate infighting, losses, and finally a reversion to functional arrangements that only worsened the situation.

Companies have attempted to "serve" customers by creating complex and beautifully efficient products or services that buyers are either too risk-averse to adopt or incapable of learning how to employ—in effect, there are now steam shovels for people who haven't yet learned to use spades. This problem has happened repeatedly in the so-called service industries (financial services, insurance, computer-based services) and with American companies selling in less-developed economies.

"Marketing Myopia" was not intended as analysis or even prescription; it was intended as manifesto. It did not pretend to take a balanced position. Nor was it a new idea—Peter F. Drucker, J.B. McKitterick, Wroe Alderson, John Howard, and Neil Borden had each done more original and balanced work on "the marketing concept." My scheme, however, tied marketing more closely to the inner orbit of business policy. Drucker—especially in *The Concept of the Corporation* and *The Practice of Management*—originally provided me with a great deal of insight.

My contribution, therefore, appears merely to have been a simple, brief, and useful way of communicating an existing way of thinking. I tried to do it in a very direct, but responsible, fashion, knowing that few readers (customers), especially managers and leaders, could stand much equivocation or hesitation. I also knew that the colorful and lightly documented affirmation works better than the tortuously reasoned explanation.

But why the enormous popularity of what was actually such a simple pre-existing idea? Why its appeal throughout the world to resolutely restrained scholars, implacably temperate managers, and high government officials, all accustomed to balanced and thoughtful calculation? Is it that concrete examples, joined to illustrate a simple idea and presented with some attention to literacy, communicate better than massive analytical reasoning that reads as though it were translated from the German? Is it that provocative assertions are more memorable and persuasive than restrained and balanced explanations, no matter who the audience? Is it that the character of the message is as much the message as its content? Or was mine not simply a different tune, but a new symphony? I don't know.

Of course, I'd do it again and in the same way, given my purposes, even with what more I now know—the good and the bad, the power of facts and the limits of rhetoric. If your mission is the moon, you don't use a car. Don Marquis's cockroach, Archy, provides some final consolation: "an idea is not responsible for who believes in it."

6

Corporate Mission Statements: The Bottom Line

Abstract

The development of a mission statement is widely accepted as essential to successful strategic planning, yet there is surprisingly little evidence that a well-formulated mission statement enhances organizational performance. Furthermore, the value of one component in a mission statement over another is virtually unexplored.

Some benchmark components against which to conduct further study are needed. Accordingly, the mission statements of a number of Fortune 500 companies were examined for the presence of eight desired components, and two findings resulted:

1. *The mission statements of high-performing firms exhibited more of the desired components than did those of the low-performing firms.*

2. *Significantly more of the mission statements of the highest-performing firms exhibited three particular components than did the statements of the lowest-performing firms.*

The three components significantly related to superior financial performance were the following:

1. Company Philosophy: *A disclosure of the organization's basic beliefs, values, aspirations, and philosophical priorities.*

2. Self-Concept: *The organization's view of its own competitive strengths.*

3. Public Image: *An expression of consideration for social concerns and desires.*

Although the findings do not suggest that well-formed mission statements will improve organizational performance, they do lend support to the notion that higher-performing firms work to build worthwhile statements of mission, presumably benefiting from the process. The research also contributes empirical data to the challenge of linking strategic planning with corporate performance.

Corporate Mission Statements: The Bottom Line

John A. Pearce II and Fred David

Developing a mission statement is an important first step in the strategic planning process, according to both practitioners and research scholars.[1] Several recent books on strategic management include entire chapters on mission statements, which attest to their perceived importance in the strategy formulation process. Nevertheless, the components of mission statements are among the least empirically examined issues in strategic management. No reported empirical studies describe the composition of business mission statements, only a few conceptual articles suggest desirable component characteristics, and no reported attempts have been made to link mission statements to corporate performance.

This neglect is surprising since several studies have concluded that firms that engage in strategic planning outperform firms that do not.[2] Thus, the research reported in this paper focused on the nature and role of mission statements in organizational processes; its goal was to improve our understanding of the link between strategic planning and firm performance.

The Mission Statement

Function

An effective mission state defines the fundamental, unique purpose that sets a business apart from other firms of its type and identifies the scope of the business's operations in product and market terms.[3] It is an enduring statement of purpose that reveals an organization's product or service, markets, customers, and philosophy. When prepared as a formal organizational document, a mission statement may be presented under a maze of labels, including "creed statement," "statement of purpose," "statement of philosophy," or a statement "defining our business." Yet regardless of the label, a mission statement provides the foundation for priorities, strategies, plans, and work assignments. It is the starting point for the design of managerial jobs and structures. It specifies the fundamental reason why an organization exists.

A mission statement should create an organization identity larger than the limits placed on the firm by any individual. An effective statement helps to satisfy people's needs to produce something worthwhile, to gain recognition, to help others, to beat opponents, and to earn respect. Thus, it is a general declaration of attitude and outlook. Free from details, a mission statement has breadth of scope; it provides for the generation and consideration of a range of alternative objectives and strategies because it does not unduly stifle management creativity.

Components

A mission statement may be the most visible and public part of a strategic plan. As such, it is comprehensive in its coverage of broad organizational concerns. Although no empirical research has been published to guide corporate mission statement development, the limited evidence available suggests eight key components of mission statements:

1. The specification of target customers and markets.
2. The identification of principal products/services.
3. The specification of geographic domain.
4. The identification of core technologies.

5. The expression of commitment to survival, growth, and profitability.
6. The specification of key elements in the company philosophy.
7. The identification of the company self-concept.
8. The identification of the firm's desired public image.

A Study of Mission Statements

Based on previous theoretical and conceptual work focusing on the composition of mission statements, the present empirical investigation was undertaken to assess the relationship between mission statements with the eight components listed above and corporate financial performance. The present study specifically addressed the following hypothesis: The mission statements of high performing *Fortune* 500 companies will exhibit more of the desired components than will those of low performing *Fortune* 500 firms.

Our rationale for this hypothesis was prior theoretical and conceptual writing suggesting that eight components characterize an effective mission statement. Prior research also suggested that firms that engage in strategic planning outperform firms that do little or no planning. We reasoned that because a mission statement is increasingly perceived as an indication of a high-quality strategic planning effort, firms that have developed a comprehensive mission statement should outperform those with a weak or no mission statement. Such a finding would not, of course, indicate causation, because many diverse factors affect organizational performance. However, a comprehensive mission statement, we reasoned, should provide a basis for making better strategic decisions which, in turn, should contribute to improved organizational performance.

Survey Results

Response Raters

Completed surveys were returned by 218 of the *Fortune* 500 companies mailed the research instrument. Of the respondents, 61

(28%) supplied mission statements that were analyzed for this report. As indicated in Exhibit 1, of the remaining respondents, 40.4% replied that their organization did not have a mission statement; 5% replied that their mission statement was confidential; and 26.6% sent material, such as an annual report, from which a statement of mission could not be confidently extracted.

Nature and Prevalence of Components

One of the most valuable insights the survey results provide is a realistic portrayal of the components of corporate mission statements. For managers who are asked to participate in constructing or modifying a firm's mission, such information is helpful for comparative purposes. In this section, we will review the survey results for popularity of each of the eight components identified above. We will also present examples of each component excerpted from the corporate mission statements we evaluated.

Number of mailings	**500**
No response	282 (56.4%)
Responses	218 (43.6%)
Responses replying:	
That the organization had no mission statement	88 (40.4%)
That the organization had a confidential mission statement	11 (5.0%)
With material that we could not use	58 (26.6%)
With usable mission statements	61 (28.0%)

Exhibit 1. The Survey Responses

1. *Target customers and markets.* Did the mission statements specify the firm's intended major customer or market targets? Many did—48%. We were somewhat surprised that more firms were not willing to commit openly to customers and markets. Those we questioned provided three reasons for this intentional omission: First, specifying certain groups might unintentionally signal "no interest" to others; second, merger and acquisition activity might violate any predetermined definition of customers or markets; and third, the various markets of many diverse business units effectively dictated a worldwide corporate market focus, and limiting that focus in any way could be confusing to some readers acquainted with smaller markets for individual product lines.

From the mission statements of Johnson & Johnson and CENEX came these clear commitments to specific customer groups:

> We believe our first responsibility is to the doctors, nurses, and patients, to mothers and all others who use our products and services. (Johnson & Johnson)
>
> . . . to anticipate and meet market needs of farmers, ranchers and rural communities within North America. (CENEX)

2. *Principal products or services.* Did the mission statements convey the firm's commitment to major products or services? Yes—a solid majority, (67%) were unequivocal in specifying their major products or services.

Consider, for example, the following excerpts from the mission statements of **AMAX** and Standard Oil Company of Indiana, respectively:

> AMAX's principal products are molybdenum, coal, iron ore, copper, lead, zinc, petroleum and natural gas, potash, phosphates, nickel, tungsten, silver, gold, and magnesium.
>
> Standard Oil Company (Indiana) is in business to find and produce crude oil, natural gas and natural gas liquids; to manufacture high quality products useful to society from these raw materials; and to distribute and market those products and to provide dependable related services to the consuming public at reasonable prices.

3. *Geographic domain.* Did the mission statements specify the firm's intended geographic domain for marketing? Only 41% did.

Those who talked to us about the omission said it seemed unnecessary to state the "obvious" global nature of their marketing efforts. "This is undoubtedly an important issue to smaller firms" was the frequent comment of the *Fortune* 500 spokespersons.

Exemplary statements that included this component were the following by Corning Glass and Blockway:

> We are dedicated to the total success of Corning Glass Works as a worldwide competitor. (Corning Glass Works)
>
> Our emphasis is on North American markets, although global opportunities will be explored. (Blockway)

4. *Core technologies.* Did the mission statements describe the firm's core technologies? Overwhelmingly, they did not. By far the least frequently included component in the 61 mission statements we evaluated was the "core technology" component, which was specified by only 20% of the firms. The principal reasons company spokespersons gave to our follow-up questioning about the omission were (1) the impossibility of succinctly describing the many technologies on which their multiple products depended, and (2) the inappropriateness of trying to describe the core technologies of their service-based business units. Once again, this component was judged to be far more relevant to smaller, more narrowly focused businesses.

Two of the corporations providing noteworthy exceptions were Control Data and NASHUA, which clearly specified their core technologies:

> Control Data is in the business of applying micro-electronics and computer technology in two general areas: computer-related hardware; and computing-enhancing services, which include computation, information, education and finance. (Control Data)
>
> The common technology in these areas relates to discrete particle coatings. (NASHUA)

5. *Concern for survival, growth, and profitability.* Did the mission statements specify the firm's plans regarding survival, growth, and target levels of profitability? Overwhelmingly, they did. The most popular component in the mission statements was an organizational commitment to survival, profitability, and growth. Of the 61

firms, 55 (90%) included statements at least as explicit as the following excerpts from Hoover Universal and McGraw-Hill:

> In this respect, the company will conduct its operations prudently, and will provide the profits and growth which will assure Hoover's ultimate success. (Hoover Universal)
>
> To serve the worldwide need for knowledge at a fair profit by gathering, evaluating, producing, and distributing valuable information in a way that benefits our customers, employees, authors, investors, and our society. (McGraw-Hill)

6. *Company philosophy.* Did the mission statements disclose the firm's basic beliefs, values, aspirations, and philosophical priorities? Yes—more than three-fourths (79%) of the respondents did include clear indicators of the firm's strategic, operating, and human resources philosophies. Several did so by attaching elaborate statements of philosophy to more product/market-oriented statements.

The following brief excerpts from two statements provide a sense of how philosophies were embedded in the mission statements:

> We believe human development to be the worthiest of the goals of civilization and independence to be the superior condition for nurturing growth in the capabilities of people. (Sun Company)
>
> It's all part of the Mary Kay philosophy—a philosophy based on the golden rule. A spirit of sharing and caring where people give cheerfully of their time, knowledge, and experience. (Mary Kay Cosmetics)

7. *Company self-concept.* Did the mission statements express the company's view of itself? Did they provide an explanation of the firm's competitive strengths? The answer to these questions is "yes" for 77% of the respondents. As part of their corporate self concept, Hoover Universal and Crown Zellerbach stated the following:

> Hoover Universal is a diversified, multi-industry corporation with strong manufacturing capabilities, entrepreneurial policies, and individual business unit autonomy.
>
> Crown Zellerbach is committed to leapfrogging competition within 1,000 days by unleashing the constructive and creative abilities and energies of each of its employees.

8. *Desired public image.* Did the mission statements express the firm's desired public image? They clearly did in 87% of the cases, which makes this the second most included component in 61 formal statements. Among the ways in which desired public images were expressed were the following statements from Dow Chemical, Sun Company, and Pfizer:

> To share the world's obligation for the protection of the environment. (Dow Chemical)
>
> Also, we must be responsive to the broader concerns of the public including especially the general desire for improvement in the quality of life, equal opportunity for all, and the constructive use of natural resources. (Sun Company)
>
> . . . to contribute to the economic strength of society and function as a good corporate citizen on a local, state, and national basis in all countries in which we do business. (Pfizer)

Mission Statements and Financial Performance

In summary, the analysis of the 61 mission statements revealed some common characteristics. Specifically, the 90% and 87% values (55 and 53 of 61 firms, respectively) indicate that nearly all of the corporate statements included the "concern for survival" and "desired public image" components. In contrast, the 19% and 41% values (12 and 15 of 61 firms, respectively) suggest that sample corporate statements tended to omit discussions of "core technology" and "geographic domain." As shown in Exhibit 2, significantly more of the mission statements of the highest performing *Fortune* 500 firms exhibited three of the eight components than did the statements of the lowest performing firms. Further, mean scores of the highest performers were greater than those of the lowest performers for six of eight components. These findings were all supportive of the research hypothesis. Thus the inclusion of the desired mission statement components was positively associated with a firm's financial performance.

Of course, many variables affect organizational performance, so the present findings do not suggest that the inclusion of desired components in a firm's mission statement will directly improve organizational performance. Quite to the contrary, a firm may have a

A Comparison of Mission Statements of Fortune *500* Companies			
Component	High Performers' Mean Score[a]	Low Performers' Mean Score[a]	Statistical Difference Between Mean Score?[b]
Philosophy	.8947	.6000	Yes
Self-Concept	.8947	.5333	Yes
Public image	1.0000[c]	.7333	Yes
Customer/ market	.4737	.6000	No
Product/ service	.5789	.8667	No
Geographic domain	.4211	.3333	No
Technology	.1579	.0667	No
Concern for survival	.9474	.8667	No

[a]High performers were firms in top quartile of a profit margin distribution of all responding *Fortune* 500 companies. Low performers were the lower quartile firms.

[b]A "Yes" indicates a t-value significant at less than .05.

[c]A mean value of 1.00 indicates that all 61 mission statements included the evaluative criterion.

Exhibit 2. A Comparison of Mission Statements of
Fortune 500 Companies

comprehensive mission statement and still experience declining sales and profits for any number of reasons. Thus, it would be inappropriate, based on this study alone, to label the desired components as "essential" characteristics of mission statements. Rather, further research is needed to determine particular industries, conditions, and situations when specific components are most desirable.

However, the current findings are important for two major reasons. First, they lend empirical support to the notion that higher performing firms have comparatively more comprehensive mission statements. Specifically, for the organizations included in the study, higher performing firms more often exhibited the components suggested as important in the literature. Second, the findings suggest that corporate philosophy, self-concept, and public image are especially important components to include in an organizational mission statement.

Discussion

Developing a Mission Statement

An intended practical and immediate contribution of the present research was to provide some benchmarks against which future studies could gauge the nature and direction of mission statement development. Because such large sample baseline data are otherwise unpublished, the information gathered in this research effort may provide a useful standard of comparison for managers responsible for coordinating the development of mission statements.

This research disclosed that 40% of the 218 responding *Fortune* 500 companies did not have written mission statement. If mission statements are so important to the strategic development process, why is this so? The respondents may have provided an unsolicited answer, in that 10% of all corporate CEOs specifically requested guidance from the researchers in helping them develop effective mission statements. It may well be that a lack of knowledge about desirable components hampers or even prevents mission statement development.

This initial attempt at empirical research in the area of mission statement composition provides some encouraging evidence of the accuracy of previous conceptual writings and case studies. All eight of the components described as desirable in the normative literature were found to exist in the mission statements; in fact, they appeared with an average frequency of 66%. This finding is important because evaluators of mission statements—such as industry analysts, stockbrokers, and directors of investment funds—may express as much concern for components that are excluded as for those that are included. With the general and macro-nature of mission statements, perhaps it is at least as important for a firm to demonstrate concern for a particular content issue as it is to express a particular preference for outcomes.

It may in fact be that the findings of this study understate the importance of a carefully and comprehensively developed mission statement. It seems reasonable to theorize that organizations differ dramatically in such areas as profit motive, stakeholders, and geographic marketplaces would also differ in the components included in their mission statement. In fact, had the corporations responding to the study been more homogeneous, or had business units rather than corporations been contacted, the observed differences might have been greater both in number and in magnitude. For optimal effectiveness, mission statements may need to be as distinctive as the relatively unique competitive situations in which organizations conduct their strategic planning.

Questions Remain

Not only is additional research needed to assess the degree to which the findings of this initial empirical effort can be generalized, but several critical questions about mission statements merit special attention. Three of the more intriguing questions are the following:

1. *What is the nature of the link between mission statements and organizational performance?* An important likely finding is that comprehensive mission statement development sets the stage for comprehensive planning efforts. Since such efforts have been associated with improvements in organizational performance, mission statements may be found to act as outlines for top managers to use to direct and focus their own planning and that of their subordinates.

2. *In what ways should the composition and intent of useful corporate and business-unit mission statements differ?* Corporate missions must often reflect the diverse concerns of several distinct strategic business units, even though corporate and business unit missions may differ in their contributions to performance. Corporate missions may be best used to establish organizational values and strategic planning priorities, while business missions may be best when they suggest more specific directions that business strategies should incorporate.

3. *How closely associated are publicly pronounced mission statements and "in-house" strategic planning documents?* Our discussions with strategic planners revealed that public statements of corporate mission are designed to be of little value to other firms as a basis for competitive planning. Thus, they are unlikely to spell out specific plans for strategic action. It is perhaps more likely that public statements provide only competitively harmless overviews of competitively potent strategic intentions. In such cases, the mission's strategic substance, which serves as the framework for competitive action, may be communicated among key managers on a classified basis.

Conclusion

Practitioners and researchers alike believe there is value in mission development and in the written statements that result. Perhaps it is asking too much to prove that they guarantee direct financial consequences. However, it is not unreasonable to demand empirical evidence of the presumed integral role of mission statements in linking strategic planning with corporate performance. The research we have described puts the first piece of that evidence in place.

Endnotes

1. Among recent authors who have stressed the critical role of mission statements as the starting point in strategic management are W. A. Staples and K. U. Black in their article, "Defining Your Business Mission: A Strategic Perspective," *Journal of Business Strategies*, 1984, 1, 33-39; V. J. McGinnis in "The Mission Statement: A Key Step in Strategic Planning," *Business*, November-December 1981, 39-43; and D. S. Cochran, F. R. David, and C. K. Gibson in "A Framework for Developing an Effective Mission Statement," *Journal of Business Strategies*, 1985, 2, 4-17.

2. For the reader interested in a better understanding of the nature of the empirically evidenced positive relationships between strategic planning and firm performance, three articles should be of particular interest: (1) G. G. Dess and P. S. Davis's "Porter's (1980) Generic Strategies as Determinants of Strategic Group Membership and Organizational Performance," *Academy of Management Journal*, 1984, 3, 467-488; (2)

J. W. Fredrickson and T. R. Mitchell's "Strategic Decision Processes: Comprehensiveness and Performance in an Industry with an Unstable Environment," *Academy of Management Journal*, 1984, 2, 399-423; and (3) R. B. Robinson, Jr. and J. A. Pearce II's "The Impact of Formalized Strategic Planning on Financial Performance in Small Organizations," *Strategic Management Journal*, 1983, 3, 197-207.

3. Probably the most often referenced work on mission statements, the one on which strategic management texts heavily rely, and the one that provided much of the impetus for the present study, is an article by J. A. Pearce II, "The Company Mission as a Strategic Goal," *Sloan Management Review*, Spring 1982, 15-24.

Research Methodology

The Research Sample — A letter requesting a copy of the organization's mission statement was mailed to the chief executive officer of each of the *Fortune* 500 corporations. Responses were received from 218 of the 500 companies, producing a 44% response rate. Of the respondents, 61 companies supplied a mission statement that could be evaluated.

Content Analysis — To evaluate the 61 corporate mission statements, content analysis, a qualitative research technique for analyzing message contents, was used. Specifically, content analysis involves selecting a written message to be studied, developing categories for measurement, measuring frequency of appearance of the categories by using coding rules, applying an appropriate statistical test to the data collected, and then drawing conclusions. The mission statements were evaluated to determine whether they exhibited the eight components identified from the literature review. Three independent raters evaluated each of the 61 usable statements to determine the degree to which they contained the eight desired components. Prior to conducting their evaluations, the raters read and discussed mission statement articles; they also rated and discussed their ratings of several example mission statements.

When a rater determined that a mission statement contained a specific component, a value of "1" was assigned to the statement. When a particular mission statement did not "clearly" exhibit the component, a "0" was assigned. Inter-rater reliability coefficients revealed no significant differences ($p < .01$) among the three independent raters on their evaluations of the corporate statements' total scores.

Statistical Analyses—Pearson intercorrelations of the eight mission statement components disclosed that only one of the 28 computations ("concern for survival" with "public image") was statistically significant, and only one of the coefficients was above .2701. Thus, the evaluated mission statement components were considered distinct variables. In addition, the low intercorrelations lend some empirical support for the heretofore theoretical notion that mission statements may be examined in terms of their components.

Parametric t-test analyses were performed to test the hypothesis that mission statements of high performing companies would exhibit more of the components than those of low performing firms. The selected indicator of performance was the profit margin of each of the sample *Fortune* 500 companies. The distribution was first divided into quartiles; then mission statements of the top quartile firms were compared with those of lower quartile firms. The results are discussed in association with Exhibit 2.

7

Making Quality a Fundamental Part of Strategy

Abstract

Quality has replaced price as the key determinant of both market share and profit margins. Technological sophistication, shortened life cycles, and more rigorous competition, combined with increasing consumer awareness, are factors that have increased the importance of quality as a competitive advantage. Quality is cost effective, profitable, promotes corporate longevity, and builds an important company value system. The quality issue should be a fundamental part of management's responsibility in the organization and an integral part of strategy.

Two issues need to be addressed in American businesses: (1) management inattention and (2) the system of quality management in use, or misuse, in many firms. Management inattention is due in part to the overriding focus on production over quality; plant managers will tolerate substandard quality in order not to compromise output. The system of quality assurance and control in use by many firms contributes to poor quality. The dominant form of both incoming supplier control and outgoing manufacturing control is by inspection; but you cannot inspect quality into a product—it must be built in.

The key to defect-free production is a manufacturing process that is "in control." The worker, according to some estimates, is responsible for only 15 percent of defects; 85 percent are due to the system. A system that is not "in control" encourages defects. It is much better to improve the system for prevention of defects than to hire costly inspectors to find defects. People perform to the standards of their leaders. If people have a picture of quality that is clear enough for them to see where they fit in, then strategy can be formulated, implemented, and achieved.

The customer defines quality and usually gives it a high priority. The only starting point for defining the business purpose and mission, therefore, is the customer.

Making Quality a Fundamental Part of Strategy

Joel E. Ross
Y. Krishna Shetty

Few strategic challenges have caused as much concern among American chief executives as the recent movement to product and service quality, the other side of the productivity coin. This movement has been called both a quality and a managerial revolution. Whatever the label, it is clear that the focus on quality is far reaching and promises to become the competitive advantage of the 1980s and beyond. It may have a profound effect on the way we manage.

Concern with quality is not new but more and more firms are restructuring their competitive approach to make it a load bearing element in their strategy. More and more are attempting to change corporate culture both on the shop floor and in the executive suite. This revision of competitive strategy is partly the result of new evidence that quality has a direct impact on both market share and profit margins. Indeed, quality has replaced price as the key determinant of both. For example, a study of 2000 business units by the Strategic Planning Institute, of Cambridge, Massachusetts, shows

Reprinted by permission. "Making Quality a Fundamental Part of Strategy," by Joel E. Ross and Y. Krishna Shetty in *Long Range Planning*, February 1985, pp. 53-58.

that improving quality is an effective way to gain market share and that companies with high quality and high market share typically have profit margins five times greater than companies at the opposite extreme. And a recent study by McKinsey *et. al.* concluded that 'successful midsized companies compete on quality . . . they charge a higher price.' (1)

Nor is quality confined to manufacturers. It has become a potent marketing tool in service industries as well. 'Service is our most strategic marketing weapon', says Louis Gerstner Jr., chairman and CEO of American Express' Travel Related Services Company, 'It's the only way we can differentiate our product in the marketplace.' (2) Hospitals, schools, transportation systems, financial and retailing firms are among those to be affected.

Technological sophistication, shortened life cycles and more rigorous competition, combined with increasing consumer awareness, are among those factors that argue for a strategy that includes quality as a competitive advantage. As more and more firms adopt policies and programs in response to this movement there will be a ripple effect as suppliers to these firms and then suppliers to those suppliers join the quality movement out of necessity.

The Lesson from Japan

The story is told about the Frenchman, the Japanese and the American who were to be shot before a firing squad. Asked if they had any last requests, the Frenchman asked to be allowed to sing La Marseillaise and the Japanese requested that he be allowed to deliver a lecture on Japanese management. The American pleaded, 'please, let me be the first to be shot. I can't take another lecture on Japanese management!'

Many Western managers are tired of hearing about the Japanese system. Nevertheless, when it comes to quality management perhaps we should listen and learn. John Naisbitt is his popular book *Megatrends*, (3) traces the downfall of American competitiveness with Japan and attributes it to high-quality imports and the relative lack of emphasis on quality by U.S. firms and managers. A rethinking of our approach to product and service quality as a competitive edge may be in order, and although a number of causes of substandard quality have been identified,[1] it appears that two considerations related to strategy development and implementation need to be addressed in American businesses. These are management inattention and the system of quality management in use, or misuse, in many firms.

The basic differences between product quality management in the two countries, Japan and the U.S., for a 'typical' manufacturer is summarized in Table 1.

Management inattention is due in part to the overriding focus on production as quality takes a back seat. In order to meet schedules and stay within budgets, plant managers will tolerate substandard quality or high reject rates in order not to compromise output. This problem is tacitly approved by higher management and financial personnel who tend to focus on short term results. Harold S. Geneen, former CEO of ITT, summed it up this way: 'Operating managers know they cannot get into deep trouble for creating non-conformance products or services. They will be frowned at for these difficulties, but they can really be put down only for profit loss. Therfore, they concentrate on financial and schedule matters. Quality is third.' (4) (In a separate comment Geneen said, 'Quality is the most profitable product line we have'.) Professor W. Edwards Deming, a folk hero in Japan for his work on statistical quality control, writes that two of the major obstacles to quality and productivity are the detachment of top management and acceptance of defects as a way of life. (5)

The *system of* quality assurance and control in use by many firms contributes to poor quality. Surveys have shown that the dominant form of both incoming supplier control and outgoing manufacturing control is by inspection; incoming for raw materials and supplies and outgoing for finished goods. This approach is not conducive to defect prevention. It is an 'after the fact' discovery of defects. It is too late at that point in the process. You cannot inspect

---

[1]Other causes include (1) overlooking the customer, (2) acceptable quality level as a way of life, (3) quality control by final inspection, (4) inadequate defect prevention, (5) inadequate measures and standards, (6) true cost of quality not known, (7) not organized for quality assurance, and (8) involvement of people. See Joel Ross, The Quality Gap: Causes and Cures. *Industrial Management* (Forthcoming).

Table 1. Product quality management, Japan vs. U.S. ('average' manufacturer)

Item	Japan	U.S.
National policy*	Company wide activities QC audit Education in quality QC circles Statistical techniques	No national policy
Company policy	Quality during life cycle of the product *Marketing* Market research R & D Planning *Design* Design Trial production Evaluation *Production* Planning Purchasing Production Inspection *Usage* Shipping Usage Service	Various policies adopted by U.S. firms but in general it consists of an in many cases is limited to quality inspection of: (1) incoming materials, (2) work in process, and (3) final inspection

Table 1. (continued)

Item	Japan	U.S.
Standards	Zero defects Focus on quality	Acceptable level (AQL) Focus on production
Suppliers	Supplier is partner Automaker has 300–400 suppliers Supplier education Quality is No. 1 criteria for selection	Supplier may be partner Automaker has 2500 suppliers Incoming inspection Lowest cost is criteria for selection
Organization	Team approach (QC, design, engineering, manufacturing, service, marketing, etc.)	Adversarial relationship between QC an manufacturing. QC is policeman
Quality control	Process control for prevention of defects using process control charts. Do it right the first time	Final inspection to discover defects
Raw material and parts inventory	Kanban-Just in time	30–90 days supply

*This is national policy in the sense that it is promoted by the Japanese Union of Scientists and Engineers (JUSE), a quasi-official organization that is encouraged by the federal government. Thus JUSE oversees quality in the manufacturing industries.

quality into a product, it must be built in ! The solution, of course, is a process control system that *prevents* defects. You do not have to sample incoming material or outgoing product if both processes are stabilized and under control.[2]

There seems to be a tendency to blame many quality problems on workers. Yet the key to defect-free production is a manufacturing process that is 'in control'. To paraphrase Professor Deming again, 85 per cent of defects are due to the system and are 'normal' because of the inadequate system of defect prevention. The worker can only control the 15 per cent that are 'abnormal'.

A system that is not 'in control' encourages defects. The tendency of many operators is to pass it along on the assumed probability that the inspector may miss it or rework it, or the supervisor may send it through production to avoid being caught short at a later stage down the line. The operator and the supervisor are getting paid to produce defects. The system is at fault. Note also that station to station production outside of manufacturing and between departments is subject to the same effect. In both cases it is much better to improve the system for *prevention* of defects rather than hiring costly inspectors to find them.

Improving Product Quality

The good news is that a growing number of American companies are joining the quality revolution, some by choice and others by necessity. The latter group includes the automakers. Although they are enjoying dazzling profits in 1984, as opposed to a $4·2 bn loss in 1980, they still have not proved that a successful defence of home markets can be made. The problem is the high quality and the low price of Japanese imports.

In his book *Quality is Free*, (6) Philip Crosby suggests five measurement categories for determining your quality management maturity:

---

[2]For a brief but excellent primer on process control in manufacturing see Howard S. Gitlow and Paul T. Hertz, Product Defects and Productivity, *Harvard Business Review*, September–October (1983).

- management understanding and attitude;
- quality organization status;
- problem identification and prevention;
- control of costs of quality;
- quality improvement actions.

In our experience with managers from over 100 manufacturers, the average quality maturity score is 2½ on a scale of 1–5, something less than we had expected. For those firms scoring low on these criteria, they might want to take a lesson from those American firms with a reputation of doing an outstanding job now and in the past. In their highly successful book, *In Search of Excellence*, (7) Peters and Waterman say that the excellent companies are obsessed with quality and reliability and that these characteristics comprise an essential part of the *value system* and strategy of the organizations. Consider Caterpillar Tractor ('we guarantee 48 hour parts delivery anywhere in the world'), McDonalds ('quality, service, cleanliness and value: Q.S.C. & V.'), Maytag ('ten years trouble-free operation'), Holiday Inns ('no surprises'), Proctor & Gamble ('a reverence for quality') and so on with the excellently managed firms.

American firms can win the race but quality must receive top billing in corporate strategy.

The Cost of Poor Quality

If you are not convinced that quality deserves a prominent place in corporate strategy, consider the cost of poor quality, a cost that is rarely calculated in real terms. In 1 year faulty cheques cost U.S. banks about one-half of all cheque-processing costs. Firestone's radial tire recall cost $135m, more than net income for that year. But these are unusual examples. Nevertheless, it is estimated that the cost of quality (COQ) for the average U.S. firm is *10–20 per cent of sales*, (8) more than profit before tax in most cases. In the automobile industry it is as much as 25 per cent. (9) Despite this, many American managers continue to believe that high quality is not cost effective and that it reduces productivity.

Hewlett-Packard (who incidentally reports that quality of U.S. manufactured semiconductors is equal to Japanese products) describes the damage a 2¢ resistor can do: 'If you catch the resistor before it is used and throw it away, you lose 2¢. If you don't catch it until it has been soldered into a computer component it may cost $10 to repair the part. If you don't catch the component until it is in a computer user's hands the repair cost will amount to hundreds of dollars and may exceed the manufacturing costs.' (10)

Overlooking or underestimating the cost of quality (COQ) is widespread for two main reasons. First, the quality cost reporting systems are usually installed by QC personnel and the reports lack consistency, confidence, and accuracy. (11) Many are misleading. Second, most quality costs computations use 'after the fact' criteria such as scrap and repair costs, vendor rejections, and quality costs vs. product costs. Most managers would be shocked if they computed all costs associated with: (1) *prevention* (e.g. design review and preventative maintenance), (2) *appraisal* (e.g. receiving and inspection, inspection and quality labour), and (3) *failure* (e.g. redesign, warranty, rework, repair).

Strategy is Market Driven

We have no qualms about complaining to the people who make the items and provide the services we buy in our own personal life. Why should we expect our customers to treat us differently? Quality considerations have historically focused on the production process and motivation of the worker. Now, strategists are realizing that success is a function not only of a defect-free product but the consumers' perception of high quality and service.

The Strategic Planning Institute of Cambridge, Massachusetts, in a study of over 1000 major manufacturing businesses whose performances are contained in their PIMS data bank, concluded that 'quality, defined as customers' evaluation of the businesses product/service package as compared to that of competitors, has a favourable impact on all measures of financial performance.' In other words, businesses selling high quality products or services are generally more profitable than those with lower quality. Both return on investment and profit as a per cent of sales, increase as relative quality increases.

Given the correlation between quality and success as measured by financial performance, growth and market share, one would expect a greater definition and understanding of quality between company and customer. However, there is a gap between the perceptions of executives and their customers. A number of surveys have indicated how wide this gap is. (12) In our own research, based on a questionnaire of 336 front line supervisors and non-supervisory employees in over 300 manufacturing and service firms, respondents' perception of quality in their own company varied considerably. Indeed, of the 70 per cent who attempted a definition, few could provide a quantitative measure (see Table 2).

Part of the problem relates to differing definitions of quality and the difficulty of measuring the customers' perception of it. Although the measure and the perception is elusive, an effort can be made to identify the criteria by which the customer makes a choice. These criteria may include the classic ones of reliability, delivery, availability of spare parts or response time for service. Remember that the customer defines quality—you don't. And finally it is worth noting that it is not usually necessary to exceed competitive quality by a wide margin. However, maintaining this competitive edge margin requires quantitative measurements of all aspects of quality.

Determining how customers define quality is no easy task. Consumers' priorities and perceptions change over time and most of them have difficulty articulating a definition. Many use a yardstick that simply measures one product against another product as 'better than' or 'worse than'. If yours is perceived as 'worse than', you are in trouble. Promotional tactics (e.g. 'quality is job one') must ultimately be backed up with true quality as the buyer perceives it.

Monitoring available information, both internal and external, through a normal market research method is part of the answer for keeping a finger on the pulse of the market. Specific data, as well as more general information regarding societal trends and attitudes, should be included. Notice, for example, the trends during recent years toward 'quality, not quantity' and 'life-cycle buying'. These trends reflect an emphasis on such values as durability, reliability, craftsmanship and longevity. To illustrate, some people might prefer

Table 2. Employee perception of product/service quality. (336 respondents in over 300 companies)

Definition or perception	Respondents	
	Number	Percentage
Quality is the ability of a product or service to satisfy the needs of customers (needs not specified)	73	22
Quality means efficient, friendly, helpful and fast service to customers	33	10
Quality refers to the ability of a product or service to perform the functions for which it is designed	30	9
Quality is the ability of a product or service to conform to the design/engineering/ manufacturing/blueprint specifications	29	9
Quality is the ability of a product or service to perform its intended functions in a reliable, dependable and defect-free manner	23	7
Quality implies the substance or characteristics of a product or service that makes it best in the market	18	5
Quality of a product or service is what it gives its customers—their money's worth	15	4
Quality refers to the characteristics of a product or service that induces customer loyalty, goodwill, repeat purchase, and positive perception about the product and the company	13	4
Cannot define	102	30

*Front-line supervisors and non-supervisory employees.

a $10 light bulb, which uses one-third as much electricity and lasts four times as long, over the conventional bulb that costs $1.

Making Quality a Fundamental Part of Strategy

Peter Drucker reminds us that there is only one focus, one starting point for defining business *purpose and mission,* the prerequisite to strategy. That starting point is the customer. (13) The customer defines the business, you don't. All that the customers are interested in are their own values, and there is abundant evidence that customers, whether industrial or end users, give quality a high priority.

Product Scope includes both a definition of 'what we are selling' as well as supporting product policies. The definition of what you are selling should relate to some problem-solving utility for the customers and fulfilling whatever they perceive as value. Policy might state that each individual is expected to perform like the requirement or cause the requirement to be changed to what you and the customer really need.

IBM sells information for decision making, not computers. In their Entry Systems Division (PC) in Boca Raton, Florida, their policy is termed Excellence Plus Commitment and states that 'IBM Boca Raton will deliver defect-free, competitive products and services on time, to all customers. Quality will be the primary consideration in all decisions related to cost and delivery. Likewise, each department will provide defect-free work to the next user of its output or service.'

Key performance areas (major objectives) are an essential part of strategy and the point at which quality requirements can be established at the top for subsequent cascading throughout the organization. The requirements should, as a minimum, meet world class standards. Major Japanese manufacturers have set a standard of zero defects (ZD) and measure discrepancies in parts per million. Compare this with the majority of U.S. manufacturers who use the 'acceptable quality level' (AQL) system and suggest that zero defects as a standard represents overkill and is statistically impossible to attain. Impossible, yes, but it is the attitude that counts. ZD becomes a target to shoot for and if you do not shoot for 100 per cent you are tolerating mistakes. You will get what you asked for. Zero defects is the attitude of defect prevention. It means doing the job right the first time. And this attitude should pervade all departments. Quality problems arise not only in manufacturing but throughout the organization—market research, design, manufacturing, procurement, sales and service; indeed, throughout the life-cycle of the product.

Douglas Fraser, formerly head of the United Automobile Workers, has long contended that U.S. workers are the best in the world. 'They will deliver peerless quality, but only if management asks them.' (14)

There comes a time when someone has to implement strategy and actually get the job done. People conduct the business of every company, whether manufacturing or service. For the unfortunate firm with a history of poor quality in products or services, the sometimes insurmountable problem is competing head-on with the excellent company. Indeed, the real barrier to entry is the investment that the excellent company has made in gaining acceptance of quality and service as *the* organizational value system and getting employees to live service, quality and customer problem solving.

Quality should be an easy company value to sell because it is a matter of leading people to what they already know is right. People perform to standards of their leaders. If management thinks people do not care, they will not care. But if the machine operator, the bank teller, the flight attendant or the retail salesperson has a picture of quality that is clear enough for them to see where they fit in, then strategy can be formulated, implemented and achieved.

Everything we know about strategy and strategic planning argues for the adoption of quality as a major component of mission and competitive advantage. In some organizations it may be the most important component. It is cost effective, profitable and promotes corporate longevity. Additionally, such a strategy builds a company value system that is so important when considering the people dimension. President Clemenceau of France once observed that war was too important to be left to the generals. Perhaps quality is too important to be left to quality control personnel or planners. The development of strategy is a responsibility that is peculiar to the chief executive.

References

(1) Quality: The U.S. drives to catch up, *Business Week,* 1 November (1982). See also, McKinsey & Company, *The Winning Performance of Midsized Growth Companies* (1984).

(2) Making service a potent marketing tool. *Business Week.* 11 June (1984).

(3) John Naisbitt, *Megatrends.* Warner Books, New York (1982).

(4) H.S. Geneen, Fourteen steps to quality, *Quality Progress,* March/April (1972).

(5) W. Edwards Deming, *Quality Productivity and Competitive Position,* Massachusetts Institute of Technology, Center for Advanced Engineering Study (1982).

(6) Philip B. Crosby, *Quality is Free,* McGraw-Hill Book Company (1979).

(7) Thomas J. Peters and Robert H. Waterman, Jr., *In Search of Excellence,* Harper & Row (1982).

(8) Jack W. Schmidt and Jerry F. Jackson, Measuring the cost of product quality, *Proceedings of the February 1982 Meeting of the Society of Automotive Engineers.* February (1982). See also, Quality: The U.S. drives to catch up, *Business Week* 1 November (1982), also Philip B. Crosby, op. cit., also Harold P. Roth and Wayne J. Morse, Let's help and report quality costs, *Management Accounting* (1983).

(9) *Business Week.* op. cit.

(10) Jeremy Main, The battle for quality begins, *Fortune,* December (1980).

(11) Harold P. Roth and Wayne J. Morse, op. cit.

(12) Hirotaka Takeuchi and John A. Quelch, Quality is more than making a good product, *Harvard Business Review,* July-Aug. (1983).

(13) Peter Drucker, *Management Tasks, Practices, Responsibilities.* Harper & Row (1973).

(14) *Time,* 26 March (1984).

8

Competitive Advantage: The Cornerstone of Strategic Planning

Abstract

A competitive advantage is one that offers the opportunity for sustained profitability relative to competitors. The idea of competitive advantage emerged in the late Seventies to describe the success of the Japanese in penetrating world markets.

Increased uncertainty in the business environment and increased intensity of global competition are the two predominant forces with which management must deal with in future years. Competitive advantage offers the best general approach for achieving business success given these two factors. In pursuing competitive advantage, management should choose arenas where victories are clearly achievable. The competitive arena must be sheltered from change in the business environment and from global competition. The purpose is not to retreat from competition, but to compete selectively from an advantageous strategic position. Competitive advantage can be achieved through a number of different avenues, including: concentrating on particular market segments; offering products which differ from, rather than mirror, the competition; using alternative distribution channels and manufacturing processes; and employing selective pricing and fundamentally different cost structures. In each instance, the goal is to establish a clear and favorable differentiation from competitors.

It is desirable to instill throughout the organization a discipline for critically examining businesses to identify current or future opportunities to achieve advantaged positions. Two-day workshops involving all managers can be especially useful to train them to ask the key questions of strategic thinking: What business am I in? What makes the difference between success and failure in this business? Where do I and my competitors stand? Who has a competitive advantage? How should I use my advantage? What support will my strategy require? Is the investment of resources worth it in terms of expected returns? Who will implement the plan and how?

Competitive Advantage: The Cornerstone of Strategic Thinking

Stephen E. South

There are signs that a new management philosophy is emerging. As the 1980s began, a general approach for dealing with the central business challenges of the time already was being incorporated into management practice. From an historical perspective this is to be expected, since in previous decades new management philosophies have evolved to accommodate the fundamental forces which were then influencing business success.

During the coming decade there will be in all likelihood two predominant forces with which management must deal: uncertainty in the business environment and intensity of global competition. While other developments will also be important, these two are likely to shape the prevailing management philosophy of the decade. Under these circumstances it is becoming more and more evident that the idea of competitive advantage—the philosophy of choosing only those competitive arenas where victories are clearly achievable—offers the best general approach for achieving sustained business success. It does so by prescribing a concentrated

Reprinted by permission. "Competitive Advantage: The Cornerstone of Strategic Thinking," by Stephen E. South in *Journal of Business Strategy*, Spring 1981, pp. 15-25.

investment of resources in those enclaves of competitive activity which, because they are sheltered from the changing business environment and protected from intense global competition, offer the best opportunity for continuing profitability and sound investment returns.

This general approach to the management task is more selective than that of previous decades and is providing the underlying philosophy for the dominant management practice of the 1980s: strategic management. The process of strategic management is coming to be defined, in fact, as the management of competitive advantage—that is, as a process of identifying, developing, and taking advantage of enclaves in which a tangible and preservable business advantage can be achieved.

This article will first deal with the idea of competitive advantage, how it developed and where it fits in the evolution of management practice. Then we will deal with a key question: Is it achievable in real-life business situations? And, by example, we will demonstrate its value as an effective basis for building strategies and plans. Finally, we will discuss an approach used for instilling this philosophy in a large multinational organization, including group learning exercises used in strategic management workshops conducted around the world.

How the Notion of Competitive Advantage Emerged

The idea of competitive advantage emerged in the late 1970s, articulated by McKinsey and Company and based on the success of the Japanese in penetrating world markets under changing business circumstances. It is an interpretation of the approach which brought competitive success to a wide range of Japanese companies. These companies achieved high levels of operating efficiency based in part on cultural differences which are now widely discussed. But they were successful also in artfully selecting competitive arenas in which they could do battle from a position of strength. In short, they succeeded as strategists—winning strategic as well as operating victories.

In a sense the Japanese experience offered a preview of the 1980s, confronted as they were with the necessity of becoming worldwide competitors at a time when world markets were shocked by the uncertainties of oil shortages, recession, rapid escalation of oil and other prices, and floating exchange rates. The Japanese have already experienced and dealt with the forces which are recognized as the important management challenges of the 1980s. These forces clearly have a direct impact on day-to-day operations, and many tactics have evolved for dealing with the difficulties they create. But they are also impacting the fundamentals of what it takes to make a business successful, necessitating a rethinking of the basics of business success.

Rethinking Business Success

In rethinking the basics of superior performance relative to competitors, managers in Japan and elsewhere have come to distinguish between two fundamental elements of business success: operating effectiveness and competitive position. It is now widely recognized that effective management of operations is not the only key, and that competitive position in an industry is frequently the dominant factor in determining which businesses are most successful.

Competitive position, determined not only by market share but also by manufacturing process, distribution approach, product offering and the like, frequently overwhelms differences in operating effectiveness to determine which competitors are most successful. So while the combination of strong competitive position and effective operations almost always guarantees success, a strong competitive position makes relative success highly likely even if operating performance suffers in comparison with competition. On the other hand, a weak competitive position combined with poor operating effectiveness virtually assures failure relative to competitors. And the chances of offsetting a weak position with more effective operations are questionable at best.

Interestingly, evidence suggests that this has always been an important distinction. But, in a world of slower change and more isolated competitive arenas, competition tended to focus on operations, with competitive positions tending to be very similar except for differences in volume and market share.

Reciprocal vs. Strategic Competition

Because of this, only recently have we come to recognize that there are really two very different forms of competition. The first and most familiar, and still the most prevalent, is reciprocal competition. In this instance, which most frequently occurs in mature industries, companies compete from very similar strategic positions, relying on operating differences to separate the successful from the unsuccessful.

The new form of competition, effectively pursued by the Japanese, is strategic competition. In this approach the competitive struggle is pursued, first and foremost, on a strategic basis. The choice of market segments, product offering, distribution channels, and manufacturing process becomes the paramount consideration.

Competitive Advantage: The Key to Strategic Competition

The notion of competitive advantage suggests that the key to successful strategic competition is the selection of competitive arenas which meet two criteria: First, that they can be sheltered from change in the business environment and, second, that an advantaged position can be achieved as protection from intense global competition. The purpose is not to retreat from competition, but to compete selectively from an advantageous strategic position.

Competitive advantage can be achieved through a number of different avenues:

- By concentrating on particular market segments.
- By offering products which differ from, rather than mirror, the competition.
- By using alternative distribution channels and manufacturing processes.

- By employing selective pricing and fundamentally different cost structures.

In each instance, however, the goal is to establish a clear and favorable differentiation from competitors. This can be achieved in very direct ways, including patent protection or trade barriers, for example, and indirectly through competitor inaction or aggressive pursuit of advantage by a competitor more willing to take risks.

Regardless of the basis for competitive advantage, the central considerations are whether the advantage is tangible and measurable and whether it is preservable, at least for a period of time. In short, a competitive advantage is one which offers the opportunity for sustained profitability relative to competitors rather than a circumstance in which profits are competed away by firms with similar positions fighting for volume and market share.

Strategic Management

The idea of competitive advantage is a powerful one because it identifies what to look for in developing strategies and plans—namely, a fundamentally advantageous position from which to compete. The management approach which it prescribes is a continuing process of identifying, developing, and exploiting advantageous business positions. To accept anything less than a tangible and preservable advantage in the competitive arena, especially during the 1980s, is to virtually insure that sustained business success will be sacrificed to changed business conditions and aggressive global competitors.

Is Competitive Advantage Really Achievable?

With regard to this philosophy of management, or any other for that matter, the key question is not whether the approach appears to fit the needs of the times or is conceptually appealing, but whether it is a practical and useful tool for managing businesses. And in this instance, the specific question is whether it is practical to achieve advantaged competitive positions in real business situations.

From our experience in capital goods businesses at Clark Equipment Company, the answer is yes. The internal consulting group in our corporate planning department has dealt with business situations around the world using competitive advantage as the guiding philosophy for developing strategies and plans. And this experience has convinced us that, at least for many of our businesses, it is possible to achieve tangible and preservable business advantages which can be the basis for sustained profitability relative to competitors.

As suggested earlier, there are two primary considerations in identifying or developing competitive advantage in real-life business situations:

- To select or establish business arenas which are relatively sheltered from the vagaries of environmental change.
- To achieve a protected or advantageous competitive position within that arena.

Sheltered Business Arenas

The first of these considerations tends to be more subjective and subtle, more a matter of degree. However, there are examples of successfully achieving sheltered business situations which are relatively immune from economic, political, and technological change.

An Example: Going Local.—In a Latin American subsidiary, for example, a number of steps were taken over the years to shelter the operation from substantial changes in government policy. Early on it was recognized that the only avenue for successfully participating in that market on a continuing basis was to develop an operation indigenous to the country, one which was in concert with the basic aims and interests of the government and which could comfortably adapt to and contribute to changes in policy. This was accomplished through a series of steps, including shared ownership with local investors, local manufacture of virtually all products sold in the market, high local content to provide maximum employment and to develop local suppliers, and export programs to support government trade policies. In short, these steps were taken to establish an operation which was relatively immune from changes in economic policy directed at outsiders and, in that sense, one which was sheltered from some of the uncertainties of that market.

Other Opportunities: Technology and Finance.—There are, moreover, other opportunities for developing sheltered business enclaves, including technologically stable product and manufacturing situations which are not susceptible to abrupt technological change, financial structures which can help to neutralize the impact of currency changes, the development of a business mix which neutralizes the impact of economic cycles, and the establishment of a funding mix which minimizes the impact of interest rate cycles. In each case, the common denominator is a deliberate effort to establish a business arena which is not directly vulnerable to major changes in the environment.

Advantaged Competitive Positions.—As these examples suggest, the philosophy of blanket participation in all markets, products, and technologies related to a business can give way to selective participation in those arenas with enough stability to insure profitable return on investment. And this more selective approach carries over to the second consideration in arriving at competitive advantage. That consideration is whether, within a chosen business enclave, there is an opportunity to establish a clearly advantageous business position. This may be accomplished either through a fully protected situation where no competition exists, or one in which competition is present but is clearly at a disadvantage.

Patents and Trade Barriers.— The most obvious illustration of a fully protected business position is patent protection. Trade barriers are another avenue for achieving similar levels of protection. In some industries and countries, businesses still enjoy relatively complete protection from imports and few if any local competitors. This provides clearly protected situations with uncontested access to these markets and, importantly, a period of time in which to develop a strong competitive position. Other opportunities for fully protected situations range from high tariffs to single-source contracts.

Early Market Entry.—Time can often be as effective in protecting a business position as the presence of an artificial barrier. Early market entry is the most obvious example. There are still many opportunities in world markets for exclusive involvement for extended periods before competitors enter. In countless instances in the capital goods industry, companies have entered markets in which there was little or no competition for five or ten years, and more. These protected positions, achieved through individual company initiative and inaction by competitors, provide an extended period in which to achieve brand identification and customer loyalty, develop distribution networks, achieve manufacturing scale, and to enjoy considerable flexibility in pricing and product offering.

Product Leadership.—Product leadership—being the first to introduce a product in a certain class or size range—can also provide a protected position. In one of our North American markets, there was a clear pattern of new product introduction from year to year as competitors launched products with greater and greater capacity in two product classes. Three or four manufacturers led the way and, typically, there was a six-month-to-two-year lag from the time one manufacturer introduced a model until the others followed suit. During that period of time, for that capacity machine, the leader enjoyed a protected business position.

As attractive as protected positions are, they tend to break down over time regardless of whether they are based on government policy, competitor inaction, or other factors. However, they are important not only for the immediate profit opportunity they provide, but also for the opportunity to develop an advantageous position for the longer term. In the case of product leadership, for example, the temporary absence of competition provides the opportunity to gain market share and brand loyalty, which tends to continue over a long period of time. Across the board, the first entrant in a size class tended to maintain a significant share advantage over competition.

Innovative Product Features.—There are many other examples, however, of advantageous competitive positions which are not developed under protected circumstances, such as introduction of innovative product features. In one such case relatively competitive machines were available from a number of manufacturers, but the first to introduce a new feature enjoyed an advantageous position for more than two years, with an opportunity for profitability and market share until the others followed suit and neutralized the advantage.

Pricing.—Pricing can often be the vehicle for maximizing competitive advantage. In one interesting example,[1] a company holding a small share of industry volume recognized that in certain applications the fuel consumption of its product was materially lower than competitors, providing a measurable advantage in operating cost. From this basic advantage, the company was able to establish a price premium for its product which materially improved profitability. Yet, by focusing on these applications and limiting the price advantage to less than the product's true value to the customer, the company was also able to gain market share.

Cost Structure.—Price advantage can also frequently be the vehicle for reaping the rewards of an advantageous cost position. The advantage may be based on scale or experience and volume. Advantages are also obtainable through parts commonality and concentration of product lines into fewer models and, of course, through vertical integration. Making fundamental shifts in manufacturing process—for example, shifting from bay-build to moving line—can also achieve significant cost advantage.

Financial Structure.—Finally, in addition to product, market, price, and cost-based advantages there are other opportunities which involve parts and service support, financial merchandising, and even the financial structure of the company. The impact of an aggressive financial structure—a highly leveraged balance sheet—on competitive cost position is sometimes overlooked. The willingness to

----

[1]William E. Johnson, "Trade-Offs in Pricing Strategy," *Pricing Practices and Strategy* (The Conference Board, 1977).

take financial risk through greater leverage can mean that margins and prices can be reduced without sacrificing shareholder profitability relative to competitors. And the price advantage this provides can be the basis for gains in market share.

These are just a few examples which illustrate the range of possibilities for achieving competitive advantage. In some cases, they represent actions which might have been pursued for other reasons, but the important point is to take full advantage of such situations.

Instilling the Idea Throughout an Organization

Our experience in applying the idea of competitive advantage in some of our divisions suggested to us the value of instilling throughout the organization a discipline for critically examining businesses to identify current or future opportunities to achieve advantaged positions.

The vehicle we used to instill this philosophy on a worldwide basis was a series of two-day workshops in strategic management. These sessions involved all general managers, managers of marketing, manufacturing and engineering, controllers and planners. The purpose of these workshops was to:

- Develop a common strategic thought process—a shared way of thinking among the management group of each division which focused on strategic competition and what to do about it.

- Establish an understanding of competitive advantage as the centerpiece of strategic thinking and as the underlying philosophy of strategic management.

- Communicate realistic examples of competitive advantage taken from our businesses.

- Discuss techniques of business analysis which could help in identifying competitive advantage.

Thinking Strategically: The Key Questions

The method we used for developing among participants a common strategic thought process based on competitive advantage was a simple framework—or outline—consisting of a series of questions to be answered for individual businesses. This approach was prompted by similar frameworks used in developing military strategy. In fact, strategic thinking is a thought process probably first developed centuries ago by military organizations. And these organizations have found it useful to develop aids to strategic thinking which help them focus on the right issues, suggest a sequence for the thought process, and provide a common frame of reference for discussing and reviewing strategy. The questions which make up our framework serve as aids in developing business strategy, with one question building on another, leading to conclusions regarding the strategies and plans most appropriate for the business.

What Business Am I in?—The approach begins with the question: What business am I in? At least at the outset, the definition can be straightforward. The key elements will be products offered, geographic or other boundaries of the market, and a listing of major competitors. These elements will generally define the current scope of the business, although in some instances it may be necessary to elaborate on technologies involved or other factors. However, there can be more to this question than you might think.

First, some concern usually arises over how narrowly or broadly to define businesses. This is a matter of judgment, but the basic principle is to isolate a unique competitive situation which can be dealt with on a relatively uniform basis.

A second important consideration is whether to define the business as it presently stands or as it can be in the future. For example, a railroad might consider itself to be in the business of providing rail service utilizing a given route structure or, alternatively, as a transportation company employing rail and other modes to transport goods within a geographic area.

The choice of business definition, more than any other element of strategy, depends on the personality, leadership qualities, and vision of the individual general manager. In those instances in which

168   II. Clarifying the Mission

he is pursuing a new and different direction, his definition of the business can itself be the central element of a business strategy.

Regardless of how a business is defined at the outset, however, it is likely to be redefined as actual strategies are considered. Often the definition will be broadened to encompass the full range of available opportunities, which may not have been recognized initially.

What Spells the Difference Between Success and Failure?—Once the scope of the business is clear, the next question is: What makes the difference between success and failure in this business? Answering this question involves sorting through all the complexities of the business, and boiling them down to a limited number of factors which will make one competitor more or less successful than the others.

Two approaches can help in arriving at sound answers. In the "top-down" or "macro" approach, one begins by considering those factors which are generally important to the profitability of any business—market share, investment intensity, and the like. Then a broad-gauge comparison of the industry with others helps to narrow the list. Finally, from that broad perspective it is possible to formulate a short list of factors which are keys to success for the specific business in question, based primarily on judgment and industry experience.

The second method, a "bottom-up" or "micro" approach, involves looking more intensively and perhaps more analytically at the particular industry segment in which the business competes. One technique is to compare the way competitors do business and to separate the successful from the unsuccessful, identifying what the first group does or does not do compared to the second. A complementary approach is to focus on the ultimate customer, rethinking his needs and the role the product plays in the economics of his business or in his value system. This is important because prevailing industry practices may, in fact, be missing the mark entirely.

The important thing to keep in mind is that success is relative. A winning strategy is one which places a business among the most successful in its industry segment. Those factors which make the difference between the more and less successful must, therefore, become the focal point for the strategic thought process.

Where Do Competitors Stand?—Identifying these key success factors sets the stage for the next question: Where do I and my competitors stand? For those key factors which really make the difference, what is the true market and competitive situation? The purpose in answering this question is to develop an objective evaluation of the situation.

From the strategic perspective there are two important elements of a business situation: competitive circumstances and the market environment. Two questions need to be asked:

- Relative to competitors, what are my strengths and weaknesses?
- In the marketplace, what are the primary opportunities and threats?

Some factors to consider in answering these questions are product offering, distribution networks, manufacturing processes, technological changes, and political developments.

The analysis of strengths/weaknesses and opportunities/threats is now a relatively conventional approach to situation analysis. In thinking through a basic strategy for the business, however, it is useful to limit this evaluation to those key factors which make the difference between success and failure. For example, if distribution coverage is the key to success, the evaluation of competitors and market changes should focus on implications for the distribution network.

Who Has Competitive Advantage?—From this objective self-analysis some conclusions can be reached to the question: Do I or my competitors have any unique competitive advantages?

The real problem in identifying competitive advantage is to distinguish it from the vague notion that "we are better than they are." Identifying current competitive advantage can begin from the analysis of strengths and weaknesses relative to competitors. But a strength will represent an advantage and a weakness a disadvantage only if it:

- Involves a key success factor.
- Is definable, measurable, and significant.
- Is preservable.

The question of competitive advantage has a second aspect which extends beyond the current situation. That involves identifying potential advantages that can be developed for the future. Assessing future moves, based on opportunities and threats in the market environment, provides a list of possibilities to consider in arriving at a strategy for the future of the business.

How Should I Use My Advantage?—Once competitive advantage has been identified, the question is then: How do I most effectively employ the advantages I have, counter those of my competitors, and develop or acquire greater advantage? Managing a business strategically means continually asking and answering this question in an effective way.

This question not only defines business strategy in a specific way—as the management of competitive advantage—but also identifies the elements necessary for a comprehensive strategy. These include not only a rationale for making the most of current circumstances but also for minimizing competitive inroads and, importantly, for building a position of advantage for the future. Without each of these elements a strategy is incomplete.

Answering the strategy question provides the important ingredient frequently missing from conventional planning approaches: namely, a clear and explicit rationale for achieving competitive success, based on a clearly defined scope for the business, an understanding of those factors which make for success in the industry, an objective assessment of the market and competitive situation, and a clear understanding of competitive advantage.

What Support Will This Strategy Require?—With this rationale in mind the planning question can be asked from a strategic viewpoint: What will this strategy require in terms of product development, marketing, and manufacturing?

This approach differs from the conventional approach to planning because it provides a clear purpose for developing plans. That purpose is to devise a practical way of achieving competitive advantage; that is, a concrete group of actions which will implement the rationale for competitive success. It may involve product specifications which meet needs served ineffectively by competitor products, marketing priorities which focus on market segments in which competitor presence is missing or ineffective, a change to a different manufacturing process, unused by competitors, which provides unique cost or quality advantages, a pricing policy which exploits a competitor price umbrella, or a parts and service policy which reflects an advantage in field population. In short, this approach helps to shift the planning effort away from the conscious or unconscious mimicking of competitors.

Is It Worth It?—The next important consideration is the financial question: Is the investment of resources—financial and otherwise— worth it in terms of expected returns and, for the company as a whole, is it affordable? The important point here is that the total investment in a strategy, not simply the capital equipment portion, be subjected to thoughtful analysis as an integral part of the strategic thought process.

A full financial analysis may, however, interrupt the strategic dialogue. But a simple balancing of costs involved and benefits expected, even without being reduced to the common denominator of discounted investment returns, can generally separate the practical from the impractical. The important consideration is to identify all of the major impacts of a strategy. For example, aggressive pricing in a particular market segment must be reflected in lower gross margins. Once the strategic impacts are identified, costs can be weighed against benefits judgmentally, with detailed analysis to follow when appropriate.

Who Will Implement the Plan and How?—The final question, and an important element of strategy is: Who will implement the plan and how? What are the principal goals and objectives individuals must achieve to successfully implement the strategy? Can they survive the test of competing priorities? This is a crucial question because many strategies and plans fail for lack of effective implementation.

This final question completes the basic elements of thinking through a comprehensive strategy for a business. Taken together, they suggest a sequence for developing, reviewing, and discussing business strategy.

A Practical Exercise in Strategic Thinking

As an aid to strategic thinking the questions just outlined are simple and straightforward. As a practical matter, however, considerable effort is required to instill this discipline throughout an organization. And the best way to introduce this approach, in our experience, is for individual managers to apply this framework directly to their own businesses in a workshop setting. As a vehicle for doing so we have devised an exercise (Exhibit 1) which serves as a convenient way of recording thoughts and conclusions regarding each of these questions. During the workshops, a moderator elaborates briefly on each question and discusses examples. Individual participants then answer each question as it pertains to their own business, developing a strategy rationale for the business as they proceed.

However, in all but the most autocratic organizations, strategy planning is a collective, not an individual, undertaking. It is a collective process of thinking and communicating which involves not only the general manager, but also managers of major business functions such as engineering, manufacturing, and marketing.

Combining Individual and Group Exercises

For this reason, the exercise has been used not only as an individual learning experience but also as a group learning process—again, using a real business situation. The approach is for individual members of a division's management group to first complete the exercise independently. Then a group discussion session is convened. The exercise begins again, starting with the question of business definition. In time, each question is discussed and, where possible, a consensus or common view is developed. This group exercise helps develop a common framework for discussing and arriving at business strategy based on competitive advantage. And it can help to identify issues to be resolved and conflicting perceptions of the business which could hamper implementation of the general manager's strategy.

Of course, no simple framework can do justice to the complex thought process involved in developing a business—or military—

BUSINESS DEFINITION
What Business Am I in?

KEY SUCCESS FACTORS
What makes the difference be-
tween success and failure in this
business?

SITUATION ANALYSIS
For most factors which make a
difference, where do I stand?

COMPETITION Strengths/Weaknesses	Market Opportunities/Threats

EXHIBIT 1. Strategic Thinking Exercise

COMPETITIVE ADVANTAGE
Do I or my competitors have any
unique competitive advantages?

Present Advantage/Disadvantage	Potential Advantage/Disadvantage

STRATEGY
How can I most effectively employ the advantages I have/counter those of my competitors—either present or potential—and develop or acquire future competitive advantage?

Exploit Current Advantage, Minimize Disadvantage	Develop Future Advantage, Counter Potential Disadvantage
Summary Statement	

EXHIBIT 1 (continued). Strategic Thinking Exercise

FORECASTS
Is it worth it and can I afford it?

Benefits Volume, Financial Returns, Cost Reduction, Etc.	Costs Product Development, Ex- penses, Capital Investment, Etc.

Summary, Benefits vs. Costs

GOALS AND OBJECTIVES
What must be done to implement the strategy and plans?

Marketing	Engineering	Manufacturing

EXHIBIT 1 (continued). Strategic Thinking Exercise

PLANS
What will this strategy require in terms of
Marketing, Product Development, Manufacturing, and Parts Credit?

Marketing Pricing, Distribution, Marketing Focus, Etc.	Product Development Product Offering, Timing, Etc.

Manufacturing Location Source, Manufactur- ing Process, Etc.	Parts Credit Availability, Pricing Rates and Terms, Etc.

EXHIBIT 1 (continued). Strategic Thinking Exercise

strategy. But it can help to focus and channel the process in a constructive way and provide a common language for the planning dialogue.

A common framework for thinking about and communicating strategies is perhaps the central discipline which contemporary planning practice is bringing to business organizations. An approach such as the one just outlined, however, can also provide a useful framework for developing another important planning discipline: the creation of strategies and plans which are soundly based on data, facts, and analysis. And that is the final purpose of the strategic management workshops.

Strategic Management Workshops

The two-day workshops begin with an explanation of the company's planning process. Most of the first morning is devoted to the exercise in strategic thinking, first for individuals and then for teams of managers. For the remaining day and a half each of the strategic questions is again discussed. These discussions focus on real-life examples from businesses other than those represented at the workshop, and on techniques of business analysis which can most appropriately be used to arrive at sound answers to these questions. For example, techniques of market analysis ranging from survey research to econometric forecasting are discussed as vehicles for arriving at a sound assessment of the market environment.

A Strategic Management Culture

These workshops, then, are a basic vehicle for developing a common strategic perspective among operating managers—a perspective based on competitive advantage as the underlying philosophy of strategic management. The development of such a perspective can contribute greatly to an organization's ability to think strategically about its businesses. And, it can provide a common base of understanding which is central to effective communication on issues of business strategy and, ultimately, to the development of a strong and effective management process. As organizations grow larger, more complex, and more distant from the competitive realities of the marketplace, this understanding—communicated widely through an organization—can help create a management culture focused on achieving competitive success in the turbulent business environment of the 1980s.

References

Banks, Robert L., and Wheelwright, Steven G., "Operations vs. Strategy: Trading Tomorrow for Today," *Harvard Business Review,* May-June 1979.

"Effective Strategies for Competitive Success," *The McKinsey Quarterly,* Winter 1978.

Hayes, Robert H., and Wheelwright, Steven G., "The Dynamics of Process-Product Life Cycles," *Harvard Business Review,* March-April 1979.

Johnson, William E., "Trade-Offs in Pricing Strategy," *Pricing Practices and Strategy* (The Conference Board, 1977).

Strategic Leadership: The Challenge to Chairmen (McKinsey & Co., 1979).

III.
Creating a
Strategy

Introduction

The heart of the strategic planning process involves making specific plans for how the overall mission of the organization will be attained through identifying what is needed to be successful in the business(es) the organization is in, how that success will be measured, and what activities will specifically be done to achieve that success.

"Identifying Strategic Issues," the first article in this section, contends that firms that incorporate pertinent environmental information into their strategic planning have the brightest prospects of long-term survival. The second article, "Achieving Excellence in Strategic Planning Systems," attempts to show how high-performing companies have used the strategic planning process to achieve or sustain a competitive edge. The author analyzed the process in fifty organizations and presents his conclusions in seven major points.

Strategic Business Modeling

An important stage of the strategic planning process is known as strategic business modeling. This modeling involves two parts: (1) the strategic profile, or quantified business objectives, in which the strategic planning team identifies the businesses the organization should be in within the next three to five years, including specific quantitative indicators of success, such as profitability, market penetration, and liquidity; and (2) statements as to how the quantified business objectives will be achieved in each specific business segment.

When stating how the quantified business objectives will be obtained, many firms focus on analyzing critical success factors (CSFs), characteristics, conditions, or variables that can have a significant impact on the success of a firm. CSFs are discussed at length in "Identifying and Using Critical Success Factors," the next article in this section. The authors stress that CSFs can be instrumental in several stages of the strategic planning process, including the performance audit, environmental scanning, and evaluation of strategic choices.

Many operations managers overstress the quantified portion of the business plan, resulting in an exaggerated emphasis on short-term financial gains made at the expense of longer-term strategic goals. In "Operations vs. Strategy: Trading Tomorrow for Today," this trade-off dilemma is discussed. The authors outline the problems that arise from such trade-offs and recommend specific techniques to keep long-range objectives viable, including: setting more realistic goals, increasing the emphasis on long-term goals in the measurement of managerial performance, increasing the awareness of long-term goals with lower-level managers, stressing the importance of planning and review, and changing managers when long-term strategies are changed.

Strategic business modeling also involves envisioning the future organization and determining what potential new services and products will be offered and in which markets. Also included in this scenario is an estimate of what degree of risk will be allowed in which areas of the business, how competitors and customers will be approached, and any other fundamental changes in the way the company conducts its business operations as reflected in the earlier values analysis and the formulation of the mission statement of the firm.

Note that this modeling process is done prior to a specific examination of the current performance and existing markets in which the business is involved, so as not to overlook new possible markets that are congruent with and build on the identified values, agreed-on mission of the organization, and expertise and resources of the firm.

The Performance Audit

The performance audit is an examination of the recent and current performance of the organization in the business areas identified in the strategic profile. It serves as a starting point in determining in which areas there are "gaps" between what is realistic, feasible, and attainable and what initially seems to be overly optimistic in strategic modeling. This step requires adequate time for the collection of necessary data, analysis of those data, and adjustment of strategic objectives. It also requires a large amount of honesty and openness about what is feasible and what is realistic for the organization.

The performance audit makes use of any and all available data on both internal and external factors, such as the firm's products, markets, competition, employee work force, facilities, and inventory. This information is necessary to determine as well as possible the feasibility and capability of the organization to successfully implement its strategic plan and mission. A thorough and effective performance audit takes considerable time in the collection of necessary data, analysis of those data, and adjustment of strategic objectives.

An important and often overlooked part of the performance audit is a thorough competitive analysis. This process starts with an examination of current competitors (those that are in the same business or marketing to the same customers or market segment) but then should go much further to include, for example, an analysis of products or services that are marketed for similar reasons (or, what will not be purchased if a customer buys a particular product). "Down-boarding," or evaluating competitors' possible responses to the organization's actions in the market, is an integral part of competitive analysis. In addition, the risk of future competitors in the market (new firms, expansions of large corporations, or new international competitors) should be considered.

Gap Analysis

Gap analysis is the process of adjusting the planning objectives to fit the reality as described in the performance audit. This process can take several iterations as the planning team tests the newly revised objectives against the information base and determines the feasibility of achieving the desired objectives. The process is repeated until the "gaps" are closed and the objectives are clearly attainable, given the resources and projected time estimates. Gaps also need to be closed in regard to objectives that are inconsistent with the underlying values and mission statement that the planning team developed.

Contingency Planning

A strategic plan is not completed unless it contains plans for threats and opportunities that might occur during the course of the plan. Potential events that have either a negative or a positive potential impact on the organization are identified. Plausible scenarios that might develop from those events are analyzed from the perspective of how the company would be affected. Contingency activities are evaluated in light of such changes. The probability of such an occurrence is estimated and key indicators are identified that can be monitored to allow for the greatest degree of advance warning possible. Well-done contingency planning can keep management from panicking if the business environment in which the firm operates becomes unstable. Note that such plans are for unlikely events; if an event that will significantly impact the business is highly probable, it should be prepared for within the context of the plan.

9

Identifying
Strategic Issues

Abstract

Research suggests that the nature and rate of environmental change directly influence the results of an organization's strategic-planning effort. Therefore, firms that incorporate pertinent environmental information into their planning have the brightest prospects of long-term survival.

The literature on scanning for such environmental information suggests that scanning must be an integral part of both planning and decision making to be successful. In practice, most scanning systems are not well integrated with planning, nor is the application of scanning activities well defined. As a result, current scanning seldom produces viable alternatives to existing strategy.

A strategic issue scanning system (SIS) offers a five-step approach for correcting many of the weaknesses of current environmental scanning:

1. **Preparation.** This step involves selecting people who will be responsible for scanning and orienting them to the scanning process. These individuals must be made familiar with the organization's current performance and its immediate operating environment.

2. **Mission and Key Success Factors.** The mission statement and the key success factors are used as the focus of the scanning process.

3. **Stategic Issue Identification.** Environmental threats and opportunitites are identified, rated as to their probable impact, examined with regard to the likelihood of their occurrence, and culled according to their perceived importance.

4. **Cross-Impact Analysis.** In this procedure the impact of one possible environmental event on another is considered in depth. This procedure validates assumptions made previously and clarifies the relationship of the organization with its environment.

5. **Strategic Option Identification.** This final step is taken to integrate the results of scanning into the organization's planning and decision-making processes. Strategies are developed to address the scanning issues with the highest perceived and most probable impact on organizational performance.

Identifying Strategic Issues

J. J. Murphy

Introduction

In 1976 Louis Gerstner[1] wrote: "One of the most intriguing management phenomena of the late 1960s has been the rapid spread of the
corporate or strategic planning (SP) concept."

Few management techniques have swept through corporate and
governmental enterprise more rapidly or completely. Yet in recent
years, doubts about the value of SP which had once only been whis-
pered have become more vocal and persistent. Walter Kiechel[2] puts
the question: "Doesn't the fact that hardly anyone can carry it out say
something about the value of strategy?"

Paul *et al.*[3] quoting some examples (General Foods, Rohr
Industries, Mattel, Outboard Marine, etc.), come to the conclusion
that "as one examines the growing list of companies that have
become entangled in financial misfortunes because of decisions
apparently made in accordance with the principles of strategic
planning, it seems that strategic planning may not always produce
expected results." There are many probable and/or possible reasons
for this, with no easy answers to a problem of this magnitude and
complexity. A statement that can, however, be made without fear of
contradiction is that the rate and nature of environmental change
has accelerated.[4,5] That environmental change has a direct linkage
to the strategic planning process has also been established.[6] Perhaps

Reprinted by permission. "Identifying Strategic Issues," by J. J.
Murphy in *Long Range Planning*, vol. 22, no. 2, pp. 101-105, 1989.

SP has failed in some cases, not because of inherent weaknesses but because of inadequate scanning of environmental changes.

In such conditions of change there is a growing sense of urgency to develop more effective ways of providing environmental intelligence to strategic decision-makers.[7] If current research on organizations is correct, firms that can successfully introduce pertinent information about their changing environments into strategic decision-making processes have the brightest prospects of long term survival.[7]

Against this background a research project was launched in 1983 to develop a methodology for use in environmental scanning. The backdrop to this research in South Africa is a First and Third World economy functioning side by side in one country, a sophisticated top management but generally weak middle management, and a rapidly changing socio/political structure.

This paper addresses the following aspects: (1) a literature survey referring to the essential characteristics of scanning, the rules of scanning, the time horizon of scanning and scanning in practice; and (2) the development of a strategic issues scanning system, highlighting some of the problems encountered.

Literature Survey

Essential Characteristics of Environmental Scanning

It is necessary to identify the essential characteristics of environmental scanning. In the first place, it should be integrative. It is vitally important that the environmental scanning system should form an integral part of the planning and decision making system of the corporation. Wilson et al.[8] state that interpretation of the present and speculation on the future make no real contribution to corporate success if they result merely in interesting studies. The relevance which environmental scanning should have to strategic planning can perhaps be best defined as (a) a focus on strategic issues and (b) assistance in making today's strategic decisions with greater environmental sensitivity and with a better sense of precognition. Finally, scanning should also have a holistic approach—so as not to miss any signals the corporate radar must do a 360° scan.

The Rules of Scanning

Aguilar[9] states: "The rules of scanning must be framed with reference to the economics of this activity, and costs must be weighed against benefits. Thus, we can argue that the primordial rule of scanning—to which all other rules relate—is the rule of efficiency." This basic rule is subdivided into a number of more specific or "operating" rules. These include the scope or magnitude, urgency or timeliness of the issue, the extent to which it constitutes a problem, the types and levels of scanning skills available in the organization and the interests and values of the people who do the scanning.

The Role of Top Management in Environmental Scanning

The fundamental purpose of environmental scanning is to "provide information about events and relationships in a company's outside environment, the knowledge of which would assist top management in its task of charting the company's future course of action." This theme is continued by Nanus,[10] who states that to manage the firm's interaction with its many outside environments " . . . it is first essential to understand how those environments are changing in ways that will have major impacts on the organization."

In most cases the management team's collective view of the environment is fairly accurate, since each manager is in touch with a variety of constituencies and brings years of experience to bear upon the significance of external events to the corporation. Mintzberg[11] makes the statement that "the manager who needs certain environmental information establishes channels that will automatically keep him informed."

There are numerous studies which center on the information gathering activities of senior level executives.[9,12] As of late these activities are referred to as boundary spanning activities.

Time Horizon

It is important to decide as soon as possible on the question of the time horizon to be used in the environmental scanning process. Research seems to indicate a bi-modal distribution in terms of the long range planning time horizon, viz 3 to 5 years. Naylor[13] comes to the conclusion that forecasting can, at best, really be credible only over the short range—about 5 years into the future.

In our experience, if we limit the time horizon to 5 years, managers tend to get hung up on present trends and also to identify only threats. Very few opportunities are identified. As a rule of thumb we now establish a time horizon twice that of the strategic plan.

Scanning in Practice

Ten years after Aguilar published his work, Fahey and King[14] published the results of a study of 12 firms undertaken to identify environmental scanning processes and activities and assess the relationship of the activities to corporate planning. The results showed that the firms had "not devoted extensive attention to specifying those areas of the environment that are of the greatest importance to them and, despite the fact that two of the 12 firms have established formal scanning units, none of them have succeeded in effectively integrating environmental scanning into their strategic planning process."

Their findings were largely confirmed in a longitudinal extension of their study by Charles Stubbard.[15] He also lists five other important findings:

- Low marks for futurism
- Instability of scanning units
- Incompatibility of scanning units with existing organizational arrangements
- Inability of scanning units to define required information
- Legitimacy of scanning function questioned by many managers.

In his study of 26 companies, Bhatty[16] found that all their corporate planning systems inadequately addressed the strategic problem of adapting the organization to its environment and failed to consider alternative futures. An analysis of corporate planning processes of 31 companies by Nick Binedell[17] revealed that 28 of them undertook environmental scanning on an irregular basis and were dependent on published and "informally" collected information. Only two of the respondents published their analyses and presented them as a starting point for the planning cycle.

It is reasonable to conclude that, in comparison with internal analysis (strengths and weaknesses), external analysis (issue scanning) has lagged behind in the development of analytical techniques and models, not only in the development of techniques and models but also in its integration into the strategic planning process.

In summary, scanning in practice lacked integration with decision making processes, used inadequate scanning units and methods, and did not create viable alternatives.

The Strategic Issue Scanning System

In view of the above shortcomings of strategic scanning systems, a research effort was launched to overcome these obvious impediments. The Strategic Issue Scanning (SIS) technique developed during our research combines many well known and established techniques such as:

(a) QUEST—Quick Environmental Scanning Technique developed by Burt Nanus[10]

(b) Delphi, O. Helmer[18]

(c) X-Impact [cross-impact] Analysis—Modified version of Gordon and Hayward model[19]

(d) Likelihood of Events Modified Assessment Process (LEAP) —John F. Prebble[20]

SIS, like QUEST, is a futures research process designed to permit executives and planners in an organization to share their views on trends and issues in future external environments that have strategic implications for the organization. It is a systematic, intensive and relatively inexpensive way to develop a shared understanding of high priority issues and focus management's attention rapidly on strategic areas.

SIS basically consists of the following phases:

(a) Preparation

(b) Mission and Key Success Factor Analysis

(c) Key Issue Identification

(d) X-Impact Analysis

(e) Strategic Option Identification

Preparation

This phase consists of selecting the managers to participate in the exercise and supplying them with information regarding the actual performance of and trends in the organization. An intelligence report is compiled, containing obvious trends and events in both the company and the industry. This information is drawn from readily available trade association, governmental, financial analysis and other standard sources.

It is interesting to note that in QUEST, Nanus[10] advocates that 12 to 15 executives participate in the exercise. In our experience, executives resist this limitation on numbers, stating that participation in such exercises is beneficial to management development and the commitment to finally developed strategies. However, as we make extensive use of the nominal group and Delphi techniques, large numbers of participants create problems in the voting procedures, affect group affiliation and promote clique formation. The facilitator has to circumvent these problems.

Mission and Key Success Factor Analysis

Definition of the business is a crucial first step in any strategy development process. However, identifying the mission (what business I am in, and what business I want to be in) is also essential if the strategic issues to be identified are to be rational and applicable.

Identifying the key success factors is also a prerequisite to identification of the strategic issues, the reason being that the KSFs are the benchmarks against which the impact is measured.

Strategic Issue Identification

If environmental analysis is a starting point for strategic planning, issue identification is its control focus. The essential question of this phase is: what are likely to be the positive or negative impacts of macro and micro environmental forces on the business? This suggests defining issues and opportunities or threats and assessing the potential impact of such opportunities and threats on the key success factors of the business.

During this phase extensive use is made of a modified nominal group technique (NGT)[21] and also a modified Delphi Technique.[18]

As both of these techniques are well known, it will be more appropriate to relate some of the problems which surfaced during our research than to discuss the process of issue identification.

(a) Because of the number of participants (on CEOs' insistence) the normal NGT proved cumbersome. The original group was thus subdivided into smaller groups. This created unexpected problems, however, such as group affiliation to their specific issues, which tended to cloud the final voting.

(b) The voting procedure had to be modified. It was noted that participants found it difficult to reduce the number of issues from n to 15 (n = total number of issues identified by group) without an intermediate step. The voting thus typically went from n to $n/2$ to 15 issues.

(c) This step-down voting procedure, plus the greater number of participants, made the voting procedure time consuming. Special equipment and micro software had to be developed to speed up the voting procedure and analyze any significant deviations from the norm.

(d) It was also found that in the process of identifying the 15 most important issues, i.e. those which would have the highest impact, it became necessary to define "impact." Was it to be ROI, ROE, market share, survival, etc.? After much deliberation and many literature surveys, it was decided to look specifically at the impact of the issues on the key success factors.[22]

(e) Assigning probabilities and date of occurrence to the issues presented another problem. It was found that management's understanding of such concepts as probability, cumulative probability distributions, etc. could create problems. The researchers therefore used a variation of the Delphi technique[18] in conjunction with a modified version of John F. Prebble's "Likelihood of Events Assessment Process" (LEAP)[20] to determine the probabilities and likely dates of occurrence of each issue.

(f) Another finding of our research has been that it is better to structure the strategic issue scanning process. For example, a major petroleum company which went through a scanning exercise failed to identify the fall of the oil price to below $10 a barrel as a strategic issue. On reflection it was agreed by the research team that, had Michael Porter's[23] "Five Forces" model of competition been used as a vehicle for identifying micro environmental issues, this oversight would not have occurred. In essence, then, in identifying strategic issues both at the macro environment, i.e. political, economic, socio/demographic and technology (PEST) as well as in the micro environment, represented by Porter's model, we very carefully structured the issue identification exercise. In this way the researchers found that structuring the nominal group's brainstorming exercise rationalized the process, accelerated the step-by-step ranking procedures and ensured a much higher validity rating.

X-Impact Analysis

By this stage, the participants had estimated the probability of occurrence of all the identified events. However, it is a well known fact and subject of much research that the occurrence (or non-occurrence) of any event has an influence on the occurrence of others.

The model used in the X-impact analysis is based on the classic formula by Gordon and Hayward.[19] Participants fill out a cross impact matrix relating each chosen issue in the previous phase to each of the others. Three items of information are required:

(a) Direction of impact—does the occurrence of event A enhance or inhibit the probability of occurrence of event B or will it have no direct effect?

(b) Strength of impact.

(c) Predecessor relationship. Is event A an essential prerequisite for event B to occur or not?

For points (a) and (c) open consensus is sought. The strength of impact is determined by each participant individually on a scale from 1 to 9. The tri-mean of all the individual responses is used as a representative figure of strength. This contains more information than the median whilst avoiding outliers which can distort the mean.

This information is then used in a Monte Carlo simulation model to update the individual probability estimates.

It should be mentioned here that the X-impact analysis is a very rewarding but exhausting exercise. Dealing with a 15 x 15 matrix typically takes 6-8 hours of intensive discussion. However, at the end of this session Wilson and Tomb's[24] first principle of planning—"Understanding the business and the way it reacts to change"—is fully met. Looking at each issue 15 times from different viewpoints generates an enlightened understanding of the business and its interaction with the environment.

The shifts in probabilities resulting from the simulation also proved enlightening at times. For example, a tendency was sometimes evident to play down the probability of threats whilst boosting the probability of favorable events. The cross-impact exercise has a sobering effect on this.

A skillful facilitator is needed to ensure that the X-impact discussion progresses at a satisfactory pace, that there is wide participation, and that the group retains its focus. If properly conducted, such a session can be very intensive, stimulating and productive.

Development of the Issues Priorities Matrix

With the available data, a X-impact simulation model is utilized to calculate the final probabilities of each issue, taking into account the X-impact of every issue on the others. We then have enough information to compile an issues priorities matrix.

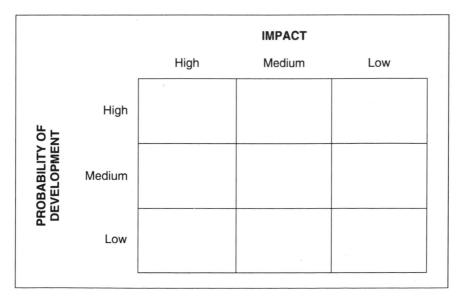

Figure 1. Issue Matrix

On the one axis we have probability—low, medium and high, and on the other we have impact—low, medium and high. Issues having a high probability of occurrence and a high impact on KSFs automatically select themselves for utilization in planning the development of strategic options. Issues with low probability and low impact are rejected. There are, however, issues with high impact but low probability. These we refer to as "flag" items. They are red-flagged and assigned to a specific individual manager to monitor. (A monitoring technique was developed by Bright.[25]) It is essential that any movement, longitudinal, horizontal or both, on the issue priority matrix, should be picked up early and brought to the notice of the CEO, since it could warrant a strategic response.

Strategic Option Identification

Strictly speaking, strategic option identification is not part of the strategic issue scanning process. It is, however, an important element in the total strategic planning system, in that it is during this phase that all the variables of the strategic jig-saw are assembled. It is through the interlocking of the identified opportunities and threats with the strengths and weaknesses, key success factors etc., that innovative alternative strategies can be identified.

It is our experience that management finds the interlocking and innovation process difficult to achieve. This inevitably results in problem solving action plans (internal focus) rather than the generation of innovative strategies (external and internal focus). Thus, once again, we have a need for a structured approach. After much deliberation, the use of field force analysis coupled with Ishikawa diagrams was decided upon as a possible solution. Although this phase of the research has not been completed, preliminary results seem promising.

Summary

Strategic planning might not always produce the expected results. The probable and/or possible reasons for this are legion. However, research exposes at least one common denominator, namely the rate and nature of environmental change as directly influencing results.

In this paper we have discussed a research project centered on the development of a methodology for environmental scanning. The first half of the paper looks at some of the existing theory that legitimates the model developed in the second half. Rather than discuss well known techniques, we have tried to indicate some of the practical problems encountered during our research.

Like most research projects, this one opened a Pandora's Box and created more research questions than answers. However, these questions are regarded as a challenge by the research team, which is actively planning Phase II of the research project.

References

1. Louis V. Gerstner Jr., Can strategic planning pay off? in Richard D. Irwin, *Marketing Management—Perspectives and Applications*, p. 174, Homewood, IL (1976).
2. Walter Kiechel III, Corporate Strategists, *Fortune*, 27 December (1982).
3. Ronald N. Paul, Neil B. Donovan and James W. Taylor, *Harvard Business Review*, May/June (1978).
4. A. Toffler, *The Third Wave*, Bantam Books, New York (1981).
5. J. Naisbitt, *Megatrends*, Warner Books, New York (1982).
6. Charles W. Hofer and Dan Schendell, *Strategy Formulation: Analytical Concepts*, West Publishing Company, St. Paul, MN (1974).
7. R.T. Lenz and Jack L. Engledow, *Environmental Analysis: The Applicability of Current Theory*.
8. Ian Wilson and Kenneth M. Albert, *The Strategic Management Handbook*, McGraw-Hill (1983).
9. F.J. Aguilar, *Scanning the Business Environment*, Macmillan, New York (1967).
10. Burt Nanus, Quest—quick environmental scanning technique, *Long Range Planning*, **15** (2), 39 (1982).
11. Henry Mintzberg, The manager's job: folklore and fact, *Harvard Business Review*, July/August (1975).
12. Donald C. Hambrick, Specialization of environmental scanning activities among upper level executives, *Journal of Management Studies*, **18**, 3 (1981).
13. Michael E. Naylor, in Kenneth M. Albert, *The Strategic Management Handbook*, McGraw-Hill (1983).

14. Liam Fahey and W. R. King, Environmental scanning for corporate planning, *Business Horizons*, August (1977).
15. Charles Stubbard, Are environmental scanning units effective? *Long Range Planning*, **15**, (3), 139 (1982).
16. Egbert F. Bhatty, Corporate planning in medium sized companies in the U.K., *Long Range Planning*, **14** (1), 60 (1981).
17. N. A. Binedell, Corporate Planning—The need for Environmental Analysis in the South African Context (Unpublished Report), University of Cape Town (1982).
18. O. Helmer, Problems in futures research, *Futures* (1977).
19. T. J. Gordon and H. Hayward, Initial experiments with the cross-impact matrix method of forecasting, *Futures* 1 (2), December (1968).
20. John F. Prebble, Futures forecasting with LEAP, *Long Range Planning*, **15** (4), 64, August (1982).
21. A. L. Delbecque, A. H. Van der Venn and D. H. Gustafson, *Group Techniques for Program Planning: a Guide to Nominal Group and Delphi Processes*, Scott-Foresman, Glenview, IL (1975).
22. Kenichi Ohmae, *The Mind of the Strategist*, McGraw-Hill, New York (1982).
23. Michael E. Porter, *Competitive Strategy*, The Free Press, New York (1980).
24. S. R. Wilson and John O. Tomb, *Improving Profits Through Integrated Planning and Control*, Prentice-Hall, Englewood Cliffs, NJ (1986).
25. J. R. Bright, Evaluating signals of technological change, *Harvard Business Review*, January/February (1970).

Further Reading

Kenneth M. Albert, *The Strategic Management Handbook*, McGraw-Hill (1983).
Walter Kiechel III, Playing by the rule of the corporate strategy game, *Fortune*, 24 September (1979).

Acknowledgment—An earlier version of this paper was presented at the Sixth Annual Strategic Management Society Conference in Singapore, October 1986.

10

Achieving Excellence in Strategic Planning Systems

Abstract

The author set out to determine how high-performing companies have used the strategic-planning process to achieve or sustain a competitive edge. He presents seven major points:

1. The success of a strategic plan is not dependent on whether the planning process is formalized. *Instead, it is dependent on how comprehensive that process is in terms of identifying environmental opportunities and threats, analyzing organizational strengths and weaknesses, determining managers' individual values, establishing the organization's social and ethical responsibilities, and creating and evaluating alternative strategies.*

2. The line managers responsible for implementing the strategic plan should be involved in creating that plan. *They can contribute valuable information that strategic planners at other levels may not have; also, they are more likely to implement the plan if they feel a sense of ownership about it.*

3. Budgeters should interact with strategic planners. *For example, include the chief financial officer on the strategic-planning team.*

4. The strategic plan should be translated into a separate action plan for each functional area. *Examples of functional areas are marketing, finance, production, and operations.*

5. The chief planning executive (in most organizations, probably the CEO) should take an active role in the strategic-planning process. *The role might include generating ideas, acting as devil's advocate, evaluating the individual functional plans as well as the corporate strategic plan, and consolidating the functional plans and checking them for consistency.*

6. The period between implementation of one strategic plan and implementation of another should be at least two years. *Completing the planning process more frequently not only depletes the planning team's creative energy but also robs the previous strategic plan of the time it needs to reap benefits.*

7. The strategic plan should include specific statements of the organization's mission, performance goals, competitive strategy, functional policies, and basic planning assumptions. *The resulting strategy should be articulated throughout the organization.*

Achieving Excellence in Strategic Planning Systems

Luis Ma. R. Calingo

Building a better mousetrap so that the world can beat a path to your door is still a primary goal of executives in today's high-performing organizations. The management literature abounds with illustrations of the importance of achieving a sustainable competitive advantage. For example, Porsche AG decided to build its "better mousetrap" by positioning its sports cars as a discretionary purchase—"built to be enjoyed instead of just used," competing with sailboats, summer homes and airplanes.[1] A significant portion of Lincoln Electric Company's leadership in the arc welding industry derived from its strategy of coupling production efficiency with a unique management system, both of which enabled it to compete on price without sacrificing quality.[2]

How do companies like these develop effective strategies for success in their particular situations? It is easy to find prescriptions about what constitutes a "good" strategy for a company.[3] But these prescriptions do not help a manager organize or structure the *process* by which strategies are formulated. The available advice rarely tells a manager whether the methods and procedures of strategic planning should be formalized, how much autonomy to give line or

---

Reprinted by permission, *SAM Advanced Management Journal*, Spring 1989, Society for Advancement of Management, Vinton, VA 24179.

operating managers, how often the process should be undertaken, or addresses a number of other design questions.

To find answers to these questions, I looked at how managements of 50 companies structure their strategic planning processes. (See the appendix for a description of the study's methodology.)

The results of this research are discussed under the seven points below.

1. Formalizing the planning process does not necessarily lead to better strategies.   It is more important that the process be sufficiently comprehensive so that, at the minimum, activities fostering a "good" strategy are performed. In brief, these activities are 1) identifying opportunities and threats in the company's environment, 2) appraising the company's strengths and weaknesses, 3) assessing managers' personal values and preferences, 4) acknowledging the company's social and ethical responsibilities, and 5) developing and evaluating alternative strategies.[4] Firms are wont to document all these activities and attendant detailed procedures in the form of a thick corporate planning manual. While standardization ensures consistency in planning processes and procedures, too much formalization tends to inhibit creative thinking—the essence of strategic planning.

2. The managers who will implement the strategic plan should be actively involved in its formulation.   Corporate planning executives often raise two arguments in favor of line managers' substantive participation in the planning process. First, due to their frequent contacts with customers and the marketplace, line managers possess strategy-relevant information which is not necessarily known by corporate managers. Thus, participation is justified from the standpoint of information sharing or reduction of uncertainty. The second argument concerns the importance of giving line managers a "sense of ownership" of the strategic plan. If line managers realize they have a stake in the plan's success, they will be more motivated to implement it. Although my study showed that the appropriate extent of participation depends on the company's situation, my findings also suggest the importance of building the most participative planning process the situation will allow.

3. The manager(s) responsible for strategic planning should interact with those responsible for budgeting.   Although the development of creative thinking is a desirable characteristic of strategic planning, realism is an integral part of strategic thinking.[5] In planning, as elsewhere, one's reach shouldn't exceed one's grasp.

What the company might do in terms of the available opportunities must be balanced by what the company can do, based on its competence and resources. To achieve this balance between creativity and realism, it is not unusual to find companies including their controllers or chief financial officers as active participants in the strategic planning process.

4. The strategic plan should be tightly coupled with the company's action plans or programs for different functional areas. Another way to achieve the needed balance between creativity and realism is to translate the strategic plan into "tactics" or activities for the different functional areas (e.g., marketing). This process is typically referred to as "programming." It is mainly through the efforts of people within these functional areas that the strategic plan is eventually implemented. A majority of the companies in my study included in their corporate strategic plans long-term programs for six functional areas: marketing, finance, production/operations management, personnel, research and development, and management information systems.

5. The chief planning executive should assume a more active, substance-related role. The role of the chief planning executive has traditionally been to facilitate the process through which strategic plans are formulated. Under this conception, the planning director "plans the planning process" and is often the main source of broader strategic issues, environmental assumptions, and financial forecasts. In this view, the planner is a detached, neutral (value-free) observer, rather than an active participant—and perhaps an advocate—in the planning process.

The planning practices of the high-performing companies in my study suggest otherwise: A passive, process-oriented role is not always the best role for the chief planning executive. In these companies, the planning director—presumably a manager with experience or formal education in strategic planning—performed more active, substantive roles. Typically, the planner's role was to be an "idea generator" or a "devil's advocate" for top management as they thought about the company's future. Other roles considered appropriate were evaluating corporate and divisional strategic plans and consolidating divisional plans and checking them for interdivisional consistency prior to top management consideration.

6. The strategic plan should not be reviewed or revised more frequently than every two years.   Re-examining the company's mission, changing corporate strategy, and revising divisional charters too frequently reduce strategic planning to a monotonous, bureaucratic exercise. Such a bureaucratic exercise, and the voluminous paperwork that accompanies it, are antithetical to the essential development of creative thinking. Unfortunately, annual planning cycles have been traditional in firms that practice strategic planning. Organizations should give the strategic plan enough time to produce its benefits. Otherwise, they will fall into the trap of committing a Type II Error: rejecting a strategic plan before its effectiveness can be shown.

7. The strategic plan should explicitly state the company's mission, performance goals and objectives, competitive strategy, functional policies, and key planning assumptions.   This enables an explicit strategy to be communicated throughout the organization and eventually institutionalized.

I realize there is a school of thought that does not favor publicizing strategy or even articulating it.[6] However, other studies have consistently shown that articulating strategy is almost an absolute essential. In their best seller, *In Search of Excellence*, Tom Peters and Bob Waterman identified "stress on a key business value" (an element of strategy) as the fifth attribute of excellent companies.[7] Further, numerous studies about goal setting have consistently shown that, overall, explicit goals are better than "no goals" or "do your best" goals.[8]

In conclusion, I have recast the study's findings into a five-point "Plato" recommendation to general managers initiating strategic planning in their organizations.

P—The *process* should be comprehensive and participative.

L—The *linkage* between strategic planning and operational planning (i.e., programming and budgeting) should be tight.

A—The manager responsible for the *administration* of the strategic planning process should perform more active, substance-related roles.

T—The *timing* aspects of the planning process should be such that the plan is not revised more frequently than once every two years.

O—The *output* of the planning process should be an explicit and complete statement of the organization's strategy, including how the company intends to pursue a sustainable competitive advantage.

Given the limited size of my sample, managers need to apply the above recommendations with caution. Prescriptions that are counterintuitive or do not appear to be reasonable in a given situation probably are not. But what is more important than the individual recommendations is the recognition that *the character of the process by which a strategy is formulated is as important as the strategy itself*. If managers do not pay sufficient attention to these process considerations, even the most logical of strategies can fail.

Appendix
The Research: Method and Analysis

The paper is based on a study, completed in 1984 and supported in part by the North American Society for Corporate Planning (Pittsburgh chapter), to determine specific relationships among corporate strategy, the design of strategic planning systems (SPS), and organizational performance. The analytical investigation was the basis of my Ph.D. dissertation at the University of Pittsburgh.

Data for the study came from a combination of personal interviews and mail-questionnaire surveys involving chief corporate planning executives of 50 business organizations in the Northeast (Pittsburgh, Philadelphia, Cleveland and New York). A majority of the firms represented are large i.e., sales of at least $600 million. The number of participants represents 53 percent of the 94 eligible firms contacted for the study.

While the participating companies did not constitute a random sample of the general population of U.S. firms, the sample possessed attributes that appeared to be characteristic of a large part of American corporations. The distribution of the firms by broad industry groups (industrials, public utilities, transportation and financial) closely approximated the distribution of these groupings in the Standard & Poor's 500 Index. The S&P 500 is generally used as a proxy for the composition of the entire stock market.

The informants were asked to describe their firms' strategies, the design characteristics of their SPS, and their organizations' performance. The criterion validity and internal consistency of the measures used were confirmed from the results of correlation analysis and factor analysis where variables were found to be related to each other and to load on the same factors in the expected manner.

I conducted the analysis for this paper using multiple linear regression, with performance (either achievement of strategic planning purposes or organizational effectiveness) as the criterion variable and SPS design characteristics as predictor variables. To control for their effects, I included measures of business diversity and growth orientation (stability, expansion or retrenchment) in the right-hand side of the equation. The regression equations accounted for about 39 percent of the variation in performance (F test; *alpha* < 0.001); predictors significant at the 0.10 level are reported in this paper.

Endnotes

1. David E. Gumpert, "Porsche on Nichemanship: Interviews with Peter Schutz and Jack Cook." *Harvard Business Review* 64 (March-April 1986): 98-106.

2. Arthur D. Sharplin, "Low-Cost Strategies to Improve Workers' Job Security," *Journal of Business Strategy* 5 (Fall 1985): 90-93.

3. The state-of-the-art of these prescriptions is summarized in the following works by Professor Michael E. Porter of the Harvard Business School: *Competitive Strategy* (New York: Free Press, 1980) and *Competitive Advantage* (New York: Free Press, 1985).

4. See Kenneth R. Andrews, *The Concept of Corporate Strategy*, rev. ed. (Homewood, IL: Richard D. Irwin, 1980) for the classic treatment of the strategy formulation process.

5. The original discussion of the required creativity-realism balance is found in John K. Shank, Edward G. Niblock, and William T. Sandalls, Jr., "Balance 'Creativity' and 'Practicality' in Formal Planning," *Harvard Business Review* 51 (January-February 1973): 87-95.

6. H. Edward Wrapp, "Good Managers Don't Make Policy Decisions," *Harvard Business Review* 45 (September-October 1967): 91-99, is a widely read account of incrementalist thinking.

7. For an extended account of the eight attributes of excellent companies, see Thomas J. Peters and Robert H. Waterman, Jr., *In Search of Excellence: Lessons from America's Best-Run Companies* (New York: Harper & Row, Publishers, Inc., 1982).

8. A comprehensive review of goal-setting research can be found in Edwin A. Locke, Karyll N. Shaw, Lisa M. Saari, and Gary P. Latham, "Goal Setting and Task Performance: 1969-1980," *Psychological Bulletin* 90 (1981): 125-52.

11

Identifying and Using Critical Success Factors

Abstract

Critical Success Factors (CSFs) are those characteristics, conditions, or variables that when properly sustained, maintained, or managed can have a significant impact on the success of a firm competing in a particular industry. CSFs are often difficult to identify and rank in relative importance, but are important in helping an organization assess external threats and opportunities and internal strengths and weaknesses.

Identification. *CSFs are not easily identified by any one method; three levels of analysis have merit: (1) firm specific, which focuses on internal factors; (2) industry level, which focuses on factors in the basic structure of the industry; and (3) economic sociopolitical environment, which examines factors beyond industry boundaries. These three levels have special links to several of the steps found in a typical strategy development model; specifically, they can be instrumental in environomental scanning (assessing social, political, economic, and technological variables and their impact on the industry and the potential of significant threats and opportunities facing the firm), resource analysis (an inventory of a firm's strengths and weaknesses), and strategic evaluation (comparing the organization's strategic alternatives with the specific goals and objectives of the firm and its various constituencies).*

The authors present eight techniques for identifying CSFs: (1) environmental analysis; (2) analysis of industry structure; (3) industry/business experts; (4) analysis of competition; (5) analysis of the dominant firm in the industry; (6) company assessment; (7) temporal/intuitive factors; and (8) profit impact of market strategy results.

Relative Importance. *Once the CSFs are identified, a means of establishing their relative importance is presented. Four criteria are suggested: (1) CSFs are usually found in the major activity of the business, (2) CSFs usually involve large dollars, (3) CSFs usually have a major profit impact, and (4) CSFs often accompany major changes in the company's performance.*

Identifying and Using Critical Success Factors

Joel K. Leidecker
Albert V. Bruno

Daniel first discussed Critical Success Factors (CSF's) in an article in the early 1960s. The concept received little attention until a decade later, when Anthony, Dearden and Vancil[1] utilized the concept in the design of a management control system. Anthony and Dearden pointed out that the management control system, in addition to measuring profitability, identifies certain 'key variables (also strategic factors, key success factors, key result areas and pulse points)' that significantly impact profitability. These authors suggest, among other things, that there are usually six different variables; these variables are important determinants of organizational success and failure; they are subject to change and this is not always predictable.[2,3] The concept of critical success factors has also been used to assist in defining the CEO and General Manager's information needs.[4] This approach forces the key decision maker to identify those information needs that are critical or important to the success of the business. The factors identified become the basis for the company's management information system

---

Reprinted by permission. "Identifying and Using Critical Success Factors," by J.K. Leidecker and A.V. Bruno in *Long Range Planning*, February 1984, pp. 23-32.

and provide the standards for subsequent performance measurement and control systems. While Rockart and Anthony *et al*, believe the critical success factors approach can be an important tool in the two management areas cited above, we contend that another beneficial application of the concept is in the strategic planning and the business strategy development area. The identification of critical success factors provides a means by which an organization can assess the threats and opportunities in its environment. CSPs also provide a set of criteria for the strengths and weaknesses assessment of the firm. These two elements (assessment of environmental threats and opportunities and specific firm resource analysis) are corner-stones of the strategic planning and strategy development process.[5-8]

The purpose of this article is three-fold. First is to define and discuss the concept of critical success factors. Second is to link the concepts to the strategic planning/strategy development process, and third, the major focus of this paper, is to assist the reader with CSF identification and use. This is accomplished through discussion of various techniques for determining CSF's and by providing examples of usage applied to specific industries and/or firms.

Critical Success Factors

Definition

What is a critical success factor? Rockart observes:

> Critical success factors thus are, for any business, the limited number of areas in which results, if they are satisfactory, will insure [sic] successful competitive performance for the organization. They are the few key areas where 'things must go right' for the business to flourish. If results in these areas are not adequate, the organization's efforts for the period will be less than defined (p.85).[4]

According to Hofer and Schendel:

> Key success factors are those variables which management can influence through its decisions that can affect significantly the overall competitive positions of the various firms in an industry. These factors usually vary from industry to industry. Within any particular in-

dustry, however, they are derived from the interaction of two sets of variables, namely the economic and technological characteristics of the industry involved . . . and the competitive weapons on which the various firms in the industry have built their strategies . . . (p. 77).[7]

Hofer and Schendel argue that such factors are obvious, easily identified through a combination of sensitivity and elasticity analysis; they contend that the major problem is assessing relative importance.

We contend that critical success factors are not as obvious as Hofer and Schendel imply. While sensitivity and elasticity analyses are useful identification tools they are by no means sufficient nor are they the only useful methods for identifying a critical success factor. A substantial portion of this paper deals with these issues: factor identification and the determination of relative importance.

Because some definitional differences exist across the three applications identified above (MIS, control system, or planning system), we will use the following definition in this paper. Critical Success Factors (CSF's) are those characteristics, conditions, or variables that when properly sustained, maintained, or managed can have a significant impact on the success of a firm competing in a particular industry. A CSF can be a characteristic such as price advantage, it can also be a condition such as capital structure or advantageous customer mix; or an industry structural characteristic such as vertical integration (see Table 1 for some examples).

The concept of critical success factors has been applied at three levels of analysis (firm specific, industry, and economic sociopolitical environment). Analysis at each level provides a source of potential critical success factors. Firm specific analysis utilizes an internal focus to provide the link to possible factors. Industry level analysis focuses on certain factors in the basic structure of the industry that significantly impact any company's performance operating in that industry. A third level of analysis goes beyond industry boundaries for a source of critical success factors. This school of thought argues that one needs to perpetually scan the environment (economic, socio-political) to provide sources that will be the determinants of a firm's and/or industry's success. We believe all three levels of analysis have merit as sources for critical success factors. We note that the more macrooriented approaches are of lesser importance when designing a firm's management information system or internal control system.

Table 1a. Critical Success Factors—Industry

Automobile[1] Industry	Semi-Conductor Industry	Food Processing	Life Insurance
Styling	Manufacturing process: cost efficient, innovative, cumulative experience	New product development	Development of agency personnel
Strong dealer network		Good distribution	Effective control of clerical personnel
Manufacturing cost control	Technological competence: adequate technical	Effective advertising	Innovation in policy development
Ability to meet EPA standards	Capital availability product development		Innovative advertising Marketing strategy

Table 1b. Critical Success Factors—Firms in Semi-Conductor Industry

National Semi-Conductor	Intel	AMD	Avantek
Broad product line	Innovator and leader in technology	Proprietary innovative products	Strong transistor product line
Large, efficient production capacity	Strong product development and customer Service	Does not compete in price sensitive markets	Solid customer range High yield manufacturing
Vertically integrated	Capability	Effective location of fabrication and assembly	
Innovative packaging and assembly operations	High margin proprietary devices	Operations strong technical marketing capabilities	

[1]Adapted from Daniel, 1961.

Strategic Planning and the Strategy Development Process

Hofer and Schendel after reviewing a majority of strategy formulation models, indicate that strategy development is a seven step process (Strategy Identification, Environmental Analysis, Resource Analysis, Gap Analysis, Strategic Alternatives, Strategy Evaluation, Strategic Choice).[7] We will use these seven steps as a generally accepted representation of the strategy development process as well as the basis for our discussion of fit with critical success factors.

CSF analysis can aid the strategy development process at three specific junctures. The three are environmental analysis, resource analysis and strategy evaluation. Environmental analysis includes an assessment of the social, political, economic and technological climates and their general impact on an industry and/or firm. In addition this analysis usually will focus on the competitive environment. Environmental analysis is used to identify the significant threats and opportunities facing a firm. CSF analysis, specifically at the macro and industry level, aids in the determination of threats and opportunities. CSF analysis provides a means to identify the essential competences, resources and skills necessary to be successful in a particular industry or specific economic climate. This type of information can assist the analyst responsible for identifying threats and opportunities. For example, if analysis indicates that vertical integration is a critical success factor for the soft drink industry, any firm in that industry or that is contemplating entry into that industry will evaluate this either as a threat to or opportunity for itself.

Resource analysis involves an inventory of a firm's strengths and weaknesses. Firm-level CSF analysis should go beyond inventorying. It identifies those variables that have been instrumental to a firm's success in a particular industry. This approach leads to a level of sophistication that provides greater depth and insight than a mere listing of a firm's strengths and weaknesses. This level of input provides more useful information for assessing a firm's competitive advantage (a firm's competencies vs. its competitors). In addition, firm-specific CSF's can be compared with threats and opportunities to aid with identification of strategic options.

Another element in the strategy development process is strategy evaluation. Strategy evaluation involves comparing your strategic alternatives with the specific goals and objectives of the firm and its various constituencies, as well as any other evaluation criteria deemed pertinent. One 'other' evaluation criteria could be the critical success factors for an industry. For example, one available strategic option may be entry into the soft drink industry and, as before, vertical integration may be a CSF. Now that this fact is known, the evaluation becomes whether the firm can negate this factor (minimize its impact) or replicate it (do we have the resources, financial and otherwise, to become vertically integrated?). Obviously, the viability of the alternative is influenced by the firm's 'where-with-all' relative to the CSF.

When a strategic alternative is tested as to its 'CSF FIT' the strategy evaluation process becomes more rigorous and comprehensive.

Earlier in this paper three levels of CSF analysis (macro, industry, firm) were discussed. In this section the strategy development process was outlined and the linkages to critical success factor analysis were set forth. Figure 1 shows the linkages between the three levels of CSF analysis and the strategy development process. This linkage completes the discussion on CSF importance and usage. The focus of the paper shifts to its third and most important objective: techniques for the identification of a critical success factor.

Identification Techniques

Identification of CSF's can be an important element in the eventual development of a firm's strategy as well as an integral part of the strategic planning process. Eight techniques for identifying CSF's are set forth below. In addition, we will present their respective advantage and disadvantages, discuss ways of applying them, and present examples of their usage (see Table 2).

1. Environmental Analysis.—This broad category includes a variety of approaches that identify the economic, political and social forces that will be and are impacting an industry and/or firm's performance.

Environmental scanning, econometric models (such as the Chase Econometric Service or the Wharton models based upon key

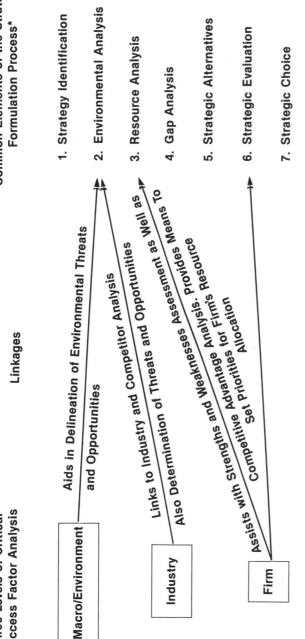

Three Levels of Critical Success Factor Analysis

Linkages

Common Elements of the Strategy Formulation Process*

Macro/Environment

Aids in Delineation of Environmental Threats and Opportunities

Links to Industry and Competitor Analysis

Industry

Also Determination of Threats and Opportunities as Well as Assessment as Means To Provides Firm's Resource

Assists with Strengths and Weaknesses Analysis. Competitive Advantage for Set Priorities Firm's Resource Allocation

Firm

1. Strategy Identification

2. Environmental Analysis

3. Resource Analysis

4. Gap Analysis

5. Strategic Alternatives

6. Strategic Evaluation

7. Strategic Choice

Strategic Alternatives Can Be Evaluated Against Critical Success Factors and the Relative Importance of CFS's May Influence Prioritization of Strategic Alternatives

Figure 1. Critical Success Factor Analysis and the Strategy Formulation Process

*Adapted from Hofer and Schendel, *Strategy Formulation and Analytical Concepts*, p. 47.

Table 2. Critical Success Factors: Identification Techniques

Technique	Focus	Sources	Advantages	Disadvantages
I Environmental analysis	Macro	Environmental Scanning (Corp. staff) Econometric models Socio-political consulting services	Future Orientation Macro orientation: analysis goes beyond industry-firm focus Can be linked to threats/opportunity evaluation	More difficult ot operationalize into specific industry or firm CSF's Results may not lend themselves to incorporate usage in current time frame (today's CSF's)
II Analysis of industry structure	Industry Macro	A variety of industry structure frameworks	Specific focus is on industry Frameworks allow user to understand interrelationships between industry structural components Can force more macro level focus (beyond industry boundries)	While excellent source for industry wide CSF's not as useful in determining firm-specific CSF's
III Industry/business experts	Industry Micro	Industry association executives Financial analysts specializing in industry Outsider familiar with firms in industry Knowledgeable insiders who work in industry	Means of soliciting conventional wisdom about industry and firms Subjective information very often not discovered with more objective, formal and analytical approaches	Lack of objectivity often leads to questions of verifiability/justification
IV Analysis of competition	Industry Micro	Staff Specialists Line Managers Internal Consultants External Consultants	Narrowness of focus, offers advantage of detailed, specific data Depth of analysis leads to better means of justification	Narrowness of focus, CSF development limited to competitive arena (as opposed ot industry structure approach)

Table 2. (continued). Critical Success Factors: Identification Techniques

	Technique	Focus	Sources	Advantages	Disadvantages
V	Analysis of the dominant firm in the industry	Industry Micro	Staff Specialists Line managers Internal consultants External consultants	Dominant competitor may in fact set industry CSF's Understanding of No. 1 may assist in corroborating firm specific CSF's	Narrow focus may preclude seeking alternative explanations of success Mary limit individual firm's strategic response and focus
VI	Company assessment (comprehensive firm-specific)	Micro	Internal staff line organizations (detailed analyses by organization function—checklist approach)	A thorough functional area screening reveals internal/strengths and weaknesses that may assist CSF development	Narrow focus of analysis precludes inputs of more macro approaches Checklist approach can be very time consuming and become data bound
VII	Temporal/ intuitive factors (firm-specific)	Micro	Internal staff Brainstorming CEO/General Mgt. observation	More subjective and not limited to functional analysis approach Leads to identification of important short run CSF's that may go unnoticed in more formal reviews	Difficulty in justifying as CFS if of short term duration Important may be overstated, if in fact a short-run phenomena
VIII	PIMS results	Industry Micro	Articles on PIMS Project results	Empirically based Excellent starting point	General nature Applicability to your specific firm or industry Determination of relative importance

environmental/economic variables), socio-political consulting services, and governmental affairs departments are but a few of the diverse approaches used to monitor and assess environmental impact on the industry and the firms comprising that industry. The analysis is macro in approach and the data obtained do not always provide a clear linkage to the determination of industry, let alone firm-specific CSF's. The major advantage is the breadth of analysis. That is, the scope goes well beyond the industry/firm interface. This is particularly important to those industries whose survival is dependent upon forces outside the control of the industry competitive environment.

2. Analysis of Industry Structure.—Much of the strategic planning literature offers techniques to analyze the structure of an industry. The framework of analysis set forth in a recent effort by Michael Porter provides an excellent example of this approach. This particular frame-work consists of five components (barriers to entry, substitutable products, suppliers, buyers and inter-firm competition). The evaluation of each element and the interrelationships between them provide the analyst with considerable data to assist in the identification and justification of industry CSF's.[9] One advantage of the analysis of industry structure approach is the thoroughness that the classification scheme provides. Another positive characteristic is the facility to schematically depict the industry's structural components as well as the critical interrelationships between elements (Figures 2 and 3 are examples of this technique).

3. Industry/Business Experts.—This category includes inputs from people who have an excellent working knowledge of the industry/business. Although this technique may not be as objective and thorough as others, it does offer the advantage of obtaining information or a perspective not always available or discernable using the more standard analytical techniques. The 'conventional wisdom', insight, or 'intuitive feel' of an industry insider often is an excellent source of CSF's and, coupled with more objective techniques, provide the analyst with a two-fold data source to substantiate other CSF identification.

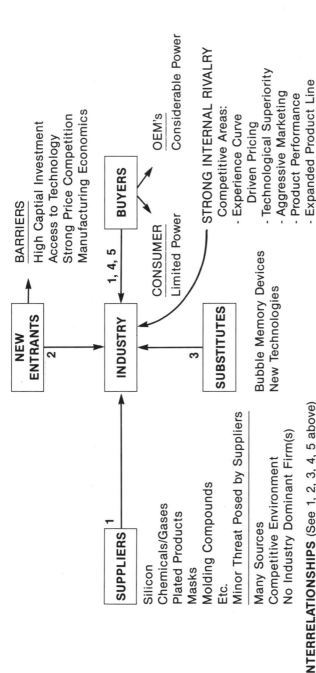

BARRIERS
High Captial Investment
Access to Technology
Strong Price Competition
Manufacturing Economics

NEW ENTRANTS

2

SUPPLIERS

1

Silicon
Chemicals/Gases
Plated Products
Masks
Molding Compounds
Etc.
Minor Threat Posed by Suppliers

Many Sources
Competitive Environment
No Industry Dominant Firm(s)

INDUSTRY

1, 4, 5

BUYERS

OEM's

Considerable Power

CONSUMER
Limited Power

STRONG INTERNAL RIVALRY
Competitive Areas:
- Experience Curve
  Driven Pricing
- Technological Superiority
- Aggressive Marketing
- Product Performance
- Expanded Product Line
- Retention of Skilled Technical Labor
  Force

SUBSTITUTES

3

Bubble Memory Devices
New Technologies

INTERRELATIONSHIPS (See 1, 2, 3, 4, 5 above)

1. Increasing emphasis on forward and backward integration.
2. In recent years high barriers have been bridged by foreign competitors (European through purchase of U.S. companies, Japanese through government support/sponsorship and technology adaptation).
3. Constant threat in this industry is the development of new technology.
4. Pressure by both buyer groups for backward integration.
5. Through marketing and product demand manufacturers can create demand.

Figure 2. Industry Structure Analysis: Semi-Conductor Industry

This approach is being used by the Center for Information Systems Research at MIT to identify firm CSF's that ultimately will be incorporated into a management information system.[4] We believe this technique is an equally rich, though subjective, source of CSF's to be utilized in the strategy development process. The disadvantages are obvious. The inputs may be no more than biased opinion and, therefore, result in a tenuous base for strategy development. Application is relatively straightforward but not simple: all that the analyst must do is to ask the 'right' questions of the 'right' knowledgeable sources and make the 'right' interpretations.

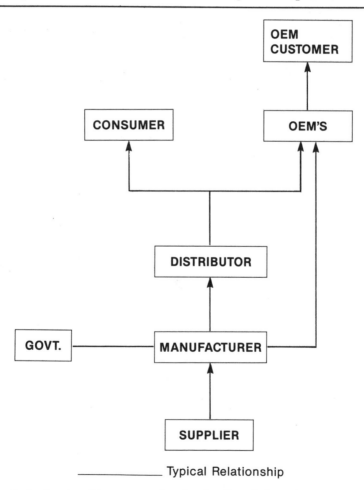

_____ Typical Relationship

Figure 3. Industry Structure Analysis: Semi-Conductor Industry

4. Analysis of Competition. The focus here is a narrow one. It is limited to the competitive environment (or how firms compete) as opposed to the industry structure approach which includes analysis of competition as one of the five structural elements to analyze.[9] The rationale for this approach is one of 'homing in on the target'. Its proponents argue that competitor analysis is one of the most important, if not the most important, source of CSF's. By concentrating analysis on *competition,* how firms compete, one does not dilute effort, and possibly under-analyze competitive forces as users of broader industry structure approaches may do. The advantage of this approach relates to the specific nature of the firm; that is the thorough understanding of the competitive environment and each firm's competitive posture allows a firm using this approach the facility to readily incorporate this information into the strategy developments process. The major disadvantage is the inability to identify CSF's not linked to the analysis of how firms compete. Discussion of the importance of competitor analysis and approaches to competitor analysis can be found in the literature.[10-11]

5. Analysis of the Dominant Firm in the Industry. Often the way the leading firm in the industry conducts itself can provide significant insights into an industry's CSF's. This method is very useful in industries dominated by one or a few firms. The careful analysis of firms such as: IBM, in the mainframe computer industry; H & R Block, in the tax preparation business; and Boeing in the commercial jet aircraft business, would provide valuable information to identify and justify specific industry CSF's. Figure 4 is an example of this type of analysis for a leading firm in the electronic components distribution industry. The advantage of this approach is that if the dominant firm establishes the traditional success pattern for an industry, a thorough understanding of what the firm does successfully would aid in one's own internal analysis as well as in determining strategic posture. The major disadvantage is the narrow focus of this type of analysis. To say the way 'so and so' does it establishes the industry CSF's and this is the only path to success in the industry can be too limiting. The strategic decision to emulate the dominant firm is fraught with danger. There are many examples of how firms have found ways of neutralizing or avoiding CSF's dictated by the

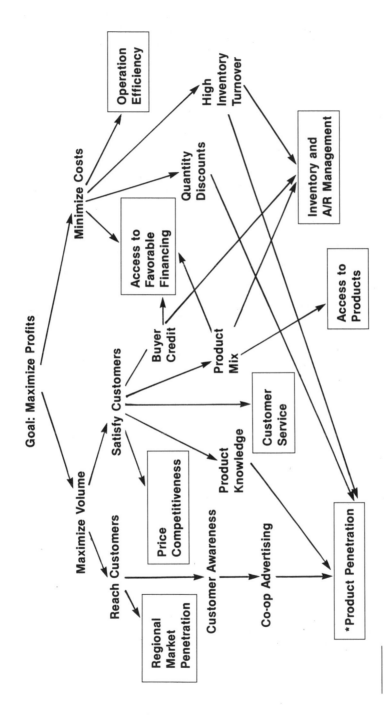

*Product Penetration—All the Sales/Marketing Activities Which Make the Distributor the Preferred Supplier for the Customer, by Creating Awareness of Firm's Product Mix, Depth and Potential to Benefit the Customer Through Dissemination of Product Knowledge, Value-Added and Purchase Discounts.

Figure 4. Electronic Component Distribution Industry: Critical Success Factors

dominant firm in the industry (e.g. the by-passing of existing distributor networks by direct selling in the microwave components industry, the leasing of aircraft to offset capital intensiveness in the jet air freight business). However, the industry leader should be analyzed before deviations from its success pattern can be formulated.

6. Company Assessment.   This approach is firm specific. The purpose of the analysis would be to identify the CSF's for a particular firm. While this is a worthwhile analytical exercise in itself, the results should be analyzed in light of industry and competitor CSF's. A variety of approaches have been articulated: strengths and weaknesses assessment, resource profiles, strategic audits, and strategic capabilities. All have one characteristic in common; that is, the analyst must thoroughly explore what the firm does well and not so well. The positive aspects of the firms's operation may provide the means to determine a firm's critical success factors. Any of the approaches above, if applied by a good analyst, will most likely result in a useful set of CSF's. One specific method of application is the comprehensive checklist approach. This is a series of questions, by functional area, designed so that the answers will provide the information necessary to determine a firm's CSF's. The specific questions to ask and the weight given to each question will vary by firm. An evaluative priorization scheme for the firm is a necessity. Also the set of questions must be tailored to each firm's specific requirements. Starting points would include check lists provided by CPA and consulting firms and the business literature.[10,13-15]

The step-by-step approach is methodical and time consuming, but will result in a very comprehensive analysis of each functional area. The narrow focus and the time to complete are the two disadvantages identified earlier; however, the major disadvantage is the possible exclusion of obvious industry level CSF's not uncovered with this approach. Moreover, the analyst/planner is constrained by the set of topics/questions that are available or that can be developed.

7. Temporal/Intuitive Factors.   This is another approach with a firm-specific outlook. This, like its industry level counterpart (Item 4 above), focuses on the intuition and insight of an individual(s) very familiarity with the firm. While very subjective, this approach often uncovers subtleties about CSF's that the more conventional and objective techniques overlook. The temporal issue deals with firm-specific occurrences, that in the short run may have a significant impact on performance and hence constitute a CSF (e.g. key management people leave for a new company; purchasing fails to order enough of a critical material; in a non-capital intensive industry a new technological breakthrough in equipment design forces a financially weak firm into a disadvantaged position).

An example of how this approach can result in the determination of an important CSF is as follows: the founder/president of a local solar energy firm, discussing 'The Key Ingredients That Make His Firm Successful', identified two important factors from his point of view. An earlier analysis utilizing a more conventional objective approach failed to discern there two important aspects, machine design and manufacturing process. Both were people specific, each gave the firm a competitive advantage that was not available in the open market. The more conventional approach did not identify the major importance of either factor.

8. PIMS Results.   In recent years the PIMS (Profit Impact of Market Strategy) project data indicates among other things, that relative market share, degree of vertical integration, new product activity, capital intensity, and ratios of R & D and marketing to sales play a major role in determining profitability.[16,17] Profitability is certainly one of an industry's or firm's measures of success, if not the only one. If the PIMS results identify the key determinants of profitability, then these inputs provide a starting point for CSF analysis (other techniques may be used to substantiate).

The major advantage appears to be the empirical basis of the project results. The major disadvantage, as an identification technique, is the very general nature of the factors. The PIMS result do not provide a method of analysis to indicate whether the data are directly applicable to a specific firm or industry and/or what their relative importance may be.

The relative importance of a CSF is something that must be determined and periodically evaluated. Some CSF's are obviously more important than others. In the next section we discuss an identification and prioritization scheme for critical success factors.

Determination of Factor Importance

The profit impact of an activity or condition is usually the most significant factor for CSF identification as well as determination of factor importance. While other areas may be important the authors suggest four starting points for the profit impact analysis which will assist in determination of factor importance.

Major Activity of Business

Usually CSF's are found in major areas of the business. For example, if a wholesaler were under examination, many of the factors that influence overall performance should be found in and around the inventory and warehousing function as opposed to say, the advertising activity. If the opposite were true and most firms in a particular industry were concerned with marketing to consumers, then the advertising function might deserve closer scrutiny.

Large Dollars Involved

Major factors probably have relatively large dollar amounts associated with them. For example, in a manufacturing firm, direct labor may be a large dollar amount and the productivity of the workforce might be a CSF. Improving workforce productivity might lead to improved bottom-line performance. This compares to the wholesaling activity described immediately above, where improved workforce productivity might not significantly improve bottom-line performance since most wholesale operations are not labor intensive.

Major Profit Impact

Another way of looking at a business is to assess the sensitivity of overall results to changes in certain activities. For example, in some circumstances, a small change in price might have enormous bottom-line impact, whereas doubling the advertising effort might have little impact. 'Value Added Analysis' would be an excellent tool to utilize for this level of analysis.

Major Changes in Performance

Sometimes it is a good idea to follow up on significant changes in the company's performance: e.g. dramatic drop in sales, major profit reversal in a segment of the operation, sizeable increases in margins. A significant change often will eventually be linked to a major CSF. Whether it will be of short or long run term duration is to be determined by the analyst. Another aid to the determination of relative factor importance and subsequent CSF usage would be a prioritization scheme. The basis for establishing CSF priorities should be linked to the industry and or firm's success criteria (economic or otherwise). When classifying *industry CSF's,* the factor importance and profit impact analysis discussion above is relevant; the classification of *firm specific CSF's* can be influenced by 'other,' non economic firm objectives. The discussion above provides the basis for prioritization. The decision as to how to prioritize the CSF's is, of course, up to the individual analyst. In the examples in Tables 3 and 4 we have used a four-factor scheme.

In most cases, the type of company or the nature of the industry will determine which CSF's are important. For example, the success of a retail business is heavily influenced by factors such as store location, effectiveness of the merchandising and inventory control. The wholesaler(s) selling to this same retailer would normally not expect a CSF to be location-oriented. Tables 3 and 4 provide examples of how the prioritization scheme can be utilized with a set of potential CSF's. On the vertical axis, various stages in the production distribution process are identified; on the horizontal axis, for comparative purpose, various industries or firms are listed; at the intersection of each category the analyst would assess the relative importance of the factor for the respective firm or industry. This method of focusing the search provides more comprehensive CSF analysis and will assist with subsequent application.

Summary and Conclusions

Critical success factors, their identification, importance and use have been the focus of this paper. The authors cite literature that links the use of CSF's to management information systems design and management control system design. The paper concerns itself with a discussion of the application of CSF's in the strategic planning process. The authors argue that CSF's can be particularly instrumental in three areas of the strategy development process: environmental analysis, resource analysis and strategy evaluation. After establishing the importance of CSF analysis in the functions of management information systems, management control systems and strategic planning, the authors conclude that the identification of critical success factors is a very important step in the application process. For the practitioner, eight identification techniques are discussed and examples of usage presented. In addition, a means of establishing the relative importance of a critical success factor is set forth.

References

1. Robert N. Anthony, John Dearden and Richard F. Vancil, Key economic variables, In *Management Control Systems,* pp. 138-143, Irwin, Homewood, Illinois (1972).
2. Robert N. Anthony and John Dearden, *Management Control Systems Text and Cases,* Irwin, Homewood, Illinois (1976).
3. Robert N. Anthony and John Dearden, *Management Control Systems Text and Cases,* Irwin, Homewood, Illinois (1980).
4. John F. Rockart, Chief executives define their own data needs, *Harvard Business Review,* pp. 81-92, March-April (1979).
5. Igor Ansoff, *Corporate Strategy,* McGraw-Hill, New York (1965).
6. William Glueck, *Business Policy and Strategic Management,* 3rd edn., McGraw-Hill, New York (1980).

Table 3. Importance of CSF's: Industry Comparison

	Soft drink Industry (Bottler's)	Semi-Conductor Industry (Manufacturers)	Ferrous Metals Distribution Industry	Tax Preparation Industry
Basic R & D	PF[1]	MF[1]	NF[1]	NF[1]
New product development	SF	MF	PF	NF
Manufacturing	MF	MF	SF	NF
Distribution	MF	SF	MF	PF
Customer service	MF	SF	MF	MF
Advertising	SF	NF	NF	SF
Post sales service	SF	PF	PF	MF

[1]Classifications are for purposes of discussion.

Major factor (MF)—An activity or condition that has a significant impact on company or industry results. This factor is usually linked directly to profit performance, but other success measures may be employed.

Secondary factor (SF)—An activity or condition which has, in most cases, modest impact on a company's results. Analysis shows this factor has an indirect link to profit performance or other success criteria. The magnitude of the impact is obviously less than a "major factor."

Possible factor (PF)—An activity or condition that could influence a company or industry results but it is not likely. This category could also be utilized when analysis does not turn up sufficient data to warrant classification in the two previous categories (the importance is not clear or future impact is probable).

Non factor (NF)—This activity of condition has very little impact on the company or industry results. Analysis indicates that there is no historical data or future expectations that link this activity with profit performance or other success criteria.

Table 4.   Importance of CSF's: Firms—Semi-Conductor Industry

	National Semi-Conductor	Intel	Signetics	Texas Instruments
Basic R & D	PF[1]	MF[1]	PF[1]	SF[1]
New product development	SF	MF	SF	MF
Manufacturing	MF	MF	MF	MF
Distribution	MF	SF	SF	MF
Customer service	MF	SF	SF	MF
Advertising	PF	PF	PF	SF
Post sales service	NF	NF	NF	SF

[1]Classifications are for purposes of discussion.

Major factor (MF)—An activity or condition that has a significant impact on company or industry results. This factor is usually linked directly to profit performance, but other success measures may be employed.

Secondary factor (SF)—An activity or condition which has, in most cases, modest impact on a company's results. Analysis shows this factor has an indirect link to profit performance or other success criteria. The magnitude of the impact is obviously less than a "major factor."

Possible factor (PF)—An activity or condition that could influence a company or industry results but it is not likely. This category could also be utilized when analysis does not turn up sufficient data to warrant classification in the two previous categories (the importance is not clear or future impact is probable).

Non factor (NF)—This activity of condition has very little impact on the company or industry results. Analysis indicates that there is no historical data or future expectations that link this activity with profit performance or other success criteria.

7. Charles W. Hofer and Dan E. Schendel, *Strategy Formulation: Analytical Concepts,* West Publishing Company, St. Paul, Minn. (1978).

8. Arthur Thompson and A. J. Strickland, *Strategy Formulation and Implementation,* Business Publications Inc., Dallas, Texas (1980).

9. Michael E. Porter, *Competitive Strategy,* The Free Press, New York (1980).

10. Stephen C. South, Competitive advantage: the cornerstone of strategic thinking, *Journal of Business Strategy,* 1 (4), 15-25, Spring (1981).

11. Jerry L. Wall and Bong-Gon P. Shin, Seeking competitive information in *Business Policy and Strategic Mangement,* 3rd edn., pp. 144-153, McGraw-Hill, New York (1980).

12. Jerry L. Wall, What the competition is doing: you need to know, *Harvard Business Review,* 227, November-December (1974).

13. Robert R. Buchele, How to evaluate a firm, *California Management Review,* pp. 5-17, Fall (1962).

14. R. T. Lentz, Strategic capability: a concept and framework for analysis, *Academy of Management Journal,* 5 (2), 223-234 (1980).

15. Howard H. Stevenson, Defining strengths and weaknesses, *Sloan Management Review,* 17 (3), 51-68, Spring (1976).

16. Schoeffler *et al.,* Impact of strategic planning on profit performance. *Harvard Business Review,* pp. 137-145, March-April (1974).

17. Buzzell *et al.,* Market share: a key to profitability, *Harvard Business Review,* pp. 19-106, January-February (1975).

18. D. Ronald Daniel, Management information crisis, *Harvard Business Review,* pp. 110-119, September-October (1961).

19. Subash Jain, Self appraisal and environmental analysis in corporate planning. *Managerial Planning,* pp. 16-28, January-February (1979).

12

Operations vs. Strategy: Trading Tomorrow for Today

Abstract

There is constant pressure on operating management to produce ever-increasing annual profits regardless of long-term strategic implications. Long-range goals, however, often require resource commitments that may adversely affect profits in the current period, even though these objectives may provide significant returns in later years. Based on a study of six major corporations, an examination was made of the short/long-term trade-offs, the rationale for the trade-offs, and methods that may be employed to control the trade-offs.

Trade-offs. *The need to make trade-offs can arise at almost any level of the organization. Four categories of problems that most frequently arise include: (1) postponing capital outlays; (2) deferring operating expenses; (3) reducing operating expenses; and (4) other operating changes, especially price changes. Each of these trade-offs can be detrimental to achieving strategic objectives.*

Rationale. *Managers make trade-offs primarily because of how their performance is evaluated and secondarily because of an imbalance in emphasis on short-term goals in most organizations. Successful performance is measured in most organizations by both status and compensation.*

Control. *Trade-offs can be controlled by counterbalancing the tendency to emphasize the short term in decision making and limiting the frequency and severity of pressure on managers to achieve short-term earnings. Structural controls are the internal and external conditions that affect the organization and are difficult if not impossible to alter. Variable controls are the products of managerial decisions. The variable controls most frequently used are: (1) setting more realistic goals, (2) increasing the emphasis on long-term goals in the measurement of managerial performance, (3) increasing the awareness of long-term goals with lower-level managers, (4) stressing the importance of planning and review, and (5) changing managers when long-term strategies are changed.*

Operations vs. Strategy: Trading Tomorrow for Today

Robert L. Banks
Steven C. Wheelwright

The end of the year was approaching with frightening speed. Sales were off because of an unexpected downturn in the economy, and profits were below projection. The pressure was on from top management. "You'd better make your profit projections, George, or you'll never make the spring cuts," was how the boss had described the situation.

What to do? Only one thing was possible. Dramatically cut costs by laying off a third of the work force. If the downturn continues, George reasoned, we'll be in good shape to ride it out. If it isn't as bad as we think it will be, then after the holidays we can rehire many of the workers laid off. Most important, my division will make its last-quarter profit goals. Considering the kind of year it has been, that could mean a bonus and a promotion!

No doubt managers everywhere have sweated over this kind of pressure at one time or another and have reacted as well as they knew how in the face of adversity to salvage profits—and maybe, like George, even their careers. In this particular case, as so often happens, George was hailed as a hero for saving the company's profits, a significant feat in the light of top management's optimistic promises to stockholders and the financial community.

But George's decision turned out to have devastating consequences for his company later on. A crucial building block in the company's strategy had long been to remain nonunion in order to avoid the costs associated with stringent work rules, restrictive hiring and promotion covenants, wildcat strikes, and the like—problems which plagued most major competitors. But not long after George's Christmas layoff, angry workers held a representation election, and by May the company had been unionized—not just George's division, but the entire company. George had made his short-term profit goals, but in the process had traded away one of the company's strategic competitive advantages.

Continual Tug-of-War

While this example is extreme, the occurrence of detrimental tradeoffs is an everyday reality. In a study of six major U.S. companies, we documented numerous examples of short-term operating decisions that adversely affected long-term goal achievement. The tug-of-war between short-term and long-term goals is a dilemma that corporations face recurrently.

The conflict is basic. The attainment of long-range goals often involves resource commitments that may adversely affect profits in the current period, even though these investments may provide significant returns in later years. Additionally, achievement of long-range goals may require adherence to a specific strategy—such as a market, product, or labor relations strategy—that in certain economically difficult years might cause higher-than-normal expenses. In the short run, these expenses reduce profits; but, in the long run, they are "investments" designed to pay off.

There is constant pressure on operating management to produce ever-increasing annual profits regardless of long-term strategic implications. Sometimes the pressure is a result of overoptimistic promises made by top management to stockholders and to the financial community. At other times it is a matter of poor forecasting, either by the corporation or by the manager. Occasionally, a sister division fails to make its targets and another division must make up the difference in profits. However, regardless of the cause, the pressure is always there.

Our study shows that, compared with 10 or 15 years ago, there is growing awareness of the problem of short-term versus long-term conflicts in operating decisions—what we shall call, for ease of reference, the S/L trade-off. Our finding is consistent with the results of a recent study by the Conference Board.[1] [See the section on research methods at the end of this article.]

For one thing, S/L trade-offs are now more obvious than they used to be. Through the expansion and development of formal strategic planning processes during the past decade, top managers have become more aware of where their corporations should be going, and deviations from the prescribed course are more noticeable. For another, the consequences of inappropriate S/L trade-offs can be more significant as companies continue to grow in size and complexity. Managers receive greater authority and responsibility, especially in highly diversified firms, and decisions made favoring the short run over strategic goal achievement may have serious financial consequences.

In addition, it appears that the effects of unrelated S/L trade-offs can be cumulative. When viewed independently, many S/L trade-offs appear to have relatively mild consequences for a company. But even apparently minor S/L trade-offs may adversely affect a corporate strategy. Moreover, they can have a serious effect on the entire corporation. For instance, in the example about George, there had been earlier layoffs at certain divisions. George's decision provided the proverbial straw that broke the camel's back.

Many managers and planners we interviewed also feel that changes in the external business environment are occurring at a more rapid pace than in the past. These changes create increased pressure for short-term performance and make accurate forecasting more difficult. Compounding this problem, competition is U.S. and foreign markets seems greater. With slower growth rates in major

---

1. See Rochell O'Connor, *Planning under Uncertainty: Multiple Scenarios and Contingency Planning,* Conference Board Report No. 741 (1978), p. 23.

economies of the world, many companies find themselves having to compete more vigorously to meet short- and long-term goals than was the case in years past. This intensified competition stretches divisional management capabilities. As short-term profit commitments become more difficult to make, strategic objectives can suffer.

Where Trade-Offs Occur

The need to make trade-offs can arise at almost any level of the corporate structure and can affect a multitude of operating areas. In all of the six companies we studied, executives were able to contribute problematic examples of actual or potential S/L trade-offs. The problems can be divided into four categories, each of which we will discuss. For each category we will also give a detailed example of a trade-off situation. Sometimes, since the divisions are necessarily arbitrary, an example overlaps a couple of categories.

Postponing Capital Outlays

Capital expenditure programs are one of the most vulnerable areas for detrimental S/L trade-offs. The horizons for returns are more than a year off; yet the costs associated with implementing the programs can easily reduce near-term profits. Postponements can almost always free up capital and manpower resources needed to produce immediate operating profits.

Since almost any capital program is susceptible to this dilemma, we studied examples concerning new plant construction, additions to existing plant, new equipment purchases, upgrading of old equipment, production-process improvements, cost-reduction investments, and long-term product-development projects. A timely example is investing in energy efficiency. Capital projects involving needs like pollution control are highly vulnerable to the S/L trade-off problem, since the investments are generally capital-consuming rather than capital-generating. Consider this case:

One of the compaines studied recently faced the prospect of replacing several relatively new and very expensive steam boilers with more efficient ones, since the company had projected a doubling of its already sizable fuel costs over the next five years. The current boiler costs were acceptable. The division manager knew that if he waited to replace the boilers until their efficiency became a serious liability in three or four years, his operating profits would remain higher in the meantime and his record would look better.

On the other hand, waiting would significantly increase the long-term cost to the company because of inflation, declining cost efficiency, and the fact that competitors (whose boilers were aging anyway) planned to add more fuel-efficient equipment within two years. Consequently, a difficult S/L trade-off had to be made.

This particular example, fortunately, had a happy ending. The division manager chose to install the new boilers right away. But suppose that a division manager in a similar situation knew his tenure would be short (for instance, he might be expecting a promotion or a transfer). Then he would be strongly tempted to decide the other way.

Deferring Operating Expenses

Many operating expenses for the current period can be postponed without causing undue harm to long-term goals. But other operating expenses can be vital to the timely accomplishment of strategic objectives. It usually is easy for a manager to postpone such expenses, since they are directly under his or her control and are often not monitored closely, if at all.

Indeed, some managers we interviewed indicated that they always overbudgeted certain operating expenses to provide a contingency fund which could be shifted around if the need arose. Only one of the six companies tightly locked managers into budgets and required formal approval of any transfers of expenses from one budget category to another. In the other companies, managers reported postponing expenses related to manpower development, advertising and public relations, maintenance, research and development, and marketing and product research.

Product-development expenses are a particularly choice target for cuts, leading frequently to detrimental S/L trade-offs. For example:

- At one company, division managers often postponed small product-development expenses, regardless of the possible significance to a marketing strategy, in order to achieve profit goals. However, these managers did not defer costs for larger projects under their responsibility because the latter had greater corporatewide visibility.

- In another company, one with several lines of well-established products, managers often had to decide whether to continue to milk existing products for maximum profit or make the commitment required to develop new products. The latter meant some sacrifice of current earnings.

    The historical tendency at this company had been for the managers to favor current products, because managerial performance was measured largely on the basis of short-term profits. Only recently had the company begun to substantially fund and require performance on the development of new products.

- In a third company, the inertia of the status quo was so strong that, in order to ensure successful development of new markets for an old product line, management had to create a new division rather than attempt to encourage product development in the existing organization. Managers simply were unwilling to trade off any part of the present for the future (though of course they did not put it so baldly).

Reducing Operating Expenses

Expenses vital to long-term goals can be pared down as well as postponed. From a strategic standpoint, this can be equally dangerous. An expense often may be postposed without forgoing the associated benefits forever. A delay in incurring the expense slows down the product development, engineering, marketing, or other objective, but does not kill it.

On the other hand, eliminating some expenses in order to salvage profits can do irreparable damage to a company's position. In the example at the beginning, George translated pressure for short-term profit into layoffs that ultimately cost his company a significant strategic advantage in labor relations. In our study, we came across other such examples in marketing, field sales, quality control, and materials purchasing.

One area that can be of critical strategic importance is customer service; yet expenses for future improvements in service are all too easy to cut when the pressure for earnings is on. In an industrial products company, for example, customer service might include having the engineering staff work closely with customers on equipment installation and operation. If this extra effort is part of the company's long-term competitive advantage, cutbacks in it can permanently damage customer relations. So, too, can cuts in warranty terms and claims handling.

Another example is the classic production-versus-marketing trade-off, either minimizing inventories to lower costs or increasing them to improve product selection and delivery time. Again, in a hotel or restaurant chain, cuts in staffing and training to achieve short-term profits can be fatal in the long run. Any such moves can easily drive customers away and into the arms of a waiting competitor.

Other Operating Changes

Current profits can be improved at the expense of long-term goals in still other ways. Common methods include changes in the product mix, delivery, suppliers, marketing strategy, and pricing (both market pricing and intracompany-transfer pricing).

Price changes, in particular, are a simple way to make a trade-off. For example, one division manager's market was extremely sensitive to price changes, and management tightly controlled pricing actions by means of a multilayered approval process. Nevertheless, the manager admitted to having successfully used price changes to boost sales and reduce inventories, improving his current operations but hurting customer service and goodwill.

Price increases can disproportionately affect market share. On the other hand, price decreases can mistakenly signal changes in strategic direction to competitors. Depending on the company and its industry, price reductions can even bring down the wrath of the federal government.

Why Managers Make Trade-offs

When a division manager decides to favor short-term profits over long-term strategic goals, he has likely been influenced by two considerations. The first, and perhaps more influential, is the manner in which his or her performance is measured by the corporation. The second is a combination of a clear lack of balance between the short and long run as emphasized in corporate communications, linkages between the long-range plan and the operating budget, and the general "culture" of the company.

Evaluation of Performance

While our study did not delve deeply into psychological factors, it is clear that performance evaluation is a key motivating factor in S/L trade-offs.[2] Naturally, managers are motivated to take actions that will reflect favorably on them personally, either immediately or in the future. Division managers at major corporations hold their positions largely because they have succeeded over time in managing their tasks the way the company decreed they should. They are very aware of how success is measured in their organization in terms of both status (e.g., peer evaluation, supervisor evaluation, rank, perquisites) and compensation (e.g., salary, commission, or bonus).

At the companies studied, it appears that the more important of the two performance evaluation motivators is status. Trade-offs appear to be made not so much with remuneration in mind (although it is important in a few instances) as with a careful eye on how the decision will be viewed by peers and superiors.

It comes as no surprise that, in general, the more a company emphasizes performance in the short run as a determinant for reward, the greater the tendency for managers to favor the near term. However, if a company allocates equal emphasis to both short-term and long-term goals, decisions appear to put the short and long terms in better balance. Two of the companies studied fell in the latter category and benefited from such a perspective:

---

2. For a detailed analysis of executive compensation and performance evaluation, see Alfred Rappaport, "Executive Incentives vs. Corporate Growth," HBR [*Harvard Business Review*] July-August 1978, p. 81.

- One assigned specific responsibilities to managers for strategic goal accomplishment (along with operating responsibilities) and measured the managers frequently on performance in both areas.
- The other company divided the annual bonus for a manager between specific strategic and operational objectives (e.g., 60% of bonus on operational goals; 40% on strategic ones). It also examined the manager's performance on both measures periodically during the operating year.

Imbalance in Emphasis

In the absence of other controls, there appears to be a natural tendency for operating managers to lean toward achieving short-term goals instead of long-term ones. Short-term goals are visible and easily comprehended. Clearly, they become dominant unless firm measures are taken to put them in perspective.

In most of the companies studied, this perspective is not fostered in communications. Division and lower-level managers are not always fully aware of their corporation's strategic aims. More important, the managers do not always understand exactly how their operations fit into the company's grand plans.

Methods for communicating a balanced emphasis can take a variety of forms, such as publications about goals and meetings with upper-and lower-level managers to discuss strategy. Whatever the method, several managers told us that "well-informed managers make good decisions, decisions that take into account the long-term good of the corporation."

Managerial perspectives are influenced also by the linkages between operating budgets and long-range financial plans. Considerable research has been done on the relative merits of loose and tight linkages.[3] We find that a tight link between the two appears to favor a balanced decision process.

The question of linkage usually arose during our interviews when we were probing weaknesses in planning processes. Generally,

---

3. For example, see John K. Shank, Edward G. Niblock, and William T. Sandalls, Jr., "Balance 'Creativity' and 'Practicality' in Formal Planning," HBR January-February 1973, p. 87.

the long-range plan is the essential financial manifestation of the corporation's strategic objectives and is its intended accomplishment over a span of five or ten years. The operating budget, meanwhile, does double duty. It is the operating manager's road map for a small part of that time span. Also, it is an instrument to assist in the accomplishment of the long-term financial performance levels described in the long-range plan.

However, at three of the companies examined, the operating budgets were not developed as a specific part of the long-term plan. In fact, in one case, the operating budget was developed and locked into operations before the long-range plan (including the current year) was finalized.

Operating managers indicated to us that when the operating budget was developed peripherally to the long-range financial plan, they found it difficult to relate their performance to the company's long-term goals and objectives. In short, they lacked a sense of belonging to the larger and more important effort of attaining the strategic objectives.

Finally, imbalance in short- and long-term emphasis is affected by top management pressure to produce current earnings. By applying pressure, top management may virtually force division-level managers to make S/L trade-offs that may have adverse results later. In the companies studied, a division suffered from top-down pressure about earnings most commonly when a sister division did not perform according to plan, leading top management to attempt to squeeze more profits from other divisions.

Controlling Trade-offs

The number and importance of S/L trade-offs that managers make depend on two conditions, one given and one the direct result of top management action.

Structural controls are the "facts of life"—the internal and external conditions that affect managerial perceptions. Some of them cannot be altered at all; others can be altered over time. Examples of structural controls outside the organization are the capital intensity of the industry, rates of technological change, rates of new-product introduction, end-consumer product orientation, industry maturity, and other factors. Examples of internal structural controls are the nature of the organization (e.g., the formal and informal power structure) and the basic culture or operating climate (e.g., workload norms and peer pressures).

In short, structural controls are the "givens" under which a company elects to operate, and they appear to determine the frequency with which managers encounter significant S/L trade-off decisions.

By contrast, *variable* controls are the product of managerial decisions. We found many of them in our study. It became clear that the companies most satisfied with their S/L trade-off balance had systematically considered the extent, type, and basic causes of trade-offs likely to occur and then had tailored their selection of variable controls to the needs of the situation. Before taking action the top executives usually considered questions like the following:

1. Is the necessity for S/L trade-offs recognized as a major problem at the company? If not, is it because executives are unaware of the occurrence of such trade-offs, or because they already have sufficient controls on them?

2. Do controls exist to minimize the likelihood of detrimental S/L trade-offs?

3. Is top management getting the proper information it needs regarding both the long- and short-term consequences of the alternatives faced by division managers?

4. Does the planning and review system motivate managers to keep long-term corporate goals in sight?

5. Does the planning and review process of each division take into account the structural controls that affect decision making there?

To assist managers in assessing their own corporate situations, the accompanying *Exhibit* shows the many types of variable controls observed and indicates at what stages of planning and review development the controls are most effective. The designated development stages are somewhat arbitrary, but they serve to identify the course of evolution that companies are likely to experience and they offer some insight into the uses of variable controls. As for the controls themselves, they can be grouped under five headings.

Exhibit

Most Effective Controls on S/L Trade-offs

Method of control or influence	Typical characteristics of stage of planning				
	1. Preplanning	II. Initial	III. Intermediate	IV. More complete	V. Advanced
	Top management does strategy; Narrow product/market segmentation; Largely centralized decision making; Some pressure from division level for long-term planning	Long-range planning largely financial; Staff develops system; does most of work; Some lower management resistance; Planning accompanies decentralization	Long-range planning system in place and accepted; More emphasis on issues; Large staff involvement; Not used at lower management levels for decision making	Decisions made and performance evaluated according to accomplishment of plan; High commitment to plan; Short- and long-term performance tied directly to plan in reviews; Line management does planning; Postaudits utilized	Explicit contingency planning; Tactical operating plans used; Lower management levels involved in planning; System encourages creativity in identifying opportunities; Rolling financial forecasts
Establishment of realistic goals					
Top management revises and adjusts submitted budget figures as needed to assure realism	▓		▓	▓	▓
Incorporate economic-cycle predictions in budgets to avoid undue profit pressure				▓	▓
Incorporate historical-trend analysis in budget-setting process	▓		▓	▓	▓
Establish appropriate time horizons for fixed portion of budget and keep up to date			▓	▓	▓
Allow some flexibility in budget beyond fixed time horizons for unforeseen events				▓	▓
Establishment of management performance measures that reflect S/L considerations					
Split goals, performance evaluation, rewards into discrete short- and long-term components					▓
Establish quarterly performance reviews for accomplishment of long-term strategic goals					▓
Perform postaudits on capital expenditures and other projects	▓		▓	▓	▓

Limit time horizons on capital spending authorizations to minimize postponements

Increased managerial knowledge of long-term strategy goals

Increase lower-level management involvement in strategy formulation

Increase discussions about strategic goals between top- and lower-level management

Line management develops long- and short-range plans

Hold explicit discussions on S/L trade-offs and the need for balanced decision making

Establishment of planning and review process elements that reflect S/L trade-off considerations

Top management reviews lower-level decision alternatives and recommendations

Analyze industry, other long-term trends to judge the "reasonableness" of plan

Increase linkage between operating budget and first year of strategic long-term plan

Use planning process as integral part of management decision-making process

Utilize monthly closings and reviews to minimize adverse S/L trade-offs

Disseminate planning "issues" from the top down; build issue-based plans bottom up

Develop explicit tactical operating plans for operational goal accomplishment

Use explicit contingency plans with well-defined "trigger points" for implementation

Implementation of organization and staffing changes

Create new strategic business units to focus on strategic goals

Undertake long-term commitments and joint ventures with other firms

Replace managers who consistently miss achievement of operating goals

Change managers when long-range strategies change

Realistic goals

The most frequent situation in which detrimental S/L trade-offs occur arises when an operating manager fails to meet the budget goals agreed on for his or her division or cost center. In our study, several companies found that one way to reduce the frequency of such trade-offs was simply to establish more realistic goals for the mangers, either during the initial goal setting or in later periods when goals or plans of action are adjusted.[4] Indeed, as is evident from the exhibit, establishing realistic goals is the step that appears most applicable to companies in any stage of development of their planning processes.

More realistic goals can be developed in several ways. Increased accuracy in the budget numbers themselves can be achieved by incorporating economic-cycle predictions and historical-trend analysis in setting budgets. Additionally, since budgets are little more than sophisticated guesses of what will happen in the future, an allowance of some flexibility for unforeseen problems can ease short-term pressures on managers.

Most businesses can predict accurately for, say, a few months away, but beyond that the crystal ball gets hazy. Several companies studied compensated for this difficulty by making a short portion of the budget—for instance, three months—inflexible but by allowing for some fluctuation in performance beyond that time. Concurrently, the budget was updated on a regular basis.

Finally, at a few companies the "final" budget numbers submitted by divisions were altered by top management to reflect either perceived optimism or conservatism on the part of division managers. In one case, the chief executive even lowered the budget projections for presentation to the board of directors while leaving the higher numbers as goals for the divisional personnel.

Longer-Range Evaluations

Another way of minimizing detrimental S/L trade-offs is to increase the emphasis on long-term goals in measurement of managerial performance. This helps to compensate for the inevitable pressure to

---

4. See Ronald N. Paul, Neil B. Donovan, and James W. Taylor, "The Reality Gap in Strategic Planning," HBR May-June 1978, p. 124.

produce short-term results. In the goal-setting process, for example, objectives can be split into discrete short- and long-term portions, with performance evaluation and rewards likewise divided.

To ensure performance on long-range objectives, management can conduct milestone reviews on a regular basis (e.g., quarterly) along with normal operating reviews. Management can also review important capital projects to ensure they are developed according to plan. In addition, it can make audits to verify the timely expenditure of funds and conduct "postaudits" to examine returns on the projects after they are completed.

Several companies in our study impose time limits on capital spending authorizations in order to prevent postponements. If a manager does not spend the funds authorized before the deadline, he or she must reapply for funds.

Awareness of Strategies

Closely related to the establishment of performance measures that reflect both long- and short-term considerations are attempts to make lower-level managers knowledgeable about long-term corporate goals and how operating managers contribute to the achievement of those goals. The underlying philosophy for these actions appears to be that good managers will more likely make appropriate trade-offs when they have a sound understanding of long-term plans.

To achieve this increased involvement, the companies emphasize the development of strategic and operating plans by line management and not by planning staffs. Additionally, some managements attempt to involve lower-level managers more in creating long-range plans (normally the lower levels merely concentrate on short-term budgets).

To improve communications, some companies increase the number of meetings between top and lower-level managers to discuss the corporate goals and how each person fits into the grand plan and to focus attention on S/L trade-off problems and the need for balanced decisions.

Planning & Review

The companies in our study use the planning and review process to stimulate better S/L trade-off decisions. Companies that have reached the intermediate development stage (see the exhibit) are the ones most likely to develop more balance in this way. The actions they take can be classified as follows:

Philosophical—Management may stress the use of planning as an integral part of managing the business rather than as an adjunct of managing per se. It may evaluate the overall "reasonableness" of the long-range plan by analyzing long-term industrial and other trends. It may set a policy of reviewing managers' recommended actions on given decisions as well as the alternatives considered.

Specific—At a more workaday level, management may take advantage of monthly closings and reviews to keep short-range concerns from dominating S/L trade-offs. It may increase the linkages between the first year of the long-range plan and the operating budget. It may develop explicit how-to tactical plans to ensure accomplishment of goals. It may design carefully delineated contingency plans with clearly defined "trigger points" for switching to alternate programs and strategies.

Staffing Changes

As pointed out earlier, the managements in our study do not try to influence S/L trade-offs by changing the organization scheme—it takes too long. However, management can make headway with revisions and variations of the organization plan. As also noted, one company, in an attempt to focus more narrowly on objectives when conditions changed, set up new strategic business units to manage new projects instead of working through the old organizations.

Similarly, this company changed managers when the long-term strategies of an operation changed, a move which helped avoid a tendency to emphasize historical trade-off considerations and the status quo. Another obvious—but not always used—action was to replace managers who consistently missed their operating goals. Poor performance tends to increase short-term emphasis in decision trade-offs, and the longer such performance continues, the higher the probability of poor decisions.

Finally, one of the managements set up joint ventures and made other long-range commitments with outside companies. By so doing, it limited the options and possibilities for making detrimental S/L trade-offs. For instance, the schedule of production commitments to a joint venture might make it difficult for a manager to manipulate his budget for the sake of a strong short-term profit showing.

Conclusion

The tendency toward achieving short-run gains at the expense of timely accomplishment of long-term strategic objectives is a significant and surprisingly common problem, our study shows. Clearly, though, there are steps which top executives can take to identify the extent of the problem in their companies and to ensure that managers make decisions with a view toward the proper balance between long- and short-term goals.

We have described some of these steps. Which one or ones should be selected depends on the relative maturity of a company's planning and review process. Some of the steps help to counterbalance the tendency to emphasize the short term in decision making. Others limit the frequency and severity of pressure on managers to achieve short-term earnings regardless of long-term considerations.

Together, these steps provide a basic pool of tactics for managers to use in developing their plans of action. There is a "George" at every company, but he *can* be encouraged to keep the company's long-term objectives in sight when making operating decisions.

Research Methods

This article is based primarily on in-depth interviews with managers and planners at different organization levels in six major U.S. companies. We chose the interview approach because it provides the best opportunity to examine many examples of short-term and long-term conflicts in decisions made under widely varying circumstances but within the limited time frame of the study.

We selected the companies to provide a broad sampling of current planning and management review systems, along with a diversity of such significant characteristics as capital intensity, nature of industry, nature of production process, type of products sold, type of market served, organizational structure, and competitive strength. Because of the subjective nature of our interviews, we could not make statistical comparisons of the companies, their planning processes, or their relative success in their industries.

Companies participating in the study included two natural resource-based organizations, each serving a different industry; a large (more than $10 billion in sales) diversified corporation with worldwide distribution of products to industrial and consumer markets; a large diversified company serving electronics-related markets; a medium-sized industrial products company; and a smaller ($200 million sales) manufacturer of limited lines of consumer and industrial products. Since certain of the data gathered are confidential, only those data which preserve anonymity are included in the article.

In the interviews, we focused on the S/L trade-off problem largely at the business level—that is, at the level where a whole area of related products is managed. However, some of our talks concerned planning at the corporate or strategic level and the *activity* or *functional* levels.[5]

The business level corresponds closely to the division level at the participating companies and includes managers with responsibility for the profit center of significant-cost center. The corporate or strategic level is where the corporation's long-term strategy is determined; at some of the companies studied this means the chief executive, at others it means the group vice president. The activity or functional level (e.g., plant or marketing managers) is where most decision making becomes shorter term and operational in nature.

In addition, we held interviews at two staff levels; the corporate staff level, which includes high-level planners and staff consultants, and the functional staff level, which includes mostly persons (e.g.,

---

5. See Richard F. Vancil, "Strategy Formulation in Complex Organizations," Sloan Management Review, Winter 1976, p. 1.

division controllers) who assist division managers with staff responsibilities. In total, we conducted more than 50 interviews.

To provide information beneficial to corporate managers, we have attempted to pinpoint in what areas and under what circumstances adverse S/L trade-offs are likely to be made by identifying examples of several different types of trade-off decisions at the companes. In addition, we have examined those elements of the planning and review process, as well as structural constraints imposed by the industry and the organization, which work to minimize the number or suboptimal trade-offs actually made. From this information, we have formulated recommendations as to how corporations in various stages of planning and review might approach S/L trade-off problems, determine their significance, and design actions to improve decision making.

This study was funded by an Associate of the Harvard Business School, the Mead Corporation. We gratefully acknowledge its assistance.

IV.
Implementing
Strategic Management

Introduction

The strategic plan comes to life in the implementation stage. For a plan to be effective and accepted by the organization, implementation considerations need to be an integral part of any planning effort. Each step of the strategic planning process has implementation considerations that should be addressed as they arise, rather than after a written plan is completed. Incorporating these steps along the way makes placing the plan into action more feasible. The final implementation involves the initiation of action plans designed at the functional level that are consistent with plans for the entire organization.

Integrating Action Plans

Once the gaps have been minimized in the strategic-business-modeling stage of the model, the planning effort should be delegated to functional units of the organization. Each unit should develop a detailed narrative functional plan that fits the organizational mission and strategic objectives. Once the narratives are approved by the CEOF (chief executive officer function), these functional plans should then be completed with forecast/budget data and timetables for execution. All functional plans then need to be shared among all departments and a consensus reached regarding the allocation of corporate resources to the various functional units.

An example of this integration process is described in "Strategic Planning and the Marketing Process," our first article in this section. In it the author shows how the marketing plan — an important part of every firm's success — should be integrated with the organization's strategic plan. The article discusses elements of environmental scanning and, in particular, how the marketing plan should be designed to take the best advantage of opportunities as they arise in the market.

Integrating with Organizational Activities

The most important test of the success of a strategic plan is the degree to which organizational members integrate the plan into their everyday actions. Effective implementation involves activity at all levels of the organization aimed at bringing about the successful completion of the stated mission of the organization. Managers especially need to be able to refer to the strategic plan for direction on daily decisions. Although guidelines for every decision will not be provided by the strategic plan, a successful plan should serve as a source of direction.

The integration of the strategic plan on a daily basis by all employees is the main focus of "Strategy Follows Structure: Developing Distinctive Skills," our second article in this section. In it the author suggests that strategy evolves from inside the organization from the cumulative effect of many informal actions and decisions taken daily over the years by many employees. Top companies have a distinctive set of "skills" that are integrated into all activities of the organization to such a degree that they become an integral part of the organization's culture.

Keeping Strategic Planning Effective

Many strategic plans fail to be successfully implemented. Many plans end when the planning process ends and a formal written planning document is completed. The document is simply stuffed into a drawer and forgotten. Visionary leaders are needed to keep the planning effort viable. The third article in this section, "Visionary Leadership and Strategic Management," lists five styles of visionary leadership and discusses ways to train managers to become visionary leaders.

The last article in this section, "Becoming PALs: Pooling, Allying, and Linking Across Companies," shows organizations how to improve their ability to compete without adding internal capacity: by pooling resources with other organizations, by forming strategic alliances for exploiting opportunities, and by linking their systems with those of other organizations.

13

Strategic Planning and the Marketing Process

Abstract

Every organization must evolve both a corporate strategy and a marketing process if it is to survive and grow. The environment undergoes rapid change, and the organization must fit its objectives, strategy, structure, and systems into a viable relationship with the environment. Management is the entrepreneurial agent that interprets market needs and translates them into products and services; it does this by planning strategies and by marketing.

The strategic-planning process describes the steps taken at the corporate and divisional levels to develop long-run strategies for survival and growth. This provides the context for the marketing process, which describes the steps taken at the product and market levels to develop viable marketing positions and programs. The strategic planning process consists of defining the organization's mission, objectives, and goals; a growth strategy; and portfolio plans. The process then calls for developing a set of objectives such as sales and market-share growth, profitability, and innovation to support the organization's mission. These objectives should be hierarchical, quantitative, realistic, and consistent.

To achieve growth, the organization must identify market opportunities where it would enjoy a differential advantage over competitors.

Finally, strategic planning must define, for each strategic business unit in the organization's portfolio, whether it will be built, maintained, harvested, or terminated.

Within this context, the marketing process can be enacted. The first step consists of generating, evaluating, and recommending marketing opportunities. For any sound opportunity, the next step is to examine the product/market structure and identify the best target market. The third step is to decide on the best competitive position and marketing mix strategy for the organization within the target market. The fourth step calls for designing major marketing management systems for effectively carrying out the intended marketing effort.

Strategic Planning and the Marketing Process

Philip Kotler

In trying to cope with an ever-changing and challenging environment, modern companies use two key processes to build their future. The first is strategic planning, which enables top management to determine what businesses it wants to emphasize. The second is the marketing process, which enables the company to proceed in a systematic way to identify and turn specific opportunities into profitable businesses. Although companies differ considerably in the degree to which they use these two processes, the most outstanding companies use both.

An organization's performance in the marketplace depends on the degree of creative alignment between the organization and its environment. The ideal organization examines its environment for opportunities, sets appropriate objectives, develops a strategy to achieve them, builds a framework to carry out these objectives, and designs management systems to support the organization's ability to carry out its strategy.

Of all the elements in the picture, the environment is the one that changes the fastest. Even bringing everything into alignment

Reprinted by permission from the author and from *Business* Magazine. "Strategic Planning and the Marketing Process," by Philip Kotler, May-June 1980.

with this year's environment is not enough. A sophisticated corporation such as IBM or Xerox will attempt to forecast what its business environment will be, say, five years ahead. Given this environmental forecast, it will set objectives that describe where it wants to be then. It will then formulate a strategy to achieve these objectives in that time frame. It will begin to alter the organization and its systems so that these will support the new strategy, rather than act as a drag on its fulfillment.

Although environments change, not all industries and companies are exposed to the same rate of environmental change. Some companies operate in a fairly *stable environment;* other companies operate in a *slowly evolving environment;* and still others operate in a *turbulent environment.* It seems that companies will increasingly find themselves operating in turbulent environments, and this will call for much more strategic flexibility.

In the face of a rapidly changing environment, companies need to operate an intelligence system that continually monitors major developments and trends in the environment. Each development should be assessed as to its implications for company planning and marketing decision making. Some trends and developments will represent threats to the company; others will represent opportunities; and still others will represent both. It is important that managers in charge of various divisions, products, and markets not only recognize the major threats and the major opportunities that surround their business but take steps to deal with them.

Not all threats warrant the same attention or concern. Managers should assess each threat according to two dimensions: (1) its potential severity as measured by the amount of money the company would lose if the threat materialized and (2) its probability of occurrence.

Similarly, not all opportunities are equally attractive. An opportunity can be assessed in terms of two basic dimensions: (1) its potential attractiveness as measured by the amount of profit it might yield to an average company and (2) the probability that this particular company will be able to outdo its competitors in carrying out this venture. Furthermore, management may want to dismiss certain financially attractive opportunities if they are unattractive on social grounds.

Each business unit can seek to better its situation by moving toward its major opportunities and away from its major threats. With respect to opportunities, the firm must carefully appraise their quality. There is a whole profession of "futurologists" who conjure up wonderful products and services the public needs. Levitt has cautioned business executives to judge opportunities carefully:

> "There can be a need, but no market; or a market, but no customer; or a customer, but no salesman. For instance, there is a great need for massive pollution control, but not really a market at present. And there is a market for new technology in education, but no customer really large enough to buy the products. Market forecasters who fail to understand these concepts have made spectacular miscalculations about the apparent opportunities in these and other fields, such as housing and leisure products."[1]

In general, management has to pay attention to the key concepts of *market evolution* and *strategic fit.* All markets undergo evolutionary development marked by changing customer needs, technologies, competitors, channels, and laws. The firm should be looking out of a *strategic window* watching these changes and assessing the requirements for continued success in each market.[2] There is only a limited period when the fit between the requirements of a particular market and the firm's competencies is at an optimum. At these times the strategic window is open, and the firm should be investing in this market. In some subsequent period the firm will find that the evolutionary path of this market is such that it can no longer be effective and efficient in serving this market. It should then consider disinvesting and shifting its resources to areas of growing opportunity.

The major processes that a company uses to adapt to its environment are summarized in Exhibit 1. The company gathers information on broad macroeconomic forces, publics, competitors,

---

1. Theodore Levitt, "The New Markets—Think Before You Leap," *Harvard Business Review,* May-June 1969, pp. 53-67 (esp. pp. 53-54).

2. See Derek F. Abell, "Strategic Windows," *Journal of Marketing,* July 1978, pp. 21-26.

marketing channels, markets, and target markets. This information plays an essential role within the company in carrying out two major adaptive processes, namely, the strategic-planning process and the marketing process.

Strategic Planning

Strategic planning is the managerial process of developing and maintaining a strategic fit between the organization and its changing marketing opportunities. It relies on developing a clear company mission, objectives and goals, a growth strategy, and product portfolio plans.

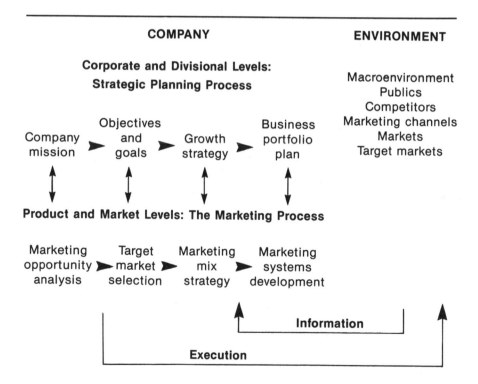

Exhibit 1: Strategic-Planning Process and the Marketing Process

Company Mission

An organization exists to accomplish something in the larger environment. Its specific purpose or mission is usually clear at the beginning. Over time, however, one or more things happen. Its mission may become unclear as the organization grows and develops new products and markets. Or the mission may remain clear but some managers may no longer be interested in it. Or the mission may remain clear but may lose its appropriateness because of new conditions in the environment.

When management senses that the organization is drifting, it is time to renew the search for purpose. It is time to ask the following questions:[3] *What is our business? Who is the customer? What is value to the customer? What will our business be? What should our business be?* These simple-sounding questions are among the most difficult the company will ever have to answer. Successful business firms continuously raise these questions and answer them thoughtfully and thoroughly.

More and more organizations are developing formal *mission statements* to answer these questions. A well-worked-out mission statement provides corporate personnel with a shared sense of opportunity, direction, significance, and achievement.

Unfortunately, it is not easy to write an effective company mission statement. Some organizations will spend a year or two before they come up with a satisfactory statement about the purpose of their firm. In the process they will discover a lot about themselves and their latent opportunities.

The company's mission statement should serve it for many years. The company mission is not something that should be revised every few years in response to environmental changes or new unrelated opportunities. On the other hand, sometimes a company has to reconsider its mission if it no longer works or if it does not define an optimal course that the company can follow.

---

3. See Peter Drucker, *Management: Tasks, Responsibilities, Practices* (New York, Harper & Row, Pub., 1973), Chap. 7.

Company Objectives and Goals

The company's mission should be defined into a finer set of supporting objectives for each level of management. Each manager should know his or her objectives and be responsible for their accomplishment. This system is known as *management by objectives.*

As an illustration, the International Minerals and Chemical Corporation is in a number of businesses, among them the fertilizer business. The fertilizer division does not say that its mission is to produce fertilizer. Instead, it says that its mission is "to fight world hunger." This mission leads to a definite hierarchy of objectives.[4] The mission to fight world hunger leads to the company objective of increasing agricultural productivity. Agricultural productivity in turn can be increased by researching new fertilizers that promise higher yields. But research is expensive and requires improved profits to plow back into research programs. So a major company objective becomes "profit improvement."

Now profits can be improved by increasing the sales of current products, reducing current costs, or both. Sales can be increased by increasing the company's market share in the domestic market and entering new foreign markets. These two objectives are adopted by the marketing department as its current marketing objectives.

The next step is to develop marketing strategies to support these marketing objectives. To increase its domestic market share, the company will increase its product's availability and promotion. To enter new foreign markets, the company will cut prices and concentrate on large farms. These are the broad marketing strategies.

Each marketing strategy will be spelled out in greater detail for different marketing specialists within the marketing department. For example, increasing the product's availability will be given not only to the sales force as an objective for which they have to find a sales strategy but also to the advertising department as an objective for which they have to find an advertising strategy. The increased

---

4. For a useful discussion of objectives setting, see Charles H. Granger, "The Hierarchy of Objectives," *Harvard Business Review,* May-June 1964, pp. 63-74.

sales objective will also be turned into manufacturing objectives, financial objectives, and personnel objectives for these respective departments. In this way the mission of the firm becomes translated into a specific set of objectives for the current period.

To determine whether the department was successful, all the objectives have to be turned into specific quantitative *goals.* The objective "increase our market share" is not as satisfactory as "increase our market share to 15 percent by the end of the second year." Managers use the term *goals* to describe an objective that has been made highly specific with respect to *magnitude* and *time.* Turning the objectives into goals facilitates the process of management planning and control.

Company Growth Strategy

Among the various objectives that companies adopt, growth is one of the most common. Companies want to grow in sales, profits, and other dimensions. To accomplish this, companies have to select a target growth rate and formulate a strategy for achieving it.

Growth comes about in two ways. It is achieved through managing current products for growth and adding new products to fill the remaining growth gap. We will examine a particular company to determine how it can systematically search for growth opportunities with its current products and possible new products.

Modern Publishing Company (name disguised) publishes a leading health magazine that has a monthly circulation of three hundred thousand copies. The company's marketing environment is changing rapidly in terms of consumer interests, new competitors, and rising publishing costs. It is attempting to formulate a systematic plan for company growth during the next ten years.

A growth strategy can be generated by a company by moving through three levels of analysis. The first level identifies those opportunities available to the company in its current sphere of operations *(intensive growth opportunities).* The second level identifies those opportunities available through integration with other parts of this marketing channel system *(integrative growth opportunities).* The third level identifies those opportunities lying outside the current marketing channel system *(diversification growth opportunities).*

Intensive growth.   Intensive growth makes sense if a company has not fully exploited the opportunities in its current products and markets. Ansoff has proposed a useful device for generating ideas for intensive growth opportunities, a *product/market expansion matrix.*[5] This matrix, shown in Exhibit 2, focuses on three major types of intensive growth opportunities:

1. *Market penetration consists of the company's seeking increased sales for its current products in its current markets through more aggressive marketing effort.* This includes three possibilities:

   a. Modern can encourage current subscribers to increase their *purchase quantity* by giving gift subscriptions to friends.

   b. Modern can try to *attract away competitors' customers* by offering lower subscription rates or promoting its magazine as being superior to other health magazines.

   c. Modern can try to *convert new prospects* who do not now read health magazines but who have the same profile as current readers.

2. *Market development consists of the company's seeking increased sales by taking its current products into new markets.* This includes three possibilities:

   a. Modern can distribute its magazine in *new geographical markets*—regional, national, or international—where it has not been available.

   b. Modern can try to make the magazine attractive to new types of individual readers by developing new features that appeal to these segments.

   c. Modern can try to sell its magazine to new types of institutional subscribers, such as hospitals, physicians' offices, and health clubs.

3. *Product development consists of the company's seeking increased sales by developing new or improved products for its current markets.* This includes three possibilities:

---

5. H. Igor Ansoff, "Strategies for Diversification," *Harvard Business Review,* September-October 1957, pp. 113-124.

	Existing products	New products
Existing markets	1. Market penetration	2. Product development
New markets	3. Market development	4. Diversification

Exhibit 2: Product/Market Expansion Matrix

---

  a. Modern can develop one or more new health magazines that will appeal to the present readers of its health magazine.
  b. Modern can create different *regional versions* of its health magazine to increase its appeal.
  c. Modern can develop an abbreviated cassette edition of its monthly magazine as an alternative for certain markets that prefer listening to reading.

Integrative growth.   Integrative growth makes sense if a company's basic industry has a strong growth outlook and/or the company can increase its profitability, efficiency, or control by moving backward, forward, or horizontally with the industry. Three possibilities can be defined as follows:

  1. *Backward integration consists of a company's seeking ownership or increased control of its supply systems.* Modern might consider buying a paper supply company or a printing company to increase its control over supplies.
  2. *Forward integration consists of a company's seeking ownership or increased control of its distribution systems.* Modern might see an advantage in buying some magazine wholesaler businesses or subscription agencies.
  3. *Horizontal integration consists of a company's seeking ownership or increased control of some of its competitors.* Modern might consider acquiring other health magazines or health magazine publishing companies.

Diversification growth.   Diversification growth makes sense if a company's marketing channel system does not show much additional opportunity for growth or profit, or if the opportunities outside the present marketing system are superior. Diversification does not mean that the company will take up any opportunity that comes along. The company would attempt to identify fields that make use of its distinctive competences or help it overcome a particular problem. There are three broad types of diversification moves:

1. *Concentric diversification consists of the company's seeking to add new products that have technological and/or marketing synergies with the existing product line; these products will normally appeal to new classes of customers.* Modern, for example, might consider starting a paperback division to take advantage of its network of magazine distributors.

2. *Horizontal diversification consists of the company's seeking to add new products that could appeal to its current customers though technologically unrelated to its current product line.* For example, Modern might decide to open up a series of health clubs in the hope that readers of its health magazine would become club members.

3. *Conglomerate diversification consists of the company's seeking to add new products that have no relationship to the company's current technology, products, or markets; these products will normally appeal to new classes of customers.* Modern might want to enter new business areas, such as real estate, hotel management, and fast-food service.

Thus we see that a company can systematically identify growth opportunities through application of a marketing systems framework, looking first at current product/market opportunities, then at opportunities in other parts of the marketing channel system, and finally at relevant opportunities outside the system.

Company Portfolio Plan

After management examines the company's various growth opportunities, it is in a better position to make decisions with respect to its current product lines. Management must evaluate all of the company's current businesses so that it can decide which to build, maintain, phase down, or phase out. Its job is to keep refreshing the company's portfolio of businesses by withdrawing from poorer businesses and adding promising new ones.

Management's first step is to identify the key businesses making up the company. These can be called strategic business units (SBUs). An SBU ideally has the following characteristics: (1) it is a single business; (2) it has a distinct mission; (3) it has its own competitors; (4) it has a responsible manager; (5) it controls certain resources; (6) it can benefit from strategic planning; and (7) it can be planned independently of the other businesses. An SBU can be one or more company divisions, a product line within a division, or sometimes a single product or brand.

The next step calls for management to rate all the SBUs in a way that would reveal how much resource support each SBU deserves. The two best-known evaluation schemes are those of the Boston Consulting Group and the General Electric Company. [Due to space limitations, we have chosen to pass over detailed descriptions of these evaluation schemes in this article. Please refer to...the...article by Ben Enis (*Business,* May-June, 1980, pp. 11-12) for more complete descriptions.]

Whether the BCG, GE, or some other analysis of the company's current portfolio of business is used, the main point is that the company must evaluate its SBUs as a basis for setting objectives and resource allocation priorities. The result of the analysis enables management to decide on the business objective for each SBU and on what resources it will be given. Then the task of the SBU's management and marketing personnel will be to figure out the best way to accomplish that objective. Marketing managers in certain businesses will find that their objective is not necessarily to build that business! This is somewhat contrary to their traditional mandate, which is to build sales. Their job may be to hold the existing volume in spite of fewer marketing dollars, or actually to reduce demand. Thus the generic task of marketing management is not to build demand but to manage demand. Marketing has to take its cue from the objective developed for the business in the course of strategic planning at the corporate level. Marketing contributes to the evaluation of the business's potential and where it stands in the matrix, but once the business's objective is set, marketing's task is to carry it out efficiently and profitably.

Marketing Process

We will now examine the other major process, the marketing process, which plays a key role in the company's ability to adapt creatively to its changing environment. We define *marketing process* as follows:

The marketing process is the managerial process of identifying, analyzing, choosing, and exploiting marketing opportunities to fulfill the company's mission and objectives. More specifically, it consists of identifying and analyzing marketing opportunities, segmenting and selecting target markets, developing a competitive marketing mix strategy, and designing supporting marketing management systems for planning and control, information, and marketing personnel.

Marketing Opportunity Analysis

The marketing process begins with the company's effort to find attractive opportunities. In this quest the marketing department plays a major role. Although new opportunities can be spotted by various persons in the company, marketers bear the major responsibility for generating, evaluating, and selecting attractive opportunities.

Marketers use several techniques to spot new opportunities. They make sure that various ideas arising in the firm flow to the marketing department where they can be evaluated. Marketers often conduct brainstorming sessions to develop new ideas. They make use of systematic techniques such as the product/market expansion matrix discussed earlier for locating growth opportunities. They watch a number of industries, which they rate on their attractiveness by using the GE approach [discussed in the article by Enis, mentioned earlier].

It is important to distinguish between *environmental opportunities* and *company opportunities.* There are attractive environmental opportunities available in any economy as long as there are unsatisfied needs. Currently there are great opportunities to develop new sources of energy, new food products, improved agricultural methods, improved forms of transportation, new forms of leisure, and improved teaching technology. There are opportunities in refuse disposal, low-cost legal services, containerization, prefab housing, water purification, day-care centers, and biomedical instruments. But none of these necessarily represent opportunities for any specific company. Fast-food restaurants are probably not an opportunity for U. S. Steel, nor are biomedical instruments an opportunity for Kentucky Fried Chicken.

To be successful, the company should be concerned with attractive environmental opportunities for which it has the required business strength. We call these *company opportunities.* The company must be able to bring to an attractive environmental opportunity more business strength than its potential competitors can. We make the following assumptions:

1. Every environmental opportunity has specific *success requirements.*
2. Each company has *distinctive competences,* that is, things that it can do especially well.
3. A company is likely to enjoy a *differential advantage* in an area of environmental opportunity if its distinctive competences outmatch those of its potential competition.

The combination of attractive company marketing opportunities can be called the *company opportunity set.* Given these opportunities, the marketer's task is to evaluate each opportunity. Who would buy the product? How much would they pay? What would be the optimal features? How many units would be bought? Where are the buyers located? Who would the competition be? What distribution channels would be needed? The answers to these and other questions will lead to an estimate of the marketing opportunity's sales potential. Financial and manufacturing executives would add their estimates of costs. This information will enable the marketers to rank the opportunities and recommend those that should be selected for further development.

Target Market Selection

The second step of the marketing process is called target market selection. Suppose the company has spotted an especially attractive market. The issue becomes how to enter that market. Every market is filled with many more customer groups and customer needs than one company can normally serve, or serve in a competitively superior fashion. The task calls for market segmentation, that is, dividing the market into segments that differ in their requirements, buying responses, or other critical characteristics. Once a useful segmentation approach is developed, the company can consider which is the best part of the market to enter. The part of the market that the company decides to enter is called the *target market—a well-defined set of customers whose needs the company plans to satisfy.*

We will illustrate market segmentation and target market selection by the following:

A successful manufacturer of snow removal equipment is looking for a new product line. Management reviews several opportunities and finds the idea of manufacturing snowmobiles to be attractive in terms of market growth, sales potential, and company business strength. The marketing vice-president thoroughly investigates the structure of the snowmobile industry to determine whether the company could find a viable niche in this industry.

A useful approach to segmentation is to develop a *product/market grid.* Exhibit 3 illustrates a product/market grid for snowmobiles. The company can decide to manufacture any of three

Markets

	Consumer	Industrial	Military
Gas-driven snowmobiles			
Diesel-driven snowmobiles			
Electric-driven snowmobiles			

Products

Exhibit 3: Product/Market Grid for Snowmobiles

product types: gasoline, diesel, or electric. And it can design a snowmobile for any of three markets: consumer, industrial, or military. The marketing vice-president will proceed to estimate, for each of the nine product/market segments, its degree of market attractiveness and the company's degree of business strength. Suppose the segment that looks best is the "diesel-driven snowmobile for the industrial market segment" that is shaded in Exhibit 3.

Even this market segment may be larger than the company can serve, in which case *subsegmentation* is warranted. Exhibit 4 shows a subsegmentation of this market by customer use and customer size. Snowmobiles can be designed for use as delivery vehicles (i.e., used by business firms and the post office), as recreation vehicles (i.e., rented at resort hotel sites), or as emergency vehicles (i.e., used by hospitals and police forces). Their design will also be affected by whether the company will try to sell them to large, medium, or small customers. After evaluating the various subsegments, the marketing vice-president concludes that the "large customer, delivery segment" looks best. Thus management has arrived at a clear idea of its target market.

This target market may constitute the total ambition of the company in this market or may be viewed as a launching pad for later

Customer Use

	Delivery	Recreation	Emergency
Large			
Medium			
Small			

Customer Size

Exhibit 4: Subsegmentation by Customer Use and Customer Size

expansion to other market segments. Companies will usually consider any one of the following five *market coverage strategies.*

1. *Product/market concentration* consists of the company's niching itself in only one part of the market, here making only diesel-driven snowmobiles for industrial buyers.
2. *Product specialization* consists of the company's deciding to produce only diesel-driven snowmobiles for all customer groups.
3. *Market specialization* consists of the company's deciding to make a variety of snowmobiles that serve the varied needs of a particular customer group, such as industrial buyers.
4. *Selective specialization* consists of the company's entering several product markets that have no relation to each other except that each provides an individually attractive opportunity.
5. *Full coverage* consists of the company's making a full range of snowmobiles to serve all the market segments.

Marketing Mix Strategy

The third step in the marketing process consists of developing a competitively effective marketing mix strategy for the target market. Marketing mix is one of the major concepts in modern marketing. It is that particular blend of controllable marketing variables that the firm uses to achieve its objective in the target market.

What variables make up a company's marketing mix? There are actually a great number of marketing mix variables. Fortunately they can be classified into a few major groups. One of the most popular classifications has been proposed by McCarthy and is called the "four *P's*": *product, price, place,* and *promotion.*[6]

---

6. E. Jerome McCarthy, *Basic Marketing: A Managerial Approach,* 4th ed. (Homewood, Ill., Richard D. Irwin, 1971), p. 44 (1st ed., 1960). Two alternative classifications are worth noting. Frey proposed that all marketing decision variables could be divided into two factors: (1) *the offering* (product, packaging, brand, price, and service), and (2) *methods and tools* (distribution channels, personal selling, advertising, sales promotion, and publicity). See Albert W. Frey, *Advertising,* 3rd ed. (New York, Ronald Press, 1961), p. 30. Lazer and Kelley proposed a three-factor

The company arrives at its marketing mix by deciding on the competitive position it wants to occupy in the target market. We can illustrate competitive positioning by returning to the company that has decided to produce snowmobiles for business firms that will use them as delivery vehicles. Suppose this company learns through marketing research that business customers are primarily interested in two snowmobile attributes: size and speed. The company can ask prospective customers and dealers where they perceive competitors' snowmobiles to be located along these dimensions, and the results can be plotted in the *product space map* shown in Exhibit 5. Competitor A is seen as producing small/fast snowmobiles; B, medium-size/medium-speed snowmobiles; C, small-to-medium-size/slow snowmobiles; and D, large/slow snowmobiles. The areas of the circles are proportional to the competitors' sales.[7]

Given these competitor positions, what position should the new manufacturer seek? The company has two basic choices. One is to take a position next to one of the existing competitors and fight to obtain the customers who want that type of snowmobile. The company might choose to do this if it feels that (1) it can build a better snowmobile of this type, (2) the market buying this type of snowmobile is large enough for two competitors, (3) it has more resources than the existing competitor, and/or (4) this position is the most consistent with the company's reputation and competence.

The other choice is to develop a snowmobile that is not currently offered to this market, such as a large/fast snowmobile (see empty northwest quadrant of Exhibit 5). The company would gain instant leadership in this part of the market, since competitors are not offering this type of snowmobile. But before making this decision, the company has to be sure that (1) it is technically feasible to build a large/fast snowmobile, (2) it is economically feasible to

---

classification: (1) *goods and service mix,* (2) *distribution mix,* and (3) *communications mix.* See William Lazer and Eugene J. Kelley, *Managerial Marketing: Perspectives and Viewpoints,* rev. ed. (Homewood, Ill., Richard D. Irwin, 1962), p. 413.

7. These maps must be interpreted with care. Not all customers share the same perceptions. The map shows the average perception. Attention should also be paid to the scatter of perceptions.

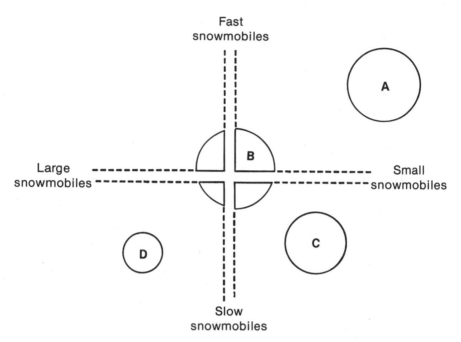

Exhibit 5: A Product Space Map Showing Perceived Offers of Four Competitors

build a large/fast snowmobile at the planned price level, and (3) there are a sufficient number of buyers who would prefer a large/fast snowmobile to any other kind. If the answers are all positive, the firm has discovered a "hole" in the market and should quickly move to fill it.

Suppose, however, the company decides there is more profit potential and less risk in building a small/fast snowmobile to compete with competitor A. In this case the company would study A's snowmobile and other aspects of A's offer, seeking a way to differentiate its offer in the eyes of potential buyers. Instead of competitive positioning through *product/feature differentiation,* it might seek competitive positioning through *price/quality differentiation.* Suppose competitor A's snowmobile is of average quality and carries an average price. The company can offer a better-quality snowmobile than A's at a somewhat higher price, on the familiar argument "You pay more and get more." Or it can offer a better-quality snowmobile but charge the same as A on the argument "More quality for the same price." Or it can design an average-quality snowmobile and charge less on the argument "Same quality for less money." Other price/quality strategies are also possible, and the company will have to choose its strategy carefully.

The company's decisions on the product's quality, features, price, advertising budget, marketing channels, and other marketing variables for this target market make up its *marketing mix.* The marketing mix is the means by which the company defines and supports the competitive position it seeks to occupy in the target market.

Marketing Management Systems Development

Once the company has chosen a target market and has defined its competitive position, it is ready to undertake *marketing management systems development.* Marketing cannot be carried out effectively unless certain management systems are created to support the marketing effort. The three principal systems needed by a company in managing its marketing effort can be described as follows:

1. *Marketing-planning and control system.* Every company should develop plans for the coming period covering its goals, strategies, marketing programs, and budgets. Companies vary considerably in how formally they do their planning, although most of them are moving toward increasingly formal planning. It is the author's position that a formal marketing-planning system is essential to achieving the maximum results sought in the marketplace. Formal marketing planning also requires the design of a marketing control system for checking on whether marketing goals are being achieved and what corrective actions, if any, are needed to improve marketing performance.

2. *Marketing information system.* The job of effectively planning and controlling marketing effort calls for a great amount of continuous information about the macroenvironment, customers, marketing intermediaries, competitors, and other forces in the company's marketing environment. The gathering, processing, and dissemination of this information calls for a marketing information system that is accurate, timely, and comprehensive.

3. *Marketing organization system.*   The company must design an organization that is capable of effectively carrying out many and diverse marketing tasks. This includes a number of things. First, the company must design an organizational structure that leads to integrated, innovative, and responsible marketing planning and control. This usually means appointing a vice-president of marketing, who supervises several marketing executives and coordinates their reports. Second, each marketing job position—such as advertising manager, product manager, and sales manager—must be described in terms of the job's purpose, functions, tasks, and responsibilities. Third, the jobs must be filled by individuals who have adequate skills and motivation and the kind of personality that will enable them to do their marketing job effectively.

Summary

Every organization must evolve a corporate strategy and marketing process if it is to survive and grow. The environment undergoes rapid change, and the organization must fit its objectives, strategy, structure, and systems into a viable relationship with the environment. The organization must continuously identify and evaluate marketing opportunities and threats and take the necessary actions.

Management is the entrepreneurial agent that interprets market needs and translates them into satisfactory products and services. To do this, management goes through a strategic-planning process and a marketing process. The strategic-planning process describes the steps taken at the corporate and divisional levels to develop long-run strategies for survival and growth. This provides the context for the marketing process, which describes the steps taken at the product and market levels to develop viable marketing positions and programs.

The strategic-planning process consists of defining the company mission, objectives, and goals, a growth strategy, and portfolio plans. Developing a sound mission statement is a challenging undertaking, if it is to serve its purpose of directing the firm to its best opportunities.

Strategic planning then calls for developing a set of objectives such as sales and market-share growth, profitability, and innovation to support the company mission. These objectives should be hierarchical, quantitative, realistic, and consistent.

To achieve growth, the company must identify market opportunities where it would enjoy a differential advantage over competitors. The company can generate relevant opportunities by considering intensive growth opportunities within its present product/market scope (such as market penetration, market development, and product development), integrative growth opportunities within its marketing channel system (such as backward, forward, and horizontal integration), diversification growth opportunities outside its marketing channel integration), and diversification growth opportunities outside its marketing channel system (such as concentric, horizontal, and conglomerate diversification).

Finally, strategic planning must define, for each strategic business unit (SBU) in the company's portfolio, whether it will be built, maintained, harvested, or terminated. As aids to doing this, companies can use either the BCG growth-share matrix or the GE strategic business-planning grid.

Within this context, the marketing process can be enacted. The first step consists of generating, evaluating, and recommending marketing opportunities. For any sound opportunity, the next step is to examine the product/market structure and identify the best target market. The third step is to decide on the best competitive position and marketing mix strategy for the company within that target market. The fourth step calls for designing three major marketing management systems—a planning and control system, an information system, and an organization system—for effectively carrying out the intended marketing effort.

14

Strategy Follows Structure: Developing Distinctive Skills

Abstract

Successful strategy implementation is almost entirely a function of the execution of details on a day-to-day basis by all employees. Execution is strategy. The secret to success of the so-called excellent companies is almost invariably mundane execution. The top firms in any industry each have a distinctive set of "skills." In aggregate, these skills form a distinctive strength (usually innovation, service, or quality) that forms a virtual unassailable barrier to competitor entry. Neither strategy nor structure is adequate to explain organizational differences. "Management style" or culture can subtly direct habitual forms of organizational behavior; "guiding values" can significantly direct institutional energy.

Skills—or distinctive competences—describe the variance between successful companies and their less effective competitors. Distinctive competence is not a new concept. In recent years, however, the focus on distinctive competence has been downgraded in favor of quantitative methods. Quantitative and analytic tools can be useful, but only in a secondary way, otherwise they lead to "thought without implementation."

There are only three truly distinctive skill packages. They are: (1) A focus on total customer satisfaction, (2) A focus on continuous innovation, and (3) A focus on an all-out commitment.

These three skills are virtually the only effective sources of sustainable, long-term advantage. Strategies follow skills.

"Revenue line enhancement"—the distinction created by superior service or quality—is more important to a company's success than a slavish devotion to "low cost at all costs."

What then is the leader's role? A creator or shaper or keeper of skills. The creators of effective organizations are unabashed enthusiasts whose love for the job at hand was transmitted and transmuted into excitement, passion, enthusiasm, and energy. The winning companies are ruled by somewhat channeled passion in pursuit of distinctive skill building and maintenance.

Strategy Follows Structure: Developing Distinctive Skills*

Thomas J. Peters

David Ogilvy, in his delightful new book, *Ogilvy on Advertising,* quotes Marvin Bower, McKinsey & Co.'s legendary leader:

> If a company rests its policy of not letting its agencies serve competitors on the need for security of information, it does not have a very solid base. As a matter of realism, the interests of competing clients would not be harmed by an almost complete exchange of information among the people serving the two competing companies. Of course, no responsible service firm would do that—and indeed they go to great lengths to avoid even inadvertent exchanges. Nevertheless . . . the history, make-up, ways of doing business, attitudes of people, operating philosophy and procedures of even directly competing companies are ordinarily so different that information could be exchanged between them with no harm to either. (1)

Or, strategy follows structure. Distinctive organizational performance, for good or ill, is almost entirely a function of deeply

© 1984 by the Regents of the University of California. Reprinted from *California Management Review,* Volume XXVI, No. 3, pp. 111-125 by permission of the Regents.

*I would like to acknowledge the crucial contribution by Bob Waterman to my sensitivity to this subject.

engrained repertoires. The organization, within its marketplace, *is* the way it *acts* from moment to moment—not the way it thinks it *might* act or *ought* to act. Larry Greiner recently noted:

> Strategy evolves from inside the organization—not . . . a manipulable and controlable mechanism that can easily be changed from one year to the next. Strategy is a nonrational concept stemming from the informal values, traditions, and norms of behavior held by the firm's managers and employees—not a rational, formal, logical, conscious and predetermined thought processes engaged in by top executives. Strategy emerges out of the cumulative effect of many informal actions and decisions taken daily over the years by many employees— not a "one shot" statement developed exclusivley by top management for distribution to the organization. (2)

Of course we understand, at one level, exactly what Greiner is saying; few would disagree with it. At the same time, however, we more often than not manage as if the principal variable at our command—in order to bring about an adjustment to a changing environment—is the "strategy lever."

Execution Is Strategy

SAS (Scandinavian Air System) just completed a monumental "strategic turnaround." In a period of 18 months, amidst the worst recession in 40 years, it went from a position of losing $10 million a year to making $70 million a year (on $2 billion in sales), and virtually the entire turnaround came at the direct expense of such superb performers as SwissAir and Lufthansa. The "strategy" (he calls it "vision") of SAS's Jan Carlzon was "to become the premiere business person's airline." Carlzon is the first to admit that it is a "garden variety" vision: "It's everyone's aspiration. The difference was, we executed." Carlzon describes SAS as having shifted focus from "an aircraft orientation" to a "customer orientation," adding that, "SAS *is* the personal contact of one person in the market and one person at SAS." He sees SAS as "50 million 'moments of truth' per year, during each of which we have an opportunity to be distinctive." That number is arrived at by calculating that SAS has 10 million customers per year, each one comes in contact with five SAS employees on average, which leads to a product of 50 million "opportunities."

Perdue Farms sells chickens. In the face of economists' predictions for over 50 consecutive years (according to Frank Perdue), Perdue Farms has built a three-quarter billion dollar business. Margins exceed that of its competitors by seven or eight hundred percent, yet Perdue Farms maintains market shares in the fifties and sixties in every major area in which it competes—even in tough markets such as Richmond, Baltimore, Philadelphia, Boston, and the New York metropolitan area. Frank Perdue argues, and a careful analysis of his organization would lead one to argue, that his magic is simple: "If you believe there's absolutely no limit to quality [remember we're talking about roasters, not Ferraris] and you engage in every business dealing with total integrity, the rest [profit, growth, share] will follow automatically." Interestingly, Perdue's number one customer is Stew Leonard's, "the Disneyland of dairy stores," as it is called by *The New York Times.* Leonard, too, engaged in a most mundane business—selling dairy products in a giant Norwalk, Connecticut, store—yet his results are nothing less than astonishing.

A colleague of mine once said, "Execution *is* strategy." The secret to success of the so-called excellent companies that Bob Waterman and I looked at, and the ones that I have looked at since, is almost invariably mundane execution. The examples—small and large, basic industry or growth industry—are too numerous to mention: Tupperware, Mary Kay, Stew Leonard's, Mrs. Field's Cookies, W.L. Gore, McDonald's, Mars, Perdue Farms, Frito-Lay, Hewlett-Packard, IBM, and on it goes.

My reason for belaboring this point is to suggest that, above all, the top performers—school, hospital, sports team, business— are a *package of distinctive skills.* In most cases, one particularly distinctive strength—innovation at 3M, J&J, or Hewlett-Packard; service at IBM, McDonald's, Frito-Lay, or Disney; quality at Perdue Farms, Procter & Gamble, Mars, or Maytag—and the distinctive skill—which in all cases is a product of some variation of "fifty million moments of truth a year"—are a virtual unassailable barrier to competitor entry or serious encroachment. David Ogilvy quotes Mier Van Der Rohe as saying of architecture, "God is in the details." (3) Jan Carlzon of SAS puts it this way, "We do not wish to do one thing

a thousand percent better, we wish to do a thousand things one percent better." Francis G. (Buck) Rodgers, IBM's corporate marketing
vice-president, made a parallel remark, "Above all we want a reputation for doing the little things well." And a long-term observer of
Procter & Gamble noted, "They are so thorough, it's boring." The
very fact that excellence has a "thousand thousand little things" as
its source makes the word "unassailable" (as in "an unassailable
barrier to entry") plausible. No trick, no device, no sleight of hand,
no capital expenditure will close the gap for the also rans.

Distinctive Competence—The Forgotten Trail

The focus on execution, on distinctive competence is indeed not
new. Philip Selznick, as far as I can determine, talked about it first:

> The term "organization" suggests a certain bareness, a lean, no-
> nonsense system of consciously coordinated activities. It refers to an
> *expendable tool,* a rational instrument engineered to do a job. An
> "institution," on the other hand, is more nearly a natural product of
> social needs and pressures—a responsive adaptive organism. The
> terms institution, organizational character, and distinctive competence
> all refer to the same basic process—the transformation of an
> engineered, technical arrangement of building blocks into a pur-
> posive social organization. (4)

Early thinking about strategy, which was the focus of my MBA
schooling a dozen years ago at Stanford, was driven by the industry
standard: Edmund P. Learned et al.'s textbook, *Business Policy.* (5)
The focus of strategy-making at that point was clearly on analyzing
and building distinctive competences.

In the years since Selznick and Learned et al., the focus on
distinctive competence has been downgraded. Analysis of strategic
position within a competitive system has all but butted out concern
with the boring details of execution (which sum up to that elusive
competence). Presumably the "people types" (the OB faculty) take
care of such mundane stuff. The experience curve, portfolio
manipulation, competitive cost position analysis, and the like have
reigned supreme for the last decade or so.

I have no problem with the usefulness of any of these tools. Each is vital and few of them, indeed, were used very thoughtfully or regularly just a dozen years ago. However, we seem to have moved (rushed?) from a position of "implementation without thought" (analyzing structures on the basis of span of control, rather than on the basis of external forces) to "thought without implementation." We have reached a wretched position in which Stanford, annually voted by the business school deans as America's leading business school (and thus the world's), has only *three* of 91 elective MBA courses focusing on the making (manufacturing policy) or selling (sales management) functions of business. (6) This distortion of priorities was poignantly brought home to me late last school year. A local reporter attended my last class (an elective based on *In Search of Excellence*) and asked my students if the course had been useful. One student, quoted in the subsequent article, tried to say the very most complimentary thing he could: "It's great. Tom teaches all that soft, intangible stuff—innovation, quality, customer service—that's not found in the hard P&L or balance statements." Soft? Hard? Has that youngster got it straight or backwards—is there a problem here?

Roots

Let me backtrack for a moment, and describe my own odyssey. I became involved in the issue of "doing strategy" in 1976. Returning to McKinsey & Co. from a sabbatical during which I completed my business Ph. D. at Stanford, I was given a project that dealt with "looking for the next generation of organizational structure." (Prior to 1976, I had been a garden variety strategy consultant, dealing mainly with oil exploration simulation models.) McKinsey's new managing director asked me to undertake the study for three reasons:

- The matrix structure—which was the kneejerk structure being installed by every company, especially if the company called in McKinsey—was clearly showing that it was less than ideal in practice (it was great on paper) and we needed to know why—quickly.

- McKinsey's new managing director had earned his own stripes primarily by being a champion of radical decentralization and was thus a proponent of the critical importance of organizational structures to business success (i.e., strategy execution).

- McKinsey was, without much conscious thought, going willy-nilly down the path of becoming a "strategy boutique," in response to competitive threats (the first serious ones in the company's history) from the Boston Consulting Group and Bain & Company. Indeed, McKinsey in the mid-seventies was populated by young men almost totally enamored with the nuances of the ideological debate going on amongst strategists—the Porter view, the PIMs view, and the McKinsey (or GE) portfolio/nine box, versus the BCG/four box versus the ADL/24 box.

I began my search rather randomly and traveled from Stockholm, to London, to Dusseldorf, to Detroit, to Palo Alto. As time went by, it became obvious that neither strategy nor structure—nor even the two together—was sufficient to explain organizational differences. I began to focus on "management style" (which, as I defined it at the time, would fall under the heading of "culture" today), on the subtle role of management systems in directing habitual forms of organizational behavior, and on "guiding values" which seemed to somehow be the most significant in directing institutional energy (these have now come to be called by many, myself included, such things as "vision," "superordinate goals," "shared values," or, again, "culture").

Eventually, in mid-1978, my colleague Bob Waterman and I, with the help of Anthony Athos and Richard Pascale, developed the so-called "McKinsey 7-S framework." (7) In a nutshell, it was a response to a single phenomenon that we had all observed: what I now call the "strategy-execution gap." The 7-S structure, as many doubtless know, consists of the following variables: strategy, structure, systems, style, shared values (called superordinate goal originally), staff (people), and skills.

The 7-S structure was once a 5-S structure, then a 6-S structure, and then the last variable to be added was skills. When writing the first lengthy description of the model, (8) I went through each of the variables in what was then a "6-S" model. I was trying to figure out, since our sole objective was to do better organizational diagnosis, "what the six S's added up to." It was not a very rigorous or perfectly logical question, but it was a very pragmatic one. Did some five of the S's add up to the sixth—strategy? That didn't feel right. Or did five of the S's add up to an alternate sixth—style, or another, staff (people)? All told, nothing felt quite right. As a product of frustration, more than inspiration, I decided to add the term "skills." My observations seemed to suggest, above all, that organizations were packages of "somethings"—skills?—perhaps just another term for habitual ways they acted or reacted to crisis and opportunity alike. On the one hand, these things called "skills" seemed the most important of all—the most distinctive encapsulation of the organization's way of doing business. On the other hand, they seemed to be the things that, above all, dropped through the cracks in any analysis—typically reductionist analysis which usually focuses on structure, control systems, or strategy formulation processes. Fiddle with the structure, change the strategy, think about the style, work on the development of staff (people), articulate a new system. But just *what* was it that you were really up to? It is of course an unanswerable question, but skills seemed to fit the bill acceptably well.

At the time our objective was simply to (in Bob Waterman's words, I believe) "enhance the pile of variables beyond the simple structure-strategy or structure-strategy-systems formulation." We wanted to do better—richer—diagnosis. We wanted to reduce the strategy-execution gap.

We Blow It Again

The chain of circumstances is unimportant, but a year or so later, in 1979, we began the so-called "excellent company research," that of course resulted, among other things, in the publication of *In Search of Excellence.* And what did we observe in those companies? Well, history—i.e., our shortcomings—repeated itself. We began with a very extensive, systematic 27-page interview guide. Our focus was on differences in sales force organization and differences in compensation or informal reward systems. The questionnaire, though we religiously followed it in all of our settings, turned out to be of little value in unearthing differences. The respondents, from top to bottom in the organizations we polled, were talking about the other things. I *now* believe that what they were talking about was *skills*—or distinctive competences. Moreover, a la the opening quote by Marvin Bower, they talked freely about them, explicitly aware that to copy "the 3M way" is a virtual impossibility for others. David Ogilvy, in his new book, has a brief chapter solely devoted to the ins and outs of competing with Procter & Gamble. He has just two points. The first is a suggestion: Don't. The second is the reason why: They make better products. The same "oversimplifications" are true of virtually all the companies we looked at. IBM has a three-value set of beliefs. The driving force (in addition to the focus on people from whom it all emanates), is "to provide the *best* service of *any* company in *any* industry in the *world*." Mars, Inc., Perdue Farms, Maytag, and others—along with P&G—all focus slavishly on superior quality. Frito-Lay, Disney, Sysco, and the like focus on superior service. Raychem, Hewlett-Packard, Johnson & Johnson, and 3M focus on continuous innovation. The late Ray Kroc, McDonald's founder, once said, "If I had a brick for every time I've said Quality, Service, Cleanliness and Value, I could pave a two lane road to the moon." Debbie Fields of the remarkably successful Mrs. Field's Cookies says, "I am not a businesswoman. I'm a cookie person." To our utter—and growing—astonishment, these simple (albeit excruciatingly hard to execute), yet very distinctive skills turn out to describe a shockingly high percentage of the variance between these companies and their less effective competitors. Procter & Gamble understands brand management to be sure, and it manages and invests in advertising beautifully, but its 150-year dedication to absolutely unparalleled, top quality at the head of every category in which it chooses to compete is the true reason for its unparalleled effective performance (e.g., seven of the top ten package good products in the U.S.).

The Simple Substance

As best I can determine, there are only *three* truly distinctive "skill packages." They are evident in virtually all of the institutions which are top performers. They are:

- a focus on total customer satisfaction,
- a focus on continuous innovation, and
- a common denominator—the notion that the first two require "all hands," and virtually every one of these companies shares a bone-deep belief in the dignity and worth and creative potential of the individual person.

Total Customer Satisfaction

The most frequent accusation I face is that Waterman and I discovered "mere common sense." It is an accusation that I relish. What kinder thing than to be accused of having discovered common sense! The miracle, as I'm fond of pointing out, is that so few apply it, or are *able* to apply it in large, complex businesses. Nothing is more common sensical than TCS—total customer satisfaction. And yet seldom do more than one or two companies in any segment provide truly distinguished service and quality of product. IBM's corporate marketing vice-president, Buck Rodgers sadly comments, "If you get satisfactory service today, it's a darned miracle."

The superior service and/or quality provider is the winner wherever one turns. In 65 of the 70 companies that we looked at, the competitive distinction comes from what I've come to call "revenue line enhancement," which is apparently more important than a slavish devotion to "low cost at all costs."

An IBM officer makes a vital distinction, not found in the microeconomic texts: "There's a big difference between 'competitive cost' and 'low cost.' The former is vital. But I've never known a winner over the long haul with a 'low cost attitude.'" His point *is* the key point, as it relates to distinctive competence, or skills. On paper, there's no earthly reason a business can't be the "high value added, industry-leading innovator, low-cost producer." However, it is nigh on impossible for big companies to be best at all things, to walk and chew gum simultaneously. The obsession necessary to do any one thing well is enormous. The whole debate focuses on paper possibilities (first at everything) versus real world skills (where first at any one thing is miracle enough).

A recent extensive study for the American Business Conference, the new lobby representing America's "mid-size growth companies" (those between $25 million and $1 billion in sales, which have doubled or more in size over the last five years), concludes exactly the same way. Forty-three out of 45 of its top companies focus on revenue enhancement.

> Winners almost always compete by delivering a product that supplies superior value to customers, rather than one which costs less. Most strategists believe that the business winners are those who capture commanding [market] share through lower costs and prices. The winner mid-size companies compete on the value of their products and services and usually enjoy premium prices. (9)

The act of differentially focusing on quality, service, and nicemanship (revenue enhancement) would not be newsworthy, except for the fact that in the "real world" it is rarely practiced. Moreover, business schools and consultants have been a major part of the problem. Carlzon's transformation of SAS was an unabashed attempt to focus on revenue enhancement. He tells a wonderful story:

> I didn't learn much at business school. To be frank, I simply learned that if you had a problem, there were only two strategies that could be used to extract yourself from it—increase revenue or decrease cost. I made that apparently simplistic comment in front of a large [Swedish] group recently. One of my former economics professors, to my surprise, happened to be in the audience. He stood up and said, "Mr. Carlzon, as I suspected, you weren't listening. We didn't provide you with two tools, but only with one—reduce costs."

Using the venerated tool of content analysis (actions speak louder than words) and remembering my prior comments about the 91 electives at Stanford, the same thing could almost be said of at least one U.S. school, quantitatively: while only three courses at Stanford focus on selling and making, fully 34 focus on accounting, financing, and decision analysis.

Looking back at the seventies, it's amazing that we got so badly stung by the experience curve. From the mundane world of Dreyer's Ice Cream (50% equity returns and 50% p.a. growth in a $75 million business), to Mr. Perdue's chickens (with margins, remember, that are 800% above industry average), to Maytag's washers (which command top share and a $75 price premium per machine against tough competitors in a mature market), to Procter & Gamble's toilet paper (whose one-ply variety, even, sells at a full 50% price premium over generic "TP"), the higher value-added producers are the winners. Even U.S. Shoe, a tremendously successful company, calls itself the "sports car and convertible end of the shoe business." As Ted Levitt begins in his latest, very readable book, *The Marketing Imagination*, "There is no such thing as a commodity." (10) The often slavish devotion to the experience curve effect is not responsible for our forgetting all of this counter evidence, to be sure. Making more (selling at a lower price to gain share) in order to achieve a barrier to entry via lowest subsequent industry cost is certainly not a bad idea. It's a great one. But the difficulty seems to be the unintended resultant *mindset*. As one chief executive officer noted to me, "We act as if cost—and thus price—is the only variable available these days. In our hell bent rush to get cost down, we have given all too short shrift to quality and service. So we wake up, at best, with a great share and a lousy product. It's almost always a precarious position that can't be sustained." Also, I suspect, the relative ease of gaining dominant market position—first in the U.S., and then overseas—by most American corporations in the 1950s through the 1970s (pre-OPEC, pre-Japan) led institutions to take their eye off the service and quality ball. The focus was simply on making a lot of it for ever-hungry markets. Moreover, this led to the executive suite dominance by financially trained executive-administrators, and the absence of people who were closer to the product (and thus the importance of quality and service)—namely, salespersons, designers, and manufacturers.

The net result is that our strategy-making focus in the U.S. has become cost containment rather than revenue enhancement. To put it bluntly, service and quality stink to high heaven in most U.S. markets. I revel in GE's ability to have increased its share (from 7% to 75% in 26 months) in the domestic U.S. locomotive market through "better listening to its customers." Then I find out that fully 60% of GE's machines *didn't* work just three years ago. Holy Smoke: 60%! Room for improvement is enormous—from shoes to locomotives.

Continuous Innovation

The second basic skill trait is the ability to constantly innovate. Virtually all innovations—from miracle drugs, to computers, to airplanes, to bag size changes at Frito-Lay, to menu item additions at McDonald's—come from the wrong person, in the wrong division, of the wrong company, in the wrong industry, for the wrong reason, at the wrong time, with the wrong set of end-users. The assumption behind most planning systems, particularly the highly articulated strategic planning systems, of the seventies, was that we could plan our way to new market successes. The reality differs greatly. Even at the Mecca of planning systems, General Electric, the batting average of strategic planning was woefully low. In the 70s (when planners were regularly observed walking on water at Fairfield), GE's major innovative, internally-generated business successes—e.g., aircraft engines, the credit business, plastics, and the information services company—came solely as a product of committed, somewhat irrational (assumed, inside, to be crazy) champions. When Jack Welch became GE's chairman in 1980—ending a 30-year reign by accountants—he moved to enhance entrepreneurship. One of his first steps was to reduce the corporate planning staff by more than 80 percent. The most truly innovative companies—Hewlett-Packard, the Raychem Corporation, 3M, Johnson & Johnson, PepsiCo, and the like—clearly depend upon a thoroughly innovative climate. Radical decentralization marks Johnson & Johnson. Both J&J and IBM (via its new Independent Business Unit structure) give the innovating unit a Board of Directors with an explicit charter to "ignore the strictures of formal planning systems and to keep the bureaucrats out of the hair of the inventors." 3M is simply a collection of skunkworks. The highly profitable Raychem Corporation has grown to almost a billion dollars by adding over 200,000 products to its product line in a 25-year history. In the soft goods business, the extraordinary success of Mervyn's (a Dayton-Hudson subsidiary) is based upon the fact that it can remerchandise a multi-billion dollar business in ten days—an act which takes almost 10-12 weeks at its arch-competitors J. C. Penney and Sears. In the same tough business, Bloomingdale's is marked, according to its most intimate analyst, by having "more experiments going on per square foot than any other retailer in the country." It's a formula that Macy's Ed Finkelstein has copied for the last five years—resulting in Macy's extraordinary success.

The trend toward radical decentralization (as opposed to coordinated market attack via central strategic planning) as the only viable path to instilling entrepreneurship is beginning to intrude into an ever-larger number of corporations, especially mature businesses. Campbell Soup is tired of simply trading tiny fractions of share points. Its new chief executive officer, Gordon McGovern, has just reorganized the company into 50 independent business units. The objective for each of them is clear; innovate *around* their product lines rather than stick with the tried and true. Numerous other package good companies—PepsiCo chief among them—are vigorously pursuing new business development rather than relying upon grabbing another millionth of a share point (which may easily be lost next month). A most unlikely vital company is U.S. Shoe, yet the entrepreneurial vigor of this billion-and-a-half dollar company is extraordinary. A recent *Fortune* article attributed its success to "superior market segmentation." The next issue of *Fortune* carried a letter to the editor from the son of the founder which rebutted that argument: "My father's real contribution was not superior market segmentation. Rather, he created a beautiful corporate culture which encouraged risk-taking." So from Hewlett-Packard and 3M, where we'd expect it, to PepsiCo, Campbell Soup, and U.S. Shoe, we find the gospel of salvation through internal entrepreneurship increasingly being practiced.

All Hands

The third and final regularly found skill variable is the *sine qua non* that goes hand-in-glove with the first two. Superior customer service, quality, and courtesy (total customer satisfaction) is not a product of the executive suite—it's an all hands effort. Constant innovation from multiple centers is similarly not the domain of a handful of brilliant thinkers at the top. Thus, virtually all of these institutions put at the head of their corporate philosophies a bone-deep belief in the dignity and worth and creative potential of *all* their people. Said one successful Silicon Valley chief executive officer recently, "I'll tell you who my number one marketing person is. It's that man or woman on the loading dock who decides *not* to *drop* the box into the back of the truck." Said another, "Doesn't it follow that if you wish your people to treat your customers with courtesy that you must treat your people with courtesy?" Many sign up for these three virtues, but only the truly distinguished companies seem to practice them regularly.

Common Thread: The Adaptive Organism

These three skills—and these three alone—are virtually the *only* effective sources of sustainable, long-term competitive advantage. Notice that each suggests the essence of an adaptive organism. The organization that provides high perceived value—service, quality, courtesy—invariably does so by constantly listening and adapting to its customers' needs. The innovative company is similarly radically focused on the outside world. And the expectation that all people will contribute creatively to their jobs—receptionist and product designer alike—means similarly that each person is a source of external probing and a basis for constant renewal, fulfillment, and adaptation. These organizations, then, are alive and are excited— in both the "attuned" and the "enthusiastic" sense of that word. Moreover, such organizations are in the process of constant redefinition. The shared values surrounding these skills—customer listening and serving, constant innovation, and expecting all people to contribute—are rigid. But, paradoxically, the rigid values/skills are in service of constant externally focused adaptation and growth.

The excellent companies—chicken makers to computer makers—use their skills as the basis for continually reinventing adaptive strategies—usually on a decentralized basis—to permit them to compete effectively in both mature and volatile youthful markets. Skills, in a word, *drive* strategy in the best companies.

Skills versus Strategy

I tend to see the word strategy, in the sense that it's currently taught in the business schools (or practiced by the leading consultants), as *not* having much meaning at the corporate or sector level at all, but as being the appropriate domain of the strategic business unit or other form of decentralized unit (the IBU at IBM, the division at Hewlett-Packard or J&J, the merchant organization at Macy's). To return to our 7-S model, this is the classic case for what we have constantly called "soft is hard." The driving variable in the model, which creates the pre-conditions for *effective* strategizing, is, above all, skills. Strategy is the dependent variable, operable at a lower level in the business.

We view the constantly innovating, constantly customer-serving organization as one that continually *discovers* new markets and new opportunities. The notion of the learning organization, the adapting organization, the discovering organization, reigns supreme. Sound skills are the basis for "finding" or "discovering" business unit strategies in the cause-effect model that we see at play from IBM to Perdue Farms. IBM has had a giant success with the PC. The basis: IBM translated its unique view of customer friendliness into a market previously driven by engineering (technology)-run companies. 3M scored a remarkable success with Post-It Notepads. 3M is a blue-chip finder of odd-ball new markets, uniquely independent of prior category designations. By contrast, we watch the traditional "strategists" fall into the abyss time and again. Because a market looks good on paper, they believe the company should take it on. Yet they invariably underestimate the executional effort (skill base) required to do extremely well at *anything.*

Proactive Leadership

If there is some sense to all the above, what then is the leader's role? If not master strategist, then what? He or she becomes, above all, a creator or shaper or keeper of skills. Warren Bennis has called the leader of this sort a "social architect." Harry Levinson calls him an "educator." Larry Greiner coined "strategic actor." Xerox subsidiary (Versatec) CEO Renn Zaphiropoulos calls himself a "gardener." I have used terms such as role model, dramatist, and value shaper.

Above all the leader's role becomes proactive rather than reactive. Strategy formulation has usually seemed to me, as it actually gets practiced (certainly not as planned by the academics), to be a reactive process. Analyze what was and try to get ahead of the world by projecting from there. This is not the stuff of creation—of new markets in shoes or miracle drugs. I'm always reminded that Ray Kroc created McDonald's by following up on the order pattern of a single customer (when he was selling milkshake machines) who happened to be using about seven times as many machines as that store "should have been using." He learned from the store, bought it from the McDonald family, and the rest is history. A 3M executive says that the senior manager (many more than just those in the executive suite) "should above all be a *nurturer* of champions." He says that would-be champions ("monomaniacs with missions," in Peter Drucker's words) are "close to a dime a dozen." The important people are those that view their prime role as protecting the champions from the silliness of inertial bureaucracies. Former Chairman Ren McPherson, speaking of the Dana Corporation, sketches a similar role: "The manager's job is to keep the bureaucrats out of the way of the productive people." Sam Walton, founder of the remarkably successful WalMart Corporation, says, "The best ideas have always come and will always come from the clerks. The point is to seek them out, to listen, and to act." At the Rolm Corporation, an executive adds, "The leader is not a devil's advocate. He is a cheerleader." Gordon McGovern at Campbell says senior management's role is to develop "a business concept, challenging financial goals, guideline characteristics and an understanding of how to move its culture."

Larry Greiner also speaks eloquently to the proactive role, discriminating between the "trapped executive" (e.g., solves daily problems, meets formally with immediate subordinates, acts aloof and critical, pays attention to weaknesses) and his notion of a "strategic actor" (e.g., articulates philosophy, makes contact with employees at all levels, acts warm and expressive, pays attention to strengths of the business). (11) The skillbuilder, in my experience, is thus a nurturer, cheerleader, unabashed culture shaper, keeper of bureaucrats off the backs of productive people, listener, wanderer. All are direct statements about value shaping and skill building. All are proactive.

Leadership: Spirit in the Details and Daytimer

The leader is not a decision maker! Gordon McGovern describes his reorganization of Campbell Soup:

> We first broke the business into manageable parts, multiplied the number of people running to an opportunity and with the wherewithal to get things done. We then established with these people a concept which is flexible and rich and open-ended, so they can go out and grab parts of it that we at the top wouldn't even imagine. (12)

If not a decision-maker/strategist, then what? If a skill builder/value shaper, what does that mean? Awhile ago I had dinner with Andy Pearson, PepsiCo's president. Andy has a sparkling reputation in many circles as a "genius at package goods strategy." I want to argue that he's not! He's better than that. He is a skill builder in a once dormant, now vital $8 billion enterprise.

The dinner with Pearson, before a Strategic Marketing Society conference, illustrated the point. It was a lovely Montreal restaurant. The food and wine were first class. The discussion? It could have been about anything. Baseball would have been my first choice (it was October and my favorite team was in the playoffs). But no, for four non-stop hours we talked about waiting time bells in Pizza Huts, cookie shelf space acquisition tactics by Frito-Lay, a tiny new bakery PepsiCo recently acquired and so on. Andy is not "a strategist." Andy *lives* the skill he is shaping: entrepreneurial, constant, opportunistic quick attacks on a variety of markets. Test. Do. Try. Fail. Learn. Try again. Get on with it. That is the skill that Andy and Chairman Don Kendall have built into PepsiCo. When Andy visits a subsidiary, stop one is *not* the executive suite. Instead, he camps out in the offices of the associate brand managers. "What are you up to?" Over and over he probes, day in and day out, decade in and decade out. Is Pearson a master strategist? Or a master skill builder/value shaper?

At a recent seminar, a former P&G senior manufacturing manager (a 15-year veteran) takes agitated exception to an insurance executive's assertion that *In Search of Excellence* makes a case for "balancing rigid controls with some 'informal, looser stuff.' " The ex-P&Ger almost shouts: "We didn't have the MRP systems or lengthy reports. And I'll tell you how I learned about quality at P&G. As a young manager, I remember vividly the phone ringing one night at 1:30 a.m. It was a sales manager, and he screamed at me, 'George, we got a problem with a [he emphasizes "a"] bar of soap down here!' ['Here' was 200 or so miles away.] 'Could you be down here by 7:00 a.m. to look at it?' The tone told me it wasn't an invitation. After you've driven 200 miles, through the mountains, at 75 miles per hour, to look at one 35¢ bar of soap, you figure out pretty quick that these guys [P&G] are more than a little bit serious about product quality. It ain't soft or informal, I'll tell you."

P&G's stories—heroes, myths, anecdotes—are at the soul of its remarkable 145-year history of unparalleled quality. P&G's "strategy" is to maintain that skill and apply it creatively in a raft of markets, and even to fend off maturity when required (they explicitly deny that product life cycles exist and point to 100 or so reformulations of Ivory Soap as an example).

A large company president and friend states, "The maintenance of the lasting skill lives in the millions of executive actions, many or most nearly subconscious, that illustrate and dramatize a continuing, living commitment to it. It's the visits, marginal notes, and content of articles in the company bulletin that really count—not the so-called 'bet the company' decisions."

The lasting strategic skill, the distinctive competence that acts as a decades-long barrier to competitive encroachment, *is* Andy Pearson's stories and visits, *is* the simple recollection, in public, of the harrowing ride through the Tennessee hills to rescue a single 35¢ bar of soap at P&G.

Enthusiasts, Passion, and Faith

Let's really stray afield from the world of traditional definitions of strategy formulation. Ray Kroc says, "You gotta be able to see the beauty in a hamburger bun." Recall that Debbie Fields of Mrs. Field's Cookies says, "I am not a businesswoman, I am a cookie person." Sam Walton loves retailing. From Steve Jobs to Famous Amos, the creators of effective organizations are unabashed *enthusiasts.* Bill Hewlett and Dave Packard had a passion for their machines. Herman Lay had a passion for his potatoes. Forrest Mars loved factories. Marvin Bower of McKinsey loved his clients. John Madden loved linebackers. The love was transmitted and transmuted into excitement, passion, enthusiasm, energy. These virtues infected an entire organization. They created the adaptive organization—the organization aimed externally, yet depending upon the full utilization of each of its people. This seemingly simple-minded definition of effective strategy for the ages even holds in mature organizations. The fervor with which Procter & Gamble revered quality has now been passed down through many generations. The "salesman's bias" of an IBM and 3M has similarly been maintained several generations beyond the founder. The passionate belief that the dominant skill reigns supreme is at the heart of business success. Johnson & Johnson, many generations beyond the founder, credits the power and continued vitality of its brief credo for its successful (remarkably so) response to the tragic Tylenol affair. The response was not analytic. The response was to re-interpret the basic values.

So where does all this leave us? The world of experience curves, portfolios, and 4-24 box matrices has led us badly astray. George Gilder notes in *Wealth and Poverty:*

> Economists who attempt to banish chance through methods of rational management also banish the only source of human triumph. The inventor who never acts until statistics affirm his choice, the businessman who waits until the market is proven—all are doomed to mediocrity by their trust in a spurious rationality. (13)

The devilish problem is that there is nothing wrong with any of these strategy tools. In fact, each one is helpful! I think of the same thing in the area of quality: quality circles, automation, and statistical quality control are extraordinarily powerful tools—but *if and only if* a bone-deep belief in quality comes first. Given the 145-year tradition at Procter & Gamble, the tools are then helpful. Absent the faith, passion, belief, value, and skill, the tools become just one more manifestation of bureaucracy—another attempt to patch a fundamental flaw with a bureaucratic band-aid. In the same vein, if you have the well-developed skills of J&J, 3M, HP, U.S. Shoe, WalMart, or Mrs. Field's Cookies, then the strategy tools can be helpful adjuncts indeed.

But we should never forget for a moment that the analytic models are not neutral. Any analyst worth his salt, with anything from a decision tree to a portfolio analysis, can shoot down any idea. Analysts are well-trained naysayers, professional naysayers. Yet it turns out that only passion, faith, and enthusiasm win. Passion can also lead to losses—many of them, of that there is no doubt. Yet there is no alternative. We simply can't plan our way to certain success. John Naisbitt, *Megratrends* author, asserts: "Strategic planning turned out to be an orderly, rational way to efficiently ride over the edge of the cliff." I think he's not far off. Above all, the winning companies that we've observed—small and large, regulated or unregulated, mature or new—are ruled by somewhat channelled passion in pursuit of distinctive skill building and maintenance.

References

1. David Ogilvy, *Ogilvy On Advertising* (New York, NY: Crown, 1983), p. 69.
2. Larry E. Greiner, "Senior Executives as Strategic Actors," *New Management,* Vol. 1, No. 2 (Summer 1983): 13.
3. Ogilvy, op. cit., p. 101.
4. Philip Selznick, *Leadership in Administration* (New York, NY: Harper & Row, 1957), p. 5.
5. Edmund P. Learned, C. Roland Christiansen, Kenneth R. Andrews, and William D. Guth, *Business Policy: Text and Cases* (Homewood, IL: Richard D. Irwin, 1969).
6. "Course Descriptions for Electives Taught in the 1983-84 Academic Year," Stanford University Graduate School of Business.
7. Robert H. Waterman, Jr., Thomas J. Peters, and Julien R. Phillips, "Structure is Not Organization," *Business Horizons* (June 1980).
8. Thomas J. Peters, "Enhancing Organizational Capability and Effectiveness: The Never-Ending Juggling Act," McKinsey & Co., October 1978.

9. Thomas J. Peters, "On Political Books," *The Washington Monthly* (October 1983), p. 56.

10. Theodore Levitt, *The Marketing Imagination* (The Free Press, 1983), p. 72.

11. Greiner, op. cit., p. 14.

12. Gordon McGovern, Address to "1983 Midyear Executive Conference," National-American Wholesale Grocers Association, September 30, 1983.

13. George Gilder, *Wealth and Poverty* (New York, NY: Basic Books, 1981), p. 264.

15

Visionary Leadership and Strategic Management

Abstract

Strategic vision, a combination of strategy and leadership, has been touted as a way to manage complex organizations. However, efforts to train managers to be visionary leaders risk robbing the concept of strategic vision of its vitality.

One can use the metaphor of drama in training managers to be visionary leaders. Both drama and visionary leadership combine the components of repetition, representation, and assistance:

*1. **Repetition.** Just as an actor repeats lines over and over until they can be said effortlessly, the visionary leader, through practice, develops strategic perception. In other words, the leader becomes intimately involved with the business, its product, its market, and so on.*

*2. **Representation.** Through a performance, an actor transforms the repetition of rehearsal into successful drama (by presenting the material again but making it live anew). Similarly, the visionary leader articulates the vision so that it can be represented or communicated, in words and actions, throughout the organization. The way in which the vision is unveiled and communicated is as important as the content of the vision itself.*

*3. **Assistance.** In drama the term "assistance" refers to the third essential component of theatrical success: the active participation of a supportive audience. In strategic management, stakeholders fulfill the analogy. Visionary leaders need the assistance of supportive followers. Followers stimulate the leader, and the two participate in creating the final vision.*

The authors discuss five styles of visionary leadership:

1. The creator, who produces sudden, original, and holistic vision;

2. The proselytizer, who demonstrates evangelical zeal to show people the potential of the vision;

3. The idealist, whose refusal to recognize flaws or contradictions in the vision cystallizes the dreams of a constituency;

4. The bricoleur, who sees how to combine seemingly unrelated events and situations into new potential; and

5. The diviner, whose insight provides clarity to an otherwise unmanageable situation.

Visionary Leadership and Strategic Management

Frances Westley and Henry Mintzberg

A strange process seems to occur as concepts such as culture and charisma move from practice to research. Loosely used in practice, these concepts, as they enter academia, become subjected to a concerted effort to force them to lie down and behave, to render them properly scientific. In the process they seem to lose their emotional resonance, no longer expressing the reality that practitioners originally tried to capture.

Leadership is another such concept. Somewhere along the line, as Pondy has argued, "we lost sight of the 'deep structure,' or meaning of leadership" (1978: 90). In attempting to deal with the observable and measurable aspects of leadership behavior, and perhaps to simplify for normative purposes, leadership research has focused on a narrow set of styles—democratic, autocratic, and *laissez-faire*, for example. We agree with Pondy that instead "we should be trying to document the variety of styles available" (p. 90).

Strategy may also be such a concept. Much effort has been dedicated in strategic management to narrowing it, to pinning it down (as in the attention to "generic" strategies), likewise to narrowing the process by which it forms (in the attention to "planning").

Again, in attempting to dissect a living phenomenon, the skeleton may be revealed while the specimen dies.

More recently, the concepts of strategy and leadership have been combined into that of strategic vision. In academia (Bennis, 1982; Mendell and Gerjuoy, 1984) as well as practice (*Business Week*, 1984; Kiechel, 1986). This has been hailed as a key to managing increasingly complex organizations. Consultants have responded with workshops (e.g. Levinson and Rosenthal, 1984) that promise to train managers to be visionary leaders. In general, however, efforts to turn the creation of strategic vision into a manageable process, one that can be researched, taught, and adopted by managers, risk robbing it of its vitality.

Of special concern should be the tendency to subsume strategic vision under leadership in general, in other words to perceive it as just another category of leadership style (e.g. "transformative"; Tichy and Devanna, 1986). Most writings seem to agree that leadership vision, or "visioning," as the process has sometimes been called, can be broken down into three distinct stages: (1) the envisioning of "an image of a desired future organizational state" (Bass, 1987: 51) which (2) when effectively articulated and communicated to followers (Bennis and Nanus, 1985; Tichy and Devanna, 1986; Gluck, 1984) serves (3) to empower those followers so that they can enact the vision (Sashkin, 1987; Srivastva, 1983; Conger and Kanungo, 1987; Robbins and Duncan, 1987). Such a view posits enormous control in the hands of the individual leader (Bennis and Nanus, 1985: Meindl, Erlich and Dukerich, 1985; Gupta, 1984).

If the field of strategic management is to render the concept of strategic vision suitable for its own purposes it must deal with it in a unique way. That is what we set out to do in this paper, proceeding from three assumptions that differ from those of the traditional leadership literature. First, we assume that visionary leadership is a dynamic, interactive phenomenon, as opposed to a unidirectional process. Second, we assume that the study of strategic vision must take into consideration strategic content as well as the strategic contexts of product, market, issue, process, and organization. Third, we assume that visionary style can take on a variety of different forms.

In this paper we shall deal with each of these assumptions in turn. We build our description on a survey of biographical and autobiographical publications of a number of well-known leaders generally thought to be visionary, including Lee Iacocca of Chrysler, Jan Carlzon of SAS, Edwin Land of Polaroid, René Lévesque of the Parti Québecois, and Steven Jobs, formerly of Apple Computer.

Visionary Leadership as Drama

As noted, visionary leadership is increasingly being defined as a process with specific steps, by and large as follows:

vision (idea) → communication (word) → empowerment (action)

The process, in its emphasis on active leadership and unidirectional flow, may be likened to a hypodermic needle, with the active ingredient (vision) loaded into a syringe (words) which is injected into the patient (subordinate) to effect change. Stripped to its essence, this model takes on a mechanical quality which surely robs the process of much of its evocative appeal.

An alternative image of visionary leadership might be that of a drama. Here action and communication occur simultaneously. Idea and emotion, actor and audience, are momentarily united in a rich encounter which occurs on many symbolic levels. Peter Brook (1968), the legendary director of the Royal Shakespeare Company, has suggested that the magic of the theater lies in that moment when fiction and life somehow blend together. It may be brief, but it is the goal of playwright, director, actor, and audience, the result of "rehearsal," the "performance" itself, and the "attendance" of the audience. Brook, however, finds these words too static, and prefers the French equivalents "repetition," "representation" and "assistance" (p. 154), all of which, coincidentally, have special meanings in English. We wish to suggest that these words may equally be substituted to describe strategic vision, suggesting a dynamic model as follows, each stage of which we then discuss in turn.

repetition   ⟷   representation   ⟷   assistance
(idea)   (vision)   (emotion and action)

Repetition

Repetition, according to Brook, beautifully captures the endless practice in which every artist must engage. He notes that Laurence Olivier would repeat his lines again and again until he had so trained his tongue muscles to say them that he could perform effort-lessly (p. 154). Repetition is likewise the musician practicing her scales until she can be consistent every time, so that while she per-forms she can think about the music itself rather than the individual notes.

For the strategic visionary, repetition has a similar role—to develop an intimacy with the subject at hand, to deal with strategy as "craft," as one of us has noted elsewhere:

> Craft evokes the notions of traditional skill, dedication, perfection through the mastery of detail. It is not so much thinking and reason that spring to mind as involvement, a sense of intimacy and harmony with the materials at hand, developed through long experience and commitment (Mintzberg 1987: 66).

Like the craftsman, the strategic visionary would appear to develop strategic perception as much through practice and gut-level feel for the business, product, market, and technology, as through con-scious cognition. Lee Iacocca "grew up" in the auto industry. When he left Ford he went to Chrysler because cars were "in his blood" (Iacocca, 1984: 141). Jan Carlzon, hailed as a visionary for his turn-around at SAS airlines, has spent his entire career (beginning in 1968) in the travel business, since 1978 in the airline industry.

Consider how Edwin Land describes his invention of the Polar-oid camera:

> One day when we were vacationing in Santa Fe in 1943 my daughter, Jennifer, who was then 3, asked me why she could not see the picture I had just taken of her. As I walked around that charming town, I under-took the task of solving the puzzle she had set for me. Within the hour the camera, the film and the physical chemistry became so clear that with a great sense of excitement I hurried to the place where a friend was staying to describe to him in detail a dry camera which would give a picture immediately after exposure. In my mind it was so real that I spent several hours on this description (Land, 1972a: 84).

Reading this description, it is easy to focus on the element of inspira-tion, of an idea seemingly springing fully blown, from nowhere.

What might be forgotten is that Land had spent years in the laboratory perfecting the polarization process, schooling his scientific and inventive abilities, practicing and repeating, learning his craft. His inspiration fell on fertile ground, prepared by endless repetition. As Land himself said:

> It was as if all that we had done . . . had been a school and a preparation both for that first day in which I suddenly knew how to make one-step dry photographic process and for the following three years in which we made the very vivid dream into a solid reality (Wensbergh, 1987: 85).

In a sense the strategic visionary practices for the moment of vision, much as the actor practices for the moment of performance. But for strategy to become vision, craft is not enough. Repetition can become deadly, rigidifying innovation into imitation. Strategic visionaries are leaders who use their familiarity with the issues as a springboard to innovation, who are able to add value by building new perceptions on old practices.

Representation

For the actor, the performance itself is what must transform repetition into success. Brook chooses the word "representation" to describe this transformation. To represent means to take the past and make it live again, giving it immediacy, vitality. In a sense, representation redeems repetition, turning it from craft into art.

But what corresponds to the work of art for the strategic visionary? It is, of course, the vision itself. But not the vision as a private mental image. Rather, it is the vision articulated, the vision *represented* and communicated, in words and in actions. Just as a leader cannot exist without followers, so too strategic vision cannot exist without being so recognized by followers.

For this reason we equate visionary leadership not just with an idea *per se*, but with the communicated idea. Here we are concerned with the profoundly symbolic nature of visionary leadership. What distinguishes visionary leadership is that through words and actions, the leader gets the followers to "see" his or her vision—to see a new way to think and act—and so to join their leader in realizing it. *How* the vision is communicated thus becomes as important as what is communicated. Edwin Land understood this as well. He argued that inventions have two parts: the product itself, which must be "startling, unexpected and come to a world which is *not* prepared," and the "gestalt" in which the product is embedded:

> The second great invention for supporting the first invention is finding how to relate the invention itself to the public. It is the public's role to resist. All of us have a miscellany of ideas, most of which are not consequential. It is the duty of the inventor to build a new gestalt for the old one in the framework of society. And when he does his invention calmly and equitably becomes part of everyday life and no one can understand why it wasn't always there. But until the inventor has done both things [product and gestalt] nothing has any meaning (Land, 1975: 50).

And how is such a gestalt created? Here again, the metaphor of drama is useful. When the actor represents the play, he or she draws upon a variety of verbal and non-verbal resources. The voice, the face, the gesture, the language itself, the timing, the costume, the lighting, the staging, all combine in an intricate weave to arouse and inspire the audience to create a living gestalt. There is much to suggest that the visionary leader shares many of the actor's skills in representing his or her strategic vision.

For example, one is hard-pressed to find an example of a visionary leader who was not also adept at using language. Language has the ability to stimulate and motivate, not only through appeals to logic but also through appeals to emotion (Burke, 1950; Pfeffer, 1981; Edelman, 1964.) Rhetoricians since Aristotle have carefully observed the potential of linguistic devices such as alliteration, irony, imagery, and metaphor, among other things, to provoke identification and emotional commitment among listeners. The speeches of famous visionary leaders such as Winston Churchill and Martin Luther King offer good examples of the skillful use of such rhetorical devices, which allow their listeners to "see" the visions as if they were real. Analysis of Lee Iacocca's leadership in the Chrysler turnaround suggests that much of the power of his strategic initiatives resided in his use of metaphors to unite stakeholders behind him (Westley and Mintzberg, 1988). Likewise, Edwin Land inspired his employees not only with his inventions, but also with the evocative imagery with which he surrounded them. In a short statement on photography (Land, 1972a), Land suggested that it was a way of retaining the shifting, fleeting world of childhood and thus giving the child "a new kind of security." Sharing photographs was to him an act of intimacy; to show someone a photograph you took was to give them a "deeper insight into you as well as what you discerned." Land presented his new camera as follows:

> It will help [the photographer] to focus some aspect of his life and in the process enrich his life at that moment. This happens as you focus through the view finder. It's not merely the camera you are focusing: you are focusing yourself. That's an integration of your personality, right that second. Then when you touch the button, what's inside you comes out. It's the most basic form of creativity. Part of you is now permanent (Land, 1972a: 84).

In a similar fashion, Steven Jobs described the Macintosh as an "insanely great" product, which will "make a difference." He described his co-workers as "the people who would have been poets in the sixties and they're looking at computers as their medium of expression rather than language" (Jobs, 1984: 18). On the Apple Computer Company itself, Jobs said: "There's something going on here . . . something that is changing the world and this is the epicenter" (Jobs, 1984: 18). As Steve Wozniak, the co-founder with Jobs of the Apple Computer Company, tersely noted: "he can always couch things in the right words" (Patterson, 1985).

In addition to language, the visionary leader can use a range of dramaturgical devices capable of stimulating and arousing responses. Nonverbal elements such as gesture (Hall, 1959), glance (Goffman, 1959), timing (Wrapp, 1967), movement, and props are also able to evoke similar responses. For example, Steve Jobs organized the Apple office as a circle of work areas around a central foyer. There stood a grand piano and a BMW. "I believe people get ideas from seeing great products," Jobs claimed (Wise, 1984: 146).

In sum, the media of communication for the visionary are many and varied. By wedding perception with symbols the visionary leader creates a vision, and the vision, by evoking an emotional response, forms a bridge between leader and follower as well as between idea and action.

Assistance

Brook argues that for repetition to turn into representation requires more than practice, more than craft, more than the power of word and gesture. An audience is needed. But not a passive audience. It must be active, hence the importance of "assistance."

Brook tells of an ingenious experiment to show what audience assistance entails (1968: 27-29). During a lecture to a lay group he asked a volunteer to come to the front and do a reading. The audience, predicting that the volunteer would make a fool of himself, began to titter. But Brook had given the volunteer a passage from Peter Weiss' play on Auschwitz, which recounted with great clarity a description of the dead. The volunteer was too "appalled" by what he was reading to pay much attention to the titters, and something of his attitude was communicated to the audience. It became quieter. As the volunteer was moved by what he was reading, he delivered the text with exactly the right pacing and intonations, and the audience responded with "shocked, attentive silence" (p. 28).

Next Brook asked for a second volunteer. This time the text was a speech from Henry V listing the names of English and French dead at the battle of Agincourt. Recognizing Shakespeare, the volunteer launched into a typically amateur rendition: false voice, stilted phrasing, etc. The audience grew restless and inattentive. At the finish Brook asked the audience why the list of the dead at Agincourt did not evoke the same response as the description of the dead at Auschwitz. A lively discussion ensued. Brook then asked the same volunteer to read again, but to stop after each name. During the short silence the audience was to try to put together the images of Auschwitz and Agincourt. The reader began. Brook recounts:

> As he spoke the first name, the half silence became a dense one. Its tension caught the reader, there was an emotion in it, shared between him and them and it turned all his attention away from himself on to the subject matter he was speaking. Now the audience's concentration began to guide him: his inflections were simple, his rhythms true: this in turn increased the audience's interest and so the two-way current began to flow (p. 29).

Like a performance, a strategy is made into vision by a two-way current. It cannot happen alone, it needs assistance. Elsewhere we have argued that part of what made René Lévesque and Lee Iacocca effective as leaders was the temporal significance of their vision: they appealed powerfully to the specific needs of specific stakeholders at a specific time. Indeed, there are important instances when the "followers" stimulate the leader, as opposed to the other way around. In most cases, however, it would appear that leader and follower participate together in creating the vision. The specific content—the original idea or perception—may come from the leader (though it need not, as in the case of Lévesque), but the form which it takes, the special excitement which marks it, is co-created. As Brook put it: "there is only a practical difference between actor and audience, not a fundamental one" (1968: 150). Recall Land's description of hurrying to tell his friend of his vision of the camera. Why was he not content to keep the idea to himself? For the same reason an actor is not content to perform before the mirror. Vision comes alive only when it is shared.

This is captured dramatically in this century's most infamous example of visionary leadership. Shortly before Adolph Hitler came to power, Albert Speer attended one of his lectures. Arriving skeptical, Speer left a convert.

> I was carried away on the wave of enthusiasm which, one could almost feel this physically, bore the speaker along from sentence to sentence. It swept away any skepticism, any reservations . . . . Hitler no longer seemed to be speaking to convince; rather, *he seemed to feel that he was expressing what the audience, by now transformed into a single mass, expected of him.* It was as if it were the most natural thing in the world . . . (Speer, 1970: 18; italics added).

Thus the visionary leader not only empowers his audience; it also empowers him. On leaving Apple, Steve Jobs was described as "its heart and soul" (Patterson, 1985) and Lévesque was seen as speaking for the little people of Quebec, the average French Canadians whom he loved.

One final word about our analogy. The early Greek and Roman rhetoricians were particularly sensitive to the need for integrity among those who used the power of word and gesture (Burke, 1950). In this sense visionary leadership is distinct from theater. The actor can play a different person each month and still be considered a good actor. Ironically, the visionary leader who, through similar inconsistency, is labelled a good actor, risks losing credibility. Even before Steven Jobs left Apple, accusations that he was facile, inconsistent, and lacked integrity surfaced. "He should be running Walt Disney. That way every day when he has some new idea, he can contribute to something different," one Apple manager complained (Cocks, 1983: 26). In contrast, Edwin Land's belief that other people in the organization should have the same rich, varied job as himself, the fact that he used similar symbols to describe his products, his organization, and his own life (as we shall describe in greater detail below) enabled stakeholders to trust him. They knew that the same power he used to move them moved him. It is this integrity—this sense of being truly genuine—which proves crucial to visionary leadership, and makes it impossible to translate into a general formula.

In summary, the use of the metaphor of drama has allowed us to construct an alternative model of visionary leadership, one of dynamic interaction rather than unidirectional flow, a process of craft and repetition rather than simple cognition, brought to bear in the communication of affect as well as effect. Vision as leadership is a drama which takes place in time. As in theater, a leader can have a "bad house"—a passive, unresponsive organization. Only at the right time with the right audience can strategy become vision and leadership become visionary.

Varieties of Visionary Leadership

All that we have described so far we believe to be common to visionary leadership in general. But in other regards contexts vary, issues vary, leaders vary. If vision is a drama, then script, direction, actors, staging, and audience may all vary; many combinations can produce vivid, exciting representation.

What drives the strategic visionary? What is the nature of his or her particular attributes, his or her particular ideas?

Firstly, just as recent theories of the mind suggest there is not one but multiple kinds of intelligence (Gardner, 1983), so too the notion of vision seems to involve a variety of mental capacities, what can be called *visionary style*. In particular, vision has been equated with a capacity for "imagination," "inspiration," "insight," "foresight," and "sagacity" *(Oxford English Dictionary)*. An analysis of some of the visionary leaders we have encountered in our research suggest that individual leaders exhibit characteristic styles in which certain of these capacities are salient, while the others, though present, remain secondary.

Secondly, visionary style is expressed through *strategic process*. We identify two elements of this—its mental origin and its evolution. *Mental origin* refers to that combination of mental and social dynamics, particular to the individual, that gives rise to the vision in the first place. For example, vision may arise primarily through introspection or interaction, or through the combination of the two. *Evolution* refers to the deliberateness and pace of development of the vision. Some visions develop more deliberately, through controlled conscious thought. Others emerge through a less conscious learning process. Also, some appear suddenly (like a visitation), others build up gradually, piece by piece over time in an incremental process. We might also note the aspect of intensity, which refers to the degree to which the vision possesses the visionary and those surrounding him/her, and durability, which refers to the persistence of the vision, ranging even beyond the career of the visionary as it infuses the behavior of an organization for generations.

Thirdly is the *strategic content* of the vision. Vision may focus on products, services, markets, or organizations, or even ideals. This is its strategic component, the central image which drives the vision. We refer to this as the *core* of the vision. In addition to this, every vision is surrounded by a kind of halo designed to gain its acceptance. It is this component, comprising its symbolic aspects of rhetorical and metaphorical devices, which we refer to as its circumference. Often, however, unless the vision focuses on a very tangible product (such as Land's camera), the line between core and circumference is blurred. We should also note that the value added by the visionary may lie in the circumference alone, the core alone, or in the core and circumference in a gestalt combination. That is, leaders can sometimes charge rather ordinary products or markets, etc. with strategic vision, or create novel products of markets. The most exciting cases, however, inevitably involve novelty of both, integrated together.

Fourthly, and last, there are variations in *external context* that influence the visionary process. The nature of the organization itself can vary, in ownership, in structure, in size, in developmental stage, etc., for example, being public or private, developing entrepreneurial or mature turnaround. So too can the industry and the broader environment, from traditional mass production to contemporary high technology, etc.

In a previous paper (Westley and Mintzberg, 1988), we probed into the relevance especially of the contextual and stylistic factors through a comparison of the visionary leadership of Lee Iacocca and René Lévesque. Here we draw on that material and also extend the analysis to some of the other factors in considering these two visionary leaders alongside three others—Edwin Land, Steve Jobs and Jan Carlzon. Four of the people we shall discuss, Land, Jobs, Iacocca and Carlzon, are business leaders widely recognized and admired for their visionary abilities. The fifth, René Lévesque, likewise recognized for his visionary leadership, was the premier of Quebec between 1976 and 1985 who brought that province to the brink of separation from the rest of Canada. As shown in Table 1, we consider these men to have exhibited five distinct styles of visionary leadership.

The creator: Edwin Land

The creator visionary is characterized by two qualities: the originality of his or her ideas or inventions and the sudden, holistic quality of their realization. Vision for the creator occurs in moments of inspiration, which seize the leader suddenly and unexpectedly and which become, for that leader, a driving preoccupation, a singleminded focus which evokes, at least metaphorically, the notion of all eyes turned in a single direction. Such vision is often experienced as deriving from a source outside the self, as in the classic case of religious leaders who claim to be the receptacles or channels of divine inspiration.

No one we have encountered exemplifies these creative aspects of vision better than Edwin Land, the founder of the Polaroid Corporation and the inventor of the Polaroid Camera. Earlier we recounted Land's own description of his invention of the Polaroid camera. Land was clearly inspired that day in Santa Fe when, in the space of only a few hours, he constructed a complete mental image of the product. Such inspirations often possessed him. When they

Table 1. Varieties of Leadership Style

Characteristic style	Salient capacities	Content	Process	Organization content	Product/ market context	Target group
Creator (Edwin Land)	Inspiration, imagination, foresight	Product focus	Sudden, holistic; introspective, deliberate	Start-up, entrepreneurial	Invention and innovation, tangible products, niche markets	Independent consumer, scientific community
Proselytizer (Steven Jobs)	Foresight, imagination	Market focus	Emergent, shifting focus, interactive, holistic	Start-up, entrepreneurial	Tangible product, adaptation, mass market	Collective market, competitor infrastructure
Idealist (René Lévesque)	Imagination, sagacity	Ideals focus	Deliberate, deductive, introspective, incremental	Turnaround, public bureaucracy	Political concepts, zero-sum market	General population, 50% market share
Bricoleur (Lee Iacocca)	Sagacity, foresight, insight	Product/ organization focus	Emergent, inductive, interactive, incremental	Revitalization, turnaround, private and public bureaucracy	Product development; segmented, oligopolistic markets	Government (in Chrysler), union, customers
Diviner (Jan Carlzon)	Insight, sagacity, inspiration	Service focus	Incremental, sudden crystalization, interactive	Revitalization, bureaucracy	Service development and innovation, mass oligopolistic market	Employees

occurred, Land would disappear in his laboratory for 3-day uninterrupted stretches. He described these experiences as intense and almost mystical:

> I find it is very important to work intensively for long hours when I am beginning to see solutions to a problem. At such times atavistic competences seem to come welling up. You are handling so many variables at a barely conscious level that you can't afford to be interrupted. If you are, it may take a year to cover the same ground you could cover otherwise in sixty hours (Bello, 1959: 158).

Note in the above quote that Land is unclear about the sources of his own creativity. Elsewhere he suggests that such impulses are ill-understood and extremely primitive. For him the moment of inspiration had a miraculous quality of being transported to a wholly unexpected realm:

> The transfer from the field of polarized light to the field of photography was for us all a miraculous experience, as if we had entered a new country with different languages and different customs only to find that we could speak the language at once (Wensbergh, 1987: 85).

Land was also characterized by a remarkable ability to construct clear and detailed mental images of phenomena which did not yet exist. Of course, that was aided by the focus of the vision on concrete products, another characteristic we believe to be associated with creator visionaries. Their visions seem to have little to do with images of "future organizational states" (Bass, 1987).

Land's ability to "see" his products marks him as an inventive genius; but his inventions were also prophetic: he had foresight. Land knew there was a market for the Polaroid camera. In his vision the role of industry was to understand "the deep needs of people that they don't know they have" (*Time*, 1961: 88). That Land knew how to package his inventions in evocative images we have already seen as well. In this, Land the creator was also Land the proselytizer, the style to which we shall turn next.

Strategy, for Land, began with two simple but enduring preoccupations. From the time he was a teenager he was fascinated by the idea of polarizing light, and from his time at Harvard he wanted to build a world-class scientific laboratory (Wensbergh, 1987). Land deliberately set out to win over the scientific community by establishing and building on his relationship with scientists at Harvard and MIT. He also staged dramatic events both for the general media and the scientific magazines. These events were carefully designed for dramatic impact and often timed to coincide with science fairs and conventions (Wensbergh, 1987). This gave Polaroid and Land a well-deserved reputation for being both seriously scientific and innovative and helped attract first-class scientists to work on applications for polarization.

On the basis of these two enduring preoccupations the Polaroid group developed a wide variety of inventions, such as 3D glasses, polaroid sunglasses, and customized products for photography and automobile manufacture, with varying degrees of commercial success, none of them spectacular. With Land's invention of the instant camera, however, preoccupations suddenly found a focus, the core for his strategic vision: to develop and perfect that instant camera. In contrast to the sudden emergence of the core, however, the circumference of the vision developed more gradually.

As for context, here we have a case of classic entrepreneurial start-up based on invention and innovation. The products were tangible, and the markets, mostly consumer, composed of niches clearly defined by the inventions. The strategies were thus ones of differentiation, and the issues were of a technological nature, requiring Land, in his proselytizing role, to target both the individual consumer and the scientific community to accept his views. All these attributes seem to fit most naturally with the concept of the visionary as creator.

The proselytizer: Steven Jobs

Superficially, Steve Jobs would appear to be a classic visionary much like Edwin Land (who was one of his heroes). As he himself admits, he was in love with products, and his leadership centered around one particular set of them: the Apple computers.

Jobs, however, did not seem to have had the kind of creativity or concrete imagination that characterized Land's leadership. His cofounder, Steve Wozniak, boldly stated that Jobs did not understand computers, and the actual design of the machine has been widely credited to Wozniak. But as Wozniak also said, "It never crossed my mind to sell computers. It was Steve who said 'Let's hold them up in the air and sell a few.'" It was Jobs who insisted that the computer be "light and trim, well designed in muted colors." Jobs likewise pushed his engineers to "make machines that will not frighten away a skittish clientele" (Cocks, 1983: 25).

What was visionary about Jobs' approach—where he surely added value—was his evangelical zeal to show people the future potential of the product. This is vision as foresight, and has caused Jobs to be dubbed the "priceless proselytizer" (Uttal, 1985a) and the "missionary of micros." Jobs has been credited with "selling hundreds of thousands, possibly millions of Americans on the new technology" (Cocks, 1983: 25). His visionary capacity as a promoter was also widely recognized and appreciated within the company. "Apple isn't just the money," one programmer commented, "it's a giant magnifying glass that takes your great stuff and broadcasts it out to everyone" (Rogers, 1981: 54). Borrowing from Land, Jobs has compared the computer to the telephone in its significance for ordinary people (Marbach, 1984). He was determined that it should be both beautiful and usable. He once purportedly had an outburst of temper when he heard that a university to which he had donated computers was controlling access. "We don't want the use of these machines to be controlled . . . we want people to start fooling around, to let them get stolen, to let people use them at night" (*Forbes*, 1981: 32).

Jobs was a child of the 1960s, who travelled through India in search of truth, who meditates and has been a rigid vegetarian (some stories suggest that the name "apple" was chosen because at that point Jobs ate only fruit [Cocks, 1983]). His uncompromising and heartfelt ideas about what sort of place Apple Computer should be, as well as what sort of products it should produce, seem to have both made the company and led to his ouster from it (Uttal, 1985a,b).

Among the leaders we are describing here, Jobs is outstanding in his merging of foresight and imagination into the genius of the proselytizer. He shares with Land some of the capacity for inspiration, if not for true creativity. And he shares with René Lévesque an idealism and an attachment to his ideals which ultimately limited his leadership. Jobs was a perfectionist, and as the organization grew, many in Apple experienced this as intolerance and self-absorption. Said Steve Hawkins, an Apple employee:

> He's extremely ambitious, almost to the point of megalomania! He's such a perfectionist that people can never please him, and that caused a lot of trouble with morale . . . Most people weren't good enough for him and would really be in a state of shock after encounters with Steve (Butcher, 1988: 122).

The context here may also seem similar to that of Land—a consumer product based on innovation in start-up entrepreneurship. But in an important sense it was quite different, as was the market and the issue. For whereas Land created a series of niches defined by his very inventions, Jobs set out to create and conquer one very large market (he saw it as large from early on), based more on adaptations than on inventions. In a sense Land had to convince individual consumers to buy into his ideas; Jobs, in contrast, had to create a market *per se*, had to convince people *collectively* to support a new line. Any individual can put on a new pair of sunglasses or take their own pictures in a new way. But the software and service support for the personal computer meant that the collectivity had to be convinced rather than the individual. Perhaps that is why we find the proselytizer here, the creator in Land's context.

In addition, the proselytizer may prove less able to survive the transition from entrepreneurial to established organization than the creator. Jobs' capacities for foresight and imagination made him a genius in a competitive industry in its infancy. But as Apple grew in size and reputation, Jobs' capacities were less in demand and his weaknesses more evident. He was then preaching to the converted. Thus, people became suspicious of his persuasive powers and tired of his intensity (Butcher, 1988: 126).

Certainly, the proselytizer is the most dependent of the five visionary styles. While creators rely on others to *enact* their vision, proselytizers depend on others to *stimulate* their vision. Jobs' vision was based on the products others created and the patterns he observed in their activity. He added value at the circumference rather than at the core. He was able to use his vision to maneuver strategically in the interests of his company, but his dependency remained.

One of the potential pitfalls for proselytizers, however, is that they may come to forget this dependence. With success they may believe that, like creators, their vision is responsible for the existence of their products. This may be what happened to Steve Jobs. Certainly he appears to have ceased to rely on his powers of persuasion; during his last days at Apple he alienated many of the subordinates, the suppliers and the buyers he previously charmed (Butcher, 1988: 123). In doing so he severed himself emotionally from the sources of his vision before the organization finally rejected him. The industry waits to see whether Jobs can succeed with a vision as well as a new competitor in Next, the company he founded when he left Apple (O'Reilly, 1988).

The idealist: René Lévesque

An idealist is someone who speculates on the ideal, who dreams intensely of perfection and minimizes or ignores the flaws and contradictions of the real. As a visionary capacity idealism must have an appeal, it must crystallize the dreams of a constituency. But, like the creator, the source of the idealist's inspiration is essentially introspective, not interactive. He or she is inspired by ideas, his or her own or those already created. Idealism in its extreme form is no more responsive to social interaction than is the creator's inspired invention. But for the idealist this can present a problem. If the idealistic capacities characteristic of the visionary leader are overdeveloped at the expense of other more interactive capacities, the individual will not long be a leader. Thus the idealistic visionary may have to be a pragmatist, to mix considerable political sagacity with his or her idealism in order to animate the vision, and to avoid alienating stakeholders.

Of course, we are more likely to find what we are labelling the idealistic visionary in a missionary-type organization than in a conventional business corporation. René Lévesque at the head of the Parti Québecois represents that kind of visionary leader. Lévesque did not invent the notion of "sovereignty-association," his party's guiding philosophy, but rather adapted a social ideal that had long existed in Quebec. He pursued, or more exactly sought to operationalize, that ideal into political reality. The ideal was simple, almost simplistic:

The more I thought about this project, the more it seemed logical and easy to articulate. Its main lines were beautifully simple and there was paradoxical added advantage that it was far from revolutionary. In fact, it was almost banal, for here and there, throughout the world, it had served to draw together people who, while determined to be masters in their own house, had found it worthwhile to enter into associations of various kinds with others. So association it was to be, a concept that had figured for a long time in our vocabulary and a word that would marry well with sovereignty, sovereignty-association making a euphonious pair (Lévesque, 1986: 214).

What is interesting about the above quote, in addition to illustrating the abstract, idealistic nature of Lévesque's thoughts (in contrast to the concrete nature of Land's), is its suggestion that Lévesque did in fact possess the requisite political wisdom. In the notion of sovereignty-association, as Lévesque spells it out above, is married not only ideas but also political groups. Sovereignty for the radical separatists who were tired and angered by centuries of what they felt to be political oppression at the hands of the English Canadians, and association for the majority of Québecois who remained conservative and somewhat attached to Canada.

There is much evidence that Lévesque held both ideologies, and so was a man divided to represent a people divided. In the end, however, his sagacity and his idealism were at odds. In the effort to make his dream a reality he was unable to hold together the factions he first combined, and his idealism degenerated into maneuvering. As we have described elsewhere (Westley and Mintzberg, 1988), for Lévesque, strategy that began as visionary perspective reduced first to a portfolio of specific political positions, many in the form of legislation after the Parti Québecois became the ruling government of Quebec, and then to ploys as the Lévesque cabinet maneuvered on the intricacies of the wording of their referendum question on sovereignty-association. We would suggest that compromise generally poses a threat to the idealistic visionary leader. It represents the "routinization of charisma" (Weber, 1978), which can rob vision of its unique force and appeal. Without compromise the organization cannot succeed. With compromise the idealism is diluted: the vision cannot succeed.

In a certain way strategy-making for Lévesque was both deliberate and emergent, almost independently. It was deliberate in that the idealist sought to implement his vision of sovereignty-association. Lévesque's approach was fundamentally *deductive*—to reduce a vague vision to the practical realities of a rearranged political order. But it was emergent too, or perhaps more accurately, "disjointedly incremental" (Braybrooke and Lindblom, 1963), in that power evoked processes of its own, as the determined and influential people around Lévesque each maneuvered to support their own positions. In a sense, Lévesque tried to use his vision to control that disjointedness, but his was a losing battle.

We broached the issue of context above. Lévesque clearly operated in the public sector, indeed we might add, with a vengeance, given the intensity of the political battles he had to fight, with his opponents but no less with people within his own party. But some of the concepts normally associated with private sector strategic management can be applied here too. The issue—in Lévesque's vision at least—was one of turnaround: how to save a culture threatened by social pressures. Moreover, to effect that turnaround, Lévesque was prevented from operating in market niches, as Land could do, even well-developed segments, as in the case of Iacocca at Ford or Chrysler. In having to win his referendum Lévesque needed to convince a majority of the voters—in conventional strategy terms, he was engaged in a two-person zero-sum game that required a market share greater than 50 per cent.

The difficulty for the idealist, exemplified by Lévesque, is that he or she has to sell an abstract concept. While Land could promote a novel camera and Iacocca a set of tangible automobiles, even Jobs a physical machine behind his ideas, Lévesque was forced to sell an idea whose final shape was never more than a series of proposals on paper. All strategists have to manage ideas, often in the form of analysis or debates, simply because every strategy is at its roots no more than an abstract concept that has to be seen in the mind's eye. But some strategies can at least come to life in tangible ways—for example, as products that flow off assembly lines. For others, where this is not true, strategy-making becomes that much more of a vulnerable process, as we saw in Lévesque's eventual demise.

For idealists to implement their vision they must convince people to accept it in its entirety. They must convince them not only to execute a plan but also to accept the values which undergird that plan. This process may resemble a conversion. But when such an "ideal" vision is broken into distinct parts it may not be possible to reassemble it later. In the realization of ideals, unlike the construction of cameras, the whole is greater than the sum of its parts. Hence, while Land was able to turn perspective into plan, for Lévesque it degenerated into ploy. And ploy is potentially dangerous to any visionary as it opens him or her to suspicions of insincerity.

The bricoleur: Lee Iacocca

The term "bricoleur" refers to a common figure in France: a man who frequents junkyards and there picks up the stray bits and pieces which he then puts together to make new objects. This image, drawn from Levi-Strauss (1955), was originally intended to be a metaphor for myth-making. Here we use it to suggest both the myth-making capacity of certain visionary leaders and their capacity for building, whether that be organizations, teams, designs or ideologies. In contrast with the creator and to some extent the idealist, the bricoleur's genius resides not in an introspective ability to invent or imagine, but rather in an interactive, social ability to "read" situations and recognize the essential (insight), to understand and deal with people (sagacity), and to project these essential understandings into the future for promotional purposes (foresight).

We believe Lee Iacocca represents the bricoleur because, despite his visionary reputation, neither at Ford nor at Chrysler did he really present the world with anything startlingly new or original. Of his most famous success, the Ford Mustang, Iacocca freely admits that the design represented a recombination of "classic" stylistic elements, tailored to fit on existing car platforms and over existing engines. Iacocca's role here was in leading a team driven by "a market in search of a car," and in recognizing a good design when he saw one. In contrast to Land, Iacocca never imagined the product himself. But he had the sagacity to build the team, the foresight to read the market, the insight to recognize the winning design.

As for his experiences at Chrysler, the core of what Iacocca did there amounted to a classic form of operating, not strategic, turnaround. In other words, Iacocca cut costs, reorganized, rationalized, etc., rather than conceived a new image of how to compete in the automobile business. On the political dimension, however, Iacocca did exhibit sagacity in dealing with Congress and the unions, as well as foresight in selecting arguments to present the

Chrysler case. Thus his was a *political* turnaround as well as an operating one, a concept that has been missing from the literature of strategic management and, judging from the behavior of many large organizations, one that seems to be increasingly popular.

Iacocca's unique style resided not in the core vision but in his ability to create the gestalt, a powerful circumference to that core. He combined the elements he found around him—whether people, parts, processes, or operations—and then infused these combinations with intense personal affect and evocative symbolism. He was a strategist very much as Wrapp (1967) and Quinn (1980) have described, the incrementalist, but also, as Selznick (1957) characterized it, the "institution builder." The act of incrementally piecing together people, parts and processes resulted in the Mustang at Ford; the act of incrementally piecing together people and perceptions resulted in a powerful survival myth at Chrysler, perhaps the key to its turnaround. Such "bricolage" represents serendipity as an art form.

It should be obvious from the above that the bricoleur is more of a learner than the other strategists so far discussed, and his or her strategies are less deliberate, more emergent. If Lévesque was the deductive strategist, then Iacocca was the *inductive* one, combining the pieces to create the whole. Both core and circumference emerged over time and crystallized into identifiable vision only, perhaps, where looked at in retrospect.

As we characterized Iacocca in our other paper, he began with strategy as process not content: the construction of a team that itself would develop the strategy. From that process the team developed a series of positions, tangible elements about specific automobiles, loan guarantees, etc. In the Chrysler case Iacocca embodied these tangible elements in a highly symbolic ground, constructing metaphors and myths which gave him emotional appeal and heroic significance. This symbolic "circumferential" vision, supported by no shortage of more pedestrian ploys, was kept to the turnaround strategy and set it apart from other, less sensational cases.

Iacocca's context was private enterprise and largely consumer products, much like those of Land and Jobs. But the organization was quite different: in both Ford and Chrysler, large and established, dedicated to mass production in a mature industry. And Iacocca was an employee, not a substantial owner. All this perhaps explains why we see less vision at the outset, less even after all was said and done. Iacocca was not so much promoting something new as trying to improve (in the case of Ford) or turn around (in the case of Chrysler) something quite old.

Interestingly, in some respects, René Lévesque comes closest to this: his party may have been new, indeed in some sense his own, and, in the context of government, rather entrepreneurial; but that party, in order to effect its desired turnaround, had to seize the power of a very long-established and bureaucratic organization, namely the government of Quebec. Of course, in having to deal with the U.S. government in the Chrysler turnaround Iacocca faced similar political pressures. But in other ways, of course, the two contexts were very different. Iacocca headed clearly hierarchical organizations, and like Land and Jobs he had the advantage of producing tangible products through tangible processes. (Consider the advantages of strategic vision taking such tangible shape: on first looking at a clay model of what was to become the Mustang, Iacocca was immediately attracted to it with the feeling that it "looked like it was moving" (Iacocca, 1984: 67).

Moreover, while Lévesque was trying to execute radical change in a society, Iacocca was merely trying to preserve the status quo: sustain Ford and turn around Chrysler to preserve its jobs and markets. Perhaps that is the main reason why one failed while the other succeeded, also why one was the idealist, the other the bricoleur. Different personalities are attracted to different strategic contexts, although the context certainly evokes particular behaviors in the leader.

The diviner: Jan Carlzon

The salient capacity of what we are calling the diviner is insight, which comes with great clarity in moments of inspiration. In this respect the diviner is like the creator: his insights have the quality of something new and fresh, of coming into the mind like a visitation. However, unlike the creator, the insights of our diviner visionary tend to focus on process as opposed to product, for example on how to conceive or structure the organization; in fact, in the ability to use his or her capacities to build organizations, the diviner resembles the bricoleur.

Jan Carlzon is a good example of the diviner. As president of SAS, Carlzon focused not so much on product as on process and organizational structure. True, he put a great deal of emphasis on Euroclass, SAS's version of business class. But his novel insights were into the nature of service itself and the type of organizational structure most likely to deliver it. In his autobiography, *Moments of Truth*, Carlzon (1987) spells out his organizational blueprint in great detail: it includes making the front line workers—ticket agents and stewardesses in particular—into "managers," giving them the authority to "respond to the needs and problems of individual customers." Middle managers are transformed from supervisors into resources for the frontline workers. They are reprimanded for inhibiting these people's initiatives.

Like Iacocca, Carlzon obviously had the political sagacity to turn these organizational images into reality. He effected a now legendary turnaround at SAS. Unlike Iacocca, however, he seemed to orchestrate the turnaround in more than textbook fashion. The core image of service and organization seems to have originated with Carlzon, much as the image of the camera developed with Land. Carlzon describes the process of image construction quite differently from Land, however. Instead of leaps of imagination resulting in complete designs, Carlzon suggests that his organizational blueprint resulted from a number of small insights, discrete moments of inspiration, which he pieced together, bricoleur fashion, to create the whole.

The source of such moments were interpersonal experiments. Carlzon was very attentive to his interactions with others and to the effects of his words and deeds. He learned from these experiments— they inspired him, giving him a sense of his own character and the nature of his business. Carlzon recounts how, when he first took over Vingresor, Sweden's largest tour operator, he felt frightened, lost and inexperienced. He resorted to role-playing: he acted as he thought a president should act. He made firm decisions (about things he felt unsure of), gave orders and generally acted like an autocrat. One day one of his employees walked into the office and confronted him:

> "What are you doing?" he asked me. "Why do you think you became the boss here? To be someone you aren't? No—you were made president because of who you are!

Thanks to his courage and frankness, Christer helped me discover that my new role did not require me to change. The company was not asking me make all the decisions on my own, only to create the right atmosphere, the right conditions for others to do their jobs better (Carlzon, 1987: 8).

Carlzon built on this moment of insight when he moved to his new job at Linjeflyg (Sweden's domestic airline). There, instead of attempting to conceal his feelings of inadequacy, he acted on them. He began by appealing to his employees to save the company: "You are the ones who must help me, not the other way around" (p. 11). Their delighted response confirmed his perceptions: people liked a boss who gave them the authority and responsibility to act.

In the end, Carlzon's experience became a metaphor for what a service organization should be. The "moments of truth" in service are the small encounters between employees and customers, which are inspired by a true feeling of serving, by intrapreneurial zeal. Put together, hundreds of these moments make up a winning organization. Put together, Carlzon's personal moments of truth revealed the blueprint for an organization's design.

Our final type of visionary is again largely inductive, his or her vision—both core and circumference—largely emergent, followed by a more clearly deliberate period of vision enactment. A sharper vision appears here than in the case of Iacocca, the bricoleur, and certainly one that is more original. Carlzon too effected a turnaround, or perhaps more accurately a revitalization, but more strategic, less operating than that of Iacocca at Chrysler.

Otherwise, the Carlzon context seems to be rather much like that of Iacocca: a large, established, and hierarchical organization, operating in markets that were competitive yet also oligopolistic. It was a service rather than product business, but flying people and cargo between destinations remains rather tangible, certainly when compared with the philosophy of a political party.

Indeed, in addition to his interpersonal sensitivity, perhaps a key element in Carlzon's effectiveness was his ability to render the services of his airline so tangible exemplified by his concepts of the "moment of truth" in their delivery and in the intriguing notion of the manager who works for the ticket agent. Of course, while Land had to convince the individual consumer, Jobs the collective market, Lévesque the population at large, and Iacocca the government and other stakeholders (in the case of Chrysler), it was largely his own employees whom Carlzon had to convince to accept a new way of doing things. Perhaps we should add the label *ideological* turnaround (or perhaps conclude that revitalization must always involve elements of ideology) for Carlzon's actions as a diviner visionary.

Conclusions

In the above cases we have suggested that visionary leadership can vary importantly from leader to leader. The style of the leader may vary, as may the content of the leader's vision and the context in which it takes root. The core of the vision may focus on product or service, market, process, organization or ideals: its circumference involves the rhetoric and metaphor of persuasion. The envisioning process may be ignited by introspection or interpersonal interaction. It may be experienced by the leader as deliberate or emergent, and as a sudden visitation or a series of incremental revelations. It may vary in intensity and in duration. The possibilities are enormous; other leaders may reveal other categories. Our intention has not been to present any firm typology so much as to indicate the possibilities for variations in visionary style, and to map out some important dimensions of visionary leadership.

Thus, *strategic vision* is part style, part process, part content, and part context, while visionary leadership involves psychological gifts, sociological dynamics and the luck of timing. True strategic visionaries are both born and made, but they are not self-made. They are the product of the historical moment.

Our research suggests that despite their great skills, it is a mistake to treat leaders such as those discussed here as possessing superhuman qualities. They are the product of their times, of their followers, of their opportunities. As times and contexts change the visionaries of yesterday fade into obscurity, or worse, become the villains of today. Iacocca is currently in danger of losing his status as a visionary leader, Carlzon has likewise run into difficulties. Polaroid and Land eventually parted company, as did Apple and Jobs, and Lévesque lost his election and quit his party in frustration. It did not seem to be the man or his capacities that changed in these cases, so much as the needs and expectations of his followers, organizations, and markets.

We should emphasize that visionary leadership is not always synonymous with good leadership. All of our leaders had reputations for being difficult to work with in some ways. Land "wore out and exhausted his employees" (Wensbergh, 1987: 128). Some claimed that Jobs could be tyrannical and destructive (Butcher, 1987: 117-126). Leaders in many contexts can be effective without being visionary, and their organizations may be happier places.

A dramaturgical model of vision raises a number of intriguing questions for further research. What is the exact nature of the symbols and processes visionary leaders employ in their "representations"? What kind of interactions characterize the "assistance" that the visionary receives from his or her organization? What kind of psychological, social, or technical "repetition" forms the different visionary styles?

Careful analysis of speeches, reports, autobiographies, and interviews using techniques of textual analysis (Kets de Vries and Miller, 1987) should reveal similarities and differences in "representation" technique across styles. Further collection of biographical information with a larger sample of visionary leaders should be oriented toward uncovering patterns of similarities and differences in the process of repetition or rehearsal. Assistance must likely be uncovered through direct observation, or through accounts of people who worked with the visionary. We might expect to find regularities in the roles team members play in relation to the visionary, but this has yet to be established.

Overall, the study of visionary leadership and strategic vision offers the opportunity for a rewarding and revitalizing interchange between the fields of leadership studies and strategic management. Concepts of strategy introduce consideration of market forces, environmental pressures, and organizational imperatives which form the backdrop for visionary initiatives. Against these features it is to their credit that even the gifted individuals we discussed were able to have such an impact on their organizations and on history. Consideration of that impact—more attention to issues of insight and inspiration, communication and commitment—can help to humanize considerations of strategic management while restoring to leadership study itself some of the flavor that Selznick (1957) sought (largely in vain) to instill 30 years ago.

In the closing lines of his book, Brook makes an observation about the relationship between life and the theater:

In everyday life, "if" is a fiction, in the theater "if" is an experiment.

In everyday life, "if" is an evasion, in the theater "if" is the truth.

When we are persuaded to believe in this truth, then the theater and life are one.

This is a high aim. It sounds like hard work.

To play needs much more. But when we experience the work as play, then it is not work any more.

A play is play. (p. 157)

If we substitute "organization" for "life" and "vision" for "theater," we may begin to understand why strategic vision is stimulating so much interest. The visionary leader is a transformer, cutting through complex problems that leave other strategists stranded. Visionary leadership encourages innovation—fiction becomes experiment. Visionary leadership inspires the impossible—fiction becomes truth. In the book *The Soul of a New Machine*, Tracy Kidder quotes a secretary who worked for the Eagle Team under the visionary Tom West. Asked why she didn't leave when so overworked and underappreciated, she replied: "I can't leave . . . I just have to see how it turns out. I just have to see what Tom's going to do next" (1981: 58). Visionary leadership creates drama; it turns work into play.

References

Bass, Bernard M. "Charismatic and inspirational leadership: what's the difference?" *Proceedings of Symposium on Charismatic Leadership in Management*, McGill University, Montreal, 1987.

Bello, Francis. "The magic that made Polaroid." *Fortune*, April 1959, pp. 124-164.

Bennis, Warren. "Leadership transforms vision into action," *Industry Week*, 31 May 1982, pp. 54-56.

Bennis, Warren and Burt Nanus. *Leaders: The Strategies for Taking Charge*. Harper and Row, New York, 1985.

Braybrooke, David and Charles E. Lindblom. *A Strategy of Decision*, Free Press, New York, 1963.

Brook, Peter. *The Empty Space*, Penguin Books, Markham, Ontario, 1968.

Burke, K. *A Rhetoric of Motives*, Prentice-Hall, Englewood Cliffs, NJ, 1950.

Business Week. "A new breed of strategic planner," 17 September 1984, pp. 62-68.

Butcher, Lee. *Accidental Millionaire*, Paragon House Publications, New York, 1988.

Carlzon, J. *Moments of Truth*, Ballinger, Cambridge, MA, 1987.

Cocks, J. "The updated book of Jobs," *Time*, 3 January 1983, pp. 25-27.

Conger, Jay A. and Rabindra N. Kanungo. "Towards a behavioral theory of charismatic leadership in organizational settings," *Academy of Management Review*, **12**(4), 1987, pp. 637-647.

Edelman, M. *The Symbolic Uses of Politics*, University of Illinois Press, Urbana, IL, 1964.

Forbes, Vol 127, 13 April 1981, p. 32.

Fraser, Graham. *René Lévesque and the Parti Québecois in Power*. Macmillan of Canada, Toronto, 1984.

Gardner, H. *Frames of Mind*, Basic Books, New York, 1983.

Gluck, Frederick W. "Vision and leadership," *Interfaces*, **14**(1), 1984, pp. 10-18.

Goffman, Erving. *The Presentation of Self in Everyday Life*. Doubleday, New York, 1959.

Gupta, Anil K. "Contingency linkages between strategy and general manager characteristics: a conceptual examination," *Academy of Management Review*, **9**, 1984, pp. 399-412.

Hall, E. *The Silent Language*, Doubleday, New York, 1959.

Hofer, Charles W. "Turnaround strategies," in Glueck, W. F. (ed.), *Business Policy and Strategic Management*, McGraw-Hill, New York, pp. 271-278.

Iacocca, Lee with William Novak. *Iacocca: An Autobiography*. Bantam Books, New York, 1984.

Jobs, Steven. "What I did for love," *Advertising Age*, 3 September 1984, p. 18.

Kets de Vries, M. and D. Miller. "Interpreting organizational texts." *Journal of Management Studies*, **24**(3), May 1987, pp. 233-247.

Kidder, T. *The Soul of a New Machine*, Aron Books, New York, 1981.

Kiechel. W. "Visionary leadership and beyond," *Fortune*, 21 July 1986, pp. 127-128.

Land, E. "The most basic form of creativity," *Time*, 26 June 1972a, p. 84.

Land, E. "If you are able to state a problem, it can be solved," *Life Magazine*, 27 October 1972b, p. 48.

Land, E. "People should want more from life . . . ," *Forbes*, 1 June 1975, pp. 48-50.

Lévesque, René. *Memoirs* translated by Philip Stratford. McClelland and Stewart, Toronto, 1986.

Levinson, H. and S. Rosenthal. *CEO: Corporate Leadership in Action*. Basic Books, New York, 1984.

Lévi-Strauss, Claude. "The structural study of myth," *Journal of American Folklore*, **68**, 1955, pp. 428-444.

Lieberson, S. and J. F. O'Connor. "Leadership and organizational performance: a study of large corporations," *American Sociological Review*, **37**, 1982, pp. 117-130.

Marbach, W. "Reviewing the Mac," *Newsweek*, 30 January 1984, p. 56.

Meindl, James R., Sanford B. Ehrlich and Janet M. Dukerich. "The romance of leadership," *Administrative Science Quarterly*, **30**, 1985, pp. 78-102.

Mendell, Jay S. and Herbert G. Gerjuoy. "Anticipatory management or visionary leadership: a debate," *Managerial Planning*, **33**, 1984, pp. 28-31, 63.

Mintzberg, Henry and James A. Waters. "Tracking strategy in an entrepreneurial firm," *Academy of Management Journal*, **25**, 1982, pp. 465-499.

Mintzberg, Henry and James A. Waters. "Of strategies, deliberate and emergent," *Strategic Management Journal*, **6**, 1985, pp. 257-272.

Mintzberg, Henry. "Crafting Strategy," *Harvard Business Review*, July-August 1987, pp. 66-75.

Mintzberg, Henry. "Five P's for strategy", *California Management Review*, **30**, Fall 1987b, pp. 11-24.

O'Reilly, B. "Steve Jobs tries to do it again," *Fortune*, 23 May 1988, pp. 83-88.

Patterson, William P. "Jobs starts over—this time as a multi millionaire," *Industry Week*, 30 September 1985, pp. 93-98.

Pfeffer, Jeffery. "Management as symbolic action: the creation and maintenance of organizational paradoxes," in Straw, B. M. (ed.), *Research in Organizational Behavior*, Vol. 3, JAI Press, Greenwich, CT, 1981, pp. 1-52.

Pondy, Louis R. "Leadership is a language game". In McCall, M. J. and M. W. Lombardo (eds), *Leadership: Where Else Can We Go?* Duke University Press, Durham, NC, 1978, pp. 87-99.

Quinn, James Brian. *Strategies for Change: Logical Incrementalism*. Richard D. Irwin, Homewood, IL, 1980.

Robbins, S. R. and Robert B. Duncan. "The formulation and implementation of strategic vision: a tool for change." Paper presented to the seventh Strategic Management Society Conference, Boston, MA, 14-17 October 1987.

Rogers, M. "It's the Apple of his eye," *Newsweek*, 30 January 1984, pp. 54-56.

Sashkin, Marshall. "A theory of organizational leadership: vision, culture and charisma," *Proceedings of Symposium on Charismatic Leadership in Management*, McGill University, Montreal, 1987.

Selznick, Philip. *Leadership in Administration: A Sociological Interpretation*. Harper and Row, New York, 1957.

Speer, A. *Inside The Third Reich*, Macmillan, New York, 1970.

Srivastva, Suresh and Associates. *The Executive Mind*. Jossey-Bass, San Francisco, CA, 1983.

Tichy, N. and D. Ulrich. "Revitalizing organizations: the leadership role." In Kimberly, J. R. and R. E. Quinn (eds), *Managing Organizational Transitions*, Richard D. Irwin, Homewood, IL, 1984.

Tichy, Noel M. and Mary Anne Devanna. *The Transformational Leader*, John Wiley and Sons, New York, 1986.

Time. "Edwin-Herbert Land," 17 March 1961, p. 88.

Uttal, Bro. "Behind the fall," *Fortune*, 5 August 1985a, pp. 20-24.

Uttal, Bro. "The adventures of Steve Jobs (cont'd)," *Fortune*, 14 October 1985b, pp. 119-124.

Weber, M. *Economy and Society*, University of California Press, Berkeley, CA, 1978.

Wensbergh, Peter C. *Land's Polaroid*, Houghton Mifflin, Boston, MA, 1987.

Westley, F. and H. Mintzberg. "Profiles of strategic leadership: Lévesque and Iacocca," in Conger, J. and R. Kanungo (eds), *Charismatic Leadership: The Elusive Factor in Organizational Effectiveness*, Jossey-Bass, San Francisco, CA, 1988.

Wise, D. "Apple's new crusade," *Business Week*, 26 November 1984, pp. 146-156.

Wrapp, H. Edward. "Good managers don't make policy decisions," *Harvard Business Review*, **45**, May-June 1967, pp. 91-99.

16

Becoming PALS: Pooling, Allying, and Linking Across Companies

Abstract

One way for organizations to improve their ability to compete with-out adding internal capacity is to become "PALs": they pool resources with others; they ally to exploit opportunities; and they link systems in partnerships.

The benefits and drawbacks of PAL arrangements vary with the type of alliance:

1. A service alliance. *Two or more organizations form an alliance to meet a need that is too expensive or difficult to conquer alone. This alliance yields large-scale benefits; drawbacks are problems related to management and commitment.*

2. An opportunistic alliance. *This alliance is formed to gain competitive advantage. The benefits are specific and last only as long as the opportunity lasts; thus, drawbacks involve the short-term perspective and the protection of competencies.*

3. A stakeholder alliance. *An organization strengthens its cooperation with other entities with which it is already interdependent, such as suppliers, customers, and employees. The benefits are enhanced problem-solving ability and sustained competitive edge.*

The most significant change required to form PAL arrangements is in the possession and management of power. The more adversarial the partners before the alliance, the more change will be required in internal management structures and norms. Hierarchies become less effective as employees must behave more like partners.

These PAL arrangements are inherently fragile. Significant shifts in the work environment or in strategy can erode the relationship. So can an imbalance in power between or among partners. Other threats include the taking of significant action before trust has been established, conflicting loyalties, undermanagement, an insufficient allocation of resources to the partnership, and an insufficient integration of management teams or the absence of a common framework for management.

Successful partnerships are characterized by six "I's": (1) the partners see the relationship as important; (2) they agree to a long-term investment; (3) they are interdependent; (4) they are integrated; (5) each partner is informed; and (6) the relationship is institutionalized.

Becoming PALs: Pooling, Allying, and Linking Across Companies

Rosabeth Moss Kanter

One of the lessons America's mythologized cowboys supposedly learned in the rough and tumble days of the American frontier was that paranoia was smart psychology. You couldn't trust anybody. They were all out to get you, and they would steal from you as soon as your back was turned. Staking out an ownership claim to a territory or to a herd was necessary (though not sufficient) to guarantee that you would get your piece of the action. Indeed one did not even have to travel very far west to find other cultural support for the paranoid world view. "Self-reliance" was the best-known phrase associated with the influential New Englander of the 19th century, Ralph Waldo Emerson. "Good fences make good neighbors," New Englanders thought, as Robert Frost quoted to his readers a century later.

Good fences make good corporations, the translation to traditional management assumptions could read. If you don't own it, if it hasn't been branded with your mark, you don't control it, and it

---

might hurt you. What you own is "inside" the fence; everything else is "outside," to be treated as a potential enemy or adversary unless brought under your domination.

How times have changed. Today the strategic challenge of doing more with less leads corporations to look outward as well as inward for solutions to the competitive dilemma, improving their ability to compete without adding internal capacity. Lean, agile, postentrepreneurial companies can stretch in three ways. They can *pool* resources with others, *ally* to exploit an opportunity, or *link* systems in a partnership. In short, they can become better "PALs" with other organizations—from venture collaborators to suppliers, service contractors, customers, and even unions.

This friendly approach contrasts sharply with the adversarial system ingrained in American business management. The adversarial mode for dealing with "outsiders" has had a long time to take root. Like the "paranoid style of American politics" labeled by Richard Hofsteder, the "paranoid style of traditional American management" evolved as the only means of survival in the fiercely competitive atmosphere of the late nineteenth century and reflected corporate conditions then, not now. It has pervaded relationships with organized labor. It has been immortalized in folk wisdom like "caveat emptor" (let the buyer beware). The paranoid world view has even dominated textbook discussions of organization theory and behavior, in which organizations are seen as being resentful of "resource dependencies that force them into relationships with other organizations and seeking any way they can to increase their own advantage in the relationship."

The adversarial mode with its paranoid world view centers on images of domination and fear of being dominated. It stands in stark contrast to the cooperative mode better suited to the challenges of the global Olympics, a mode that seeks opportunities for growth by allying with other organizations. For postentrepreneurial strategists, distinctions such as "inside versus outside" or "us versus them" have less meaning when teaming up might produce benefits for each group.

From Adversary to Ally

In the face of heightened competitive pressures and the worldwide scope of both technology and markets, many U.S. firms have established new cooperative agreements with other organizations at home and abroad that involve unprecedented (for them) levels of sharing and commitment. While American firms, particularly small ones, have always allied with other firms for specific purposes, the extent as well as the diversity of such activity has grown in recent years, moving from the periphery to take a central place in some companies' strategies. Indeed, international alliances and partnerships are associated with competitive strength: entered into by larger firms, by those more experienced internationally, and in strategically important industries by those with strong domestic positions.[1]

In 1987, more than forty coalitions between Ford Motor Company and outside commercial entities were identified by Harvard professor Malcolm Salter. There were more than 8,000 visits by U.S.-based Ford employees to Japan—and so much traffic between Detroit and Tokyo that many U.S.-Tokyo flights now originate in Detroit rather than Chicago. Indeed, by 1986 General Electric had more than 100 cooperative ventures with other firms, and even IBM, long known as one of the "great independents," had established formal partnerships with a number of other organizations, including Merrill Lynch and Aetna Casualty and Life. IBM was also trying to ally with potential competitors through agreements making them "value-added resellers"; McDonnell Douglas Automation, for example, would sell IBM products to their customers, adding their own to the package. In some sectors, there were more joint domestic ventures announced in a single year in the 1980s than in the previous 15-20 years combined.[2]

Firms do not lose their legal identity; they retain their own culture and management structure, and they can pursue their own strategies. But they reduce their autonomy by strengthening their ties with other organizations, thus sharing authority over certain decisions. And sometimes the interpenetration makes it hard to distinguish employees of one organization from employees of the other. At Eastman Kodak, one of its suppliers staffs and runs a Kodak office supply room.

When an alliance has existed for a long time, the bonds between representatives of the two cooperating organizations can sometimes be even closer than those within their own organizations. The advanced development division of a major defense contractor I worked with has had a long-term partnership with the Department of Defense that has resulted in a joint entity that functions like a single operating unit with both corporate and government employees. In terms of any measure except formal employer, the contractor and customer form an organization with stronger internal ties than those either group has to its own official "owner." Some of the DOD program managers have been in that role more than twenty years, guiding the corporate team in decision making. Both sets of people participate fully in regular review meetings, turning them into working sessions exemplifying their joint commitment to the products. They attend each other's recreational and educational events; indeed, at a recent divisional management development retreat, it was impossible to distinguish the customers from the hosts.

Yet, despite examples such as these, the fragility of some kinds of partnerships is as striking as their growing frequency and extent. Independent studies by McKinsey & Company and Coopers & Lybrand show that perhaps 70 percent of joint ventures of formal "strategic alliances" are disbanded or fall short of expectations. Of course, dissolution of a partnership is not de facto evidence of failure; it may mean that the alliance achieved its purpose.[3] But even for those that work, the management complexities are enormous. So why would companies elect to enter into partnerships or alliances rather than choose the simpler options of building their own internal capacity or merging with another organization?

The "do-it-yourself" option has limitations in a fast-paced, highly competitive environment. It is costly in terms of both resources and time, even assuming that the organization has the capacity to handle the new task successfully. Acquisitions are similarly costly; and they entail an obligation to manage all that comes with the package. Furthermore, it is harder to move in and out of full-fledged ownership positions than more limited arrangements that offer more flexibility. Acquisition in the form of vertical integration may create organizational rigidities that prevent innovation (for example, former external vendors with so much security they lose the motivation to innovate) or make it difficult to keep up if industry technology changes dramatically. For example, automakers who were vertically integrated with carburetor manufacturers were slower to change when electronic fuel injectors began to substitute for mechanical carburetors.[4] While the power to set terms and conditions may come with ownership or domination, this strategy can also limit the flexibility required for innovation and fast technological progress.

Besides avoiding the risks and costs of acquisition, partnerships that allow organizations to retain nominal independence also provide the motivational benefits of "ownership" of each one's piece of the territory—something particularly important to smaller and more entrepreneurial companies—instead of the loss of identity that a full merger implies. And then, of course in some spheres, for some kinds of alliances, building your own substitute or taking over the other organization is not even an option. A company cannot "take over" an existing union; it is legally safeguarded. And antitrust rules still prevent some mergers while permitting alliances among those same organizations for more limited purposes.

Analog Devices, for example, has two reasons for preferring partnerships and joint ventures over outright acquisition of small companies with the new technology Analog needs. Acquisitions would require changes in Analog's organizational structure every time a company was bought, changes that would have to be undone if an acquisition turns sour; and acquisitions would soon amount to an increasing portion of the company.

Another justification for partnerships is their dynamism. Some partnerships that begin as an alternative route to gaining a capacity or a resource may end with at least one organization better able to provide that resource for itself, so that it no longer requires the partner. Dependency is decreased over time, and the partnership dissolves. But other partnerships have the opposite dynamic. What begins as a limited alliance may move toward greater degrees of interdependence, and end with the organizations merging. Some analysts have compared "strategic alliances" to marriages, but they are really more similar to living together.

There is something entrepreneurially appealing about cooperative arrangements among firms. These relationships can help little firms compete with big firms. They offer flexibility and speed of access to new capacity. Getting the benefits of what another organization offers without the risks and responsibilities of "owning" is the ultimate form of leverage.

Of course, the benefits and issues that partnerships create depend on the purpose of the alliance. I have distinguished three categories of such partnerships: multiorganization service alliances, opportunistic alliances, and stakeholder alliances. The first type involves the least overlap and smallest sphere of cooperation between the partner organizations; the latter involves the most. Yet it is the third kind of partnership that seems to have the greatest potential for enduring benefits to the allies.

Service Alliances: The Cross-Country Consortium

In service alliances, a group of organizations with a similar need, often in the same industry, band together to create a new entity to fill that need for all of them—an industry research consortium, for example. The service is one that is too expensive or difficult for a single organization to provide for itself, and it cannot be purchased on the open market. So several organizations ally to establish a new organization, which they jointly control, to meet the need.

The resulting consortium requires the fewest changes in each partner of the three types discussed here, because interdependence among partner organizations is low; at the same time, the difficulty of getting the diverse partners to agree on the service that suits all of them can make these entities very hard to manage and loss of interest or commitment a common problem. The limited purpose of the consortium makes it possible for even nominal competitors to ally (both legally and strategically) in ensuring that a service is available across the board to all members for the purpose of lifting the performance level of the whole group. By definition, a consortium is a group formed to undertake an enterprise beyond the resources of any of its members that will provide benefits to all of them.

Consortia thus try to offer the benefits of larger scale through resource pooling. Each member gains some of the benefits of larger scale while still retaining its independence with respect to every other activity. For this reason, consortia are especially attractive in areas in which the development of new technology is particularly important and particularly costly.

The National Cooperative Research Act of 1984 loosened antitrust restrictions to allow joint development through the prototype stage. By 1985, at least forty R&D consortia were being organized nationwide, taking a number of forms. Pradco—organized by Borg-Warner, Dresser Industries, Ingersoll-Rand, and TransAmerica to design new boiler pumps for power plants—spreads research tasks among its own members. The thirty-three members of the Semiconductor Research Corporation, including AT&T, GM, IBM, and DuPont, sponsor research at a number of universities, as do the seven members of the International Partners in Glass Research. The Center for Advanced Television Studies—formed by ABC, CBS, NBC, PBS, RCA, and five other companies to improve the quality of television transmission—spends its $1 million yearly research budget through MIT; and the Guided Wave Optoelectronics Manufacturing Technology Development Program, organized by six companies, conducts its research on fiber optics at the Batelle Memorial Institute in Columbus, Ohio.

While R&D consortia are by far the most identifiable, they are not the only examples of this form of organizational cooperation. In 1986, thirty-four companies, including IBM, General Electric, and Chase Manhattan, anted up $10 million each to form American Casualty Excess Insurance Company, a company that would provide them with insurance they could not otherwise obtain. Even more significant are consortia designed to allow smaller companies to gain joint purchasing or market clout—such as the Independent Grocers of America.

Consortia are stronger versions of the weaker alliances (such as trade associations) that companies in the same industry form to conduct research or take action at the industry level. Membership is generally more restricted, membership costs are higher, and the consortium itself has more strategic significance; it is expected to produce specific benefits for specific companies, rather than generalized or abstract benefits. The stake in consortia is much higher than the stake in trade associations, and participation in governance is thus a more significant issue. But still, compared with the next two types of alliances, consortia maintain the lowest degree of joint commitment. This low commitment level is often pointed out by skeptics, who claim that companies withhold their best people and their best ideas.

Opportunistic Alliances: The Joint Venture

A second cluster of partnerships is best labeled "opportunistic," with all the positive and negative connotations of that term. Organizations see an opportunity to gain an immediate, although perhaps temporary, competitive advantage through an alliance that gets them into a new business or extends an old business. The goal is venture development. The alliance opens up possibilities that would not have existed for either of the partners acting alone. Once that opportunity is exploited, it is not always clear whether there is any basis for the relationship to continue. It is this kind of alliance that the McKinsey and Coopers and Lybrand studies saw dissolving frequently.

Joint business ventures are the generic example of the opportunistic alliance. The partners get from each other a competence that will allow them to move more quickly toward their own business goals. For example, CBS formed a number of joint ventures in the 1980s—with IBM and Sears to develop and market videotex, an electronic information system; with Twentieth Century-Fox to develop videotapes; and with Columbia Pictures (Coca-Cola) and Home Box Office (Time, Inc.) to develop motion pictures. Digital Equipment Corporation strengthened its hold on the manufacturing automation market by developing an alliance with Allen-Bradley, an industrial controls company.

The addition of the partners' competence is the answer to the question of why organizations would want to pursue a business opportunity with full-fledged partners, instead of more passive lenders or investors. The ability to gain larger scale is one motivating factor, although a weak one, tending to be confined to mass production industries with lower rates of technological innovation.[5] Instead, the two principal driving forces behind this kind of alliance are competence-enhancing ones: technology transfer or market access or both, especially where technology and markets are rapidly changing. And that is often the trade: one partner contributes the technology in return for the other's access to particular markets. But then, once one of the partners has gained experience with the competence of the other, the alliance is vulnerable to dissolution—the opportunity can now be pursued without the partner.

Stakeholder Alliances: Suppliers, Customers, Employees

Stakeholder alliances are defined by preexisting interdependence. They are "complementary" coalitions among a number of stakeholders in a business process who are involved in different stages of the value-creation chain. Stakeholders are those groups on which an organization depends—the people who can help it achieve its goals or stop it dead in its tracks. They include suppliers, customers, and employees.

Suppliers. Facing imperatives to cut costs and improve quality, leading American companies are creating closer relationships with their suppliers. "Outsourcing" is one way American high-tech firms are addressing productivity issues—buying more instead of making it in-house; 41 percent of the firms in a 1988 American Electronics Association survey planned to increase the value of the product outsourced, while only 18 percent intended to decrease it. But those same firms saw quality as their number one competitive factor.[6] To ensure quality while buying from outside firms calls for a redefinition of the vendor relationship. Arm's-length relationships do not produce the motivation for suppliers to invest in technology to improve quality or manage the complexities of just-in-time inventory.

Customers. Partnerships with customers are just the flip side of supplier relationships, of course. There have always been strategic advantages to staying close to customers. Good customer relationships reverberate not only in current sales but also in future effectiveness and growth. Satisfied customers are the best source of business. Timely knowledge of changing customer requirements makes it possible to guide production more efficiently, reducing waste, inventory costs, and returns. And experience shows that customers are also one of the major founts of ideas for innovation. In some industries, as much as 80 percent of all important industrial innovations have originated with users.[7] These are among the reasons why innovation-conscious high-technology companies go beyond emphasizing customer service to create more formal ties; user councils, inviting customers to consult on R&D projects, joint promotions, and—the ultimate partnership step—joint-development projects.

Employee organizations. A third form of complementary partnership is that between labor organizations and management to set policies jointly or coadminister an area of company operations. The planning for General Motors' Saturn subsidiary, for example, has been conducted jointly with the United Auto Workers. The plans include a network of management-union committees running the plant; representatives of the UAW sit on all planning and operating committees, including the strategic advisory committee formed by Saturn's president and staff.

Union-management alliances are occurring in industries undergoing rapid change, as a means to permit innovation—to collaborate in changing work rules or job conditions to improve competitiveness. Thus, it is no surprise that telecommunications is joining autos, steel, and air transportation in seeking new relationships between labor and management organizations.

Overall, stakeholder alliances represent the closest tie among companies of all of the three forms of partnership. The relationships establish the largest sphere of jointness—the greatest area of overlap between the activities of the partners.

Putting Power into Partnerships

What does it mean to be PALs? The strategy involves more than a mere handshake. The most important degree of change is in power. The redefinition of owner begins with a rethinking of the company's role vis-á-vis its stakeholders, a re-examination implied by the very notion of "strategic partnership." "Partners" are welcome allies, not manipulated adversaries. An enhanced role for allies can be accomplished only via a sincere company acknowledgement that such influence is warranted. This requires a new attitude among those who might feel that kind gestures toward stakeholders are a management "gift," not a partnership, in which they temporarily agree to "give" the stakeholder some of the company's rightful power, to bequeath something voluntarily in order to win cooperation, something that can be withdrawn at will. Such a paternalistic attitude can undermine the core of the partnership effort and its future potential.

Even in alliances with different origins and goals, the impact on a partner's home organization is profound. This was illustrated in three partnerships I observed closely. They can be arrayed along a continuum of prepartnership status, from the most to the least adversarial. The first, the Pacific Bell-Communication Workers of America union management "business partnership," was initially a highly adversarial relationship and thus faced the greatest amount of internal change as the parties moved significantly closer. Furthermore, the sphere of cooperation was great. The second, Digital Equipment

Corporation's supplier partnerships, involved a previously arm's-length but not severely adversarial relationship now moving closer; there was an intermediate amount of change and an intermediate degree of overlap. In the third case, a joint venture, the partnership grew out of a pre-existing but limited alliance for particular products. There was, therefore, the least internal change when the joint venture was established and the least overlap, since the joint venture was a complete business separate, in large part, from the parent companies. But even so, there were concerns that a closer partnership would involve some of the same consolidation and cutbacks as a full merger.

As a general rule I found that the greater the change in external relationship, the greater the shift in internal power resulting from the partnership:

- The labor-management partnership shifted the action away from events favoring professionals in the union and toward those favoring local presidents; away from processes favoring the national union and toward those favoring local decision making; away from treatment of workers on a mass basis and toward differentiated treatment of individuals and local worksites. And the local common interest forums added new arenas for defining union strategy, arenas in which local presidents represented the union.
- The supplier-customer partnership shifted the attention of staffs from routine administration of strategic considerations, empowered the purchasing department, and necessitated a more collaborative web of interfunctional relationship across departments inside the company.
- The joint venture shifted the locus of power from the traditional management hierarchy to those who could effectively influence the partners and represent the home organization's strategic agenda.

The Shift in Power

The power that devolves on partnership managers is seen most directly in those cases where pre-existing arm's length relationships are converted into partnerships. For many of the managers and professionals involved in partnership dealing, the empowerment is clear and direct. They have increased access to top management, whereas previously they were not included in strategic deliberations. They are given information and data allowing them to understand better what drives business decisions, and they can get questions answered with a single phone call to a previously accessible executive. They are consulted on matters of business significance to the company, before decisions are made. They are handed an opportunity to educate management about the pressures on allies—suppliers, venture partners, or customers. And they increasingly know things before the rest of the company management does, even becoming a source of information and influence for others in middle management.

The Changing Nature of Staff Roles

More line-manager and senior-management involvement in partnerships does not mean a diminished role for staffs, but it does mean a different role—and often one with fewer people.

The traditional mode was characterized by a single point of contact between one organization and its "external" constituencies: the purchasing department to management procurement, the sales department to deal with customers, the labor relations department to handle the union. That manager or department served as "gatekeeper," patrolling the boundaries and influencing, if not determining, what could come "in" and what would be sent "out." All information flowed through that gate, and the gatekeepers monopolized the management of the relationship.

Partnerships, in contrast, simultaneously make the activities involved in "external" relationships more important and reduce the former gatekeeper's monopoly over them. They can increase the number of functions and the number of people involved with those "external" relationships. For example, where strong customer alliances prevail, both product designers and production workers get directly involved with customers. In a union-management partnership, line managers relate directly to union officials, without any labor-relations-staff involvement. The former "boundary managers" can gain importance from the strategic significance given to their area, but they lose monopoly power and must change how they operate. If they do not, they risk being bypassed.

The change in traditional staff roles is apparent in Digital's purchasing department. Jobs are being upgraded, as routine administration and an emphasis on meeting specifications are replaced by a need for more experienced people who can be involved in every aspect of a business process and handle complex negotiations. Instead of rewarding staff for never running out of parts, the department now emphasizes meeting broader time-to-market and profitability goals. Instead of using the purchasing staff as an opportunity to promote less-sophisticated clerical personnel, the department seeks people who can effectively take more complete business responsibility for their decisions, represent the company in strategy discussions with partners, and even carry out such specialized professional tasks as writing contracts without using lawyers. While these are more significant tasks, they can also be done by fewer people, especially as advanced technology replaces purely routine paperwork.

The Changing Nature of Job Skills

Overall, the development of strategic alliances is one more force toward politicizing the role of managers, making it essential for them to be able to juggle constituencies rather than control subordinates. The great management theorist Chester Barnard recognized long ago that the task of leaders was to develop a network of cooperative relationships among all those people, groups, and organizations with something to contribute to an economic activity.[8] Alliances and partnerships multiply the complexity of this task. For example, after leading Teknowledge, Inc., producer of expert systems software, in development alliances with six major corporations, including General Motors, Procter & Gamble, and FMC, President Lee Hecht told a *Business Week* reporter that he feels "like the mayor of a small city. I have a constituency that won't quit. It takes a hell of a lot of balancing."[9]

The balancing act was not required in the traditional corporation. Whatever its shortcomings in practice, the traditional adversarial style had one advantage for control-conscious managers: It preserved the illusion of decision-making autonomy for the corporation as a whole. Executives could move quickly, make unilateral decisions without needing to consult any of the other organizations that would be affected by the decisions. There might be negative consequences later—for example, a labor union calling a strike after an unpalatable management announcement, or customers switching to another manufacturer after a price rise—but at least there were few apparent constraints on action. It might be smarter for management to consult with stakeholders and take their interests into account in making decisions, but it was not required.

Partnerships, in contrast, require this kind of consultation as a matter of routine. The illusion of autonomy is lost. Unilateral action decreases. The number of forums for cooperative decision making increases. The shift from arm's length relationships to more intimate partnerships thus requires a different set of skills, especially for those working closely with a component of the partnership.

Unlike relationships in a hierarchy, relationships in a partnership are ostensibly more egalitarian. Representatives of one organization cannot "order" the other to do anything, the way they could issue orders or directives to subordinate divisions or employees. One Digital manager uses the image of boss-subordinate relationships to describe how partnership behavior is different:

> There is a big difference from a boss-subordinate relationship where the boss tells the subordinate, here is the task at hand and please complete it, and one where the boss says, "We have got to win and here is what winning is as we see it. Is this how you see it?" In this new relationship we say let's talk about the work that has got to get done and let's divide up the tasks in a fashion that makes sense. There is a very different way that you are going to be motivated and approach your work with that second scenario. I think the suppliers that I have visited feel that difference of inclusion, of desire to partner to get stuff done, of the desire to help each other out and be sensitive to each other's needs. I think with 60-70 percent of our vendors, there would be a vast improvement in what they think of us now as compared with five years ago.

Discussion of goals and a search for consensus, then, become more important than who has the upper hand. Indeed, even when one partner company has the power to make its will prevail, it is considered very dangerous and damaging to the relationship to try. The formation of a partnership almost by definition calls for participative skills—gathering information, resisting preconceived ideas, listening to others, testing assumptions, seeking consensus. Traditional managers sometimes find it hard to adjust when their companies build strategic alliances.

Managers who are accustomed to acting decisively and presenting full-blown plans (in part to look good to their underlings) need to learn the patience that consensus building requires, and they need to learn to present half-formed ideas for discussion *before* making decisions. "Coming in with prepared documents" and "not fully consulting and collaborating" were two reasons why union presidents came to resent and distrust one company officer in the PacBell CWA partnership. Because the process was far less amenable to packaging or control by any one player, managers accustomed always to having their homework done and their case flawlessly persuasive found that such behavior could be seen as manipulative, disingenuous, and counterproductive. Instead, the process rewarded managers who were prepared, yes, but more important, flexible, informed, forthcoming, and candid.

The participatory standard can easily make an executive who likes to look as though everything is fully under control feel vulnerable and exposed. And it creates dilemmas even for those who handle it well, because sometimes junior partners carry old expectations that senior partners always know what they want. For example, the manager of the joint venture between firms with unequal control attributed hidden agendas to the majority shareholder's CEO, who was genuinely opening up an issue for discussion—in part out of disbelief that this executive would not have a preset agenda.

Because of the premium placed on group leadership skills, those managers who had more experience with participative leadership or had received formal training in it and who felt more secure about their position in the company were better able to handle the new roles required by the PacBell-CWA relationship.

Clearly, respect in a partnership does not come automatically with rank. The same close working relationship that builds trust also gives each partner first-hand knowledge of the actual competence of the other's representatives. Participation demystifies potential authority figures by showing them as real people. Awe is replaced by data.

One union president made this clear in praising Pacific Telesis Chairman Don Guinn and Pacific Bell President Ted Saenger as people who did not need the traditional trappings of authority to win respect. He used descriptions as "not rigid, wears light-colored suits, more liberal, freer with people," and then went on to compliment them for their "job knowledge, they could walk you through the technologies, tell you how they work and why."

Thus, authority gives way to influence and command to negotiations. Success at resolving issues within a partnership and at leading discussion toward the outcome a representative seeks is dependent on both his relationships within the alliance and his personal communication skills, as well as on his understanding of how best to manage group decision making. One experienced joint venture participant recognized this important new dynamic:

> In voting by consensus, it's not whether you agree, it's what you can live with. This is not so good when strong feelings exist, or are not expressed, that push people to act independently in their own area rather than carry out a common solution they didn't feel good about— instead, you need to take the issue apart in small groups.

This dynamic also places a premium on face-to-face contact rather than communication by faceless voices on the telephone— increasing the necessity to spend time with the partners.

In negotiations, signals and symbols are very important, and partnership representatives benefit from the ability to read them— and use them. The experienced people in the partnerships I observed are very adept at "reading" signals that indicated whether partner representatives can be trusted.

Sensitivity is most important when the partner organizations are very different in culture and style. For example, the Pacific Bell officers involved in the company-union partnership are learning to perceive the nuances of union members' reactions to things company people would take for granted or regard as trivial. The managers are becoming aware of a range of details that do not "normally" or "traditionally" concern an officer—from making sure to hold meetings in unionized hotels, to being aware of protocol in terms of who gets meeting agendas first, to anticipating the reactions of union members when they see photos of their leaders smiling alongside managers. In relationships that move from hierarchical or adversarial to egalitarian, partners look for the symbols of equality, and an important one is each honoring the other's values.

Self-awareness is important to partnerships for other reasons, too. Personal styles play a greater role in arm's length transactions. "Personalities" become more important when closer working groups are established and people debate issues face to face And it is more likely that personal compatibility will make a difference in how well (and in which direction) issues are resolved.

The Challenge to Management

Strategic partnerships form because they bring value to the organizations entering into them. But their existence also changes how the individual organizations operate and how their managers manage. Unless partnership activities can be segregated from other organizational activities (as in the formation of a stand-alone, arm's-length unit that is the only sphere of cooperation), the need to relate to partners in ways that reap the benefits of partnership inevitably changes how each partner operates.

Thus, in profound ways, the new alliances may change how American business operates. I have seen evidence of a number of changes inside partners' home organizations: in the roles of top management and the behavior required to succeed; in communication and decisionmaking channels; and in the influence and role of staff functions. Furthermore, the goals and strategies of each organization now embrace the goals and strategies of the partner. Alliances with high degrees of interpenetration—in which each partner becomes involved in processes formerly "internal" to the other—change the nature of the management tasks.

Perhaps one of the major reasons that the number of interorganizational partnerships is still relatively small is the management difficulties they entail. For each partnership, there are three areas of management challenge: managing the inherently fragile relationship between partners and managing the changes in each of the partners' own organizations. Until these new management challenges are mastered, corporations will not be able to take advantage of the benefits of strategic partnerships.

The kinds of partnerships I have outlined still represent only a small proportion of all American corporate activity, by any measure. In 1985, cooperative research represented only $1.6 billion of the over $50 billion corporations spent on R&D, including the $1.4 billion spent by research organizations serving noncompetitive electric, gas, and telephone utility companies, according to Herbert Fusfield, director of New York University's Center for Science and Technology Policy.[10] Investment in joint ventures is a drop in the bucket compared with the multiple millions spent on mergers and acquisitions. Union-management partnerships are identifiable in a few large companies, but are still relatively rare. It is impossible to count those supplier-customer alliances that do not take the form of an identifiable joint venture, since they represent a more cooperative extension of an existing relationship. They are probably the most common and the most stable alliances—but they are unlikely to be announced in press releases that allow researchers to count them.[11]

Difficulties Between PALs: Vulnerabilities of Partnerships

The fragility of interorganizational alliances stems from a set of common "dealbusters"—vulnerabilities that threaten the relationship. Partnerships are dynamic entities, even more so than single corporations, because of the complexity of the interests forming them. A partnership evolves; its parameters are never completely clear at first, nor do partners want to commit fully until trust has been established. And trust takes time to develop. It is only as events unfold that partners become aware of all of the ramifications and implications of their involvement. For one thing, the very success of a partnership in transferring knowledge may threaten the relationship by making the partner less essential over time.

All relationships have vulnerabilities. But for strategic alliances, the issues arise more often, and their impact is more severe.

Strategic Shifts

An alliance is formed to suit one strategic purpose; but what then happens to it when business conditions change? Any significant shift in the strategy of the organizations forming an alliance is a potential threat to the relationship.

In the simplest case, one partner simply exits the business that provided the rationale for the alliance. Not surprisingly, the partnership of the German company Siemens with RCA ended when RCA got out of the computer business.

Uneven Levels of Commitment

The vulnerability of alliances to strategic shifts simply points to another source of fragility: differences in the commitment of the partners to their joint activity. For one partner, the alliance may be central to its business, but for the other it may simply be a peripheral activity. This asymmetry is particularly apparent in alliances between larger organizations and smaller ones, for whom the partnership matters more when it represents a larger relative proportion of their business. The success of a union-management partnership is also more important to the labor leaders than to the managers involved, or the union's only *raison d'être* involves its relationship to the company as employer, but managers have many other business areas in which they can demonstrate their prowess. Furthermore, union leaders face periodic elections.

Unevenness of commitment stems from basic differences between organizations entering into partnerships, and these differences can cause other inequities of power.

Power Imbalances 1: Resources

When richer organizations ally with poorer organizations, the richer ones often end up subsidizing the poorer ones in conducting the activities that will allow them to hold up their end of the partnership. For example, Mazda has more than 100 engineers whose full-time job is to work inside suppliers' organizations, educating the suppliers' staff, making sure their procedures match Mazda's and instituting such programs as statistical processes control. In union-management partnerships, resource imbalances frequently mean that the company pays for support services such as education and raising of staffs of facilitators to help implement joint decision making. This leads to such anomalies as General Motors undertaking to provide company-paid training to United Auto Workers members in labor history and the union ethos, along with problem solving and business decision making, as part of getting ready to work in the new Saturn facility. When management pays for courses in union matters, is union independence eroded? (But perhaps partnerships transform the very meaning of "independence.")

The additional cost incurred by richer organizations can also get them additional control. Because they are providing resources on their own terms, they may be able to ensure that they are used in ways that make the poorer organizations conform to their standards. In exchange for strengthening the poorer organization, the richer one may be intervening in its decisions.

Over time, it is likely that the structures and practices of the organizations entering partnerships with this kind of resource imbalance will develop similar structures and practices to facilitate coordination. The smaller or resource-poorer may begin to be organized more like the larger or resource-richer partner, and to internalize more of the richer party's business philosophy and operating practices.

"Qualifications" are important in a "business partner" in a way they are not in an adversary; the stronger organization wants more competent people on the other side of the table—and also the "gratitude" and cooperation of those people, since they gain strength from the first partner's resources. The stronger management is also more concerned with the continuity and stability of the partner's organization, since turnover can mean additional investments in training to bring newcomers up to speed and can also make it more difficult to work on issues requiring longer-term effort.

The creation of a strategic alliance does not equalize power, then. Resource dependencies may instead increase as the richer side contributes to the poorer side. The "stronger" party has a stake in strengthening the "weaker" party so that the latter can do the work the partnership needs (like Polaroid deploying consultants to suppliers); but this resource infusion may bring with it more control by the richer organization.

Power Imbalances 2: Information

Two kinds of information are required for effective partnership participation: technical knowledge, which permits contributions to decision making, and "relationship" knowledge—understanding of the partner, knowledge of partnership activities, political intelligence—that provides these background for successful negotiations. A common problem in union-management alliances, for example, is union leaders' lack of information about matters on which they will be deciding. As one union official put it, "Stocks, bonds, notes, debentures—that's the language of corporate types, not the working person. In that territory, they have the advantage."

One of the many reasons given for the lopsided benefits Japanese firms derive from their joint ventures with American companies —assimilating their U.S. partner's skill, then squeezing out—is a key information gap. Japanese managers tend to learn English, while very few American managers speak Japanese. Furthermore, some joint ventures have no American managers at all.[12] To address this difficulty, Celanese Corporation trained two employees in Japanese and assigned them to Celanese's joint venture with Daicel Chemical to observe and learn.

A balance of power certainly helps sustain a partnership, and at least one company has taken the next step, attributing economic benefits to the avoidance of power imbalances. Corning Glass is known as a particularly successful practitioner of strategic alliances, and Corning executives seem particularly concerned with equalizing power with their venture partners rather than monopolizing it. "Mutuality" is the operative word. Declared Vice-Chairman Thomas McAvoy, "If I tried to gain the upper hand in a joint venture, my boss would reprimand me."

Imbalances of Benefits

Even if allies begin on an equal footing, with all parties close together in resources and information, the structure of the deal may still favor some over others. The New York Times branded U.S.-foreign alliances the "high tech giveaway," claiming that they have resulted in a "largely one-way flow of technology and other critical skills from the U.S. to foreign nations, especially Japan."[13]

In joint ventures, benefits may diverge because of differences in how each partner derives revenue. In 1982 CBS, Time, Inc., and Columbia Pictures (later acquired by Coca-Cola) formed Tri-Star Pictures, a movie production studio; each partner put in a total of

$100 million in equal shares to get a steady flow of movies for Time's HBO (a cable station), CBS's broadcasting, and Columbia's theater distribution. But in less than three years, Columbia was able to take cash out of the deal (revenues of $26 million over six quarters) while CBS, and Time to a lesser extent, had to keep putting more in; Tri-Star as an entity was only beginning to move from significant losses to very modest gains. This happened because Columbia already had a large international distribution system and simply locked in a fee structure for distributing Tri-Star's movies through it, while the deal obligated CBS to keep buying $60 million worth of movies—whether it needed them or not.[14]

Premature Trust: Absence of Institutional Safeguards

"Even paranoids have real enemies." Sometimes parties to an alliance are naive in trusting their partners too soon, before a solid basis for trust is established, and without any legal or contractual safeguards. They give away too much too early. For example, Acme-Cleveland Corporation licensed Mitsubishi Heavy Industries to manufacture and sell one of its machine tools, only to watch Mitsubishi become its rival in the U.S. market. Somehow Acme-Cleveland had "understood" that Mitsubishi was going to confine its efforts to Asia. Having learned its lesson, A-C is now writing market restrictions into its licensing agreements.[15]

Conflicting Loyalties

The flexibility inherent in allying with other organizations rather than merging with them is sometimes accompanied by a singular drawback. Unless the agreement specifies an exclusive relationship, with all the additional costs that entails, each party to the partnership may still maintain relationships outside the alliance, including relationships with competitors. These other ties pose conflicts of time and attention and raise questions of how proprietary or potentially harmful information is to be handled.

Then there's the question of "insider" information. To make a partnership work, a great deal of information has to flow to and from the partners, some of it proprietary business information or information that could give competitors an advantage if it leaked out, such as the sales forecast information Ford shares with suppliers to help them plan their own production.

A solution to the problem, of course, is for the organization with multiple ties to segregate those working with the partnership from all other personnel, to create an island of concentrated attention and information security. But this may destroy the very reason for partnership—more integration between the allies. And this does not prevent the parent organization from acting in another relationship in ways that are contrary to a partner's desire.

Undermanagement

Some partnerships flounder because of difficulties of implementation and execution. They are not organized or managed well. According to a study by accounting firm Coopers & Lybrand, nearly half the time top management spends on the average joint venture goes into creating it. Another 23 percent goes into developing the plan, and only 8 percent goes into setting up management systems.

One typical management difficulty is the absence of "tie-breakers." Companies that would balk at the mere suggestion of "democracy" inside their own ranks establish alliances with equal representation from each partner and a requirement for consensus.

Hedging on Resource Allocations

Related to undermanagement is starvation of the partnership by not feeding it with sufficient resources—from inadequate levels of funding to mediocre staff to insufficient rewards for the people from each company who have to make it work. This is one way companies show their ambivalence toward a strategic alliance. Since alliances often start out of ambivalence anyway—"We're not sure we want to do it ourselves"; "Can we find someone else to share the risk?"—this is hardly surprising. Fed less than it needs, the relationship gradually atrophies because it cannot do all the things it was formed to accomplish.

Another matter for conflict involves the scope of the alliance— what is included under its purview and what is not. Partners may reserve for themselves the right to act unilaterally in certain areas, or they may define the domain of the partnership in ways that exclude certain key items. Sometimes this reflects hedging—skepticism or lack of commitment—and sometimes merely differences in partners' needs and goals.

Insufficient Integration and the Absence of a Common Framework

In addition to the potential difference in strategies, commitment, and power that I have already described, partner organizations also differ initially in organizational structures, processes, procedures, and style. Some of this difference stems from differences in generic type: big firm/small firm differences, union-management differences, or national differences in law, traditions, and language. Some stem from common cultural differences between organizations even of the same basic type.

The partners can, in fact, remain so different that common procedures are never adopted. They can fail to develop a legitimate process for joint decision making, so that every decision is slowed by misunderstanding and conflicts. Partnerships can fall apart because systems fail to match, because people fail to agree, or because no institutional supports are built around the partnership to shore it up during difficult times.

Internal Corporate Politics

If all the other vulnerabilities of partnerships are not enough, they also fall prey to the enemy of all innovation—the politics within each of their member organizations. The issue can range from someone feeling that the partnership threatens his or her territory to the partnership's chief sponsors losing power.

The "Six I's" of Successful Partnerships

Managing the fragile relationships and strategic alliances is indeed a delicate balancing act. Corning Glass Works is one of the few companies that has mastered the art. In 1987, about 50 percent of Corning's $207.5 million in net income came from more than twenty partnerships, most with 50-50 ownership. Furthermore, that year sales for such equity companies increased 16 percent while core company sales declined. Corning has had successful partnerships for more than five decades, including the venerable Owens-Corning Fiberglass Group owned with Owens-Illinois. Its largest current partnership is Dow Corning, with Dow Chemical, but it also has partnerships with Nutrisearch, with Kroger and Eastman Kodak; Ciba Corning Diagnostics, with Ciba-Geigy; Pless-Cor Optronics, with Plessy of Great Britain; and equity ventures companies in France, Australia, West Germany, and China, among others. Even its joint ventures have joint ventures: Siecor, the company formed by Corning and Siemens, has just formed an alliance with Kaiser Aluminum.

The flexibility with which Corning approaches its partnerships —letting the form be determined by the goals, and letting the ventures evolve in form over time—is one factor in its success. But even more important is the time and effort by Corning executives to create the conditions for long-lasting, mutually beneficial relationships.

From cases like Corning, we can see what it takes to make alliances work over the long term. Successful partnerships tend to have "six I's" in place. The relationship is important, and therefore it gets adequate resources, management attention, and sponsorship; there is no point in going to the trouble of a partnership unless it has strategic significance.[16] There is an agreement for longer-term investment, which tends to help equalize benefits over time. The partners are interdependent, which helps keep power balanced. The organizations are integrated so that the appropriate points of contact and communication are managed. Each is informed about the plans and directions of the other. Finally, the partnership is institutionalized—bolstered by a framework of supporting mechanisms, from legal requirements to social ties to shared values, all of which in fact make trust possible.

The I-factors reflect a different way of thinking about the management and organizational tasks of a modern corporation. For companies to gain the benefits of allying with other organizations— from the power of combination to flexibility and innovation—these must serve as the basis for a new, more cooperative philosophy for American enterprise.

"The rewards of these things must be incredible to justify all the extra short-term costs that go along with them," one of my colleagues commented at a seminar discussing organizational cooperation. Yet for the organizations forming strategic alliances, whatever the costs, the rewards are longer term but still tangible. Partnerships represent one of the ultimate postentrepreneurial balancing acts—a way for one partner to leverage its own resources by joining forces with others, a way of encouraging others to invest in developing the things that will bring future benefits to the first organization. In the future, if an increasing amount of economic activity continues to occur across, rather than within, the boundaries defined by the formal ownership of one firm, managers will have to understand how to work with partners rather than subordinates. And that alone promises a revolutionary change in the way America does business.

Endnotes

1. Michael Porter and Mark Fuller note that "While coalitions are not new in international competition, their character seems to be shifting. Coalitions are becoming more strategic, through linking major competitors together to compete worldwide. More traditional coalitions are often tactical." The quote is from Porter and Fuller, "Coalitions in Global Strategy," in M.E. Porter (Ed.) *Competition in Global Industries*, Boston: Harvard Business School Press, 1986, pp. 315-343. The evidence on usage of international coalitions comes from Pankaj Ghemawat, Michael E. Porter, and Richard A. Rawlinson, "Patterns of International Coalition Activity," in the same book, pp. 345-365.

2. Kathryn R. Harrigan, *Strategic Flexibility: A Management Guide for Changing Times*, Lexington, MA: Lexington Books, 1985.

3. The two studies are cited in "Corporate Odd Couples," *Business Week*, July 21, 1986, pp. 100-105. For data and arguments supporting the view that joint ventures may be undertaken for temporary advantage and therefore with a "self-liquidating strategy" so that dissolution or eventual merger can be a sign of success, not failure, see Benjamin Gomes-Casseres, "Joint Venture Instability: Is it a problem?" *Columbia Journal of World Business, 22*(2), 1987, 97-102.

4. Susan R. Helper, "Supplier Relations and Innovation: Theory and Application to the U.S. Auto Industry," unpublished doctoral dissertation, Harvard University, September 1987. See also Michael E. Porter, *Cases in Competitive Strategy*, New York: Free Press, 1982.

5. This is the conclusion I draw from studies such as P. Mariti and R. H. Smiley, "Cooperative Agreements and the Organization of Industry," *The Journal of Industrial Economics, 31*, 1983, 437-451. In seventy cooperative agreements identified from announcements in the European business press (in each case managers were interviewed), technology and marketing goals dominated: economies of scale and risk sharing were less common goals. But auto industry firms were more likely to be looking for cost reduction through scale economies. Computer industry firms were concerned about the speed and diffusion of technological innovation. Note that this study predated a major set of changes in the auto industry, putting pressure on firms for faster absorption of technological innovations in electronics and materials—which should cause this industry, too, to move away from scale economies toward innovation as a goal for partnerships.

6. American Electronics Association, 1988 Productivity Survey, conducted by Pittiglio Rabin Todd and McGrath and KPMG Peat Marwick, Santa Clara, CA: AEA, 1988.

7. Eric von Hippel, *The Sources of Innovation*, New York: Oxford University Press, 1988.

8. Chester I. Barnard, "Organizations as Systems of Cooperation," reprinted in Amitai Etzioni and Edward W. Lahman (Eds.), *A Psychological Reader on Complete Organizations* (3rd ed.), New York: Holt, Rinehart, and Winston, 1980, pp. 11-14.

9. "Corporate Odd Couples." Endnote 3

10. Andrew Pollack, "Uniting to Create Products," New York Times, January 14,1986, D1.

11. Newspaper articles have provided the database for several important studies of coalition activity, thereby tending to overcount those kinds likely to be announced with fanfare to the financial community (e.g., joint ventures or licensing agreements opening up totally new product-market possibilities) and undercounting those that have less intrinsic "glamour" (e.g., a closer relationship between existing suppliers and customers that improves existing products, speeds line extensions, lowers costs, brings faster innovation, etc,). For example, one major study using announcements in the Wall Street Journal found more examples of what the researchers called "Y" type coalitions (which

involved shared performance of an activity by the partners, as in a joint venture) than "X" type coalitions (which involved a division of labor, as in supplier-customer relationships); the researchers also expected the "Y" type to be longer lasting. See Ghemawat, Porter, and Rawlinson (Endnote 1). But I think these findings seriously understate the growing importance and longer-term viability of stakeholder partnerships. Because these are more difficult to identify from public sources, researchers must go directly to companies for information—a more time-consuming process, but ultimately more valid.

12. William Davidson at the University of Southern California is the source for the item about U.S.-Japan joint ventures with no U.S. managers. See also Steven Prokesch, "Stopping the High-Tech Giveaway," *New York Times*, March 22, 1987, sec. 3, p. 1. Thomas McCraw of the Harvard Business School has pointed out that for every American studying in Japan, there are fifteen Japanese—from a much smaller population pool—studying in the United States. "They simply know us better," he commented in an interview in the Harvard Business School Bulletin, "and have consequently outclassed us in all kinds of negotiations."

13. Prokesch, Endnote 12.

14. Jeffrey A. Trachtenberg, "Why Things Go Better With Coke," *Forbes*, November 18, 1985, p. 41.

15. Prokesch, Endnote 12.

16. Among Michael Porter and Mark Fuller's most important criteria for selecting a long-term coalition partner are that the partner possess the desired source of competitive advantage that would create a disadvantage if a rival had it, and that the partner is unlikely to become a competitor. See Porter and Fuller, Endnote 1.

Appendix:
- ## The History of Strategic Planning
- ## Resources

The History of Strategic Planning

The term "strategy" comes from a Greek word meaning "army leader." According to Bracker (1980, p. 219), the verb form meant "to plan the destruction of one's enemies through the effective use of resources." "Strategy" became the craft and domain of the warrior. Strategic planning can be traced to when resources and technology required by warfare made planning a necessity. A well-known British military historian, Hart (1968, p. 2), suggested that the term "strategy" is best confined to the meaning of "generalship"—the "actual direction of military force, as distinct from the policy governing its employment."

Strategic Planning in the 1800s

Strategic planning increased sharply when two key factors became important in large-scale warfare. The first was the required implements (such as ships, weapons, personnel, and supplies) that were dependent on planning. The second factor was an organizational structure that formalized the use of specialists, including planners. As the need for large quantities of interrelated resources developed in the 1800s, planners were used in a formal and elaborate manner.

The Franco-Prussian War and the U.S. Civil War saw the turning point in the adoption of formal, long-range planning in complex organizations. First in the military, then in government, and eventually in business, strategic planning became a crucial part of the management process within the organization.

The trend away from small businesses with owner-managers to corporations or large firms with professional managers in the last half of the 1800s accelerated the development of administrative management, including strategic planning. Management historians, including Ronald Shuman (1948), consider 1890 as the key division point between the operation of businesses by owner-managers and the operation by professional managers. American business since 1890 can be generally divided into three periods: From 1890 to the mid-Thirties the period was marked by a production orientation; the early Thirties to the mid-Fifties, by an operations-management orientation; and the mid-Fifties to the present, by a marketing orientation. These periods overlap, of course, particularly during the Thirties, when economic conditions made financial management vitally important.

Hax and Majluf (1984) have divided the evolution of modern strategic planning into five principal stages:

1. Budgeting and financial control
2. Long-range planning
3. Business strategic planning
4. Corporate strategic planning
5. Strategic management

We will categorize these five principal stages in the time periods where they had greatest prominence.

From 1890 to the Mid-Thirties: A Production Orientation

Most companies in this time period made a single product and focused on production, i.e., making that product more efficiently.

Budgeting and Financial Control. As management systems developed after 1890, budgeting and financial control methods and tools were created to plan and monitor the financial resources of enterprises. Because of the importance of these resources, accounting methods and practices were established and communicated within the firm. At this stage the primary focus of budgeting and financial control was internal.

From the Early Thirties to the Mid-Fifties: An Operations-Management Orientation

The more complex that businesses became, the more managerial attention had to be placed on policy making. This work came to be considered the primary task of top management. Some policies could be formalized and standardized to such an extent that they could be incorporated into policy manuals; others had to be developed on an ad hoc basis to keep pace with rapidly changing business and environmental conditions. This reactive—and primarily internal—orientation of policy making that served most businesses well from 1890 to the mid-Thirties began to lose effectiveness as change accelerated during the Great Depression, World War II, and the postwar international expansion.

Long-Range Planning. Long-range planning grew out of the need to make projections beyond a one-year planning horizon. The basic purpose of long-range planning was to examine environmental trends and opportunities and to prepare guidelines or planning parameters to shape the operations and activities of the firm. Although long-range planning has been used to some extent throughout this century, the major increase came after World War II, as companies tried to exploit the growth opportunities of the postwar boom.

The typical long-range plan of this period was simply an extension of one-year budgets into a five-year projection based on historical data. Sales were forecast for a multiyear period; and based on this forecast, other functional plans (for example, manufacturing, research and development, and personnel) were developed. Then all of these projections were combined into a comprehensive financial plan. Newly developed methods of computing cash flow and payback were used in conjunction with the financial plans to assess the feasibility of making capital expenditures. A business could then establish quantitative criteria for making positive or negative decisions on investment opportunities.

This process was appropriate if the firm was in a familiar environment, if change was usually predictable, and if the future could be anticipated. In that case, manuals could be developed for financial methods and procedures, and controls could be highly formalized. Therefore, the development of long-range planning was aided by relatively stable economic conditions. Also markets were growing, trends were fairly predictable, firms had essentially a single dominant product, and the competitive environment was not intense—particularly on an international level.

As the arena of business changed from the entrepreneurial model to a functional model and then to a divisional organizational model, approaches to planning needed to change to cope with the increasing complexities of the international environment. This change encompassed a shift from policy making to strategic planning, from a primary emphasis on functional interrelationships to a focus on internal strengths and weaknesses and external opportunities and threats—from a reactive to a proactive stance. The new planning outlook (which was replacing the incomplete outlook that was ineffective in the fast-changing environment) was described by Hofer, et al. (1985). They stated that during the twenty years after World War II, most major businesses in both the U.S. and abroad diversified their operations by expanding into markets different from their original core businesses. Therefore, it became extremely difficult to establish a single set of functional-area policies that would effectively address all of the innovative and integrative needs of the enterprise. According to the authors, the problem was "one of dynamically coordinating all of these functional areas over time in much more complex organizations. The task itself was not new, it had always existed. But in earlier, simpler times, it had been accomplished informally in the heads of top management, a management that usually had a clear conception of the business as a whole because it had either established the business or had joined it prior to the major expansions described above. However, the increasing complexity of most firms, coupled with even more rapid and pervasive environmental changes, made such informality a luxury of the past." (pp. 4-5). The authors further contend that more policies, better policies, or more rapid changes in policy were not the answer; rather, the answer lay in revising the core concepts of the business and the ways it related to the environment, i.e., in the reformulation of its strategy in a formal, explicit manner.

An examination of an annual report from a divisionalized firm—it need not be a conglomerate—will readily illustrate this transition. The crucial variable is not the size; it is the difficulty of effectively managing markedly different product lines, with markedly different product life cycles, in markedly different competitive environments.

From the Mid-Fifties to the Present: A Marketing Orientation

Business Strategic Planning. Throughout the first half of the Twentith Century fundamental economic changes began to occur in the United States. The production orientation that characterized business during the first decades of the century gradually eroded during the Thirties and then more rapidly in the Forties and Fifties. Price could no longer be the primary marketing tool, and promotion was increasing in importance. A marketing orientation was now required for a business to succeed, and with this orientation came an external focus.

Other changes were also occurring. The environment was only partially predictable and was filled with surprises. Although long-range planning was the initial response to these changes, something more was needed, and strategic planning—together with the development of strategic planning tools, concepts, and applications—has more and more been the response.

Businesses began to realize that if they could no longer extrapolate the future, they would need to "create" the future through the identification of strengths, weaknesses, opportunities, and threats. They would have to plan a strategy to use in their corporate warfare.

Corporate Strategic Planning. The same trends that influenced the development of business strategic planning influenced corporate strategic planning. The two differ primarily in the level at which they are applied. As Andrews (1971) indicated in his definition of strategy, corporate strategy addresses strategy formulation, implementation and evaluation, and control in a process that encompasses the entire organization, its stakeholders, and its environment. Hax and Majluf's (1984, pp. 44-45) identification of the basic steps in the corporate strategic planning process indicates the global nature of this process:[1]

1. The vision of the firm: corporate philosophy, mission of the firm, and identification of SBUs and their interactions.
2. Strategic posture and planning guidelines: corporate strategic thrusts, corporate performance objectives, and planning challenges.
3. The mission of the business: business scope and identification of product-market segments.
4. Formulation of business strategy and broad action programs.
5. Formulation of functional strategy: participation in business strategic planning, concurrence or nonconcurrence to business strategy proposals, and formulation of broad action programs for each function.
6. Consolidation of business and functional strategies.
7. Definition and evaluation of specific action programs at the business level.
8. Definition and evaluation of specific action programs at the functional level.
9. Resource allocation and definition of performance measurements for management control.
10. Budgeting at the business level.
11. Budgeting at the functional level.
12. Budget consolidation and approval of strategic and operational funds.

---

[1]Arnoldo C. Hax, Nicolas S. Majluf, *Strategic Management: An Integrative Perspective,* copyright 1984, pp. 44-45. Reprinted by permission of Prentice-Hall, Inc., Englewood Cliffs, New Jersey.

Two principal areas of study are emerging in strategic planning: the strategic planning process and the managerial functions supporting the process. Although different writers classify the steps of the process in different ways, the following principal components are usually identified:

1. Mission and goal formulation
2. Strategy formulation
3. Strategy evaluation
4. Strategy implementation, including processes, structures, and systems
5. Strategic control and evaluation

The second area (those traditional managerial functions supporting the process, including planning, organizing, directing, staffing, and controlling) would also encompass those managerial roles suggested by Mintzberg (1973). These include the interpersonal, informational, and decisional roles that a manager assumes when interacting with superiors, peers, subordinates, and the outside environment. Merging these two areas is the domain of strategic planning. As Hofer, et al. (1985, p.1) suggest, "The principal focus of the field is on the intersection of these two areas, i.e. on the participation of general management in the strategic management processes of the organization," because those are the tasks that are most essential to both survival and growth of an organization.

The Sixties and Seventies: "Policy" Versus "Strategy"

During the Sixties and Seventies, "business policy" was a popular term, which was derived from the policy decisions of the CEO and senior management. Stanford (1983, p. 2) continues this concept by defining policy as "a broad scope of relationship of all the major elements in a situation of comprehensive responsibility. In this sense, it is much broader than the use of the word policy (or policies) to refer to company rules or procedures." He suggests that strategy is a "relatively broad framework for top management in which desired ends (objectives) can be chosen in a firm's environment and in which strategic alternatives can be developed and employed to use the firm's resources to achieve those ends or objectives. Strategy thus can be defined as the general means to achieve those ends or objectives."

Other respected sources take a different view. For example, Grant and King (1982, p. 4) define "strategy," "strategic planning system," and "plans" in the following manner. (Although not specifically defined, "policy" is used within the context of a "guideline.")

- *Strategy*—a time sequence of internally consistent and conditional resource allocation decisions that are designed to fulfill an organization's decisions.
- *Strategic Planning System*—A set of interrelated organizational task definitions and procedures for seeing that pertinent information is obtained, forecasts are made, and strategy choices are addressed in an integrated, internally consistent, and timely manner.
- *Plans*—The documentary evidence that a strategic planning system has functioned to produce a well-conceived strategy. They provide the reference point for the continuing evaluation of progress toward goals and for the re-examination of strategy. Plans reflect the outputs of a strategic planning system—the organization's chosen mission, objectives and strategy.

The Eighties:
Recent Trends in Strategic Planning

At the turn of the century, some of the "scientific" managers urged that the planning function be separated from the actual running of the firm to allow the planning specialists time to plan. Currently there is a strong trend toward directly involving line managers in the strategic planning process, because they are the ones who have to implement the plan.

Also today more emphasis is placed on implementation. This emphasis developed because of the problems many companies experienced in trying to implement their plans. For example, gaining acceptance of the plan—with its associated changes—was difficult, and the knowledge and skills necessary to carry out the plan were not always developed. To overcome these problems, managers are playing increasingly important roles in developing strategic plans and in implementing them.

Business Policy. Although Hax and Majluf (1984) used the term "strategic management" as the fifth principal stage in the evolution of modern strategic planning, the terms "business policy," "business policy and planning," "long-term planning," and "policy and planning" have recently appeared in the management literature. The term "policy" came from the need for the owner or professional manager to establish "business policies" to integrate the various functional areas of the enterprise. When a business was small, the CEO could integrate the work of functional units through personal, face-to-face coordination. As businesses grew from small companies that offered a single product to a select set of customers into a complex entity that offered multiple products to diverse customers, business policies became the primary coordination mechanism. These policies were formalized and standarized by the senior managers of the firm. Although a few other current writers (e.g., Hofer, 1985) suggest using the term "strategic management" to identify this area, we prefer to restrict that term to the implementation aspects of an organization's strategic plan.

Conclusion

Just as strategic planning was used against opponents in warfare in ancient times, modern organizations must also plan their strategies for corporate warfare. Several insights can be drawn from our study of the history of strategic planning:

1. Strategic planning is rapidly developing in importance as a critical field of management. The increasingly dynamic environmental changes and the complexity of these changes require an organization to use the tools and concepts of strategic planning to survive.
2. The field is broadening to encompass more of the functions of management.
3. The emphasis is on strategic planning as a long-term organizational commitment, with daily support from operational managers. One indication of the total commitment that is needed is the increased attention to organizational and personal values as a shaping influence in the strategic planning process.
4. The principal steps in the strategic planning process usually include mission and goal formulation, strategy formulation, strategy evaluation, strategy implementation, and strategic control and evaluation.
5. There are three prerequisites to the final development, selection, and implementation of strategic alternatives: the development of value-driven goals, an evaluation of internal strengths and weaknesses, and the appraisal of external opportunities and threats. These three must be considered simultaneously and interactively so that their interrelationships can be studied.

STRATEGY DEFINITIONS

There are three levels of strategy within organizations: the corporate level, the business level, and the functional level.

Corporate Strategy. Chandler (1962, p. 16) was one of the first writers to apply the term "strategy" to the conduct of business. He identified both the ends and the means of strategy when he wrote that strategy is "the determination of the basic long-term goals and objectives of an enterprise, and the adoption of courses of action and the allocation of resources necessary for carrying out these goals." Then Drucker (1964) presented one of the first analyses of corporate strategy. He considered using "strategy" in the title of his book *Managing for Results,* but was advised against it because of its military and political connotations. Within a decade, however, "strategy," "strategic planning," and "competitive strategies" became prominent words in titles of books concerning corporations and other business organizations.

Although we can find many descriptions of corporate strategy, one of the most frequently cited definitions was given by Andrews (1971, p. 18), and it applies to the whole organization: "The pattern of decisions in a company that determines and reveals its objectives, purposes or goals, produces the principal policies and plans for achieving those goals and defines the range of business the company is to pursue, the kind of economic and human organization it is or intends to be, and the nature of the economic and noneconomic contribution it intends to make to its shareholders, employees, customers and communities."

Business Strategy. Business strategy—frequently called SBU (strategic business unit) strategy—focuses on how a self-contained part of an organization will compete with its competitors. In the late Fifties and early Sixties, as competition intensified, companies began to look for ways to concentrate their resources to take maximum advantage of their distinctive competencies and competitive advantages. They needed approaches for identifying and exploiting these competencies and advantages. The concept of business segmentation, or SBUs, developed; and each SBU in a company may have a different business strategy to take the greatest advantage of its resources and opportunities in its particular competitive environment. Just as strategic planning was advantageous in ancient history to warriors who were competing against their opponents, even so today it is a necessary tool for businesses that are attempting to make headway against their competition.

In 1970, when the General Electric Company was divided into discrete organizational units, a great deal of attention was given to SBUs. The following criteria were used for classifying a unit as a strategic business unit at General Electric. Each unit must:

1. Serve an external market with goods and/or services;
2. Have external competitors;

3. Have a choice over its activities of product, place, promotion, and price (i.e., be independent); and

4. Be a profit center.

This concept of strategic business units has had an important impact on the design and use of strategic planning tools that will be discussed later.

For strategic planning, it is sometimes more efficient to consider LOBs (lines of business) rather than SBUs. In some cases, of course, the LOB would be synonymous with the SBU.

Functional Strategy. Functional strategies are the means through which the functional units—such as marketing, finance, production, research and development, and manufacturing—accomplish their objectives. However, it is extremely important for the functional strategies to work in concert with and to support the business and corporate strategies.

Stanford (1983) has prepared a very comprehensive table of the strategic planning concepts introduced by several of the prominent texts. A review of Table 1 should be useful in bringing together the various viewpoints.

STRATEGIC PLANNING TOOLS

As the general field of strategic planning has grown and matured, the tools, techniques, and applications of strategic planning have also developed. Some of these, such as capital budgeting and break-even analysis, have been an important part of strategic planning for decades, whereas others, such as the directional policy matrix, are relatively new.

Many of these tools can be used at more than one organizational level. For example, cash-flow planning is useful at both the functional and business levels, and growth-share matrices can be used at both the business and corporate levels. Therefore, even though the following paragraphs discuss tools, techniques, and applications under a particular category, they do not necessarily belong exclusively to that category.

Functional. Common examples of functional applications include electronic spread-sheet analysis and cash-flow planning in the finance field, market-research techniques in the marketing field, and cost accounting in the production field.

Business. Many of the approaches used in business strategy are drawn from the portfolio concept of financial management, in which a mix of financial instruments of different characteristics are put together to ac-

Title	Author(s)	Terms Used For			Characteristics
		Broad Scope	Ends	Means	
Management Policy	Stanford	Policy	Objectives	Strategy	Strategy relates firm to objectives within environment; multilateral relationships; alternative sequences.
Strategy and Organization	Uyterhoeven, Ackerman, and Rosenblum	General Management, Business Policy	Purpose, Goals, or Objectives	Strategic Plans	Strategy external, organization internal; elements and skills; sequential process.
Corporate Strategy	Andrews	Strategy	Objectives, Purposes, or Goals	Policies and Plans	Formulation and implementation; business strategy: "how"; corporate strategy: "what."
Strategic Management	Schendel and Hofer	Strategic Management Process	Goals	Strategy	Achievement of objectives is aim of strategy; hierarchy of strategies at four levels.
Administrative Policy	Hodgetts and Wortman	Administrative Policy Science	Purpose or Mission	Strategy	Several levels in total policy structure; business one of six components of administrative policy science.
Strategic Management	Ansoff	Strategic Management	Aspirations	Strategic Thrusts	Environment serving organizations (ESOs); multiple power centers; environmental turbulence.
Policy Formulation and Administration	Christensen, Berg, and Salter	Strategy	Purposes, Objectives	Policies	Strategy formulation influenced by corporate environment, resources, and management values.
A Strategy of Decision	Braybrooke and Lindblom	Policy Making	Objectives, Values	Policy	Disjointed incrementalism; sequential and concurrent; objectives and policy considered simultaneously.
Strategy and Policy	Thompson and Strickland	Policy	Purpose, Mission	Strategy	Mission is specified as long-run objectives and short-run goals; relationships rather than sequential flow.

Melvin J. Stanford, *Management Policy*, © 1983, p. 14. Reprinted by permission of Prentice Hall, Inc., Englewood, NJ.

Table 1. Summary of Concepts

complish a financial objective. Probably because of that practice, many business strategy applications contain the idea of balancing different SBUs to meet overall corporate goals. The tools, techniques, and applications for business strategy can be divided into two categories: One is concerned with the individual characteristics of the SBU; and the other, with the strategic options of the SBU. Representative examples for each category are as follows:

Individual Characteristics:

- Break-even analysis
- Cash-flow analysis
- Experience-curve concept
- Optimum economic size
- Return on investment
- Product life cycle

Strategic Options:

- Growth-share matrix
- Business-screen matrix
- Directional-policy matrix
- Profit impact of market strategy
- Porter industry competition model

Corporate. Glueck (1980) identified four primary categories of corporate strategy: stability, growth, retrenchment, and a combination of these three. Pearce (1982) identified twelve grand strategies and organized them in a matrix to show their purposes and areas of emphasis (see Table 2). However, as Wheelen and Hunger (1983) suggest, there is usually no one strategy or set of strategies that can be used at all levels in all organizations. A firm will normally have a mix of functional, business, and corporate strategies.

References

Andrews, K.R. (1971). *The Concept of Corporate Strategy*. Homewood, IL: Dow-Jones Irwin.

Bracker, J. (1980). The historical development of the strategic management concept. *Academy of Management Review, 5*, 219-224.

Chandler, A.D., Jr. (1962). *Strategy and Structure: Chapters in the History of the Industrial Enterprise*. Cambridge, MA: MIT Press.

Drucker, P.F. (1964). *Managing for Results*. New York: Harper & Row.

Glueck, W.F. (1980). *Business Policy and Strategic Management*. New York: McGraw-Hill.

Grant, J.H., & King, W.R. (1982). *The Logic of Strategic Planning*. Boston, MA: Little, Brown.

Hart, B.H.L. (1968). *Strategy* (2nd rev. ed.). New York: Praeger.

Hax, A.C., & Majluf, N.S. (1984). *Strategic Management: An Integrative Perspective*. Englewood Cliffs, NJ: Prentice-Hall.

Hofer, C.W., Murray, E.A., Jr., Charan, R., & Pitts, R.A. (1985). *Strategic Management: A Casebook in Policy and Planning* (2nd ed.). St. Paul, MN: West.

Mintzberg, H. (1973). *The Nature of Managerial Work*. New York: Harper & Row.

Pearce, J.A., II. (1982, Spring). Selecting among alternative grand strategies. *California Management Review*, pp. 23-31.

Shuman, R.B. (1948). *Management of men*. Norman, OK: University of Oklahoma Press.

Stanford, M.J. (1983). *Management Policy* (2nd ed.). Englewood Cliffs, NJ: Prentice-Hall.

Wheelen, T.L., & Hunger, J.D. (1983). *Strategic Management and Business Policy*. Reading, MA: Addison-Wesley.

Purpose of the Grand Strategy	Areas of Emphasis	
	External (acquisition or merger for resource capability)	Internal (redirected resources within the firm)
Overcome Weaknesses	Quadrant I Vertical integration Conglomerate diversification	Quadrant II Turnaround or retrenchment Divestiture Liquidation
Maximize Strengths	Quadrant IV Horizontal integration Concentric diversification Joint venture	Quadrant III Concentration Market development Product development Innovation

Table 2. Grand Strategy Selection Matrix*

*Adapted from J.A. Pearce, II. (1982, Spring). "Selecting Among Alternative Grand Strategies." *California Management Review*, pp. 23-31.

Resources

Books

Aaker, D. (1988). *Developing business strategies.* New York: John Wiley.
 Aimed at both managers who have experience with strategic planning and those who have never used the process, this book emphasizes three elements important to the development of business strategies: (a) organizing a method for analyzing the external environment, (b) developing "sustainable competitive advantages," and (c) making wise investment decisions.

Ackoff, R. (1981). *Creating the corporate future.* New York: John Wiley.
 This is an in-depth analysis of a highly interactive planning model that involves cross-sections of the organization in the development of the strategic plan. This widely cited text is authored by an acknowledged leader in the field.

Allison, G. (1971). *The essence of decision.* Boston, MA: Little, Brown.
 This book is the widely referenced original interdisciplinary research in strategic planning, and it is cited more than fifty times annually.

Andrews, K.R. (1971). *The concept of corporate strategy.* Homewood, IL: Dow-Jones Irwin.
 This is an important analysis of the fundamental concepts and issues in strategic management by one of the principal authorities in the field. The "Andrews model" of strategic management has been a very key influence on many writers.

Ansoff, H.I. (1965). *Corporate strategy.* New York: McGraw-Hill.
 This theoretical foundation of strategic management is based on the author's experience as a manager. It condenses his own background and experience and those of his colleagues into a prescriptive approach to strategy formulation.

Ansoff, H.I. (1984). *Implanting strategic management.* Englewood Cliffs, NJ: Prentice-Hall.

Building on the theoretical foundation in his *Strategic Management,* the author offers important prescriptions for strategic management, many of which have found practical application. This is one of the significant books of the Eighties.

Bernard, C.I. (1938). *The functions of the executive.* Cambridge, MA: Harvard University Press.

Written by a senior executive of New Jersey Bell, this book has become a management classic. It was one of the first to recognize the importance of "bottom-up" and participative management, and it is very useful for today's manager.

Boston Consulting Group. (1968). *Perspectives on experience.* Boston, MA: Boston Consulting Group.

This is an early presentation of the concepts behind the use of experience curves and the Boston Consulting Group model, both of which are widely applied in business and industry.

Boulton, W.R. (1984). *Business policy: The art of strategic management.* New York: Macmillan.

Focusing on the application of theories and the development of management skills through case studies, the author presents concepts and tools to enable managers to make decisions about strategy and to work to make these decisions successful in their implementation.

Brandt, S.E. (1981). *Strategic planning in emerging companies.* Reading, MA: Addison-Wesley.

This is a long-range-planning primer directed at small emerging businesses. The author only briefly touches most of his topics but devotes significant space to the planning-related topics of corporate culture and strategic management.

Capon, N., Farley, J.U., & Hulbert, J. M. (1988). *Corporate strategic planning.* New York: Columbia University Press.

This book documents the planning practices of major U.S. manufacturing corporations as of 1980; identifies problems with those planning systems; investigates the relationships between companies' planning systems and their environment, strategy, organization structure, and organizational climate; and investigates the relationship between planning and economic performance.

Carroll, G., & Vogel, D. (1984). *Strategy and organization: A west coast perspective.* Boston, MA: Pitman.

This is a compilation of outstanding articles from the *California Management Review* by such authors as Aaker, Pascale, and Peters. It is an excellent reference to current developments in strategic management.

Chandler, A.D., Jr. (1962). *Strategy and structure: Chapters in the history of the industrial enterprise.* Cambridge, MA: M.I.T. Press.
This book is a landmark contribution to the development of strategic management, particularly in the application of strategy to business. It is a must for the serious student of strategic management.

The Conference Board. (1985). *Facing strategic issues: New planning guides and practices* (Report No. 867). New York: Author.
This provides the results of a Conference Board study of organizations' planning processes. Participating organizations were asked what changes they had made concerning their strategic plans, planning methods, and ways of documenting plans.

Cope, R.G. (1989). *High involvement strategic planning: When people and their ideas matter.* Oxford, OH: The Planning Forum, and Oxford, England: Basil Blackwell.
Cope emphasizes the importance of involving people in the strategic planning process. His book presents ways for managers and employees to assess strategic proposals. Cope asserts that traditional strategic planning, in which a small group of managers conceive an entire organization's future, is ineffective. Rather, people—who may or may not be managers—must think about the organization as a whole, then find ways to capitalize on the organization's strengths.

Cyert, R.M., & March, J.G. (1963). *A behavioral theory of the firm.* Englewood Cliffs, NJ: Prentice-Hall.
This is an important early contribution to organizational theory of the business firm. It is one of the most widely used reference works with high relevance for today's strategic management.

Deal, T.E., & Kennedy, A.A. (1982). *Corporate cultures: The rites and rituals of corporate life.* Reading, MA: Addison-Wesley.
This is a pragmatic look at one of the important topics in strategic management: corporate culture. The influence of culture on strategic processes makes this book important.

Donaldson, G., & Lorsch, J.W. (1983). *Decision making at the top: The shaping of strategic direction.* New York: Basic Books.
This is an examination of the forces that influence strategic decision making by chief executives.

Galbraith, J.R., & Nathanson, D.A. (1978). *Strategy implementation: The role of structure and process.* St. Paul, MN: West.
This book presents a useful analysis of organizational structure and process in the implementation of strategy. It includes different types of organizations and the integrating methods and devices necessary to make the structures work.

George, C.S., Jr. (1968). *The history of management thought.* Englewood Cliffs, NJ: Prentice-Hall.

This well-known and widely used review of the history and development of management thought has an emphasis on the functional approach. It is a good introduction to planning.

Grant, J.H., & King, W.R. (1982). *The logic of strategic planning.* Boston, MA: Little, Brown.

This overview of strategic planning shows how it is done in both single-product and multi-product companies. It is one of the most complete summaries of the state of the art of strategic planning as accomplished in business organizations.

Hart, B.H.L. (1968). *Strategy* (2nd rev. ed.). New York: Praeger.

This classic review of strategy is authored by a respected military historian.

Hax, A.C., & Majluf, N.S. (1984). *Strategic management: An integrative perspective.* Englewood Cliffs, NJ: Prentice-Hall.

The authors present a clear formulation of the basic issues and concepts related to strategic management, describe in detail the most relevant and up-to-date methodologies to address these issues, and offer suggestions for developing a strategic planning process. It is a solid, comprehensive reference.

Hickman, C.R., & Silva, M.A. (1984). *Creating excellence.* New York: New American Library.

The authors combine a theoretical and application approach to teach the practical skills that must be acquired before becoming "new age executives." Factual accounts of businesses, case histories, and hypothetical present-day situations are used to illustrate their ideas.

Higgins, J.M. (1978). *Organizational policy and strategic management.* Hinsdale, IL: Dryden Press.

The cases are written in an easy-to-understand manner. The book contains excellent illustrations and charts.

Hofer, C.W., Murray, E.A., Jr., Charan, R., & Pitts, R.A. (1985). *Strategic management: A casebook in policy and planning* (2nd ed.). St. Paul, MN: West.

This casebook from some authorities in strategic planning covers all the major topics. The cases involve real-world, action-oriented managerial problems and opportunities.

Lawrence, P.R., & Lorsch, J.W. (1967). *Organization and environment: Managing differentiation and integration.* Boston, MA: Graduate School of Business, Harvard University.

This significant study of the influence of a firm's internal and external environment on its organizational structure analyzes environmental differences and their relationship to effective organizational structures.

Learned, E.P., Christiansen, C.R., Andrews, K.R., & Guth, W.D. (1965). *Business policy: Text and cases.* Homewood, IL: Richard D. Irwin.
This influential Harvard case book has, through its many subsequent editions, shaped the study of strategic management.

Leontiades, M. (1980). *Strategies for diversification and change.* Boston, MA: Little, Brown.
This advanced work covers existing descriptive models of how corporations progress from simple, one-product companies to very complex corporations serving many market constituencies. It focuses on diversification, by means of unrelated acquisitions, as the dominant current process of corporate development.

Lorange, P. (1980). *Corporate planning: An executive's viewpoint.* Englewood Cliffs, NJ: Prentice-Hall.
This book presents advanced concepts for the design, implementation, and use of corporate or strategic planning systems based on both theoretical concepts and practitioner's viewpoints. It is useful for both senior executives at general management levels and staff planning executives.

MacMillan, I.C. (1978). *Strategy formulation: Political concepts.* St. Paul, MN: West.
This book offers a political perspective of strategy to help develop an understanding of the political component of business behavior and organizational strategy. It is useful for understanding nonbusiness organizations, such as hospitals, church groups, and nonprofit organizations.

Miles, R.E., & Snow, C.C. (1978). *Organizational strategy, structure and process.* New York: McGraw-Hill.
This book examines the relationships between successful strategies and an organizational form that is both internally and externally consistent. A minimal fit is suggested as necessary for survival, a tight fit is associated with corporate excellence, and an early fit is related to a competitive advantage with long-term positive consequences.

Mills, D.Q. (1985). *The new competitors.* New York: John Wiley.
A consultant and professor at Harvard Business School, the author has used his experience and hundreds of interviews to prepare this authoritative statement about American managers. Basic operating conditions of American management have changed so drastically that the author contends there must be a full-scale rethinking of the values that managers hold, as well as the way they run their companies.

Mintzberg, H. (1973). *The nature of managerial work.* New York: Harper & Row.

The author questions the traditional functional approach to work (e.g., planning and organizing) and suggests that managerial work is comprised of ten roles that are common to all managers.

Murdick, R.C., Eckhouse, R.H., Moor, R.C., & Zimmer, T.W. (1980). *Business policy: A framework for analysis* (3rd ed.). Columbus, OH: Grid.

The authors propose ways to diagnose a firm that is in trouble or potentially in trouble and how to arrive at a specific program of remedial action. Many practical examples and suggestions are offered.

Newman, W.H., Logan, J.P., & Hegarty, W.H. (1985). *Strategy, policy and central management* (9th ed.). Cincinnati, OH: Southwestern.

This widely used, best-selling strategic management text considers the functional areas of the enterprise as well as a framework for strategy. It includes both text and cases.

Pascale, R., & Athos, A. (1981). *The art of Japanese management.* New York: Warner Books.

This major contribution to the strategic management literature looks at the ways the art of Japanese management can be applied to U.S. business. It emphasizes the product and marketing strategies that help explain the success of Japanese companies, as well as their human relations techniques.

Patz, A.L. (1981). *Strategic decision analysis: A general management framework.* Boston, MA: Little, Brown.

This book presents a unified and comprehensive framework for analyzing general-management decision problems in an easy-to-follow manner. It examines the market structure and dynamics of business to the structure and dynamics of small decision-making groups.

Pearce, J.A., II, & Robinson, R.B., Jr. (1985). *Strategic management: Strategy formulation and implementation* (2nd ed.). Homewood, IL: Richard D. Irwin.

This widely accepted text introduces the critical skills of planning and managing strategic activities. It combines text, cohesion cases, and business case studies. The work of strategic management theorists, practitioners, and researchers is integrated with a strong emphasis on real-world applications.

Peters, T., & Austin, N. (1985). *A passion for excellence: The leadership difference.* New York: Random House.

This book is a continuation of the general theme of *In Search of Excellence* with additional examples of managerial excellence outside the corporate world. Four basic values are cited: taking exceptional care of customers; promoting innovation; inspiring employees; and providing visionary, impassioned leadership.

Porter, M.E. (1980). *Competitive strategy: Techniques for analyzing industries and competitors.* New York: Free Press.

This major strategic management book of the Eighties looks at generic strategies for a competitive advantage. The author is one of the best known of the current writers in this field.

Porter, M.E. (1985). *Competitive advantage: Creating and sustaining superior performance.* New York: Free Press.

This definitive work presents the concepts and the tools needed to create a competitive advantage in cost or differentiation. It shows how the choice of competitive scope (the breadth of a firm's activities) plays a leading role in creating a competitive edge.

Pümpin, C. (1987). *The essence of corporate strategy.* Brookfield, VT: Gower.

The author believes that, in order to survive and to thrive, organizations must identify the characteristics that distinguish them from and make them superior to competitors. This book describes how to identify an organization's Strategic Excellence Position (SEP) and how to make SEPs part of the organizational culture.

Quinn, J.B. (1980). *Strategies for change: Logical incrementalism.* Homewood, IL: Richard D. Irwin.

The author suggests that instead of following rigidly prescribed formal planning practices, managers in major enterprises tend to develop their most important strategies by moving forward incrementally both consciously and proactively.

Richmond, F.W., & Kahan, M. (1983). *How to beat the Japanese at their own game.* Englewood Cliffs, NJ: Prentice-Hall.

Approaches for beating the Japanese by using their own methods are presented and discussed.

Rowe, I., Mason, R., & Dickel, K. (1985). *Strategic management and business policy* (2nd ed.). Reading, MA: Addison-Wesley.

This innovative textbook combines text material with applications and readings. It places significant emphasis on the application of strategic management tools.

Rumelt, R.P. (1974). *Strategy, structure and economic performance.* Boston, MA: Harvard Business School.

This widely cited book is one of the superior empirical studies of the variables linking strategy, structure, and economic performance.

Schendel, D.E., & Hofer, C.W. (Eds.). (1979). *Strategic management: A new view of business policy and planning.* Boston, MA: Little, Brown.

This series of papers from the leading authorities in the field indicates that a new concept of the general manager's role is developing: strategic management. This is a landmark publication.

Simon, H.A. (1946). *Administrative behavior.* New York: Macmillan.
This is one of the most significant books ever written on administrative behavior. It is considered one of the classics in management and enjoys wide acceptance today. It is a must for the professional manager.

Stanford, M.J. (1983). *Management policy* (2nd ed.). Englewood Cliffs, NJ: Prentice-Hall.
This book approaches the management of the whole company from the point of view of the general manager. It encompasses and integrates all the functions of management. The text and cases are prepared or selected by one of the best case writers.

Steiner, G.A. (1977). *Strategic managerial planning.* Oxford, OH: Planning Executives Institute.
This widely used summary of strategic managerial planning systems is based on experience by many organizations in using these systems. This excellent introductory guide to strategic planning is written by one of the most respected authors in the field.

Steiner, G.A. (1979). *Strategic planning: What every manager must know.* New York: Free Press.
This book has become the standard of traditional approaches to strategic planning, and it has wide acceptance by managers. It provides planning designs to fit a variety of organizations, and special emphasis is placed on the analysis of the current internal and external state.

Summer, C.E. (1980). *Strategic behavior in business and government.* Boston, MA: Little, Brown.
The author reviews the similarities in and differences between business and government planning. He suggests that they both behave in strikingly similar ways when planning global, comprehensive strategies and implementing them.

Thompson, A.A., Jr., & Strickland, A.J., III. (1981). *Strategy and policy: Concepts and cases.* Dallas, TX: Business Publications.
This best-selling textbook includes a comprehensive text coverage and selected cases.

Thompson, J.D. (1967). *Organizations in action.* New York: McGraw-Hill.
This brief book presents a long series of propositions that attempt to identify the underlying dynamics of working organizations. This seminal book is widely quoted and serves as the source of much empirical research on organizations.

Tregoe, B.B., & Zimmerman, J.W. (1980). *Top management strategy: What it is and how to make it work.* New York: Simon & Schuster.

This is a comprehensive look at strategic management from authors with long experience in planning and decision making.

Vance, S.C. (1983). *Corporate leadership: Boards, directors and strategy.* New York: McGraw-Hill.

Using many illustrations and examples, the author contributes to an understanding of the concepts, dynamics, maturation, and interaction of governance and management processes and structures. He discusses the current issues and innovations of contemporary boards and directors in the corporate business world.

Vesper, K.H. (1980). *New venture strategies.* Englewood Cliffs, NJ: Prentice-Hall.

This approach to strategic management focuses on entrepreneurial strategies, both personal and commercial, that can be used to effectively start and operate companies. It draws from the experiences of many entrepreneurs.

Wheelan, T.L., & Hunger, J.D. (1983). *Strategic management and business policy.* Reading, MA: Addison-Wesley.

This popular strategic management text combines text and case material. It covers the main topics in the field.

Articles and Videocassettes

Aaker, D.A. (1984, Spring). How to select a business strategy. *California Management Review*, pp. 167-175.

This article contends that traditional methods of selecting a strategy may not be sufficient because projecting profit streams of a particular strategy with a high degree of accuracy is difficult. It suggests six criteria for selecting a strategy.

Aaker, D.A., & Mascarenhas, B. (1984, Fall). The need for strategic flexibility. *Journal of Business Strategy.*

The authors stress the need for flexibility in strategic plans and suggest ways in which flexibility can be achieved. They also present a flexibility audit, which is an objective assessment of the firm's strategic flexibility.

The Abilene paradox [videocassette]. (1985). Del Mar, CA: McGraw-Hill Training Systems.

This film is based on Jerry Harvey's article, "The Abilene Paradox: The Management of Agreement." It includes a diagnostic survey to determine whether an organization's problems are the result of mismanaged agreement or mismanaged conflict. A leader's guide also is available.

Allman, W.F. (1984, October). Nice guys finish first. *Science,* pp. 25-32.
Several strategies for dealing with neighbors, business rivals, and the
Soviet Union are presented with the suggestion that the best way to get
ahead is to get along.

Andrews, K.R. (1980, November-December). Directors' responsibility for
corporate strategy. *Harvard Business Review,* pp. 30, 32, 36, 40, 42.
This article gives four reasons that a board of directors should be concerned with corporate strategy and explains the directors' functions
with regard to corporate strategy.

Banks, R.L., & Wheelwright, S.C. (1979, May-June). Operations vs. strategy: Trading tomorrow for today. *Harvard Business Review,* pp.
112-120.
This article asserts that pressure for short-term profits can seriously
impede the achievement of long-range goals. It examines the trade-
offs between short-term and long-term objectives.

Berry, W. (1984, April). An action planning process for all. *Supervisory
Management,* pp. 20-25.
A seven-step action-planning process for all levels in an organization
is presented and discussed.

Boynton, A.C., & Zmund, R.W. (1984). An assessment of critical success
factors. *Sloan Management Review,* 25(4), 17-27.
This assessment of the strengths and weaknesses of critical success
factors presents guidelines for an effective application.

Byars, L.L. (1984, May-June). The strategic management process: A model
and terminology. *Managerial Planning,* pp. 38-44.
The author suggests a model for the strategic management process
and provides definitions for the principal terms used in the model.

Conley, P. (1970, June). Experience curves as a planning tool. *IEEE Spectrum,* pp. 63-68.
This is an easy-to-understand look at experience curves and the Boston
Consulting Group model by one of the key developers of this strategic
management technique.

Cummings, T., Blumenthal, J.F., & Greiner, L.E. (1983, Winter). Managing organizational decline: The case for transorganizational systems.
Human Resource Management.
This article contends that the decline faced by many organizations in
the eighties could be corrected through arrangements with outside
organizations. Five conditions of decline that can be remedied by this
form of external collaboration are identified.

David, F.R. (1984, January-February). How do we choose among alternative growth strategies? *Managerial Planning.*
Thirteen growth strategies are presented together with the conditions
that are most appropriate for each strategy.

Day, G.S. (1977, April). Diagnosing the product portfolio. *Journal of Marketing,* pp. 29-38.

The author contends that long-run corporate performance is more than the sum of the contributions of the individual product strategies. A product portfolio analysis suggests specific marketing strategies to achieve a balanced mix of products that will produce the maximum long-run effects from scarce cash and managerial resources. The concept uses a simple matrix that is easy to understand.

Diven, D.L. (1984, July-August). Organizational planning: The neglected factor in merger and acquisition strategy. *Managerial Planning,* pp. 4-8.

Four important areas for the successful implementation of mergers and acquisitions are discussed: (1) planning for organizational change, (2) culture and policy considerations, (3) reporting channels and control, and (4) management resources inventory.

Do mergers really work? (1985, June 3). *Business Week,* pp. 88-94, 96, 98, 100.

This article suggests that the answer to the title's question is "not very often." It contends that between half and two-thirds of all mergers do not work. Some of the successes and failures are described.

Drodwin, D.R., & Bourgeois, L.J. (1984, Spring). Five steps to strategic action. *California Management Review,* pp. 176-190.

Recent research is presented that suggests that effective, innovative firms capitalize on strategic initiatives that originate on the firing line at lower management levels. The authors discuss five approaches and the differences among them.

Drucker, P.F. (1985, Winter). Entrepreneurial strategies. *California Management Review,* pp. 9-25.

This well-known author looks at entrepreneurial strategies and suggests that they are important, distinct, and different.

Dymsza, W.A. (1984, Fall). Global strategic planning: A model and recent analysis. *Journal of International Business.*

A comprehensive, dynamic model is developed for use with multinational corporations. The article discusses ways that multinational corporations are coping with rapidly changing global conditions.

FitzGerald, J.P. (1979, Summer). The three levels of strategic choice. *Journal of Business Strategy,* pp. 52-58.

This article proposes that the following three elements are essential to successful corporate planning: a mission statement, objectives, and an assessment process.

Football and the art of strategic planning [videocassette]. Vision Film Associates.

This film, which portrays the highlights of a strategic planning process with the owner, manager, coach, etc., of a football team, can be effectively used as an introduction to strategic planning, in the planning-to-plan phase, or as a general discussion starter.

Gallinger, G.W. (1982, July-August). Strategic business planning. *Managerial Planning,* pp. 41-44.

The basic steps in the strategic planning process are outlined. The key point presented is that strategic planning must be a statement not only of a company's aspirations, but also of what must be done to implement those aspirations.

Gup, B.E. (1979, November-December). Begin strategic planning by asking three questions. *Managerial Planning,* pp. 28-31, 35.

The major elements of strategic planning are grouped around three questions relating to a company's direction, environment, and strategic choices.

Herbert, T.T. (1984, November-December). Pitfalls in the planning process. *Managerial Planning,* pp. 42-45.

The author discusses why some planning systems fail to forestall corporate difficulties and where the opportunities lie to improve the results of planning efforts. He contends that planning right is more important than preparing the technically correct plan.

Hunsicker, J.Q. (1980, March). The malaise of strategic planning. *Management Review,* pp. 8-14.

The author suggests that sophisticated planning systems might have led companies into a "paralysis of analysis" and that the focus should be on challenging assumptions, competition, and the generation of innovative options.

Hurd, D.A., & Monfort, E.R., III. (1979, November). Vulnerability analysis: A new way to assess future trends. *Planning Review,* pp. 31-34.

This article gives five steps for applying vulnerability analysis (a method of helping organizations identify threats through the planning process). It also contends that vulnerability analysis is usually most helpful if a company has a long history of relative prosperity.

James, B.G. (1984, Summer). Strategic planning under fire. *Sloan Management Review,* pp. 57-61.

The author suggests that in recent years, strategic planning has not had the impact that some of its proponents had hoped. He looks at the factors that have hindered its effectiveness and proposes new approaches.

Jewell, D.O., Manners, G.E., & Jewell, S.F. (1984, July). For the first-time planner. *Supervisory Management, 29*(7), 40-42.

Several specific steps to effective reasoning and thinking are suggested for the first-time planner.

Kahalas, H. (1980, May-June). Planning types and approaches: A necessary function. *Managerial Planning.*
This is a basic review of the major aspects of the planning process in a traditional approach to planning. It discusses the relationship between the competency of the plan or the planner in making a successful organization.

Kastens, M.L. (1979, July-August). The why and how of planning. *Managerial Planning,* pp. 33-35.
This practical, hard-hitting look at the benefits and pitfalls of planning is short but very meaty.

Kiechel, W., III. (1979, September 24). Playing by the rules of the corporate strategy game. *Fortune,* pp. 110-112, 114-115.
This article provides a practical look at the tools of strategic consulting and some of the problems in applying these tools. It is a good review of the basic strategy tools.

Kiechel, W., III. (1981, October 19). Three (or four; or more) ways to win. *Fortune,* pp. 181, 184, 188.
This is a review of the generic strategies suggested by Harvard Business School professor Michael Porter.

Kiechel, W., III. (1981, November 2). Oh where, oh where has my little dog gone? Or my cash cow? Or my star? *Fortune,* pp. 148-150, 152-154.
This article provides a candid look at the Boston Consulting Group's business portfolio matrix from one of the best-known popular writers in strategic management.

Kiechel, W., III. (1982, December). Corporate strategists under fire. *Fortune,* pp. 34-39.
This interesting review of strategic planning tools shows how they failed. The key is in the implementation of the tools.

King, W.R. (1983, November-December). Integrating strength-weakness analysis into strategic planning. *Journal of Business Research,* pp. 475-487.
The strength-weakness assessment process is illustrated in terms of its implications, benefits, and underlying concepts. The author asserts that it is an essential part of the strategic planning process.

Kotler, P. (1980, May-June). Strategic planning and the marketing process. *Business,* pp. 2-9.
This article provides an interesting combination of strategic management and marketing with a special focus on possible strategic alternatives. It presents a solid, practical orientation.

Leidecker, J.K., & Bruno, A.V. (1984, February). Identifying and using critical success factors. *Long Range Planning,* pp. 23-31.
This article proposes that critical success factors are important in the environmental analysis, resource analysis, and strategy evaluation. It presents a comprehensive approach to the sources of critical success factors and how they can be used.

Levitt, T. (1960, July-August). Marketing myopia. *Harvard Business Review,* pp. 45-56. Reprinted in *Harvard Business Review,* September-October 1975, pp. 26-28, 33-34, 38-39, 44, 173-174, 176-181.
This article, which has become a classic, stresses the need for organizations to properly define the businesses they are in and warns them against nearsightedness. It also emphasizes the importance of satisfying the customer's needs.

Linneman, R.E., & Kennell, J.D. (1978, March-April). Shirt-sleeve approach to long range plans. *Harvard Business Review,* pp. 141-150.
The authors suggest a simple ten-step procedure to develop flexible strategies through a multiple-scenario process.

Linneman, R.E., & Klein, H.E. (1985, January-February). Using scenarios in strategic decision-making. *Business Horizons,* pp. 64-74.
This article maintains that a large percentage of successful U.S. and international firms use scenarios in their strategic planning. Advantages and applications of the scenario approach are suggested, and practical guidelines to their use are presented.

MacMillan, I.C., & Jones, P.E. (1984, Spring). Designing organizations to compete. *Journal of Business Strategy,* pp. 11-21.
This article contends that the ability of corporations to defend or take market shares from competitors varies with the corporation's strengths and weaknesses. It recommends that organizations not attempt to design perfect organizational structures, but simply structures that are better than those of competitors.

Maher, T.E. (1985, Winter). Condemning Japan while imitating her management techniques: No solution for America's problems. *SAM Advanced Management Journal.*
The author concludes that imitating the Japanese is a dangerous game and that America should look for the reasons that this country has failed with management techniques.

Maidique, M. (1983, Fall). The new management thinkers. *California Management Review,* pp. 151-161.
This article contends that because of the success of Japanese industrial products, management scholars are taking a critical look at American

management principles, including strategic planning. The result of this critical look could bring about new approaches to management.

Mankin, R.S. (1984, September-October). Strategic planning: An overview. *Managerial Planning*, pp. 14-21.
This overview of strategic planning as a decision-making process describes the process and the eight variables that shape it. The author contends that when this approach is followed, environmental constraints, necessary organizational requirements, and appropriate techniques become clear.

McGinnis, M.A. (1984, Fall). The key to strategic planning: Integrating analysis and intuition. *Sloan Management Review*, pp. 45-52.
Six key issues that affect the ability of a firm to understand its environment and thus create strategic opportunities are examined. The need for integration of both analysis and intuition is discussed as a way to effectively manage these issues and achieve a more effective organization.

Metz, E.J. (1984, May-June). The missing "H" in strategic planning. *Managerial Planning*, pp. 19-23.
The author discusses the importance of human resources planning in building an integrated strategic planning model.

Miesing, P. (1982, May-June). Limitations of matrix models as a strategic planning tool. *Managerial Planning*.
Pitfalls that must be avoided in adapting the growth-share matrix strategic planning model are discussed. Guidelines for using the model are presented.

Pascale, R.T. (1984, Spring). Perspectives on strategy: The real story behind Honda's success. *California Management Review*, pp. 47-72.
This powerful and well-written article looks beyond the traditional dimensions of strategy (strategy, structure, and systems) and urges a multiple-dimensional approach. An example of Honda's entering the U.S. market adds special insights.

Pascarella, P. (1984, January 9). Strategy comes down to earth. *Industry Week*.
This article proposes that rapidly changing business conditions are forcing companies to devise versatile, decentralized plans; and that, as a result, line managers now assume a more aggressive role in developing and implementing strategy.

Pearce, John A., II. (1982, Spring). Selecting among alternative grand strategies. *California Management Review*, pp. 23-31.
Twelve grand strategies that might be considered by strategic planners are presented, and an approach to select from among these strategies

to achieve an optimal grand strategy is outlined. This article provides a comprehensive discussion of grand strategies.

Pearce, J.A., II, Chapman, B., & David, F.R. (1982, July). Environmental scanning for small and growing firms. *Journal of Small Business Management*, pp. 27-34.
The authors propose that techniques of environmental scanning practiced by large corporations can be useful to small and growing companies but that they need to be adapted to the specific needs of the small firm.

Peters, T. (1983, Summer-Fall). The mythology of innovation, or a skunkworks tale, parts I and II. *Stanford Magazine.*
This summary of the principal themes from *In Search of Excellence* is presented in a very interesting way.

Peters, T.J. (1984, Spring). Strategy follows structure: Developing distinctive skills. *California Management Review*, pp. 102-116.
This excellent summary of the key points of *In Search of Excellence* has a focus on strategy.

Piercing future fog in the executive suite. (1975, April 28). *Business Week*, pp. 46-50, 52, 54.
The basic concepts in this article have stood the test of time and are still relevant to today's strategic planning. Particularly important is the point that doers should be directly involved in the planning process.

Raichle, R.W. (1980, March-April). The business of business planning. *Managerial Planning*, pp. 7-10.
A down-to-earth focus on ten simple concepts of business planning and methods to be used in the process.

Ross, J.E., & Shetty, K.Y. (1985, February). Making quality a fundamental part of strategy. *Long Range Planning*, pp. 53-58.
This article contends that everything that is known about quality suggests that it should be a major component of a firm's mission and competitive advantage and that it should be an integral part of strategic planning. The authors state that quality builds a value system that is cost effective and profitable and that promotes long life for the firm. They also suggest that quality must come from the top down and should not be left to quality-control personnel.

Rothschild, W.E. (1979, July). Competitor analysis: The missing link in strategy. *Management Review.*
In recent years many U.S. companies have been outmaneuvered in domestic and world markets, often by unexpected rivals. The author suggests that overconfident American executives have done a poor job of sizing up their competition.

Royce, W.S. (1978, November-December). The problems with planning. *Managerial Planning,* pp. 1-5, 40.

This paper discusses problems that companies have had with their planning, what they are doing to solve the problems, and some of the successes in planning.

Schoeffer, S., Buzzell, R.D., & Heany, D.F. (1974, March-April). Impact of strategic planning on profit performance. *Harvard Business Review,* pp. 137-145.

This discussion of PIMS (profit impact of market strategy) provides an approach to examining the relationship among profit and other business outcomes and different strategies. The relationships are derived from studies of business firms.

Schroeder, R. (1984, August). Operations strategy: Missing link in corporate planning? *Management Review,* pp. 20-23.

This article contends that business planning could be made more effective if the operations function played a more important role. It also suggests that operations must be an integral part of strategic planning to achieve higher quality and productivity.

Schwartz, H., & Davis, S.M. (1981, Summer). Matching corporate culture and business strategy. *Organizational Dynamics,* pp. 30-48.

The authors state that organizational culture can help or hinder the successful implementation of strategy. Four means of implementing a strategy recognizing an organization's culture are presented together with a means to assess the cultural risk.

Shanklin, W.L. (1979, October). Strategic business planning: Yesterday, today and tomorrow. *Business Horizons.*

This article is useful in understanding the historical perspective of strategic business planning.

Smith, G., & Brown, P.B. (1985, January 28). Emerging growth stocks: Why so many peak so early. *Forbes,* pp. 69-75.

This article offers reasons for the dramatic plunge that often follows a peak in growth stocks.

Smith, T.A. (1979, August). The commodity-premium scale: A force in the development of successful strategy. *Management Review,* pp. 9-17.

This classic article looks at the need to determine where a company's products fall on the commodity-premium scale to enable the company to design a strategy and organization appropriate for each product.

South, S.E. (1981, Spring). Competitive advantage: The cornerstone of strategic thinking. *Journal of Business Strategy,* pp. 15-25.

This article contends that the acceptance of competitive advantage as a key ingredient in strategic planning is increasing. The author suggests eight key questions that can aid in developing a winning strategy.

Stevenson, H.H., & Gumpert, D.E. (1985, March-April). The heart of entrepreneurship. *Harvard Business Review,* pp. 85-94.
>   The authors suggest that personal characteristics strongly influence the decisions made in the strategic management process. This article contrasts the entrepreneur's state of mind with that of the administrator.

Stonich, P.J., & Wernecke, S.G. (1982, May). Strategy formulation: What to avoid; how to succeed. *Management Review,* pp. 25-28.
>   This article states that strategy formulation is not a series of gimmicks, but a process of careful planning. A diagnostic test is outlined to test the strategy formulation process.

Tersine, R.J. (1978, November-December). The structure and content of policy decisions. *Managerial Planning.*
>   This is a comprehensive review of the strategy process with emphasis on different strategies and the use of objectives.

Thomas, P.S. (1984, July-August). Scanning strategy: Formulation and implementation. *Managerial Planning,* pp. 14-20.
>   This article discusses the problems of using the correct approaches to environmental scanning and some of the problems that develop when there is a mismatch between the models and scanning systems.

Uttal, B. (1983, October 17). The corporate culture vultures. *Fortune,* pp. 67-70, 72.
>   This article stresses culture as a key word in strategic management and contends that more managers are concerned about the impact of their organizations' cultures on the development and implementation of strategy. The author suggests that it is unclear whether most corporations can consciously create a new culture for themselves—or even whether they should try.

Who's excellent now? (1984, November 5). *Business Week,* pp. 76-79, 82-83, 86.
>   This article is an appraisal of the performance of companies cited in *In Search of Excellence.* It is a critical examination of the lessons suggested by Peters and Waterman.

Periodicals

Academy of Management Executive
Academy of Management
Box 39
Ada, OH 45810
(502) 588-6443

Advanced Management Journal
Society for Advancement of Management
135 W. 50th Street
New York, NY 10020
(212) 586-8100

Business Economics
National Association of Business Economists
28349 Chagrin Boulevard
Cleveland, OH 44122
(216) 464-7986

Business Month
Goldhirsh Group, Inc.
488 Madison Avenue
New York, NY 10022
(212) 326-2600
FAX (212) 326-6982

Business Strategies
Commerce Clearing House, Inc.
4025 W. Peterson Ave.
Chicago, IL 60646

California Management Review
University of California Press
2120 Berkeley Way
Berkeley, CA 94720
(415) 642-7159

Corporate Planning
International Association for Financial Planning
2 Concourse Parkway #800
Atlanta, GA 30328
(404) 592-2040

Fortune
Time, Inc.
1271 Avenue of the Americas
Rockefeller Center
New York, NY 10020
(212) 586-1212

Harvard Business Review
Harvard University
Graduate School of Business Administration
Soldiers Field Road
Cambridge, MA 02163
(617) 495-6182

Journal of Business Strategy
Warren Gorham & Lamont
1 Penn Plaza, 40th Floor
New York, NY 10119
(212) 971-5000

Long Range Planning
Pergamon Press, Inc.
Journals Division
Maxwell House
Fairview Park
Elmsford, NY 10523
(914) 592-7700

Management Review
American Management Association
135 W. 50th Street
New York, NY 10020
(212) 586-8100

Managerial Planning
Planning Executives Institute
P.O. Box 70
Oxford, OH 45056

Planning Review
Planning Forum
5500 College Corner Pike
Oxford, OH 45056
(513) 523-4185

Political Risk Letter
International Business Communications
407 University Avenue, #107
Syracuse, NY 13210
(315) 472-1224

Research-Technology Management
Sheridan Press
Fame Avenue
Hanover, PA 17331
(717) 632-3535

Sloan Management Review
Massachusetts Institute of Technology
Sloan School of Management
1 Amherst Street
Cambridge, MA 02139
(617) 253-7170

Strategic Management Journal
John Wiley & Sons, Inc.
605 Third Avenue
New York, NY 10158

Strategic Planning Management
Commerce Communications, Inc.
5247 Washburn Avenue S.
Minneapolis, MN 55410
(612) 924-0957

Associations

Academy of Management
Business Policy and Planning Division
Box 39
Ada, OH 45810
(502) 588-6443
> The division of the Academy of Management that deals with strategic planning; sponsors seminars, papers, and symposia on strategic planning issues at the Academy's annual convention.

American Management Association
135 W. 50th Street
New York, NY 10020
(212) 586-8100
> Offers three workshops on various aspects of strategic planning. These workshops form the core of the AMA's four-day strategic planning certificate program.

Association for Corporate Growth
104 Wilmot Road, Suite 201
Deerfield, IL 60015-5195
(708) 940-7215

> Supplies services closely related to planning and growth activities for organizations that manufacture consumer and industrial products; provides a forum for the exchange of ideas.

Business and Tax Planning Board
10 Paragon Drive
Montvale, NJ 07645
(201) 573-6219

> Increases public awareness of the importance and value of business planning and analysis.

Center for Entrepreneurial Management
180 Varick Street, Penthouse Suite
New York, NY 10014
(212) 633-0060

> Serves as management resource and makes available publications on developing business plans.

The Conference Board
845 Third Avenue
New York, NY 10022
(212) 759-0900

> A not-for-profit business information service for senior executives. The Board supports an international program of research and meetings, including an annual strategic planning convention attended by over five hundred senior managers.

International Association of Business Strategy Consultants
P.O. Box 5219
Akron, OH 44313
(216) 836-4410

> Promotes highest quality standards and ethics for business-strategy consultants. Provides access to the Strategy Identification Program, which helps members determine the current and previous strategic positions of a business.

Planning Forum
5500 College Corner Pike
Oxford, OH 45056
(513) 523-4185

> An international society for strategic management and planning; the world's largest membership organization focused on strategic man-